Landscapes and Voices of the Great War

This volume aims to provide a wider view of First World War experience through focussing on landscapes less commonly considered in historiography, and on voices that have remained on the margins of popular understanding of the war. The landscape of the Western Front was captured during the conflict in many different ways: in photographs, paintings and print. The most commonly replicated voicing of contemporary attitudes towards the war is that of initial enthusiasm giving way to disillusionment and a sense of overwhelming futility. Investigations of the many components of war experience drawn from social and cultural history have looked to landscapes and voices beyond the front line as a means of foregrounding different perspectives on the war. Not all of the voices presented here opposed the war, and not all of the landscapes were comprised of trenches or flanked by barbed wire. Collectively, they combine to offer further fresh insights into the multiplicity of war experience, an alternate space to the familiar tropes of mud and mayhem.

Angela K. Smith is an Associate Professor (Reader) at Plymouth University.

Krista Cowman is Professor of History in the School of History and Heritage, University of Lincoln.

Routledge Studies in Modern History

For a full list of titles in this series, please visit www.routledge.com

14 **Longue Durée of the Far-Right**
   An International Historical Sociology
   Edited by Richard Saul, Alexander Anievas, Neil Davidson and Adam Fabry

15 **Transnational Perspectives on Modern Irish History**
   Edited by Niall Whelehan

16 **Ireland in the World**
   Comparative, Transnational, and Personal Perspectives
   Edited by Angela McCarthy

17 **The Global History of the Balfour Declaration**
   Declared Nation
   Maryanne A. Rhett

18 **Colonial Soldiers in Europe, 1914–1945**
   "Aliens in Uniform" in Wartime Societies
   Edited by Eric Storm and Ali Al Tuma

19 **Immigration Policy from 1970 to the Present**
   Rachel Stevens

20 **Public Goods versus Economic Interests**
   Global Perspectives on the History of Squatting
   Edited by Freia Anders and Alexander Sedlmaier

21 **Histories of Productivity**
   Genealogical Perspectives on the Body and Modern Economy
   Edited by Peter-Paul Bänziger and Mischa Suter

22 **Landscapes and Voices of the Great War**
   Edited by Angela K. Smith and Krista Cowman

Landscapes and Voices of the Great War

Edited by Angela K. Smith
and Krista Cowman

LONDON AND NEW YORK

First published 2017 by Routledge

2 Park Square, Milton Park, Abingdon, Oxfordshire OX14 4RN
711 Third Avenue, New York, NY 10017

Routledge is an imprint of the Taylor & Francis Group, an informa business

First issued in paperback 2018

Copyright © 2017 Taylor & Francis

The right of the editors to be identified as the authors of the editorial material, and of the authors for their individual chapters, has been asserted in accordance with sections 77 and 78 of the Copyright, Designs and Patents Act 1988.

All rights reserved. No part of this book may be reprinted or reproduced or utilised in any form or by any electronic, mechanical, or other means, now known or hereafter invented, including photocopying and recording, or in any information storage or retrieval system, without permission in writing from the publishers.

Notice:
Product or corporate names may be trademarks or registered trademarks, and are used only for identification and explanation without intent to infringe.

Library of Congress Cataloging-in-Publication Data
A catalog record for this book has been requested

ISBN: 978-1-138-07987-8 (hbk)
ISBN: 978-1-138-33193-8 (pbk)

Typeset in Sabon
by ApexCoVantage, LLC

Contents

List of Figures   vii
Acknowledgments   ix

Introduction   1
ANGELA K. SMITH AND KRISTA COWMAN

PART I
Real and Imagined Spaces   17

1 "Funny Men and Charming Girls": Revue and the Theatrical Landscape of 1914–1918   19
   ANDREW MAUNDER

2 "When Words Are Not Enough": The Aural Landscape of Britain's Modern Memory of 1914–18   41
   EMMA HANNA

3 *Maisons de Tolérance*: The Real and Imagined Sexual Landscapes of the Western Front   58
   KRISTA COWMAN

4 "The Delightful Sense of Personal Contact That Your Letter Aroused": Letters and Intimate Lives in the First World War   77
   CAROL ACTON

PART II
Voices   95

5 "A Certain Poetess": Recuperating Jessie Pope (1868–1941)   97
   JANE POTTER

6 Ventriloquizing Voices in World War I: Scribe, Poetess, Philosopher 115
MARGARET R. HIGONNET

7 Pacifist Writer, Propagandist Publisher: Rose Macaulay and Hodder & Stoughton 131
LISE JAILLANT

8 From Collusion to Condemnation: The Evolving Voice of "Woodbine Willie" 151
STUART BELL

PART III
Landscapes 173

9 First World War Nursing Narratives in the Middle East 175
NADIA ATIA

10 Cars in the Desert: Claud H. Williams, S.C. Rolls and the Anglo-Sanusi War 192
LISA REGAN

11 Murmurs of War: Grace Fallow Norton and "The Red Road" 206
HAZEL HUTCHISON

12 Landscapes of Memory in Centenary Fiction 222
ANGELA K. SMITH

Contributors 241
Index 245

Figures

1.1 Antony (Leon Morton) and Cleopatra (Dorothy Minto), *Pell Mell*, 1916. — 20
1.2 *Shell Out* (1915). Bashful Gentleman: I should like to see a male attendant. Verbeena (Fred Emney): I am a male female attendant. — 25
1.3 Gaby Deslys and Harry Pilcer, *5064 Gerrard* (1915). — 28
1.4 Gaby Deslys (Robert Hale) and J.M. Barrie (Jack Morrison), *5064 Gerrard* (1915). — 29
1.5 *Houp La!* (1916) Song: "The Place Where the Peaches Grow." 'I like the place where the peaches grow because I haven't picked a lemon yet." — 35
7.1 Advertisement for *The Lee Shore*, *Daily Mail*, 3 August 1912, 9. — 135
7.2 Hodder & Stoughton advertisement, *Times Literary Supplement*, 12 March 1914, 123. — 136
7.3 Printing and advertising figures, *Lee Shore*, *The Making of a Bigot* and *Non-Combatants and Others*. — 144
8.1 A handbill advertising one of Studdert Kennedy's addresses in the Hotel de Ville at Rouen, April 1916. — 153

Acknowledgments

The editors would like to thank the AHRC for funding and supporting the "Alternate Spaces of the Great War" network, together with Queen Mary University, London, Plymouth University and Oxford Brookes University for hosting the three symposia that brought the network together and made this collection possible. We would also like to thank all those who participated in the network and whose input helped to shape the work presented here, especially Nadia Atia, our host at Queen Mary, and Jane Potter, our host at Oxford Brookes. Particular thanks are due to Cherry Walsh, the network administrator, whose hard work made all the events run smoothly and with great success.

We would also like to thank the editors at Routledge for their assistance with the manuscript, with special thanks to Max Novick and Jennifer Morrow for their help and advice.

Correspondence of Emily Chitticks and William Martin, in William Martin Private papers, Department of Documents (2554), Imperial War Museum, London. Every effort has been made to trace the copyright holders, and the author and Imperial War Museums would be grateful for any information which might help to trace those whose identities or addresses are not currently known. Correspondence of Miss H.M[uriel] Harpin and Capt Charles 'Neville' Overton, Private Papers 3051), Department of Documents, Imperial War Museum, London. Excerpts reproduced by kind permission of Susan Overton, copyright holder. Correspondence of Cyril Newman and Winifred Newman (née Blackburn), in Cyril Newman, Private Papers, Department of Documents (03/5/1), Imperial War Museum, London. Every effort has been made to trace the copyright holders, and the author and Imperial War Museums would be grateful for any information which might help to trace those whose identities or addresses are not currently known. Correspondence of Frederic Sellers and Grace Malin, Private Papers, Department of Documents, (09/32/1), Imperial War Museum, London. Excerpts reproduced by kind permission of John Sellers, copyright holder. Correspondence of William Wooliscroft and Lily Patrick in William Wooliscroft, Private Papers, Department of Documents, (09/57/2), Imperial

War Museum, London. Excerpts reproduced by kind permission of Patricia Yacamini, copyright holder.

The image of a hand-bill advertising Geoffrey Anketell Studdert Kennedy's addresses at Rouen is reproduced with the permission of the Library of Birmingham, MS 348/7.

Every reasonable effort has been made to contact the copyright holders where required.

Introduction

Angela K. Smith and Krista Cowman

In this centenary period, the First World War, always a site of cultural interest, has come to occupy a prime place in the public imagination. Since early 2014 a seemingly infinite number of new novels, memoirs, television and radio programmes and feature films, as well as academic histories, have been produced to coincide with the four-year anniversary. These have been underpinned by hundreds of community commemorations across the country with significant support from national bodies including the Imperial War Museum, the British Broadcasting Corporation and the Arts and Humanities Research Council as the public attempts, yet again, to come to terms with the catastrophic events of 1914–18. Historians and media commentators alike now concur that the war occupies an almost unique place in popular memory as shared ways of remembering the conflict continue to develop even as those who had personal experience of the war have died.[1] Yet popular historical understanding of the war remains firmly rooted in an under-contextualised version of the Western Front, pivoting around the viewpoint of the mythologised Tommy from the parapet of the front-line trench, a landscape delineated by mud, blood and futility.

This view has not gone unchallenged by First World War scholars. Barely a decade after the Armistice, the first public criticisms emerged of a burgeoning trend in war literature that concentrated solely on the negative aspects of the war on the Western Front and paid little attention to its broader context.[2] Charles Carrington recalled:

> The first Armistice Day had been a carnival; The Second Armistice Day, after its solemn pause at the Two Minutes' Silence . . . was a day of festivity again. For some years I was one of a group of friends who met, every Armistice Day, at the Café Royal for no end of a party, until we began to find ourselves out of key with the new age. Imperceptibly, the Feast-Day became a Fast-Day and one could hardly go brawling on the Sabbath. The do-gooders captured the Armistice, and the British Legion seemed to make its principle outing a day of mourning. To march to the Cenotaph was too much like attending one's own funeral, and I know many old soldiers who found it increasingly discomforting, year by year. We preferred reunions in private with no pacifist propaganda.[3]

Recent revisionist scholarship has identified the sources of some of the main myths that fed the change in public mood Carrington found so disquieting.[4] Janet S.K. Watson has explained how "the story of disillusionment was a product of the late 1920s and early 1930s."[5] It was underpinned by a collection of works produced by writers such as Wilfred Owen, Siegfried Sassoon and Robert Graves, rather than any universal experience. Watson argues, "The remembered soldier's story with its exclusive focus on combat trench experience by men, would not have been easily recognised as the story of the war during the period itself."[6] While some historians fear that the divide between academic scholarship and popular engagement with the war is now too wide to bridge,[7] others have attempted a broader analysis that attempts to re-evaluate understandings of the war by taking account of recent findings.[8] Adrian Gregory suggests, "By a slow and hesitant process, the British have come to renounce the war. They are still renouncing it. The verdict of popular culture is more or less unanimous. . . . There is a disproportionate fascination amongst the public with the mud and blood of Flanders."[9] It is this imbalance that we hope to continue to redress in this collection.

As part of a much broader revisionist trend, the AHRC funded a research network, *Alternate Spaces of the Great War*, in 2014. The network's aim was to join a range of scholars from a variety of disciplinary backgrounds in a series of symposia where they debated and discussed less well-documented aspects of the war. A number of key themes were selected including those of Landscapes and Voices, the focus of this volume. Participants were encouraged to explore contemporary experiences in and responses to the real and imagined spaces of both home and battle front from a variety of disciplinary perspectives including art history, literary studies, cultural history, gender studies and publishing history, and to consider the different voices emerging from such spaces. This collection of essays represents key elements of this collaboration, which has resulted in the production of some exciting new ways of thinking about the conflict one hundred years on. It brings together the international work of both established First World War scholars and innovative new voices in the field, that combine to explore the alternate spaces of war that have been neglected in the past.

The war on the Western Front still lies at the core of the collection, but it is an alternate version of this war shaped by voices from the margins, in landscapes beyond the battle lines (including the Home Front) and by women as well as men. Considering the war from the vantage point of these voices and landscapes brings a fresh perspective to the familiar tropes and clichés. The volume also travels to other landscapes, to actual spaces that are further afield geographically, or to the imagined landscapes conjured by those who never saw the fighting first hand. Thus it offers an integrated set of studies aimed at providing a wider view of war experience. Building on the arguments of Janet S.K. Watson that the war, far from being a unifying experience, spawned numerous conflicting accounts even as it unfolded, each essay describes a different perspective revealed by a fresh voice or unusual landscape and explores how this encourages consideration of an alternative or an expanded war experience.[10]

The collection is divided into three parts, each one focussing on a particular type of landscape or voice. It contributes to an important body of work that has been done by scholars in the humanities since the resurgence of interest in the war in the late twentieth century. Investigations of the many components of war experience drawn from social and cultural history have looked to landscapes beyond the front line as a means of foregrounding different perspectives on the war. Often the landscapes studied have been tangible spaces with firmly fixed parameters. Women's historians, for example, have examined the war within battlefield hospitals, munitions factories, or the civilian homes of France amongst other places to reveal what being "at war" meant to women in an age before female conscription.[11] Social historians have recently begun to examine the activities of soldiers on the Western Front when they were not engaged in front-line fighting, looking at their activities in a variety of different social and cultural locations ranging from YMCA huts to music halls as a means of explaining how the army maintained morale through Anglophone or Anglo-French cultural exchanges.[12]

The essays in the first part of this collection, "Real and Imagined Spaces," question what we mean by landscapes, or "spaces" of war. The spatial boundaries surrounding the formation of contemporary perspectives on the war extended way beyond the immediate battlefield and front line. This was as true for military personnel as for civilians. In the towns and villages of the "Occupied Zone," in Paris when "French leave" was available, and over the Channel on the Home Front, a variety of different locations offered some respite from immediate danger, and somewhere where morale might be sustained. This section explores a variety of these locations—the definite space of the French brothel just behind the lines, the actual and symbolic cultural spaces of the theatre, music and concert hall on the Home Front and the wholly imagined spaces of letters through which intimate correspondents attempted to bridge the physical divide between home and front—and considers their contribution towards shaping what it meant to be "at war." Their diversity offers new ways of imagining and understanding this, moving beyond the culturally expected, and building on previous work, offering up alternative examples of "war experience."

Beyond these spatial dimensions, scholars working within new trends in First World War history have been consistently attentive to the value of different voices in helping to frame a more varied picture of what constitutes "war experience." Feminist literary scholars have emphasised the value of women's writing on the First World War as a means of opening up different approaches to the conflict.[13] Cultural history has encouraged the exploration of different sources for studying the war such as letters, war magazines, children's books and toys, which in turn open up the psychological spaces in which war experiences were sorted, filtered and made sense of.[14] More recently work on the writings of a number different groups on the peripheries of combat ranging from army chaplains to women in auxiliary branches of the armed forces has drawn attention to a wider range of perspectives.[15] Collectively, this body of work has considerably expanded our understanding of those who had "war experience," and of the variety of the spaces in which it occurred.

Drawing on these insights, the second section of this collection is constructed around "Voice." The most commonly replicated voicing of contemporary attitudes towards the war is that of initial enthusiasm giving way to disillusionment and a sense of overwhelming futility. The essays in this section invite us to listen to other voices telling different war stories. Individual case studies of a popular army chaplain, a patriotic female poet and a pacifist woman writer reveal how many did not fit within the familiar audible trajectory that moved its listeners from enthusiasm to disillusionment but took more complicated routes around this. Paying attention to these less frequently heard voices encourages us to look afresh at the criteria through which we process and understand the war.

The spatial focus of the first section returns in the final section of the book, which looks much more closely at the importance of actual landscapes. The familiar landscape of the Western Front is replaced here by other landscapes, less easily recognised as belonging to the First World War. The war in the East, in the desert, takes centre stage, inviting us to think more carefully about other ways of mapping war experience. Sand rather than mud dominates here and the impact is significant. Complementing discussion of these Eastern spaces is a literary description that gives an American's imagined view of the wartime landscape produced from a distance in the years before the United States entered the war. The final essay looks at late twentieth and twenty-first century fiction to consider how a different form of landscape, the landscape of memory, continues to be shaped for a public with no actual memory of the period in question.

The differing focus of all three sections is underpinned by their collective suggestion of alternatives to popular (and persistent) understandings of how the war looked and sounded. As Jay Winter has argued, "Remembrance is part of the landscape."[16] This is especially true of the Western Front, where the battlefield landscapes, spaces that so quickly distorted into alien places filled with unspeakable horrors, have always been significant in defining how the First World War has been recognised in cultural memory. This is still true one hundred years on as (overly) familiar images are yet again evoked to stimulate public commemoration. The most commonly reproduced photographic representations of devastated France and Flanders have shown us how the war looked. Broken trees around shell holes filled with mud, duckboards, corpses and occasional isolated figures of men and animals still haunt our collective understanding of the event. These landscapes, once meadows or copses or farmer's fields, were transformed by the machinery of war into something other and different, no longer of this world. They shifted into desolate wastelands, populated by identical, anonymous, dehumanised soldiers, displaced from their own lives for the duration and beyond. These enduring landscapes of destruction provided a starting point for our project, but the essays in this volume take us beyond into new territories.

The "look" of the war was firmly fixed in public imagination long before the Armistice. The comparatively new phenomenon of war photography (with both still and moving images available to the Home Front) had begun to plant images in the national psyche before the war had ended, furnishing a public removed from the front line with a strong collective impression of what war was like, and how it appeared.[17] Work produced under the War Artists Scheme (initiated in the propaganda bureau at Wellington House in 1916 then taken up by the Department—later Ministry—of Information) endorsed this. Artists such as Paul Nash, Christopher Nevinson and Eric Kennington, many of whom had experienced the landscape of the Western Front as combatants as well as observers, represented it to civilians in paintings made during and after the war that reinforced the photographic images but added a further commentary as each artist interpreted what he saw rather than simply reproducing it, thus developing its symbolic significance. Nash's representations of the Western Front are particularly evocative. In "We are Making a New World" (1918), for example, Nash develops his anti-war stance through depicting the desolation of a surreal, unrecognisable landscape.[18] This landscape, as noted, is, ironically, familiar to us one hundred years on, even as it passes from living memory. We all recognise the artificially rounded undulations of the shell holes in no man's land, the stark dead trees pointing to the sky, the insipid sun rising behind sinister red clouds as the Western Front. The traditional suggestions of hope implied by the sunrise are refuted by Nash's dead landscape, inhospitable, un-mappable and desolate; the broken trees symbolically represent the broken bodies of the men who lie beneath.

The men who were surrounded by these broken landscapes for months on end could react to them in different ways. Many sought to escape them altogether by moving into different surroundings wherever possible, seeking solace in the relative normality of the civilian world, in non-military spaces designed for leisure that were so surreally juxtaposed with the front line, as recent historical scholarship has begun to demonstrate.[19] A number of essays in this collection consider the war experiences formed within the alternatives landscapes within a combatant's reach. Krista Cowman's chapter describes the interior landscape of the *maison de tolérance* in and around the war zone. Prior to the war, the inner rooms of these official brothels were designed as dreamlike spaces and sites of escapist pleasure. Her essay suggests that knowledge of the appearance of these pre-war landscapes encouraged soldiers in imagining this space as a fantasy alternative to the unreal devastation not far beyond their walls, even as military and civilian authorities were shifting to create more functional designs aimed at dealing with larger volumes of customers.

These same devastated landscapes shaped a variety of different war voices. Soldier voices sometimes come back to us through multiple media.

The voices of the soldier poets are perhaps the most well-known, but they do not necessarily represent the experience or views of all soldiers, or indeed all inhabitants of the war zone. In chapter 6 of this volume, Margaret Higonnet contrasts male and female voices as she examines the words used by nurses writing for or as soldiers, women who found themselves in the unusual position of being able to transcribe and interpret the stories of soldiers' experience as they took down their words in letters to be sent home on their behalf. Higonnet's chapter disputes the implication that combatants are the sole conduits of "war experience" to suggest that nurses, close to the front, might voice their own truths about the landscapes of war.

A very different response can be heard as we listen to the personal development of trench clergyman "Woodbine Willie" Kennedy in Stuart Bell's chapter "From Collusion to Condemnation." Like many war artists, Kennedy had first-hand experience of the trenches as an army chaplain, and saw all the horrors that the landscape revealed, but his sermons and writings show that he managed to retain his commitment to the war throughout nonetheless. However, after the conflict, he began to question everything he had done and witnessed, with dramatic consequences. Through careful readings of Kennedy's wartime and post-war poetry and his political activism, Bell explores the trajectory of his change of heart, letting his unique alternative voice of the war come through.

While painting and photography literally show us the landscapes of war, other cultural representations have added to what Winter and Prost have described as "the mental furniture men and women draw on to make sense of their world at war."[20] Since the earliest days of the war, literature has played an important part in creating and defining our view of these landscapes. Literary depictions of wartime terrains have been as important as pictorial ones in "showing" us what the Western Front was like. The soldier poets, many of whom were writing and publishing during the war, were perhaps the first to make an impact in this area, giving readers a clear impression of the ways in which landscape delineated and defined "war experience." Adding a range of emotions to the visual images, these poets and artists gave voice to the process of establishing the landscapes of the Western Front as the dominant symbols of the First World War in cultural memory.

Janet S.K. Watson has suggested that the way we see the First World War today, as a primarily negative experience for all involved and as a trigger for cultural disillusionment, is a product not so much of the war itself but of the way it has been documented and remembered. She argues:

> This familiar story [of disillusionment from the trenches] was made famous through the publication and popularity of memoirs and novels, like those of Sassoon as well as Robert Graves, Edmund Blunden, and, for Germany, Erich Maria Remarque. Yet Sassoon, though he himself in 1917 made perhaps the most famous protest against the war, tells us that the disillusionment these accounts all articulate is a postwar

phenomenon, the product of distance in time and space from wartime experiences. Inseparably connected with the war in the trenches, the disenchantment of the infantry soldier retrospectively became the story of the First World War in England.[21]

Initially there were multiple understandings of war experience, civilian as well as military. Even the Imperial War Museum recognised this through its "Women at War" collection, aimed at preserving women's part in the conflict at home and abroad.[22] It was only later that the trench experience began to be seen as primary. The soldier poets and war artists contributed to this process while the war was still raging by presenting society with powerful descriptions of landscapes that captured the public imagination and came to dominate how the war was remembered. As Watson explains, "[t]his change in perspectives was connected with the rise of trench warfare as a primary symbol of the conflict. By the end of the war itself, the trench was already becoming a powerful metaphor."[23]

Gary Sheffield suggests that ideas of disillusionment really began to infiltrate society in the immediate post-war years as people began to understand the extent of the final casualty figures. The number of British Empire military dead—947,023—744,702 of whom were from the British Isles, exceeds every war before or since.[24] Samuel Hynes agrees, "Disenchantment is a condition of loss, and that was the way the war extended its presence into English Culture after the Armistice—as forms of loss."[25] Loss was a key theme in much of the prose literature that made up the "war books" boom in the late 1920s and 1930s and are still read today, standing at the forefront of centenary commemorations. This same sense of loss that colours the written testimony of veterans in the following decades was articulated in the musical works, both high- and lowbrow, inspired by the war and explored by Emma Hanna in her chapter in this volume.

While the famous prose works of the war books boom a decade after the Armistice contributed to the development of the mythology of landscapes, one work in particular illustrates the importance of landscape in memory. Edmund Blunden's *Undertones of War*, first published in November 1928 was among the most highly critically acclaimed publications about the war. Cyril Falls described it as "a masterpiece . . . the best English book of its kind."[26] One of the most striking things about the book, a curious hybrid of memoir rather than a work of fiction, is the way in which Blunden recreates landscapes, and how this impacts on our subsequent reading of the experience of war as a whole. His voice as a poet and a devotee of the pastoral had a significant impact on these representations. The spatial dimensions of Blunden's work are so pronounced that the reader can, as Huw Strachen suggests, "follow Blunden's movements on the map, while the author himself suffuses his text with rural themes of the pastoral tradition which his poetry had embraced before the war."[27] Paul Fussell explains the importance of landscape to Blunden's writing when he argues, "To Blunden, both the countryside and English literature are 'alive,' and both have 'feelings.' They are equally menaced by the war."[28] This preoccupation with landscape not only helps to develop the legacy of landscapes of the war, but also presents them with an unusually poetic voice, influencing the way the reader responds to each tableau. His description of part of the Somme line is a good illustration of Blunden's technique:

> Jacob's Ladder was a long trench, good in parts, stretching from Mesnil with many angles down to Hamel on the river Ancre, requiring flights of stairs at one or two steep places. Leafy bushes and great green and yellow weeds looked into it as it dipped sharply into the valley by Hamel, and hereabouts the aspect of peace and innocence was as yet prevailing. A cow with a crumpled horn, a harvest cart should have been visible here and there. The trenches ahead were curious, and not so pastoral. Ruined houses with rafters sticking out, with half-sloughed plaster and dangling window-frames, perched on a hillside, bleak and piteous that cloudy morning; half-filled trenches crept along below them by upheaved gardens, telling the story of wild bombardment.[29]

As Strachen suggests, the geography is very precise. It is possible to identify exactly which part of the landscape is being described here. Although these trenches have clearly seen some action with parts being very war-torn, Blunden insists on recalling their former rural status. The mechanics of the trench are contrasted with the vibrant colours of the summer countryside, which prevail despite the battle scars. Blunden's imagination imposes the harvest cart and the picturesque cow on this devastated landscape in defiance of the destruction. The remains of the village, "bleak and piteous," offer a more "realistic" representation of a battleground, but his very emphasis on the rural, the domestic, the human elements of the scene have the effect of reinforcing the idea that this "wild bombardment" is against nature. The landscape contains both the war and the pre-war ensuring that the reader understands the extent of the tragedy.

The influence of Blunden's retrospective account of the war was critical in shaping a body of literature that enabled the primacy of one particular vision of the landscape of the Western Front to triumph and endure. The book's success (it went through seven impressions) extended this. Indeed, it could be said that in some ways, *Undertones of War*, and other works of the period, set the devastated landscapes of the Western Front in a kind of literary stone. These became the "legitimate" landscapes of the First World War, and remain the main way that they are envisaged today. Yet, while it was important to Blunden to centralise the landscape as he did, as part of a broader strategy to place narrative emphasis on the overall experience of the war rather than focussing in on the individual, he was not the only writer to attempt to do this. Grace Fallow Norton's war poetry, included in her collection "The Red Road" and analysed here by Hazel Hutchinson, offers a similar emphasis. Norton's poetry, written very early in the war, and in a landscape far removed from the actual battlefields, blends the domestic with the martial to encompass both individual and collective voices, set against a backdrop of different wartime landscapes. Through considering Norton's less well-known poetry, Hutchinson approaches these familiar landscapes in new ways, attaching alternative readings to the voices within them that challenge their prominent resonance in popular memory.

Other contributors take us into a different theatre of war, far less familiar in popular imagination, where sand is more important than mud. Nadia Atia and Lisa Regan move the focus of the conflict East, away from the Western Front, to discover "oriental" and desert spaces. Atia's chapter in this volume, "First World War Nursing Narratives in the Middle East," documents the adventures of British women as nurses in Egypt and Mesopotamia, in landscapes of war that few would recognise today. She finds that the accounts kept by many women are heavily influenced by contemporary travel writing, placing the emphasis on the experience of "other" cultural encounters and voices, rather than focussing on the more traumatic experience of treating the wounded. For them, the excitement of these exotic landscapes becomes more important than the context, the war and offers opportunity as much as a threat. In her chapter in this volume, "Cars in the Desert: Claud H. Williams, S.C. Rolls and the Anglo-Sanusi War," Lisa Regan remains in the Middle East, but explores the impact of desert landscapes on actual warfare. She uses contemporary accounts to examine the mixed success of the British army, using the modern technology of armoured cars, against an enemy much better suited to the desert landscapes. Like Atia's women tourists, these colonial soldiers take the opportunity to pursue alternate ends, mapping the unknowable desert and listening to the voices that inhabit it. Their descriptions could not be further away from the landscapes depicted by Blunden and Nash, but they are nonetheless landscapes of the First World War, a far less familiar but equally legitimate location for shaping war experience as the muddied fields of France.

As social, and more recently cultural, historians have been quick to point out, experiencing the First World War was not the unique preserve of those who actually fought it. Women, children, the elderly and large numbers of men in reserved occupations lived through the war and were shaped by it in different ways. Equally important to this collection, therefore, are other landscapes of the war, those real and imagined spaces that provide the background and context for the experience of the majority of the population. Most British men and women never saw a trench. The Home Front was their line of battle, the landscape etched by a society fractured by war. Rather than focus on the binary divide between these two spaces, Carol Acton's chapter in this volume, "The Delightful Sense of Personal Contact that Your Letter Aroused: Letters and Intimate Lives in the First World War," attempts to bridge it through examining a number of complete sets of wartime correspondence between men at the front and their female wives and sweethearts at home, highlighting the importance of the epistolary act of writing as well as reading letters both for the soldier writers and the domestic recipients. Acton argues that despite the distance, geographic and emotional, the relationships between these couples were still the most important of their lives. Their correspondence, in a world where letters were the only real means of communication for those apart, offer fascinating insights into the strategies they devised to deal with separation, fear and loss, and suggest how the voices in letters could merge the distinct landscapes of home and front for readers and writers alike.

A range of different voices created the landscapes of the Home Front. Many found them to be as alien to their pre-war lives as those foreign voices encountered by combatants nearer the front line. Vera Brittain, moving to London to work as a Voluntary Aid Detachment (VAD) nurse in 1915, as she puts it, "after twenty years of sheltered gentility,"[30] draws for the reader an image of the capital that is as complex as Blunden's French pastoral tableaux.

> The nucleus of the hospital, [1st London General Hospital, Camberwell] a large college, red, gabled, creeper-covered, is still one of the few dignified buildings in the dismal, dreary, dirty wilderness of south-east London, with its paper-strewn pavements, its little mean streets, and its old, ugly houses tumbling into squalid decay.[31]

Brittain's voice in this passage echoes Blunden's in the way it juxtaposes images to present an uncomfortable wartime landscape. The quintessential Englishness of the "red, gabled, creeper-covered" college contrasts with the barren waste land of south-east London, here presented as an alternative kind of no man's land, across which the VADs must traverse to get to and from their hostel each day. The VAD hostel itself is unwelcoming, a far cry from "sheltered gentility," "a square, solid building of dirty grey stone, with gaping uncurtained windows."[32] Brittain's job as a VAD places her into the heart of working London:

> Theoretically we travelled down by the workman's trams which ran over Champion Hill from Dulwich, but in practice these trams were so full that we were seldom able to use them, and were obliged to walk, frequently in pouring rain and carrying suitcases containing clean aprons and changes of shoes and stockings, the mile and a half from the hostel to the hospital. As the trams were equally full in the evenings, the journey on foot had often to be repeated at the end of the day.[33]

The Western Front this is not. But it does illustrate the ways in which the war brought different elements of the population together in the changing landscapes of the capital. These middle-class young women should be out of place in working-class London, as Brittain admits, but as an integral part of the war they belong, and so become symbols of modernity in a traditional landscape.

Brittain's "little mean streets" are but a short tram ride away from the East End, where the landscapes of war trespassed onto the Home Front in the most violent and dramatic ways. In her 1915 article for *The Women's Dreadnought*, "The East End Air Raid," Sylvia Pankhurst describes not only the devastation caused by German bombing of civilian homes, but also the morbid fascination of "West-Ender" spectators who make their way east to witness the trauma. Different elements of society once again combine here, but with a much less egalitarian purpose. Pankhurst's is very much a political voice, intent on illustrating the injustice and inhumanity already endemic in the landscape. Her priority is highlighting the poverty that the bombing exposes, even more than showing us the consequences of the raid for the local population. But she still effectively captures the impact of war on the London landscape:

> What a sight for the pretty ladies in dainty dresses with slender delicate throats, peering from taxi cabs and for the rather too comfortable looking business men and well-groomed officers in motor cars. Miserable dwellings, far from fit for housing human creatures, poorly clad women and with sad work-worn faces, other women just covered, no more, in horrid rags, hopeless, unhappy beings, half-clothes neglected looking little children a sadder sight, this mean street that is always with us, even than the havoc of destruction wrought by German bombs.[34]

For Pankhurst, this Home Front is double edged, ripped open by the war to reveal a darker truth. The article goes on to describe an attack, by these same crowds, on a German baker's shop, a mob incited to violence by the heady combination of bomb damage and the national press. It is a bleak and disturbing impression of the Home Front intended to make us uncomfortable.

The West End too, could be dangerous, as London theatre land became a target for bombing raids. Popular revue performer, Vesta Tilley, recalls one such night performing on stage at the London Coliseum to the background voices of maroons signalling the arrival of a bombing raid. She completed her performance and the audience all remained seated throughout, despite the threat. Later the same evening she experienced a closer brush with the war.

> It was a fine clear night, and I drew the curtains slightly and looked over the Thames. The maroons started again and I saw quite plainly a machine flying overhead. At the same moment there was a terrible explosion and I was hurled across the room as the windows cracked and blew in. Luckily I was not hurt, just bruised. We all escaped, although my maid was in hysterics.[35]

Tilley's resilience was not unusual. A party-goer in Irene Rathbone's 1932 novel *We That Were Young* recounts, "My dear, I was actually *in* the Gaiety when that bomb fell close to! My hair was covered with dust and plaster. Terrified? I should think so, but I didn't dare show it. . . . Yes, the company carried on with play—amazing of them. One could hardly hear what they said, though, for the noise of the barrage."[36]

Yet despite these uncomfortable experiences, the landscapes of London and other cities could be much more welcoming, places of warmth, recreation and relaxation during the war years. The recent "Capital Cities at War" project has provided a number of case studies that move the reader away from the front line to describe the war's impact on the continuing cultural life of Paris, London and Berlin.[37] The theatres, revues and music halls of London remained open to provide a real escape for both civilians on the Home Front and service personnel on leave from the army. In this volume, Andrew Maunder builds on such approaches to consider the lighter side of Home Front culture in his exploration of the theatrical revues presented on the wartime London stage. A potential vehicle for modernity, yet at the same time a curious hangover from a pre-war world, theatres offered possible political arenas, filled with a captive audience from all areas of society, ripe for persuasion. Entertainments also feature in Emma Hanna's chapter in this volume, which examines the importance of popular song, both as a means of coping during the war and remembering afterwards, in performances at some physical distance from the front lines. And as Maunder points out, theatres and concert halls provided an ideal forum for the articulation of a range of political viewpoints, serving equally well as recruiting stations (Vesta Tilley was particularly involved in this aspect of revue), as they were locations where a temporary escape might be effected.

The range of social and political voices that could be found in the theatre could also be found in other literary forms of the war. The disillusionment that characterised later war writing was by no means the dominant voice in wartime literature. Jane Potter's chapter in this volume gives us a very different voice heard in the poetic recruitment propaganda of Jessie Pope. Potter offers some fascinating examples of Pope's wartime verse while at the same time seeking to dispel myths that have built up around this popular wartime poet. Potter considers Pope's work before, during and after the war to establish her cultural significance as a comic "versifier," rather than a highbrow poet, demonstrating that there was more to her work than her association with "Dulce Et Decorum Est" implies. More complex approaches to patriotic writing are examined in Lise Jaillant's contribution which investigates the interrelationship between women's writing and publishing, through the conflicting agendas of patriotism and pacifism. Jaillant's exploration of the complex relationship between the novelist and poet Rose Macaulay and her publishers, Hodder and Stoughton, maps Macaulay's gradual shift towards pacifism through a reading of her 1916 novel, *Non-combatants and Others*, that placed her at odds with the patriotic agenda of the publisher. As with the landscapes described in the letters in Acton's chapter, this relationship illustrates a blurring of boundaries. It further suggests that the binaries of patriotism and pacifism are unhelpful when it comes to understanding wartime interactions. They remain unhelpful today, despite their prominence in many centenary commemorations.

In the century since the First World War, novelists, poets, historians and composers have continued to write about it. Many of the significant works of literature produced in the decade following the Armistice have never been out of print, and continue to impact on our understanding of the war today. As Emma Hanna shows, it is possible to map musical interest in the war in a similar way across the decades, each composition reflecting the way the war is understood by the generation that produced it. In the years leading up to the centenary, interest in the war and publishing about the war has been on the increase again. Angela K. Smith completes this collection with an essay examining the importance of fiction and memory, a century after the war. By reading the ways in which writers have interpreted the war and its aftermath in the last two decades, she considers how we still strive to understand a war that now only exists in cultural rather than living memory.

This volume continues the trend towards expanding definitions of war experience through considering the perspectives that emerge from a number of different voices and landscapes. Not all of the voices presented here opposed the war, and not all of the landscapes were comprised of trenches or flanked by barbed wire. Chapters investigate the voices of pro-war patriots, or unusual sites of pleasure including music halls and brothels. Collectively, they combine to offer further fresh insights into the multiplicity of war experience, alternate spaces to the familiar tropes of mud and mayhem.

Notes

1. See, for example, Geoff Dyer, *The Missing of the Somme* (London: Hamish Hamilton, 1994); Jay Winter, *Sites of Memory, Sites of Mourning: The Great War in European Cultural History* (Cambridge: Cambridge University Press, 1995); Jay Winter and Emmanuel Sivan, eds., *War and Remembrance in the Twentieth Century* (Cambridge: Cambridge University Press, 2000); Jay Winter, *Remembering War: The Great War between Memory and History in the Twentieth Century* (London: Yale University Press, 2006); Michael Keren and Holger H. Herwig, eds., *War Memory and Popular Culture: Essays on Modes of Remembrance and Commemoration* (London: McFarland, 2009).
2. Douglas Jerrold, *The Lie about the War: A Note on Some Contemporary War Books* (London: Faber and Faber, 1930); Cyril Falls, *War Books: An Annotated Bibliography of Books about the Great War* (London: Greenhill, 1989 [1930] 1930).
3. Charles Carrington, *Soldier from the Wars Returning* (London: Hutchinson, 1965) 258.
4. Brian Bond, *The Unquiet Western Front: Britain's Role in Literature and History* (Cambridge: Cambridge University Press, 2002); Janet Watson, *Fighting Different Wars: Experience, Memory, and the First World War in Britain* (Cambridge: Cambridge University Press, 2004); Dan Todman, *The Great War, Myth and Memory* (London: Hambledon Continuum, 2005).
5. Watson, *Fighting Different Wars*, 308.

6. Watson, *Fighting Different Wars*, 297.
7. Gary Sheffield, *Forgotten Victory: The First World War: Myths and Realities* (London: Headline Book Publishing, 2001).
8. J. Macleod and Pierre Purseigle, eds., *Uncovered Fields: Perspectives on First World War Studies* (Leiden: Brill, 2004); P. Purseigle, ed., *Warfare and Belligerence: Perspectives on First World War Studies* (Leiden: Brill, 2005); Stéphane Audoin-Rouzeau and Annette Becker, *1914–1918: Understanding the Great War* (London: Profile, 2002).
9. Adrian Gregory, *The Last Great War: Society and the First World War* (Cambridge: Cambridge University Press, 2008) 3–5.
10. Watson, *Fighting Different Wars* (2004).
11. See, for example, Angela Wollacott, *On Her Their Lives Depend: Munitions Workers in the Great War* (London: University of California Press, 1994); Margaret Darrow, *French Women and the First World War: Stories of the Home Front* (Oxford: Berg, 2000); Christine Hallett, *Veiled Warriors: Allied Nurses of the First World War* (Oxford: Oxford University Press, 2014).
12. J. B. Fuller, *Troop Morale and Popular Culture in the British and Dominion Armies, 1914–1918* (Oxford: Oxford University Press, 1990); Craig Gibson, *Behind the Front: British Soldiers and French Civilians, 1914–1918* (Cambridge: Cambridge University Press, 2014).
13. For example, Claire M. Tylee, *The Great War and Women's Consciousness: Images of Militarism and Womanhood* (London: Palgrave Macmillan, 1990); Sharon Ouditt, *Fighting Forces, Writing Women: Identity and Ideology in the First World War* (London: Routledge, 1994); Suzanne Rait and Trudi Tait, eds., *Women's Fiction and the Great War* (Oxford: Clarendon Press, 1997); Trudi Tate, *Modernism, History and the First World War* (Manchester: Manchester University Press, 1998); Margaret R. Higonnet, *Lines of Fire: Women Writers of World War 1* (New York: Plume, 1999); Jean Gallagher, *The World Wars and the Female Gaze* (Carbondale: Southern Illinois University Press, 2000); Angela K. Smith, *The Second Battlefield Women Modernism and the First World War* (Manchester: Manchester University Press, 2000); Angela K. Smith, *Women's Writing of the First World War: An Anthology* (Manchester: Manchester University Press, 2000).
14. For example, Michael Roper, *The Secret Battle: Emotional Survival in the Great War* (Manchester: Manchester University Press, 2009); Stéphane Audoin-Rouzeau, *La Guerre des Enfants, 1914–1918* (Paris: Colin, 1993).
15. Michael Snape and Edward Madigan, eds., *The Clergy in Khaki: New Perspectives on British Army Chaplaincy in the First World War* (Aldershot: Ashgate, 2013); Krisztina Robert, "Gender, Class and Patriotism: Women's Paramilitary Units in First World War Britain", *International History Review* Vol. 19, No. 1 (February, 1997) 52–65; Jane Potter, *Boys in Khaki, Girls in Print: Women's Literary Responses to the Great War 1914–1918* (Oxford: Clarendon Press, 2005); Andrew Frayn, *Writing Disenchantment: British First World War Prose 1914–30* (Manchester: Manchester University Press, 2014).
16. Winter, *Sites of Memory, Sites of Mourning*, 1.
17. Jane Carmichael, *First World War Photography* (London: Routledge, 1989). Connections between photography and popular memory are explored in, for example, Marlene A. Briggs, "The Return of the Aura: Contemporary Writers Look Back at the First World War", in Annette Khun and Kirsten Emiko McAllister, eds., *Locating Memory: Photographic Acts* (Oxford: Berghahn, 2006) 113–134; Geoff Dyer, *The Missing of the Somme* (London: Canongate, 2016) 47–50.
18. For a discussion of this painting and its changing interpretations see Sue Malvern, *Modern Art, Britain and the Great War: Witnessing, Testimony and Remembrance* (London: Yale University Press, 2004) 18–21.

19. See Ross J. Wilson, *Landscapes of the Western Front: Materiality during the Great War* (London: Routledge, 2012); Krista Cowman, "Touring behind the Lines: British Soldiers in French Towns and Cities during the Great War", *Urban History* Vol. 41, No. 1 (2014) 105–123; Gibson, *Behind the Front*.
20. Jay Winter and Antoine Prost, *The Great War in History: Debates and Controversies 1914 to the Present* (Cambridge: Cambridge University Press, 2005) 164.
21. Watson, *Fighting Different Wars*, 2.
22. See Susan R. Grayzel, introduction to "A Change in Attitude: The Women's War Work Collection of the Imperial War Museum", Gale Cengage online collection, 1, www.gale.cengage.com/pdf/facts/womenWar.pdf.
23. Watson, *Fighting Different Wars*, 9.
24. Sheffield, *Forgotten Victory*, 6.
25. Samuel Hynes, *A War Imagined* (London: The Bodley Head, 1990) 311.
26. Falls, *War Books*, 182–183.
27. Edmund Blunden, *Undertones of War* (London: Penguin, 2010 [1928]) Introduced by Hew Strachan, ix.
28. Paul Fussell, *The Great War and Modern Memory* (Oxford: Oxford University Press, 1975) 259.
29. Blunden, *Undertones of War*, 64.
30. Vera Brittain, *Testament of Youth* (London: Virago, 1992 [1933]) 213.
31. Brittain, *Testament of Youth*, 206.
32. Vera Brittain, *Testament of Youth* (London: Virago, 1978 [1933]) 206.
33. Brittain, *Testament of Youth*, 207.
34. Sylvia Pankhurst, "The East End Air Raid", *The Woman's Dreadnought* Vol. 2, No. 12 (Saturday 5 June, 1915) cited in Angela K. Smith, ed., *Women's Writing of the First World War: An Anthology* (Manchester: Manchester University Press, 2000) 241–242.
35. Lady De Frece, *The Recollections of Vesta Tilley* (London: Hutchison, 1934) cited in Angela K. Smith, ed., *Women's Writing of the First World War: An Anthology* (Manchester: Manchester University Press, 2000) 248.
36. Irene Rathbone, *We That Were Young* (London: Virago, 1988 [1932]) 324.
37. Jay Winter and Jean-Louis Robert, eds., *Capital Cities at War. Paris, London, Berlin 1914–1919. Volume Two: A Cultural History* (Cambridge: Cambridge University Press, 2007).

Select Bibliography

Audoin-Rouzeau, Stéphane and Annette Becker. *1914–1918: Understanding the Great War*. London: Profile, 2002.
Blunden, Edmund. *Undertones of War*. London: Penguin, 2010 [1928].
Bond, Brian. *The Unquiet Western Front: Britain's Role in Literature and History*. Cambridge: Cambridge University Press, 2002.
Brittain, Vera. *Testament of Youth*. London: Virago, 1978 [1933].
Carmichael, Jane. *First World War Photography*. London: Routledge, 1989.
Carrington, Charles. *Soldier from the Wars Returning*. London: Hutchinson, 1965.
Dyer, Geoff. *The Missing of the Somme*. London: Hamish Hamilton, 1994.
Falls, Cyril. *War Books: An Annotated Bibliography of Books about the Great War*. London: Greenhill, 1989 [1930].
Frayn, Andrew. *Writing Disenchantment: British First World War Prose 1914–30*. Manchester: MUP, 2014.
Fussell, Paul. *The Great War and Modern Memory*. Oxford: OUP, 1975.

Gregory, Adrian. *The Last Great War: Society and the First World War*. Cambridge: Cambridge University Press, 2008.
Hallett, Christine. *Veiled Warriors: Allied Nurses of the First World War*. Oxford: Oxford University Press, 2014.
Hynes, Samuel. *A War Imagined*. London: The Bodley Head, 1990.
Keren, Michael and Holger H. Herwig, eds. *War Memory and Popular Culture: Essays on Modes of Remembrance and Commemoration*. London: McFarland, 2009.
Macleod, J. and Pierre Purseigle, eds. *Uncovered Fields: Perspectives on First World War Studies*. Leiden: Brill, 2004.
Ouditt, Sharon. *Fighting Forces, Writing Women: Identity and Ideology in the First World War*. London: Routledge, 1994.
Potter, Jane. *Boys in Khaki, Girls in Print: Women's Literary Responses to the Great War 1914–1918*. Oxford: Clarendon Press, 2005.
Purseigle, P., ed. *Warfare and Belligerence: Perspectives on First World War Studies*. Leiden: Brill, 2005.
Rathbone, Irene. *We That Were Young*. London: Virago, 1988 [1932].
Sheffield, Gary. *Forgotten Victory: The First World War: Myths and Realities*. London: Headline Book Publishing, 2001.
Smith, Angela K. *The Second Battlefield Women Modernism and the First World War*. Manchester: MUP, 2000.
Smith, Angela K., ed. *Women's Writing of the First World War: An Anthology*. Manchester: MUP, 2000.
Tate, Trudi. *Modernism, History and the First World War*. Manchester: MUP, 1998.
Todman, Dan. *The Great War, Myth and Memory*. London: Hambledon Continuum, 2005.
Watson, Janet. *Fighting Different Wars: Experience, Memory, and the First World War in Britain*. Cambridge: Cambridge University Press, 2004.
Wilson, Ross J. *Landscapes of the Western Front: Materiality during the Great War*. London: Routledge, 2012.
Winter, Jay. *Sites of Memory, Sites of Mourning: The Great War in European Cultural History*. Cambridge: Cambridge University Press, 1995.
Winter, Jay. *Remembering War: The Great War between Memory and History in the Twentieth Century*. London: Yale University Press, 2006.
Winter, Jay and Emmanuel Sivan, eds. *War and Remembrance in the Twentieth Century*. Cambridge: Cambridge University Press, 2000.
Winter, Jay and Jean-Louis Robert, eds. *Capital Cities at War. Paris, London, Berlin 1914–1919. Volume Two: A Cultural History*. Cambridge: Cambridge University Press, 2007.
Wollacott, Angela. *On Her Their Lives Depend: Munitions Workers in the Great War*. London: University of California Press, 1994.

Part I
Real and Imagined Spaces

1 "Funny Men and Charming Girls"[1]
Revue and the Theatrical Landscape of 1914–1918

Andrew Maunder

The established view of First World War theatre in Britain is that it responded to the declaration of war on 4 August 1914 with a flood of crude propaganda plays and never really recovered. Although historians have developed a more sympathetic approach to wartime entertainment, recognizing its importance to combatant and civilian life, much of what was shown remains ignored. A case in point is revue, a pre-war package of topical sketches, comedians and chorus girls which achieved mass appeal after 1914.[2] If revue remains neglected, it is not because of a shortage of evidence but because the form itself remains denigrated; silly, superficial, commercial, it seems to represent much that is antithetical to "serious" works produced during the conflict—the writings of trench poets, for example. Yet one of the most famous indictments in Siegfried Sassoon's poem "'Blighters'" (1917) was prompted by watching *Fall In!* at the Liverpool Hippodrome in December 1916. The poem's description of the show's "prancing/Ranks of harlots," the audience's "cackle" and Sassoon's wish for a tank to come "lurching" in and crush this unfeeling display, is often used to highlight revue's questionable attractions, not least its apparently callous disregard for the realities of war.[3]

Historians of wartime culture have tended to follow Sassoon, adopting a disparaging stance towards an ephemeral form of entertainment that sought public approval and a "fast buck." Certainly it is the disposable songs which stand out when we look at a show like the Charles Cochran-produced *Pell Mell* (1916) (Figure 1.1) which ran for 300 performances at London's Ambassadors theatre with titles including "I'm a Musical Comedy Bus'ness Man", and "I'd Like to Know what Cleopatra Did." Producers like Cochran have been accused of putting serious plays "out of action" during the war, putting on puerile comic sketches that exploited vulnerable soldiers on leave who were happy because they "were no longer under fire" and ready to be pleased by anything, as George Bernard Shaw put it.[4]

Along with Sassoon, Shaw's comments offer the best-known disapproval of populist wartime theatre but he did at least recognise its appeal. In 1919 Shaw recalled how London's theatres were "crowded every night with thousands of soldiers on leave [who] were not seasoned London playgoers," often "accompanied by damsels (called flappers)" who together drove the

Figure 1.1 Antony (Leon Morton) and Cleopatra (Dorothy Minto), *Pell Mell*, 1916.

fare on offer.[5] Another eyewitness, W. Macqueen-Pope, noted soldiers' families including parents "who had never been inside a theatre before, thinking them sinful places, went with their sons and found they were really very enjoyable."[6] Writing in 1918, George Street noted how these spaces also attracted the "great many war-workers living in London."[7] Many of these new theatregoers were women who now had their own money to spend.

These observers sounded common themes: the theatre world changing; new audiences entering unfamiliar surroundings. But they—and many others—also highlighted the extent to which London was serving as a "clearing house for the Western Front" encouraging a boom in theatre attendance.[8] A report written in November 1915 by B.W. Findon summarised how leave trains:

> discharged some three thousand officers and men per day, and weekend leave from the various camps in the country has brought to London hundreds of young officers who are bent on making the most of their Friday and Saturday. A good percentage of these . . . would have been differently occupied in the days before the war . . . but the man who has endured the monotony and mud of camp life for several weeks naturally seeks the delights of urban life.[9]

With no organised activities during leave, theatres became places for these men to find diversion. Two years later, revue producer Albert de Courville claimed that 75% of audiences were now soldiers of all ranks.[10] Among them was nineteen-year-old Australian Jack Duffell whose experience of leave at "home" in 1917 included two days in London ("civilization"), where he and another soldier saw the musical, *High Jinks*, which they "enjoyed immensely."[11] A British officer, Lieutenant F.H. Ennor, whose rank entitled him to more leave than "ordinary" soldiers, spent evenings similarly engaged. In February 1917 he saw the revues *Three Cheers* and *Zig Zag*, as well as the exotic musical *Chu Chin Chow*. This was followed by *The Bing Girls* in March, *Zig Zag* again and *Smile* before he was sent out to the Front.[12] Lieutenant Wilfred Owen's last recorded theatre trip in June 1918 was to see *The Bing Boys on Broadway*, the (mis)adventures of two British country bumpkin brothers in America.[13]

Although other entertainment held its appeal, this chapter will argue for the importance of wartime revue and highlight some of the ways in which revues were generated and played out. When J.M. Barrie's *Rosy Rapture*, starring the exotic French *danseuse*, Gaby Deslys, and featuring a kinema picture of chapters in the life of a young baby and a vicious lampoon of national treasure, Sir Herbert Beerbohm Tree, premiered in March 1915, at least one in the Duke of York's Theatre audience—H.M. Walbrook—saw it as a symptom of cultural decline, or at least that the world really was "beginning to turn upside down."[14] As will be seen, many of Walbrook's contemporaries agreed with him. Others, however, saw revues as important outlets for escapism and sociability as well as supplying a kind of black or ironic humour, which appealed to the wartime population, particularly servicemen. More recently James Ross Moore has suggested that revues should be seen as the period's most modern form of musical theatre: escapist certainly, but also "vital, influential and innovative," at the same time as being capable of offering trenchant social commentary.[15] Thus although revues have often been dismissed as theatrical froth they occupied a more complex theatrical space than we have traditionally been led to believe, involving different cultural fields and enterprises and a variety of subject positions.

A Theatre for the War

Most contemporary accounts agree that from autumn 1914 the appetite for revue became "rampant."[16] The form predated the war with producers and performers such as George Grossmith, Harry Pelissier and Charles Cochran, importing elements from France (where revue was well-established) and, after the advent of ragtime and syncopated music, the United States.[17] Notable pre-war successes included *Kill that Fly* (1912) and *Hullo Tango!* (1913). The war, however, represented a watershed in revue's popularity. Whilst "serious" plays such as Edward Thurston's shell-shock drama *The Cost* (1914) closed early, revue began to flourish—"the only theatrical entertainment for which there is still a huge public," as a writer for *Tatler* noted in June 1915.[18] In *The Other Theatre* (1947), Norman Marshall suggested that this transformation in the theatrical landscape coincided with the wartime decline of the middle-aged Edwardian actor-managers such as Herbert Beerbohm Tree, George Alexander and Fred Terry, and the purchase of theatres by uncouth "business magnates" who, by staging revues and musicals, made "money out of the completely uncritical war-time audience." Marshall felt these men viewed their theatrical properties as "impersonally" as their other holdings—"factories, the hotels, the chains of shops, the blocks of flats" with no interest in the theatre as art.[19] His interpretation says a lot about how revue has come to be positioned; promoters are judged as obscure or irrelevant and content as crude and opportunistic, yet the genre cannot be completely ignored.

More recently, Gordon Williams has found more of interest in the ways in which two forms of wartime revue—the spectacular and the intimate—overtook musical comedy as the main competitor for audiences for plays, yet became classed as "low" rather than "high" culture.[20] This label proved difficult to shake off. In 1917 *Tatler* described revues as "pantomimes without the fairytale."[21] While, on the one hand, a reference to the idea that a revue's task was to offer spectacular scenes and light-hearted escapism, on the other, it is a comment designed to suggest dumbing down. By this time the cultural landscape had altered to include such names as the aforementioned Charles Cochran (1872–1951), Alfred Butt (1878–1962), André Charlot (1882–1956) and Albert de Courville (1887–1960), well-known and reliable money-spinners who developed revue into a speciality, bringing good business to the theatres in which they had a financial interest, enabling them to keep afloat in quiet periods. As has been noted, these were "new types" of theatre professionals. As "producers" (a new term in 1914) they competed with each other and with the actor managers reliant on wartime revivals of costume dramas such as *The Scarlet Pimpernel* or *Sweet Nell of Old Drury* which audiences were believed to find comforting and uplifting but which were also old-fashioned.

The sense of the war sweeping "legitimate" drama away beneath a deluge of revues is apparent in the testimonies of theatrical critics and other theatregoers of the time. Some had expected that the war would create a new brand of patriotic drama to inspire the nation but they were disappointed. As the *Bystander* complained in March 1915, it was revues which were

> positively pouring on, and without even a particle of a pretence of seriousness of purpose about them . . . The purifying effect of war we all talked so much about—where is it? The same sort of chorus girls—and men—are taking the middle of the stage again . . . and any night of the week the Britisher whose country is fighting a very hard fight for its very existence, may be seen in his thousands absolutely absorbed in the very last touch in rag-time or the latest undressing act. . . . Where are the

popular dramas and the stage idols of this great crisis in our history? An Irving in *Hamlet*, a Benson in *King Henry V*? Not a bit of it. The attractions of the moment are such "features" as Elsie Janis at the Palace.[22]

Shakespeare, of course, represented the best part of Britain's cultural heritage, and old prejudices died hard. Nonetheless theatre managers up and down the country encouraged revues, knowing that the form had broad audience appeal. When Herbert Beerbohm Tree was quizzed about the early closure of his revival of *Henry IV Part 1* at Britain's unofficial national theatre, His Majesty's, in November 1914, he could only say "that even the splendid heroics of Hotspur [. . .] are not so appealing at the moment."[23] Instead people rushed to see Phyllis Monkman's "Pom-Pom Dance" in *Everything New? Not Likely* at the Alhambra. The actor Fred Kerr recalled how suddenly "everything was altered." "Nothing that was worthwhile seemed to interest the public . . . the only plays the soldiers home on leave would take to were the absolutely irresponsible song-and-dance kind of entertainment."[24] To secure work, Kerr wrote a comic sketch for himself and toured it round variety theatres, as did Tree, who in 1915 appeared at the Finsbury Park Empire with a condensed version of his biggest pre-war hit, *Trilby*, in which he played the villainous Svengali.

Both Kerr and Tree, at least, seem to have accepted the revue with *sang-froid*; Tree turned to another new medium—film—and left for Hollywood in 1915. The idea that revue was a more agreeable "tonic" for a nation at war than Shakespeare was a popular defence used by producers and performers anxious to flag up their patriotic credentials. When a revised version of *The Passing Show of 1915* opened at London's Palace Theatre in June 1915 much was made of the fact that there was virtually no mention of the war in it. But as one commentator noted, no-one need feel guilty; this was "as it should be." Nor did it imply a lack of patriotism. "After all, it does not mean that because we are not talking about the war we are not thinking about it. We are. But we don't want to go where it is made 'frightful' or where it is laughed at. Both jar. We go where we can get away from it."[25] This expression of the pleasure principle was repeatedly deployed to explain revue's attractions across the whole spectrum of wartime theatregoers.[26] Some theatre managers used the slogan "No Patriotic Scenes Here" to attract soldiers on leave seeking to avoid reminders of the fighting.[27] But revue's popularity was also interpreted as a sign of the British public's coolness in a crisis, something apparent in another 1915 article, "The Passing Shows of the Year." Its author, "Arkay," explained how,

> It is something purely English this turning away from realities at a moment of great national crisis. It takes an Englishman to understand that a momentary dabble with frivolity is a sign not of indifference but of real seriousness of purpose. It is this delight in the utterly inappropriate which keeps the average Englishman so sane.[28]

Much subsequent discussion of theatre's wartime role was preoccupied with the issue of "business as usual," an updated version of the code which had enabled Britain to govern her Empire. This was considered in contrast to the German theatre industry which, despite having its own pre-war tradition of revue, apparently preferred to "feed" its public's "patriotism and sense of duty" with "peals of pompous thunder," blood-thirsty plays with a strong nationalist message. It was far better to be a revue lover, to brave the Zeppelins and Gothas, and meet death "with a whimsical smile."[29]

Performances and Personalities

The responses above suggest the wartime theatre industry's debt and continuing commitment to revue, as well as the form's relatively low status in subsequent histories of the period. But why were revues popular? Escapism was part of it but so, too, from a producer's perspective, was the speed with which an efficient writer could knock up a satirical sketch or song or whole revue from topical materials. For example, *Samples* (1915), centring on the attempts by a young man, Eustace Slackitt, to find a wartime role, reputedly took only six weeks to produce from idea to opening night. Revues were also fluid; there was scope for last-minute removals and additions if something wasn't working, making them a safer bet for investors.[30] And if the revue was being written for a particular *artiste* or *ensemble*—Shirley Kellogg, Pearl White, George Formby Sr., or Will Evans—it would usually enable them to showcase the tried and tested specialisms their fans appreciated. In *Half Past Eight* (1916), the new sketch featuring Evans as the conductor of a tube train trying to eat his dinner proved the greatest draw while *Shell Out!*, which ran for 315 performances between 1915 and 1916, had Fred Emney as an old lady struggling over a stile and as "Verbeena," an underwear saleswoman (Figure 1.2). Like music halls, running order was more important than a coherent story. There was also much talk of "revuesical free and easiness."[31] Theatregoers could arrive halfway through a revue, after dinner, and still follow what was happening. "Some of them [. . .] possess a certain amount of underlying plot" noted the *Sketch*, "but, roughly speaking, this is not a thing to be generally adhered to, or even to be primarily aimed at." Some revues had male and female tour guides—*compère* and *commère*—leading the audience through the different scenes but these were secondary features. Instead, as the *Sketch* noted, revues' chief object was "to make a portion of the evening pass with a swing and a certain amount of melody."[32]

Generally speaking, however, revue processes and limits did not lend themselves to much in-depth reflection, unless those involved were forced to defend themselves to the Lord Chamberlain's Office or the law courts. For the former's staff, tasked with licensing these productions, one problem was an apparent lack of rules beyond the fact that revues were all very self-consciously modern. "A 'Revue' is simply a series of 'turns' [. . .] more often without any continuity whatsoever, produced under a comprehensive and generally irrelevant title,"

Figure 1.2 Shell Out (1915). Bashful Gentleman: I should like to see a male attendant. Verbeena (Fred Emney): I am a male female attendant.

explained the Lord Chamberlain, Lord Sandhurst.[33] What *can* be gleaned is that those in authority seem to have regarded revue as an anarchic form always liable to overstep the mark, not least because of the tendency on the part of producers to insert new "jokes and 'business'" once the show was up and running whilst keeping the original licensed title.[34]

One person who did try to explain how a revue worked was André Charlot, producer of *5064 Gerrard* (1915), *Bubbly* (1916), and *Buzz Buzz* (1917) among many others. In "Producing English Revue" (1934) Charlot defined the genre as a "medley of spectacle, topicalities, sketches, songs etc., with a full cast, consistent in size with the theatre where it is being produced, and no attempt at a plot of any kind."[35] Charlot's iteration of the absence of a coherent plot is significant because it was this which distinguished revue from its close relation, musical comedy. As a writer for *Tatler* explained in 1915, in a revue:

> [t]here is no plot to worry over, and no difficulty about leading up to any scene or song apropos of nothing that has gone before. If the heroine suddenly appears in harem trousers after being in a crinoline all evening—who asks why? . . . It is all in a night's work.[36]

Where revue scored was in its "pace," "speed," "sound" and "variety," its witty word play and its endless possibilities for the bizarre.[37] As *Tatler's* writer noted, even a "legitimate" actor of the calibre of Sarah Bernhardt could be teamed up with some performing animals to "appear in the same entertainment under the same title of *Kick Out!*, or some other exclamation of the hour, and no one . . . would ask the reason why. That could only happen, and happen quite naturally in a *revue*."[38] Thus as a creative endeavour it did not seem too much of a challenge, provided one had the financial backers—and getting these did not seem too difficult either.

Although this picture of greedy businessmen running amok in wartime theatreland has coloured perceptions of revue, decisions about what kind of revue to put on were more considered. There was, for example, the lure of smaller, "intimate" revue (in a theatre seating less than 1,000), where, as B.W. Findon noted in a review of Cochran's *More* (Ambassadors, 1915), one could expect to see "the artists flit[ting] from scene to scene of topical interest and artistic variety" like "busy bees."[39] *More* begins with a strike by four chorus girls who plead their cause in song and dance; another sketch prompted by the restrictive Defence of the Realm Act, satirises the problems of "Buying a Drink" in wartime. This was up-to-date material appealing to a sense of shared audience recognition but offered within certain safe limits. Indeed one of the points made by contemporary observers was that British revues avoided serious topics, unlike their French counterparts. *The Bystander* noted that whereas the former were "too polite to refer to the fact that we are war with the mad Kaiser," French producers were unable to "forget that one dominating feature of our daily lives" and depicted "Hun" brutality without flinching.[40] When the producers of the London revue *By Jingo if We Do*

(1915) tried a similar tactic, by including a playlet depicting a Frenchwoman defending herself from rape (not shown at matinees), press discomfort was evident. Audiences were believed to want "brightness,"[41] which for some producers meant less dialogue, more spectacle, plus music capable of making feet tap by an orchestra whose default setting was *fortissimo*.[42]

Some producers—notably de Courville and Cochran (christened "the English Ziegfeld") made no disguise of their admiration for this style of entertainment. They particularly liked brash American extravaganzas and made frequent trips to Broadway to source songs, performers and dance instructors to drill the chorus girls in the latest ragtime rhythms. As much a visual as an aural experience, the spectacular revue thus seemed to promise the kind of powerful—sometimes exotic—escapist experience wartime theatre managers rarely found in plays. This emerges in the open letter Cochran wrote to promote *As You Were* (1918). After noting that there is nothing more satisfying at the present time "than that of providing popular recreation" and thereby engaging with "a joyous consciousness of usefulness," Cochran explains that after years of trying to "acclimatise that peculiarly French form of entertainment called Revue" he has now "achieved complete and final success." He promises "a closely-knit, interesting story [. . .] scintillating with wit, keen in topical allusion [. . .] worded to beautiful music [. . .] a gem of literature and art."[43]

A slightly different, less pretentious, account of revue's appeal appears in actress Beatrice Lillie's memoirs. Describing the Alhambra's production of *Now's the Time* (1915) with sets designed by Egyptologist Arthur Brome Weignall, Lillie colourfully evokes the audience's response to the ancient Egyptian ballet: "slowly moving figures carrying urns and palms fronds like slaves in a stone freize [. . .] This was 'The Spirit of Egypt' [. . .] the drums, cymbals and flutes were pounding out pyramid-style music." As Cleopatra, Phyllis Monkman was "whirling and weaving all over the stage." When a wardrobe malfunction exposed Cleopatra's breast "there was a gasp and a cheer" but Monkman continued "holding her bare left breast in her left hand and pointing to the trophy with her right."[44] Lillie was in no doubt that while the (probably accidental) slip would have caused apoplexy in the Lord Chamberlain's Office, the 3,000 war-strained playgoers in the Alhambra Theatre's gallery left the theatre having got the show-stopping moment that they had paid to see.

Despite Monkman's and to a lesser extent, Lillie's, celebrity, it was Gaby Deslys who remained the biggest draw.[45] In 1915 the *Illustrated Sporting and Dramatic News* had no doubt that "Mlle Deslys [. . .] is a very queen of players. Women shriek wildly with joy, and strong men break down and gasp, at the glory of it."[46] The air of scandal surrounding Deslys—a former mistress of King Manuel II of Portugal—intrigued audiences. As well as wanting to know what she ate for breakfast, people wanted to see the exotic Frenchwoman in the flesh and discover whether she could actually dance (she could), sing (less so) and act (not so much). In 1915 Deslys was thus one of the attractions of *5064 Gerrard* (Figure 1.3) but she faced competition from her co-star, Robert Hale, a leader in the performance style known as "revue ragging."[47] Hale's impersonation of Deslys (Figure 1.4) where he

Figure 1.3 Gaby Deslys and Harry Pilcer, *5064 Gerrard* (1915).

claimed to have focussed on her "perpetually open mouth," followed by his "exhibition dance" with "A Revue Author" (dressed as J.M. Barrie, author of Deslys' previous flop, *Rosy Rapture*) was as much talked about as the real Deslys' dancing.[48] So, too, was the revue's "beauty chorus," exhibited in

Figure 1.4 Gaby Deslys (Robert Hale) and J.M. Barrie (Jack Morrison), *5064 Gerrard* (1915).

haute couture and then in shorts (as boy scouts). The revue's twelve scenes followed a familiar pattern. Unlike a play or musical there was no obvious narrative drive or conflict to be resolved. Instead, a central figure, Sam, a naïve young tourist, comes to London and is shown the sights by the *commère*, Miss Prim. His arrival at the railway station features a range of city "types": comic porter, snooty ticket-office clerk, waiters (who transmogrify into a knife thrower and his hapless assistant). A cross-dressing, Beatrice Lillie appeared as "The Boy from Michigan" singing about his/her home-sickness. After being fleeced by a rogue antique dealer, Sam and his guide visit fashionable Murray's night club—faithfully reproduced on stage—where an exhibition of the foxtrot precedes Phyllis Monkman performing a new dance. The appearance of sixty cast members dressed as pierrots looped round the stage formed the basis for a finale "The Pearl

Necklace." In 1915 *5064 Gerrard* set a benchmark; its team of writers aimed to be satirical and witty, tuned into current world events but also different theatrical styles. New sketches were added during its run, it carried a mixture of new and established popular songs and above all, it was aggressively marketed, helped by its title which was also the telephone number of the theatre's box-office.

The Reckoning

Although revues were popular with the public, one reason for the conflicting attitudes towards them was the flippant—sometimes insubordinate—attitudes they seemed to encourage at a time of national crisis. On the one hand, overtly serious reflections on the war were rare. The usual policy was to endorse the war effort and also, as was the case in the popular media, ridicule pacifists. Conscientious objectors were generally sources for comedy, depicted as limp-wristed shirkers. On the other hand, revues paraded women in bathing costumes and cracked subversive jokes about politicians and newspaper proprietors with abandon. The result was that some critics and moralists tended to shake their heads in horror at the irreverence and the flesh on display. They were fearful, too, about the "demoralising" messages audiences took away, and the connection between revues and immorality was the subject of many articles in the press. Public concern is clear in correspondence with the Lord Chamberlain's Office. Correspondents included regulars such as the London Council for the Promotion of Public Morality (chairman: Arthur Winnington-Ingram, Bishop of London) and private individuals outraged by what they had seen. One such was Charles Crombie, a London resident, who stormed out of a boisterous sketch about army life at the Golders Green Hippodrome in September 1914 and suggested a fine of £100 for any entertainment "casting ridicule upon the army or calculated to discourage enlistment."[49] In spring 1915, complaints were received from provincial local authorities about chorus girls in bathing costumes in touring revues ("highly objectionable"), organised by the powerful syndicate, Moss Empires. Moss were forced to write to their theatre managers stressing the need to "avoid such complaints and in this respect to ensure that the clothing of all ladies in tights shall extend from the knee upwards so as to adequately cover their thighs and breasts."[50] By this stage, even the theatre industry's trade paper, *The Era*, was forced to admit that some producers "with pornographic intent, pander to the lowest tastes, put a premium on nakedness, and do their utmost [. . .] to degrade the poor girls of the chorus by their insistence on scanty clothes" and "cunningly arranged business of an indecorous character."[51] There was a feeling that some revues were moving into different cultural spaces and, in some cases, into a different (seedier) tradition at odds with the reputation for usefulness and respectability, which the theatre industry sought to secure. The comedian Fred Karno, originator of a form of sketch comedy with no dialogue, was seen as a particular troublemaker. His touring revues bore little similarity to the versions submitted for licensing, and included "a great deal of undress" and "suggestive dialogue."[52] Besieged on all sides, the Lord Chamberlain told Lord Stamfordham, King George V's private secretary he was "doing my best to have a general clean up all round" but was hampered by the scale of the revue industry "representing I understand about five millions of capital," as well as other vested interests.[53]

For the authorities, the evidence was highly troubling, and from the outbreak of war through to 1918 the question of how best to police revues became a source of anxiety. In autumn 1914, a dispute erupted over the "premeditated wantonness" and "doubtful morality,"[54] which some revues were thought to encourage when the Lord Chamberlain's Office warned Alfred Butt, a highly respectable man responsible for twenty-five theatres, that he faced prosecution if he allowed Gaby Deslys' risqué dancing in *The Rajah's Ruby*: "These are not the times for producing performances that are likely to create difficulties."[55] While Butt, already tired of Deslys and her demands, was amenable he replied that he could do little without breaching his contract and putting other people out of work.[56] Nonetheless, he wrote to Deslys to try to extricate himself, explaining that he had received a telephone call from the Lord Chamberlain,

> from which I gather that his Lordship does not think this is an opportune time for you to re-appear in London. . . . It is therefore very necessary that I should point out to you that just now we are passing through a terrible crisis, and the public feeling is naturally quite different from what it is under normal conditions . . . any performance given should be free from offence or anything that could be considered as in doubtful taste or questionable. I am sure that you will realise the importance of this, as I have done in the preparation of your play, and will not in its interpretation introduce anything by way of action, gesture or dance that could possibly cause offence. . . . [Maybe] you would prefer to cancel your present engagement until more normal conditions exist.[57]

Were people really sufficiently impressionable to be sent over the edge by Deslys' performances? Many critics believed so, and what seems neurotic now did not seem so at the time. The Chamberlain's Office fanned the flames of overreaction by putting Deslys under surveillance, despatching one of its readers, Ernest Bendall, to a rehearsal. Disappointingly, all appeared prosaic. "I saw nothing indelicate as regards dress or undress, nor anything improperly suggestive in the way of gesture and 'business'. [Desylys'] dancing . . . is of the semi-artistic semi-gymnastic order."[58] Nonetheless Butt had to promise that there would be no slippage. Once a license had been issued, it was all too easy to break free from the agreed script with a wink here, a throwaway comment there, creating an onslaught on decency that was deemed to be hard for theatre-goers to withstand, especially at this time, when the country needed all its reserves of moral strength to defeat Germany.

Tensions between producers and regulators of theatrical taste became most apparent, however, in the furore surrounding Charles Cochran's October 1914 production of *Odds and Ends*. Cochran, as has been seen, embodied the complex symbiosis between theatre and economics as an innovator and an entrepreneur, for whom orchestrating controversy seemed to be the breath of life. He had enormous confidence in his own abilities as a showman, claiming that his were the only true revues, surpassing the usual "hotchpotch" his competitors tried to fob off onto audiences.[59] Accordingly, there was a buzz surrounding this "intimate" show at the Ambassadors, but no one was prepared for the response to the sketch "My Lady's Undress." In this piece, a burglar entered a bedroom and, hearing its owner approaching, hid behind a fireguard, which was too small. A woman, played by the French performer Alice Delysia, entered and began to undress. Having got down to her underwear, she moved behind a screen to remove everything else. Throwing across the top first her stockings and then the remainder of her clothes, she waved her bare arms above the screen and then protruded her bare leg from the side. The burglar sidled up and collapsed the screen, Delysia uttering the words "too late, too late" as she appeared fully clothed. This so-called "undressing act" was vague in its stage directions, and set off no danger signals in the Lord Chamberlain's Office. However, reports filtered back that in performance Delysia's "bare thigh beneath very short drawers" could clearly be seen.[60] There was also something not-quite-nice about the way the burglar seemed to ogle the lady and collected and counted the pieces of discarded clothing. "It is utterly impossible adequately to convey [. . .] any idea of the nastiness and undesirability of the performance" raged the Alliance of Honour, an influential social purity organisation.[61] Meanwhile the rest of the theatre went into uproar, with the bulk of the audience—many of them soldiers—cheering Delysia. Within days, postcards depicting the scene were on sale in the foyer. A newspaper campaign began claiming that those concerned were unhinged by the stresses of war and should have more important things to think about.[62] Others asked what century objectors thought they were living in.[63] But complainants argued that the sketch was a throwback to a less moral age when licentiousness was an accepted part of public entertainment. (The play followed fears about soldiers on leave being corrupted by predatory young women and the accompanying idea that promiscuity "had the capacity to help destroy the British nation.")[64] Thus the scene enacted by one of those "Continental players who . . . have sought sanctuary in this country"[65] was not only corrupting but undermined the war effort from within. There was a sense—much like that which had earlier dogged music halls—that a new line had been crossed, or at least blurred, through the voyeurism which was the sketch's *modus operandi*. West End audiences were being given the same kind of hyper-sexualised stage displays on offer in underground nightclubs and brothels, or so it was believed. Ironically, of course, the public loved the revue; it took £8,000 at the box-office and ran for 257 performances. The playwright Edward Knoblock observed how in such spaces it was possible to see "a relaxation of all former standards"; even "[m]others laughed publicly at jokes with their sons, which under peace conditions they would not have tolerated for an instant. What did anything matter so long as the dear boys were amused? They might very soon be informed officially that they were never to hear him laugh again."[66] Meanwhile, Cochran felt himself both persecuted and vindicated in equal measure maintaining that Delysia had always worn pantaloons with elastic bands which kept them tight to the knee.[67] He felt superior to those policing him, convinced that he had helped revolutionise revue with a break-through brand of sophisticated, ironic, adult entertainment which, in turn, was dragging British theatre into the modern age.

Although exaggerating the potential impact of such pieces, the voices of the wartime groups opposing revue did represent genuine concerns. These concerns continued throughout the war. Another flashpoint came in August 1916, when General Sir Horace Smith Dorrien made a much-publicised complaint about the stage's "indecent and suggestive unnecessaries"[68] and the demoralizing effects of "scantily dressed girls and songs of doubtful character" on "young officers and soldiers."[69] Managements led by Cochran protested strongly at the unfairness of it all.[70] Oswald Stoll sued Smith for libel.[71] In 1917 there were concerns, too, about the sexual jokes in Robert Hale's burlesque of the recent stage adaptation of Eleanor Glyn's erotic bestseller *Three Weeks* in the revue *Topsy Turvey* (1917) in which Hale assumed the role of the Balkan Queen seducing a young Englishman. In the same production, a jungle ballet in which an "almost naked white girl" was pawed by an excited gorilla, likewise had members of the London Council for the Promotion of Public Morality reaching for their fountain pens.[72] By 1918, even broad-minded observers like Arnold Bennett felt that revue was venturing into areas which were best kept off-limits. After seeing *As You Were* he was struck by the extent to which "[e]very scene turned on adultery, or mere copulation," and incredulous that "[t]his revue is the greatest success in London at present, and is taking about £3,000 a week."[73] Even for the open-minded there was something disturbing about these licensed antics; was this what the country was fighting for?

Staging the Spectacular

While there was little evidence that theatregoers were corrupted by revues, anxieties that they might be continued to be heard. What *is* true is that revues had started to form their own aesthetic fuelled by developments in technology and performance. The impacts of *5064 Gerard* or *As You Were* were based not only on a deliberate breach of *politesse* but also on some very ambitious staging. These were familiar features of musical comedies more generally, of course, but what seems to have excited theatregoers was not what they heard but what they *saw*. The most influential developments in presentation were those encouraged by Albert de Courville, who explained that his productions, intended for "a public that wanted 'bucking up,'" were all about creating "comfort and cheeriness, with a lack of restraint."[74] Accordingly, each of his shows would include "at least four big full-stage spectacular effects."[75] His *Razzle Dazzle* (Drury Lane, 1916) is often cited as kick-starting this kind of sensational theatrical experience, although it was not the first. Like other revues, it was centred on star performers—in this case Shirley Kellogg and George Formby Sr.—but the other main draw was the scenery: recreations of Niagara Falls, of St Moritz in which skaters waltzed on real ice, and a climactic Scottish scene with mountains, 400 pipers and female dancers wearing kilts. While de Courville boasted that these effects prompted more applause than he had ever heard in a theatre other observers found a non-too-subtle attempt to hide the thinness of the script:

> Someone always doing something [. . .] limelights are flashing in every direction [. . .] the band is nearly always playing fortissimo [. . .] you could not wish to watch a greater bustling about, and yet—and yet—it seems to be, as it were, bustle for nothing at all beyond the desire to keep everything and everyone on the move.[76]

Such scenes became commonplace as producers tried to out-do each other. But while these shows were popular with audiences, they were not, critics claimed "honest tonics." De Courville's "idea of a 'spectacle' is not the right one," claimed *Tatler*.

> If you multiply ten chorus girls by twenty you don't get splendour, you simply get a crowd. In the same way, if you commission an expensive scene, deck out fifty young women in dazzling raiment merely for the sake of one song, you don't thrill the audience into believing the song is a masterpiece if it is only a rather poor number.

The intention was to appear bright and modern but the result meant "nothing [. . .] beyond the wonder that there are so few collisions." Moreover, as another observer noted, on this occasion the show failed to divert as rumours of a German invasion distracted the audience from the stage "in spite of its being covered with the most fearfully expensive war-time scenery imaginable."[77]

Other revues with gimmicks included *Business as Usual* (1914; a mechanical horse); *Joy-Land* (1915; an ocean liner leaving Liverpool); *Hanky Panky* (1917; a Venetian gondola) and *Smile* (June 1917; a ring of fire with a girl's face in every flame). The latter was a spectacular production replete with fifteen rapidly changing scenes, including a burlesque of a charity concert in which the leading players fail to turn up, and satires on the Irish question, the awarding of military honours and the vexed question of "war economy." This last sketch critiqued Neville Chamberlain, the Government's Director of National Service, who, in a speech given to theatre mangers the previous month, had demanded more restrained productions, claiming that expensive sets and costumes removed the labour force from "work more directly concerned with the prosecution of the war."[78] Puritan critics, meanwhile, argued that fashionable clothes seen in revues (Figure 1.5) encouraged women to go out and fritter away their money.[79] How effective such calls were is unclear. Although Cochran's next revue £150 boasted that its cost was the same as its title, most were unconvinced. In the wake of Chamberlain's speech, *The Referee* observed that producers "feverishly" trying to outbid each other to secure star performers were offering higher salaries than those given Cabinet Ministers.[80] Meanwhile, at the end of 1917 the writers of retrospectives of the theatrical year saw little change; there was a shortage of talented performers which producers sought to "disguise . . . with gorgeous scenery and dresses," the resulting "sparkle" intended to distract the audience from the absence of any real substance or talent.[81] It was not simply that many experienced male performers had been called up. Instead, a performer's ability to move an audience via a song or a joke was less important than his or her ability to look good in fashionable clothes whilst avoiding getting hit by stage machinery. Commentators, ranging from J.T. Grein, champion of the pre-war "New Drama" to Marie Lloyd, famous representative of traditional music hall, expressed their hope that revue's days were numbered.[82]

Figure 1.5 Houp La! (1916) Song: "The Place Where the Peaches Grow." "I like the place where the peaches grow because I haven't picked a lemon yet."

Not everyone disapproved, however. Raymond Blathwayt found the ability to be excited or stirred by wartime revues a testament to man's essential humanity. In "*More* and Futurism" (1915), Blathwayt noted how:

> In a quaint, odd way—very quaint and odd—a Revue [. . .] reveals itself a veritable microcosm of life, a kind of distorted mirror [. . .] of this mighty world. Like the curious and maddeningly involved pattern of a Futurist painting . . . [it] hints at the craze or the weakness of the futility of the passing moment, whilst out of the dazzling mosaic of emotions with which it so endlessly sparkles and scintillates you choose that one which makes its own special appeal to your individuality [. . .].[83]

Whether watching from the stalls as an adult or recalling similar feelings he had experienced as a child in the 1880s, it *was* possible for Blathwayt to imagine that revue was offering a deeper physical-emotional—even transformative—experience than first appeared: "a revelation of things existent which I had not deemed possible heretofore." Yet beyond the impression that he was being driven towards a brave new world of the future, Blathwayt could not quite explain it. One clue, however, might be found in Gordon Williams' recent analysis of revue's dynamics. Williams argues that revue "broke away from the rigidities of the well-made play with its fraudulent implications of an ordered world,"[84] that it involved "an erosion of theatrical convention" and was designed to make people question "reality" itself. In this sense, revue's antics made it the most obvious example of *avant garde* theatre, part of a "fragmented modernist consciousness" whose associations with disorder and chaos captured the turmoil engulfing Europe. Others might argue, that revue was a form of theatre that simply went about its business, but commentaries and diaries of the time indicate that Blathwayt's reaction was not an isolated one. Many noted that revue's content and structure—or lack of it—mirrored the "topsy-turvy effects of the war."[85] Cynthia Asquith (daughter-in-law of Prime Minister Hebert Asquith) and Huntley Carter were both profoundly moved by visits to Cochran's *More* (1915). Asquith confessed that she felt more stirred by its strange "vitality" than by seeing Hamlet's life and death dilemmas in Henry B. Irving's 1915 production.[86] In *More*, one of the scenes (in between a "bathing revue" called *Wash Me* and a Shakespeare spoof) was played out on a "pitch-black" stage, with only the words "Stage Door" visible. Into this "black chaos" disembodied voices of celebrities—Beerbohm Tree, Marie Lloyd, Enrico Caruso and others (all imitated by actors) were heard arguing with each other, their bodies missing, eroded—annihilated—by the darkness in a style which anticipated Beckett.[87]

Revue thus raises a number of questions for historians of First World War culture. Most obviously, there is the disappearance from cultural history of a particular body of work. 1914–1918 saw revues produced at almost industrial speed. This fashion created particular sketches to suit "star" performers and produced subversive versions of wartime life for different kinds of audiences. Critics of wartime theatre, and of early twentieth century popular culture more generally, have paid only limited attention to the working-class appeal of personalities such as Fred Karno but it is another area which deserves to be an important part of discussions of the ways in which the war was experienced. Of course, revues served as salutary reminders, for some critics at least, of the coarsening of theatrical culture, and of original drama's loss of influence as an art form. Yet for all the ambivalent press, their presence was undoubtedly powerful. For soldiers on leave they were spaces which helped satisfy what Siegfried Sassoon called "Blighty hunger," a "longing for the gaiety and sentiment of life."[88] For some men, revues seem to have offered a utopian promise of beauty, relaxation, gaiety and feminine spectacle, an imagined, alternate space. Soldiers also took gramophone recordings of popular revues back to the Front to play in the mess as if to cling onto this.[89] Revues were thus a link with "home" but they were also an element of the anarchic and subversive in the life of the war: noisy and blatantly commercial. In this sense, revues did not necessarily damage the theatre but transformed it, forcing audiences to reconsider their own transactions with the wartime world. Even as revues borrowed from existing theatrical forms, they were being constructed in increasingly ambitious ways, adapting to different needs of the wartime population.

Notes

1. 'The Passing Shows', *Tatler*, 19 May 1915, 198.
2. 'A Review of Reviews', *The Era*, 7 March 1917, 14.
3. Siegfried Sassoon, *Collected Poems 1908–1956* (London: Faber & Faber, 1961), 21. *Fall In!* was presented in Liverpool during the week beginning 11 December 1916. The *Liverpool Post* reported its "marked success" with "lively song and rhythmic dance." Horace Jones and Miss Enniss Parkes featured in a succession of roles beginning with a sketch set at a vegetable show. See: 'Royal Hippodrome', *Liverpool Daily Post*, 12 December 1916, 3.
4. George Bernard Shaw, 'Preface', in *Heartbreak House*, ed. A.C. Ward (London: Longmans, 1961), 32.
5. Shaw, Preface, *Heartbreak House*, 30–1.
6. W. Macqueen-Pope, *The Curtain Rises* (Edinburgh: Thomas Nelson and Sons, 1961), 300–1.
7. G.S. Street, *At Home in the War* (London: Heinemann, 1918), 108.
8. Clive Barker, 'Theatre and Society: The Edwardian Legacy', in *British Theatre between the Wars, 1918–1939*, eds. Clive Barker and Maggie Gale (Cambridge: Cambridge University Press, 2000), 11.
9. B.W. Findon, 'Editorial', *Play Pictorial*, 27 November 1915, 85.
10. 'A Review of Reviews', *The Era*, 7 March 1917, 14.
11. Jack Duffell, *Soldier Boy: The Letters of Gunner W.J. Duffell, 1915–18*, ed. Gilbert Mant (Stevenage: Spa, 1992), 86–9.
12. Jerry White, *Zeppelin Nights: London in the First World War* (London: Bodley Head, 2014), 222.
13. Wilfred Owen, *Collected Letters*, eds. Harold Owen and John Bell (London: Oxford University Press, 1967), 559.

14. Henry Walbrook, *J.M. Barrie and the Theatre* (London: F.V. White, 1922), 129.
15. James Ross Moore, 'Girl Crazy: Revue and Variety in Interwar Theatre', in *British Theatre Between the Wars*, eds. Barker and Gale, 88–112 (89).
16. 'The Passing Shows', *Tatler*, 26 April 1916, 106.
17. Raymond Mander and Joe Mitchenson, *Revue* (London: Peter Davies, 1971), 13–28.
18. 'The Passing Shows', *Tatler*, 30 June 1915, 388.
19. Norman Marshall, *The Other Theatre* (London: John Lehmann, 1946), 16.
20. Gordon Williams, *British Theatre in the Great War* (London: Continuum, 2003), 22.
21. 'The Passing Shows', *Tatler*, 3 January 1917, 10.
22. 'In England Now', *Bystander*, 10 March 1915, 327.
23. 'Sir Herbert Tree on His Next Production', *Observer*, 6 December 1914, 8.
24. Fred Kerr, *Recollections of a Defective Memory* (London: Thornton Butterworth, 1930), 210.
25. 'The Passing Shows', *Tatler*, 30 June 1915, 388.
26. 'The Entertainment of Tommy', *The Era*, 2 June 1915, 13.
27. Moore, 'Girl Crazy', 95.
28. 'The Passing Shows', *Tatler*, 1 December 1915, 268.
29. Ibid.
30. *Illustrated Sporting and Dramatic News*, 15 July 1916, 562.
31. *The Referee*, 1 April 1917, 3.
32. 'About the Halls', *The Sketch*, 22 April 1914, 90.
33. H.S. Charlton to Douglas Dawson, 23 October 1914. British Library Add MS 83610.
34. William Sandhurst to Arthur Stamfordham, 16 April 1915, British Library Add MS 83613.
35. André Charlot, 'Producing English Revue', in *Theatre and Stage*, ed. Harold Downs (London: Pitman, 1934), 895.
36. 'The Passing Shows', *Tatler*, 8 September 1915, 313.
37. 'Round the Theatres', *Illustrated Sporting and Dramatic News*, 4 September 1915, 17.
38. 'The Passing Shows', *Tatler*, 8 September 1915, 313.
39. B.F. Findon, 'More', *Play Pictorial*, 27 November 1915, 86.
40. *Bystander*, 22 September 1915, 418.
41. 'The Dramatic World', *Sunday Times*, 25 October 1915, 2.
42. See: 'Mr Albert De Courville Bids Us "Smile!"', *The Referee*, 3 June 1917, 3.
43. 'Enterprises of Charles B. Cochran', *Play Pictorial* 32 (1918), 80.
44. Beatrice Lillie, *Every Other Inch a Lady* (London: W.H. Allen, 1973), 72–3.
45. See 'Mr Alfred Butt as Theatrical Manager', *The Referee*, 4 October 1914, 7.
46. JW, 'Round the Theatres', *Illustrated Sporting and Dramatic News*, 27 March 1915, 104.
47. Herbert Farjeon, 'First Nights of the Week', *The Era*, 14 March 1917, 1.
48. Robert Hale, '"Stars" I have Imitated', *The Era*, 3 January 1917, 17.
49. Charles H. Crombie to the Home Secretary, 27 August 1914, British Library Add MS 83612.
50. Frank Allen, 1 April 1915, British Library Add MS 83613.
51. 'The Lord Chamberlain's Warning', *The Era*, 12 May 1915, 13.
52. Memorandum: Fred Karno's Productions, Lord Chamberlain's Office. nd. 1915. British Library Add MS 83613.
53. William Sandhurst to Arthur Stamfordham, 16 April 1915, British Library Add MS 83613.
54. 'The Lord Chamberlain's Warning', *The Era*, 12 May 1915, 13.
55. Douglas Dawson to Alfred Butt, 6 September 1914, British Library Add MS 83612.

56. Alfred Butt to Douglas Dawson, 8 September 1914, British Library Add MS 83612.
57. Alfred Butt to Gaby Deslys, 8 September 1914, British Library Add MS 83612.
58. Ernest A. Bendall, Lord Chamberlain's Office Memorandum, 18 September 1914, British Library Add MS 83612.
59. Charles Cochrane, 'The Future of Revue', *The Era*, 24 January 1917, 13.
60. Lord Chamberlain's Memorandum, 22 October 1914, British Library Add MS 83612.
61. Alliance of Honour to the Lord Chamberlain, 17 November 1914, British Library Add MS 83612.
62. 'In England Now', *Bystander*, 13 September 1916, 454.
63. 'Shocked the Censor', *Daily Mirror*, 23 October 1914, 2.
64. Steve Nicholson, *The Censorship of British Drama 1900–1968* (Exeter: University of Exeter Press, 2003), 125.
65. Alliance of Honour to the Lord Chamberlain, 17 November 1914, British Library Add MS 83612.
66. Edward Knoblock, *Round the Room* (London: Chapman & Hall, 1939), 201.
67. See Charles Cochran to Douglas Dawson, 27 October 1914: 'She has always worn a garment which reached practically to her knee, and has never at any performance discarded this.' British Library Add MS 83612.
68. 'Sir H. Smith-Dorrien on War and Morals: The Tone of the Stage', *The Times*, 9 October 1916, 5.
69. 'In England Now', *Bystander*, 13 September 1916, 454. See also *The Era*, 6 September 1916, 11.
70. 'A Reply to General Smith-Dorrien', *The Times*, 8 November 1916, 5.
71. 'The Libel against General Smith Dorrien', *The Times*, 5 April 1917, 2.
72. "A.B.", Topsy Turvey Report, London Council for the Promotion of Public Morality, 17 September 1917, British Library Add MS 83404.
73. Arnold Bennett, *The Journals of Arnold Bennett 1911–1921*, ed. Newman Flower (London: Cassell, 1932), 237–8.
74. '"Shell Out": Mr de Courville, Producer and Part-Author Tells Why It Is a Successful Revue', *Nash's Magazine*, October 1915, 308.
75. Albert de Courville, *I Tell You* (London: Chapman and Hall, 1928), 157.
76. 'The Passing Shows', *Tatler*, 5 July 1916, 10.
77. 'The Passing Show', *Tatler*, 4 April 1917, 4.
78. 'National Service and Amusements', *The Referee*, 4 March 1917, 2.
79. 'Economy in the Theatre', *The Era*, 14 June 1916, 13.
80. 'The Variety Stage', *The Referee*, 29 April 1917, 7.
81. 'The Passing Shows', *Tatler*, 23 August 1916, 234.
82. See: J.T. Grein, 'The Future of Musical Comedy', *The Era*, 7 March 1917, 13; also Marie Lloyd, 'The Single Turn's Return', *The Era*, 21 March 1917, 13.
83. Raymond Blathwayt, '*More* and Futurism', *Play Pictorial*, 27 November 1915, 100.
84. Gordon Williams, *British Theatre in the Great War* (London: Continuum, 2003), 24; 51–2; 22.
85. '*Cheerio!* at the Pavilion', *Bystander*, 4 July 1917, 28.
86. Lady Cynthia Asquith, *Diaries, 1915–18* (London: Century, 1968), 301.
87. 'The Ambassadors. More', *The Stage*, 24 June 1915, 20.
88. Siegfried Sassoon, *The Complete Memoirs of George Sherston* (London: Faber, 1937), 740–1.
89. See G.D. Sheffield and G.I.S. Inglis (eds.), *From Vimy Ridge to the Rhine: Great War Letters of Christopher Stone* (Marlborough, MA: Crowood, 1989), 117, cited in Jan Ruger, 'Entertainments', in *Capital Cities at War*, eds. Jay Winter and Jean-Louis Robert (Cambridge: Cambridge University Press, 2007), 105–40 (120–1).

Bibliography

Asquith, Cynthia. *The Diaries of Lady Cynthia Asquith 1915–18*. London: Century, 1987.

Barker, Clive and Maggie Gale, eds. *British Theatre between the Wars, 1918–1939*. Cambridge: Cambridge University Press, 2000.

Bennett, Arnold. *The Journals of Arnold Bennett*, edited by Newman Flower. London: Cassell, 1932.

Charlot, André. "Producing English Revue", in *Theatre and Stage*, edited by Harold Downs. London: Pitman, 1934, 895–898.

Duffell, Jack. *Soldier Boy: The Letters of Gunner W.J. Duffell, 1915–18*, edited by Gilbert Mant. Stevenage: Spa Books, 1992.

Humphreys, Richard. *Futurism*. London: Tate Gallery, 1999.

Kerr, Fred. *Recollections of a Defective Memory*. London: Thornton Butterworth, 1930.

Lillie, Beatrice. *Every Other Inch a Lady*. London: W.H. Allen, 1973.

Macqueen-Pope, W. *The Curtain Rises*. Edinburgh: Thomas Nelson and Sons, 1961.

Mander, Raymond and Joe Mitchenson. *Revue*. London: Peter Davies, 1971.

Marshall, Norman. *The Other Theatre*. London: John Lehmann, 1946.

Nicholson, Steve. *The Censorship of British Drama 1900–1968*. Exeter: University of Exeter Press, 2003.

Otte, Marline. *Jewish Identities in German Popular Entertainment, 1890–1933*. Cambridge: Cambridge University Press, 2006.

Owen, Wilfred. *Collected Letters*, edited by Harold Owen and John Bell. London: Oxford University Press, 1967.

Ruger, Jan. "Entertainments", in *Capital Cities at War*, edited by Jay Winter and Jean-Louise Robert. Cambridge: Cambridge University Press, 2007, 105–140.

Sassoon, Siegfried. *Collected Poems 1908–1956*. London: Faber & Faber, 1961.

Shaw, George Bernard. *Heartbreak House*. London: Longman, 1961.

Street, George Slythe. *At Home in the War*. London: Heinemann, 1918.

Trewin, J.C. "Bernhardt on the London Stage", in *Bernhardt and the Theatre of Her Time*, edited by Eric Salmon. Westport: Greenwood Press, 1977, 111–132.

Walbrook, Henry. *J.M. Barrie and the Theatre*. London: F.V. White, 1922.

White, Jerry. *Zeppelin Nights: London in the First World War*. London: Bodley Head, 2014.

Williams, Gordon. *British Theatre in the Great War*. London: Continuum, 2003.

2 "When Words Are Not Enough"
The Aural Landscape of Britain's Modern Memory of 1914–18

Emma Hanna

Sounds and silences are integral to the history and memory of the First World War. The aural landscape of the conflict was formed from the time of the war itself, where soldiers' songs, music hall tunes and classical compositions embroidered wartime memories into the emotional tapestry of the ways in which the conflict was remembered. However, music has been a relatively neglected area in our understanding of the cultural history and legacy of 1914–18.[1] Only now are historians beginning to examine the cultural significance of the music produced both during and after the war.[2] It is already clear that music is a central part of the "thick description" of Britain's modern memory of the First World War.[3] The emotional potency of music surpasses the capabilities of the visual images or written texts; it is an intrapersonal process, an interpersonal or social phenomenon, as well as a product of cultural influences and traditions.[4] Pieces of music in their various forms are *lieux de mémoire* (sites of memory), imagined spaces that form key topographical features in the landscape of Britain's memory of 1914–18.[5]

In Britain music has long been used as a powerful tool for setting a spiritual or moral tone for remembrance. The ways in which musicians have approached remembrance has changed broadly in line with the ways in which the nature of remembrance has developed and the ways in which the war is remembered.[6] However, much of the scholarship in memory studies has perpetuated a form of binary vision which focuses on what is remembered and what is forgotten. Winter has suggested that the memory landscape should be seen in at least three dimensions; the "vertical shoreline which is stable, dynamic and, at times, intrusive," and of "hidden shapes" which he describes as "deposits below the surface of the water which emerge with the tides." These shapes are "part of the cartography of recollection and remembrance."[7] The study of the aural landscape of the memory of 1914–18 should be approached in a multi-dimensional manner. Binary notions of what has been retained, and what has been forgotten, are overly simplistic; rather we should recognise the ebb and flow of memory, and that certain themes can be brought to the surface as the tides of memory and forgetting are pulled by the political, economic and cultural necessities of the time.

Indeed, the topography of the aural landscape of Britain from 1914–18 is rich and varied. Soldiers' songs, music hall tunes, hymns and classical compositions are key features, repositories of memory in a sound world which is understood to encapsulate the emotional meaning of Britain at war.

Few examples of sound recordings remain from the war itself. The sounds of the battlefield were recorded on 9 October 1918 when recording equipment was sent by the Royal Garrison Artillery to a farmhouse near Lille, which was under attack from shelling. This recording, by the Gramophone Company, provides the only authentic sounds of the fighting now preserved.[8] In 1996, the voice of the fighting man was recovered on a recording made in 1915 with Sergeant Edward Dwyer VC called "With Our Boys at the Front." Dwyer speaks for two minutes about the retreat from Mons in 1914, and sings one of the marching songs "which kept us going" bursting into "Here We Are, Here We Are, Here We Are Again."[9] As the war was being fought it was understood that the voice of Tommy Atkins was distilled in the songs that were sung by the troops. In October 1917, 2nd Lieutenant F.T. Nettleingham of the Royal Flying Corps published *Tommy's Tunes: A Comprehensive Collection of Soldiers' Songs, Marching Melodies, Rude Rhymes, and Popular Parodies, Composed, Collected and Arranged on Active Service with the B.E.F.* He prefaced the collection with the assertion that "if [we] knew a nation's songs, [we] could write their history [. . .] a nation's songs and other musical effort [. . .] reveal the actual character and culture of a nation in a way that is unapproached by any other art or by rule of thumb."[10]

Along with songs such as "Here We Are Again," "Let 'Em All Come" and "Are We Downhearted? No," "Tipperary" was one of the most popular anthems sung by soldiers on the Western Front during the early stages of the war in the autumn of 1914. *Tipperary* became popular because George Curnock, a newspaper war correspondent, heard a Guards band play it for the first ship of British soldiers to disembark in Boulogne in August 1914. He made a great deal of the song in his despatches and within a few days a great number of newspapers had printed the lyrics and they were shown on the screens in cinemas. It was quickly taken up by the music halls and thousands of performances followed. To hum or sing the song became the patriotic thing to do but ubiquity soon bred contempt. By the winter of 1914, although civilians retained their affection for the song, the soldiers were sick of it, and any attempts to sing *Tipperary* were soon whistled down. In 1917 Lieutenant Nettleingham was incredulous that *Tipperary* was seized upon by music publishers and publicised so widely because "it was never Tommy's song." Despite its popularity in France where "most of the street urchins and *parigots* sing it with equal exuberance in French and English" Nettleingham lamented that Curnock had heard *Tipperary* "instead of another, equally popular, which the same troops started up a few miles further on."[11] By January 1916 it was reported that "Pack Up Your Troubles" had also "won for itself a front place in the affections of the public. The chorus is conceived in the spirit of melodious optimism, and possesses the infectious quality so essential in a song if it to stand any chance of becoming a great popular favourite."[12] A journalist reported his astonishment when he heard a sermon where the preacher had quoted the song's lyrics, saying that they "contained much more healthy and helpful teaching than any sermon he could preach."[13] "Pack Up Your Troubles" was regularly performed in concert parties and music halls on the home front, and was translated into several different languages. "Tipperary" and "Pack Up Your Troubles" were quickly established as dominant features in the aural landscape of 1914–18.

In public remembrance rituals during the immediate post-war years soldiers' songs were replaced by the silence of mourning and religious music. Ceremonial music, hymns, requiems and silences created the sound world of British public mourning rituals. The first Festivals of Remembrance were staged annually on Armistice Night from 1923, with John Foulds' sizeable *World Requiem*. By 1927, however, it was felt by the Home Office, War Office and Admiralty that the ex-service community should be more fully represented at the cenotaph.[14] Foulds' piece was dropped from the national programme of remembrance as it was deeded too middlebrow for the establishment and too elitist for many of the veterans and general public.[15] In its place the *Daily Express* secured the Royal Albert Hall for its own Armistice Night concert, and the paper's two-year tenureship of the event marks a clear but temporary change in tone of the character of British national remembrance. Backed by the British Legion, the event was described as a "rally" which would feature the "community singing" of old wartime songs. This coming together of ex-servicemen in organised singing allowed them to continue to define their identities as combatants which could then be reinforced in pageants, memorials, rituals and Community Singing.[16] The writer and war veteran H.V. Morton, whose review was printed in both the *Daily Express* and the *British Legion* journal, recalled that once the music started—with *Pack Up Your Troubles*—Morton and his fellow ex-servicemen "found ourselves back in 1914."

> How many of the millions in every corner of the earth guessed until last night how intense is the emotion stored in these strange songs: for strange they are, strange as the British temperament, full of self-satire, pungent with humour directed against our own dignity. We did not realise until last night that the songs we sang in the Army are bits of history. In them is embalmed in that comic fatalism which carried us through four years of hell. We sang "Take Me Back to Dear Old Blighty" and "Who's Your Lady Friend?" Thirteen years fell from us. We ceased to see the Albert Hall and the thousands of white faces in the arc lights; we looked into an abyss of memories where the long columns passed and repassed over the dusty roads in France, where the grotesque, unthinkable things of war happened day and night—the brief joys, the sharp sorrows of those days, the insane injustices of Fate, and, above all, the memory of the men we knew so well, men better than we were, nobler, finer, more worthy of life, who slipped into the silence of death.[17]

By the late 1920s it is clear that veterans wanted to reclaim their war experiences by revisiting the aural landscape of their memories. Charles Carrington, for example, recalled that many veterans found attending remembrance services "too much like going to one's own funeral."[18] By singing the songs that they believed helped them through the war at a public event, not just a regimental reunion, veterans' voices were heard not as victims but survivors. Perhaps in response to a concern that these songs would one day be forgotten, in 1930 John Brophy and Eric Partridge published *The Long Trail: What the British Soldier Sang and Said in The Great War of 1914–18*.[19] Their survey of soldiers' songs found that most came from private soldiers, and like medieval ballads the methods of their composition are a mystery. Some are rearrangements of popular music hall songs, but Brophy and Partridge underlined that they are songs "of homeless men, evoked by exceptional and distressing circumstances; the songs of an itinerant community, continually altering within itself under the incidence of death or mutilation."[20] The idea of these songs being keystones of the aural landscape of Britain's war was well established.

It is the persistence of this musical tradition by the community of serving soldiers which places the songs and melodies at the highest peak of Britain's aural landscape of 1914–18. The therapeutic benefit of creating spaces for singing *en masse* had been discussed during the war itself. The composer Henry Walford Davies, who in 1918 was appointed the first director of music to the newly created Royal Air Force, underlined the power of singing to reinforce the team spirit of fighting men:

> A brass band is all very well in its way, but it does not come near the male voice choir in the production of the best music [. . .] Get the men to do something together and you have started an *espirit de corps* among them which will have a tremendous influence for good, and will do more than any of us imagine to make life in camp, in barrack, or billet, or in the outpost more tolerable.[21]

The *Daily Express* harnessed the power of what became known as Community Singing on 11 October 1926. The declared purpose of the new Community Singing Movement was to create an imagined space that would foster "a New Merrie England," "Making Everybody Friendlier."[22] Indeed, at a time of great political and economic difficulties in the aftermath of the General Strike, the scheme's social benefits were underlined as "the levelling of all sorts and conditions, rubbing shoulder to shoulder—with no class distinction—must exert great influence on society in general."[23] The *Express* convened a committee headed by Sir Hugh Allen, director of the Royal College of Music, Professor Music at Oxford University, a leader of the so-called "South Kensington Club" of composers.[24] The organiser of the annual Promenade concerts, Sir Henry Wood, was also involved. With Allen at the helm the Community Singing Movement was an outreach project of the English musical renaissance. This is particularly evident with the choice of repertoire focussing on English folk songs and "the visions of thousands of people coming together in the towns and cities throughout England in order to sing, and by the idea of the villagers of the countryside reviving the days of 'Merrie England' by community singing."[25] Other leading British musicians, including Dr John B. McEwen, Principal of the Royal Academy of Music, added that "community singing has always been used for ecclesiastical purposes because it has bound the singers together with the same feeling, and soldiers sing together because community singing gives them courage." It was also stated that Community Singing would benefit health, educate the masses about old English folk songs, bring greater social cohesion and even empty the divorce courts.[26] The act of gathering groups of people to sing together were effective in both physical and emotional terms.

On 30 November 1926 an inaugural Community Singing concert was held at the Albert Hall where it was not the singing of folk melodies which was most memorable, but the massed rendition of old war songs. Gibson Young, the conductor, recalled that "[t]he deepest impression, emotionally, of the whole concert, was the singing of the chorus of *Tipperary* at the request of the disabled occupants of the royal box. There was a lump in my throat as these gallant men waved their appreciation."[27] The momentum of the Community Singing Movement continued with a Christmas Festival, on 18 December 1926, in the Albert Hall with Malcolm Sergeant as one of the conductors. The programme and lyrics were printed in *Daily Express*, and the concert was also broadcast on radio.[28] However, Community Singing was most popular outside the concert hall, at football matches and local theatres. On Boxing Day 1926, 40,000 singers convened at Craven Cottage.[29] A few days later in Birmingham the singing crowd numbered 70,000.[30] The *Daily Express* reported that although the singing at the St Andrew's ground

> was strictly timed to stop promptly at 2.30pm as the match could not otherwise be finished before dusk.... The vast crowd of 45,000, stirred into a frenzy of song, did not care a jot about the clock and went on singing *Tipperary* and *Pack Up Your Troubles* after the twenty-two players ... had appeared.[31]

January 1927 witnessed a number of Community Singing events before football matches in other towns such as Southampton and Brighton.[32] "Tipperary" and "Pack Up Your Troubles" were perennial favourites. The songs were also sung at a Reading versus Manchester United match at Elm Park on 9 January 1927, and the crowd also whistled *The British Grenadiers* march to the band of the actual Grenadier Guards who were accompanying the singing.[33] The *Daily Express* believed that the popularity of Community Singing was evidence of a new spirit across the country. A Liverpool businessman was quoted as saying,

> it is possible to discern, even through our present difficulties, evidence of a new spirit at work among our people. One of the happiest signs that

the British people are at last beginning to recover their true and better selves is the remarkable growth of community singing throughout the country. [. . .] it has an old 'merrie England' ring about it [. . .] will also help to usher in the new era of peace and prosperity in industry.[34]

The popularity of the activity was such as that the *Daily Express* printed and sold copies of music and song books.[35]

BBC radio broadcast the annual Armistice Night singing every year from 1927, but by 1936 Corporation staff were referring to the annual event as a "British Legion sing-song." They suggested that more appropriate music should be played, along with readings from the Bible, to "wash out the taste of the super-sentimental orgy from the Albert Hall and reset the frame for these readings."[36] However, the songs, which had by the 1930s become seen as "sentimental," were already key features Britain's aural landscape of 1914–18. The popular music of the Great War was ever-present in the interwar period. In Winifred Holtby's novel *South Riding*, written and set in the mid-1930s, a character listens to children sing wartime songs: "Like many women of her generation, she could not listen unmoved to the familiar tunes which circumstances had associated with intolerable memory [. . .]. A joke, a picture, a tune, could trap her into a blinding waste of misery and helplessness."[37] Nevertheless, the popular music of the First World War continued to have a marginal position in official remembrance rituals, certainly those produced by the BBC.

"Tipperary" proved to be popular with troops in the Second World War and in other Allied countries too. "Pack Up Your Troubles" appeared in a number of pantomimes and musical performances, and soldiers returning from fighting in France in September 1944 reported that "Tipperary" "is still war song number one in France." *The Long Long Trail* was also mentioned.[38] Of the 1940 song "We're Going to Hang out the Washing on the Siegfried Line," which had been popular with some troops during the battle of France, it was said that "[e]ven if circumstances had not put a short, sharp end to its career [. . .] [it] would never have become another 'Tipperary'."[39] Veterans of the First World War still clearly felt an attachment to their old marching songs. One veteran in 1940 recalled that "Tipperary" "stands out in my memory, it was used as a 'livener' on entering the French villages during our forced marches, weary and footsore."[40] "Tipperary" was recognised internationally. When Anthony Eden attended a summit in Athens in March 1941 he was greeted by a military band playing the tune followed by Greek national songs.[41] The song was an accepted signal of triumph over adversity. British and American prisoners of war making their way home through Germany were heard singing "Tipperary" on the march, and it was reported in 1945 that Italian radio was playing "Piave," explained as "the Italian 'Tipperary,'" being "the signature tune of Rome radio and other Free Italian stations."[42]

The popular songs of the First World War featured in productions around the fiftieth anniversary commemorations but the official commemorations were dominated by music of a more elite nature. However, the work of composers who had served and/or died in the conflict was often overlooked in favour of more contemporary work. Benjamin Britten, a composer who had been a conscientious objector in the Second Word War, composed *War Requiem* for the consecration of the new Coventry Cathedral after the bombing of the original building in 1940. First performed in 1962, Britten used the newly discovered poetry of Wilfred Owen. The most popular aural representations of 1914–18 in the 1960s were Charles Chilton's radio series *The Long Long Trail* (BBC Home Service, 1961) which contrasted the songs sung on the Western Front with those performed at home. Theatrical producers Gerry Raffles and Joan Littlewood were among the millions of listeners of *The Long Long Trail* and they were inspired to use the wartime songs in their own production *Oh What a Lovely War*, first performed by Littlewood's Theatre Workshop in 1963, and made into a film directed by Richard Attenborough in 1968. The stage version of *Oh What a Lovely War* is a highly critical view of the war. The original meanings of the popular wartime songs are inverted and saturated with bitter irony. Attenborough's film retains much of the cynicism of the play but the tone is more mournful.[43] The pull of the political tide changed the special dimensions which submerged the original sentiments of wartime songs. Britten's *War Requiem* and both versions of *Oh What a Lovely War* spoke more to the younger generation campaigning for nuclear disarmament than they ever did the generation who experienced 1914–18.

In the same period the new BBC 2 channel opened with the flagship commemorative series *The Great War* (BBC, 1964). The title music by Wilfred Josephs was commissioned for the series and performed by the BBC Northern Orchestra under the direction of Sir Malcolm Arnold. Producer Tony Essex wrote the opening sequence that sought to combine the musical score with images selected for their power to move.[44] Essex directed that rising timpani strokes should accompany the images of rough wooden crosses silhouetted against the sky to encourage the feeling of a "sombre building of tension." As the "music is sizzling and growing in stridency" the camera shots appear to fall with increasing speed to images of a trench full of dead bodies with a single soldier staring into the camera "with a strange tired appeal."[45] The dramatic scoring combined with images of death and mourning had a significant impact on the audience. With audiences averaging 8 million people per episode, the BBC received thousands of letters from viewers detailing their emotional responses to the series. One woman wrote of

> how superbly perfect was the opening scene and the accompanying music, like the voice of Destiny itself. Truly, this was the epic of series, on a scale and a comprehension that will never be approached again, not even by the space explorers. Its ending has left a gap in our lives [. . .].[46]

A male correspondent was moved when "Josephs' threnody builds up to a climax, to the last harrowing, terrible expression on that man's face, will long be remembered by many among us."[47]

Tony Essex was remembered as a "very aesthetic" producer.[48] He was known for writing copious amounts of notes to film editors and he relished getting involved in all aspects of his film-making. It was Essex who contacted Wilfred Josephs, a London-based dentist who was making a name for himself as a composer after his *Requiem*, composed in memory of the victims of the Holocaust, won a prestigious international award in 1963. Essex asked Josephs to compose several musical themes for *The Great War* including a "March Victorious" and "Tragedy," In addition to Josephs' compositions Essex (an admirer of Russian composers) used a great deal of music by Shostakovich, Prokofiev and Kachaturian.[49] Essex's use of such music is typical of his production style which was driven by the aesthetic need for high drama to fit the scale and destruction of the war. In this way the music of *The Great War* mapped out the emotional peaks and troughs of the aural landscape of 1914–18, underlining that music is of vital importance to the television medium as an atmospheric device. It is the most potent of non-diegetic sounds on television, a signal that cues moments of drama, helping to evoke the appropriate emotion in the mind of the viewer.[50]

In the 1970s, televisual monuments to the conflict began to make use of music which was composed during the war by musicians who had direct wartime experience. The music for the BBC's sixtieth anniversary commemoration *Battle of the Somme* (BBC, 1976) brought Ralph Vaughan Williams' *Pastoral* symphony (No.3), George Butterworth's *A Shropshire Lad* and Gustav Holst *The Planets* suite to the forefront of its soundtrack to enhance its elegiac televisual narrative. The use of the trumpet motif from the slow movement of Vaughan Williams' *Pastoral* is particularly effective in evoking the aural landscape of the conflict over images of the actual wartime location. Written while the composer was serving in the Royal Army Medical Corps, and grieving for the loss of his friend George Butterworth, the out-of-tune partials directed by the score are echoes of Vaughan Williams' wartime memories. His biographer wrote that

> [l]odged in the composer's mind was a recollection of camp life with the RAMC at Bordon in Hampshire where the bugler hit the 7th as a missed shot for the octave [. . .] in so far as any particular locality is depicted in the symphony it is northern France, where he went after being commissioned in the Royal Garrison Artillery in 1917.[51]

The presenter-narrator of the programme, the actor Leo McKern, underlines how similar the soldiers thought the landscape of Picardy was to that of Southern England, and Vaughan Williams' music is underscoring this comparability by his imagined interpretation of the pastoral which reflects the reality of the actual wartime landscape.

Vaughan Williams' use of the trumpet motif and its use in *The Battle of the Somme* is a mediation of the Last Post bugle call; played at every Armistice Day service and at the Menin Gates in Ypres every evening, it is the ultimate trope in the aural landscape of British remembrance. Vaughan Williams well understood that "music uses knowledge as a means to the evocation of personal experience in terms which will be intelligible to and command the sympathy of others [. . .] those of his own nation, or other kind of homogeneous community."[52] That the programme also features the setting of A. E. Houseman's poems in *A Shropshire Lad* to the music of George Butterworth, who was killed during the battle of the Somme, adds pathos to an already moving piece of televisual commemoration. As the programme concludes, the *Mars* movement of Holst's *The Planets* fades in as present-day images of the Somme region dissolve into a rostrum camera shot of Paul Nash's painting *We Are Making a New World*. The reference to Mars the Greek god of war, and a planet that is distant, barren and inhospitable draws parallels between descriptions of areas of the Western Front as being cratered and desolate. Another friend of Vaughan Williams, Holst was prevented from enlisting in the forces due to his poor health. His enforced distance from the actual wartime landscape inspired his writing of *The Planets*, in part a war imagined in sound, during the first half of the war. In 1918 Holst was appointed as the YMCA's musical organiser for the Near East, based in Salonica.[53]

In 2003, the work of the composer Cecil Coles was used for the title music of *The First World War* (Channel 4). A friend of Gustav Holst, Coles enlisted in September 1914 and served as a sergeant in the London Regiment (Queen Victoria's Rifles) on the Western Front. A bandmaster by trade, like Vaughan Williams he continued to compose music while he was on active service. He was killed rescuing casualties on the Somme in April 1918, aged 29. However, more than 50 years after his death, Coles' daughter discovered a manuscript written by her father. She gave the producers of *The First World War* permission to use the melody contained in her father's manuscript which was then arranged by Orlando Gough. The notes that accompany the DVD of the series assert Coles' wartime pedigree; that he "died humming Beethoven" and that "the manuscript still bears the marks and mud of shrapnel," thus drawing a clear link between the music of the programme together with the actual and aural landscape of the Western Front.

Television's use of music as a "voice" of the First World War is an essential component of Britain's aural landscape of the war. These pieces of music resonate with meaning and emotion, and this resonance adds high levels of pathos to television as a medium which cannot rely on visual images alone. By presenting the emotional, aural and physical links between the former Western Front and Britain's modern memory, the pastoral device engages the horror of war by invoking a code to describe the indescribable.[54] Music is therefore a most effective emotive device for television to render the war's colossal scale of destruction and loss within viewers' understanding. However, the focus on a relatively small and well-connected group of composers draws a parallel with the over-emphasis placed on certain poets' voices in Britain's modern memory of 1914–18. This has encouraged the view of a "lost generation" which is not supported by the fact that approximately 90% of men who served in Britain's armed forces returned home. The voice of the ordinary soldier and his songs have been lost in Britain's emotional reliance on the cultural outpourings inspired by the war, and in the men who produced them shortly before their own deaths such as George Butterworth and Wilfred Owen, telling us a great deal about the ways in which the war continues to be re-remembered in contemporary Britain.

Versions of the aural landscape of the war are perpetuated through their communication to children. "Remember Me: echoes from the lost generations"[55] is the education section of the Commonwealth War Graves Commission's website providing learning resources for teachers in history, citizenship, English, ICT, design & technology and music. The music resource is called "Requiem." The unit outlines that it will help students to examine music composed by soldiers killed in the First World War and that of more contemporary composers who have responded to war through their work. There is also a short exercise which focuses on popular songs of the wartime period, and the activity concludes by inviting students to compose an anthem for remembrance.[56] These activities are introduced by the premise that:

> The experience of war can be traumatic, both for those involved in the fighting at first hand and for those left behind, struggling to come to terms with the horror of it all and the agony of personal or public loss. It is not always easy to tell others how we feel in moments of extreme emotion such as these and music can be a powerful means of expression when words are not enough.[57]

The details of four musicians and their work are given as examples of musical responses to war; George Butterworth and *The Banks of the Green Willow* (1913), Michael Tippett and *A Child of Our Time* (1944), Mark-Anthony Turnage's contemporary works *Silent Cities*, *The Torn Fields* and *The Silver Tassie*, and the violinist Hugh Gordon Langton whose headstone in Poelcapelle cemetery has inscribed upon it the musical notation for an American song "After the Ball" (1891). Of Butterworth the site says that "[h]is music captured the spirit of the English countryside that he fought for, and died to preserve." After hearing "The Banks of the Green Willow," which is held as a product of a time when "[m]any people lamented the passing of the old way of life and looked back fondly to what they saw as the days of innocence before the corrupting influence of the war" students are asked to compare the music with the poetry of Edward Thomas, "one of several poets of the war years who concentrated on the effect of the war on rural England," with the poem "As the Team's Head-Brass" (1916). The links between music and literature continue when students are asked to listen to Turnage's works before reading a range of war poetry including Wilfred Owen's "Disabled," and then choose a war poem to set to music of their own composition.

The popular music of the First World War is still present in contemporary Britain. The Harry Lauder song "Keep Right on to The End of the Road," written in the wake of his son's death on the Western Front in 1916, is still sung on the terraces of Birmingham City Football Club.[58] Academic and public interest in wartime music has increased during the centenary period with a number of conferences, new performances and publications.[59] *Oh What a Lovely War* continues to be performed by professionals and amateurs, and *War Horse*, a musical based on a book by Michael Morpurgo, has been running at the National Theatre for eight years and was made into a film by Steven Spielberg. Ninety-three years after the first Festival of Remembrance, the event in 2014 combined several musical styles by bringing together the Massed Bands of the Household Division, and the Bands of HM Royal Marines and the Queen's Colour Squadron with actors from the popular musical *War Horse* and popular music performers including the singer Joss Stone and guitarist Jeff Beck. Stone and Beck performed "No Man's Land (Green Fields of France)," a single produced in support of the Royal British Legion. The video release of the song, which was written by the folk singer Eric Bogle in 1976, sees Stone at the Tower of London walking amongst the art installation *Blood Swept Lands and Seas of Red* by Paul Cummins.[60] In the final scenes the shadowy figures of soldiers marching are projected onto the grey stone walls of the Tower, where Stone sings with the backing of a gospel choir. Bogle wrote that while he "would have wished for a version of my song that could have been truer to my original intentions in writing it: illustrating the utter waste of war while paying tribute to the courage and sacrifice of those brave young men who fought." He went on to say that if the modern interpretation "makes some people reflect, perhaps for the first time, on the true price of war, then [it] will have a measure of validity and value."[61]

Music has also been used by centenary projects such as The Last Post by Bristol-based organisation Superact, funded by the Heritage Lottery Fund, that brings communities together to play the Last Post on a variety of different instruments at commemorative musical events. The playing of the music was linked to an individual or group connected to the local area in the form of a musical commemoration.[62] However, the project proved to be contentious. In July 2014 a petition was created on the government's Number 10 website (Petitions: UK Government and Parliament) with the motion that "The Last Post bugle call must not be rearranged for First World War commemorations." The petition stated that "[w]hile we applaud [the government's] commitment to this commemoration by the use of the music and songs of the time, it is our belief that to rearrange the Last Post would make it unrecognisable to the service personnel it is used to remember." It was claimed the project "would destroy the meaning of [the Last Post] and render it worthless." The campaign received 2,275 signatures.[63] Nevertheless, the project went ahead and involved more than 40,000 people, 93% of whom stated that the musical commemoration had brought their communities closer together and fostered a more active interest in the history of 1914–18.[64]

The Last Post, and the two minutes' silence which follows, remain sacred in Britain's memory of the First World War. In the same way, selected pieces of classical music are also understood as musical monuments in the aural landscape of 1914–18. In museums and visitors' centres soundtracks can be utilised to set the tone for what is to follow. At the visitors' centre for the Memorial to the Missing at Thiepval, on the Somme, the first movement of Edward Elgar's concerto for cello in E Minor is played on repeat. This work was written in the spring of 1918 on the Sussex coast where the composer could hear the sound of "[I]ncessant gun fire (distant cannon)."[65] As Elgar is regarded as one of the foremost British composers of the wartime period, this elegiac piece of music is an immediate emotional prompt which sets the tone of mourning and remembrance at a site of a battle so central to Britain's modern memory of the war. However, it is the soldier's songs of 1914–18 that are signposts of memory in the aural landscape which evoke the spirit of wartime Britain. At the Wellington Caves in Arras, for example, a soundtrack of soldiers talking, laughing and singing popular wartime marching songs is played to visitors in the lift as they descend into the caves system built by New Zealand soldiers before the battle of Arras in 1917. It is as if the walls of the chalk tunnels absorbed the sounds of chatter and music, an aural prompt for visitors that tells them they are about to enter a space which has seen little change since the time of the war itself. It is the "lofty cynicism" and "confirmed fatalism" evinced by the songs—which Lieutenant Nettleingham identified in 1917—that demonstrate "the peculiarity of British humour to be derogatory to its own dignity, to wipe itself in the mud, [and] to affect self-satire to an alarming extent."[66] It is the distillation of the British national character which has enabled the soldiers' songs such as "It's a Long Way to Tipperary" and "Pack Up Your Troubles in Your Old Kit Bag" to form fault lines in Britain's aural landscape in our contemporary memory of the First World War.

Notes

1. Jeffrey Richards, *Imperialism and Music: Britain 1876–1953* (Manchester: MUP, 2002); J.F.G. Fuller, *Troop Morale and Popular Culture* (Oxford: Clarendon, 1990); Glenn Watkins, *Proof through the Night: Music and the Great War* (Berkeley: U of California Press, 2003).
2. For the first dedicated batch of articles on this theme see a special issue edited by Kate Kennedy and Trudi Tate, 'Literature and Music of the First World War', *First World War Studies*, 2, 1 (2011), 1–6.
3. Clifford Geertz, *The Interpretation of Cultures* (New York: Basic Books, 1973). Since the 1980s this approach has been adopted by New Historicists who have sought to understand literary texts through their historical and cultural contexts, for example see H. Aram Veeser, *The New Historicism* (London: Routledge, 1989).
4. Nico Frijda's Foreword in *Handbooks of Music and Emotion: Theory, Research, Applications* (Oxford: OUP, 2010).

5. Pierre Nora (ed), *Lieux de Mémoire* (Paris: Editions Gallimard, 1984–92).
6. See Peter Grant & Emma Hanna, 'Music & Remembrance: Britain and the First World War' in *Remembering the Great War* (London: Routledge, 2014), 110–126.
7. Jay Winter, 'Thinking about Silence' in *Shadows of War: A Social History of Silence in the Twentieth Century* (Cambridge: CUP, 2010), 3.
8. Gramophone Company, *Gramophone Records of the First World War: An HMV Catalogue 1914–18*, Introduced by Brian Rust (Newton Abbot: David & Charles, 1975). This recording 'Gas Shells Bombardment, British Troops Advancing on Lille' can be heard at http://www.firstworldwar.com/audio/1918.htm (accessed 27/05/2016).
9. Sergeant Edward Dwyer VC, 'With Our Boys at the Front' voice recording can be heard at http://www.firstworldwar.com/audio/1916.htm (accessed 18/05/2016).
10. RAF 025350: 2nd Lieutenant F.T. Nettleingham, *Tommy Tunes: A Comprehensive Collection of Soldiers' Songs, Marching Melodies, Rude Rhymes, and Popular Parodies, Composed, Collected and Arranged on Active Service with the B.E.F.* (London: Erskine Macdonald, 1917), 13–14.
11. Ibid.
12. 'Vesta Tilley's Verdict', *Liverpool Echo*, 4 February 1916, 6.
13. 'Your Old Kit Bag', *The Era*, 25 October 1916, 14.
14. Royal British Legion: General Secretary's Monthly Circular for November 1927 *British Legion*, Vol.7, No.5, November 1927, 1.
15. James G. Mansell, 'Musical Modernity and Contested Commemoration at the Festival of Remembrance, 1923–1927', *The Historical Journal*, 52, 2 (2009), 433–454.
16. Eric Leed, *No Man's Land: Combat and Identity in World War I* (Cambridge: CUP, 1979), 212.
17. *British Legion*, Vol.7, No.6, December 1927, 149.
18. Charles Carrington, *Soldier from the Wars Returning* (London: Hutchinson, 1965), 296.
19. John Brophy & Eric Partridge, *The Long Trail: What the British Soldier Sang and Said in the Great War of 1914–18* (Tonbridge: Andre Deutsch, 1965 [1930]).
20. Brophy & Partridge, *The Long Trail*.
21. Cadbury Special Collections: YMCA/K/6/1: Major H. Walford Davies 'Music and Arms', *The Red Triangle*, Vol.1, September 1917—August 1918, 97.
22. *Daily Express*, 11 October 1926, 1.
23. Ibid.
24. Meirion Hughes & Robert Stradling, *The English Musical Renaissance 1840–1940: Constructing a National Music (second edition)* (Manchester: MUP, 2001 [1993]), xiii.
25. *Daily Express*, 5 October 1926, 9.
26. Ibid.
27. *Daily Express*, 22 November 1926, 2—also see photographs of hall and soldiers in royal box, 1.
28. *Daily Express*, 18 December 1926, 3.
29. *Daily Express*, 3 January 1927, 9.
30. Ibid.
31. Ibid.
32. Ibid.
33. *Daily Express*, 10 January 1927, 3.
34. *Daily Express*, 31 January 1927, 6.
35. *Daily Express*, 12 September 1928, 15.
36. BBC: Internal memo, A.D.M. to Herbage and Reybould, 21 August 1936, R 34/227/2.

37. Winifred Holtby, *South Riding* (London: Virago, 1936).
38. *Buckingham Advertiser & Free Press*, 10 February 1940, 3; *Western Daily Press & Bristol Mirror*, 30 September 1944, 3.
39. *Yorkshire Evening Post*, 10 January 1941, 4.
40. *Manchester Evening News*, 12 February 1940, 4.
41. *Daily Record*, 4 March 1941, 3.
42. *Lancashire Evening Post*, 26 February 1945, 1; *Gloucestershire Echo*, 26 April 1945, 1.
43. Dan Todman, *The Great War: Myth and Memory* (London: Hambledon, 2005), 62–63.
44. See Emma Hanna, *The Great War on the Small Screen: Representing the First World War in Contemporary Britain* (Edinburgh: Edinburgh University Press, 2009).
45. BBC WAC T32/1139/1: 'Music and Visuals Script', Tony Essex to Malcolm Arnold (undated).
46. BBC WAC T32/1, 145/1: *The Great War* programme file, letter from Mrs M. Booth, Notts, 10 April 1965.
47. BBC WAC T32/1, 145/5: *The Great War* programme file, letter from John Tripp, London, 16 March 1965.
48. Interview with Anne Jarvis (née Dacre), Assistant to Producers, *The Great War*, by telephone with author, 8 March 2004.
49. Ibid.
50. Nick Lacey, *Image and Representation: Key Concepts in Media Studies* (London: Macmillan, 1998), 54.
51. Frank Howes, *The Music of Ralph Vaughan Williams* (Oxford: OUP, 1954), 22–23.
52. Ralph Vaughan Williams, *National Music and Other Essays* (Oxford: OUP, 1963), 1.
53. Jon Mitchell, *A Comprehensive Biography of Composer Gustav Holst, with Correspondence and Diary Excerpts* (Lewiston, NY: E Mellen Press, 2001), 161.
54. Paul Fussell, *The Great War and Modern Memory* (Oxford: OUP, 1975), 235.
55. http://www.cwgc.org/resources.aspx (accessed 27/05/2016).
56. CWGC: Teachers' Notes: Requiem, http://www.cwgc.org/education/anthem.htm (accessed 19/05/2016).
57. Ibid.
58. Birmingham City Football Club: http://www.bcfc.com/club/keep_right_on_anthem.aspx (accessed 19/05/2016).
59. Conferences have included "The Music of War," British Library, August 2014 and "Pack Up Your Troubles: Performance Cultures in the First World War," University of Kent, April 2016. Performance works include "War, Women & Song" (Harvest Media), a play with music telling the story of a First World War concert party on the Western Front, *Battle of Boat* (Jenna Donnelly & Ethan Maltby) and *The Forgotten of the Forgotten* (Daniel York Loh) on the Chinese Labour Corps.
60. This involved the 'planting' of 888,236 ceramic poppies in the Tower's moat with the proceeds going to charity. This public art work captured the imagination of the British public; by 11 November 2014, more than 8 million people had visited what came to be regarded as a contemporary, albeit temporary, war memorial. Parts of the installation later went on a tour of sites across the UK.
61. Eric Bogle, 'I Don't Like Joss Stone's Cover of No Man's Land but I Won't Sue', *The Guardian*, 12th November 2014: http://www.theguardian.com/music/musicblog/2014/nov/12/eric-bogle-responds-to-joss-stones-cover-of-his-song-no-mans-land (accessed 19/05/2016).
62. The Last Post Project, Superact, 2013–2015: http://www.superact.org.uk/projects/the-last-post-project/ (accessed 27/05/216).

63. 'The Last Post Bugle Call Must Not Be Rearranged for First World War Commemorations', Petitions, UK Government and Parliament: https://petition.parliament.uk/archived/petitions/59688 (accessed 27/05/2016).
64. The Last Post Project, Superact, 2013–2015: http://www.superact.org.uk/projects/the-last-post-project/ (accessed 27/05/216).
65. Edward Elgar Diary, 30 May 1918 as quoted in Toby Thacker, *British Culture and the First World War: Experience, Representation and Memory* (London: Bloomsbury, 2014), 201.
66. RAF 025350: 2nd Lieutenant F.T. Nettleingham, *Tommy Tunes: A Comprehensive Collection of Soldiers' Songs, Marching Melodies, Rude Rhymes, and Popular Parodies, Composed, Collected and Arranged on Active Service with the B.E.F.* (London: Erskine Macdonald, 1917), 13–14.

Bibliography

Primary Sources

BBC T32/1139/1: 'Music and Visuals Script', Tony Essex to Malcolm Arnold (undated).
BBC WAC T32/1, 145/1: *The Great War* programme file, letter from Mrs M. Booth, Notts, 10 April 1965.
BBC WAC T32/1, 145/5: *The Great War* programme file, letter from John Tripp, London, 16 March 1965.
BBC R 34/227/2: Internal memo, A.D.M. to Herbage and Reybould, 21 August 1936.
Cadbury Special Collections: YMCA/K/6/1: Major H. Walford Davies 'Music and Arms', *The Red Triangle*, Vol.1, September 1917–August 1918, 97.
RAF 025350: 2nd Lieutenant F.T. Nettleingham, *Tommy Tunes: A Comprehensive Collection of Soldiers' Songs, Marching Melodies, Rude Rhymes, and Popular Parodies, Composed, Collected and Arranged on Active Service with the B.E.F.* (London: Erskine Macdonald, 1917).
Royal British Legion: *British Legion*, Vol.7. No.6, December 1927, 149.
Royal British Legion: General Secretary's Monthly Circular for November 1927.

Newspapers

Buckingham Advertiser & Free Press, 10 February 1940, 3.
Daily Express, 5 October 1926, 9.
Daily Express, 11 October 1926, 1.
Daily Express, 22 November 1926, 2.
Daily Express, 18 December 1926, 3.
Daily Express, 3 January 1927, 9.
Daily Express, 10 January 1927, 3.
Daily Express, 31 January 1927, 6.
Daily Express, 12 September 1928, 15.
Daily Record, 4 March 1941, 3.
The Era, 25 October 1916, 14.
Gloucestershire Echo, 26 April 1945, 1.
Lancashire Evening Post, 26 February 1945, 1.
Liverpool Echo, 4 February 1916, 6.

London Evening News, 8 May 1919, 1.
Manchester Evening News, 12 February 1940, 4.
Western Daily Press & Bristol Mirror, 30 September 1944, 3.
Yorkshire Evening Post, 10 January 1941, 4.

Interviews

Anne Jarvis (née Dacre), Assistant to Producers, *The Great War*, by telephone with author, 8 March 2004.

Websites

Birmingham City Football Club: http://www.bcfc.com/club/keep_right_on_anthem.aspx (accessed 19/05/2016).
CWGC: Teachers' Notes: Requiem, http://www.cwgc.org/education/anthem.htm (accessed 19/05/2016).
Eric Bogle, 'I Don't Like Joss Stone's Cover of No Man's Land but I Won't Sue', *The Guardian*, 12th November 2014: http://www.theguardian.com/music/musicblog/2014/nov/12/eric-bogle-responds-to-joss-stones-cover-of-his-song-no-mans-land (accessed 19/05/2016).
'The First World War in the Classroom: Teaching and the Construction of Cultural Memory' was a study led by Dr Catriona Pennell (University of Exeter) and Dr Ann-Marie Einhaus (University of Northumbria)—http://ww1intheclassroom.exeter.ac.uk/.
'Gas Shells Bombardment, British Troops Advancing on Lille' can be heard at http://www.firstworldwar.com/audio/1918.htm (accessed 27/05/2016).
'The Last Post Bugle Call Must Not Be Rearranged for First World War commemorations', Petitions, UK Government and Parliament: https://petition.parliament.uk/archived/petitions/59688 (accessed 27/05/2016).
The Last Post Project, Superact, 2013–2015: http://www.superact.org.uk/projects/the-last-post-project/ (accessed 27/05/2016).
Sergeant Edward Dwyer VC, 'With Our Boys at the Front' voice recording can be heard at http://www.firstworldwar.com/audio/1916.htm (accessed 18/05/2016).

Secondary Sources

Articles

Emma Hanna, 'A small screen alternative to stone and bronze: "The Great War" (BBC, 1964)', *European Journal of Cultural Studies*, 10, 1 (February 2007), 89–111.
James G. Mansell, 'Musical modernity and contested commemoration at the festival of remembrance, 1923–1927', *The Historical Journal*, 52, 2 (2009), 433–454.

Books

Efrat Ben-Ze'ev, Ruth Ginio & Jay Winter (ed), *Shadows of War: A Social History of Silence in the Twentieth Century* (Cambridge: CUP, 2010).

John Brophy & Eric Partridge, *The Long Trail: What the British Soldier Sang and Said in the Great War of 1914–18* (Tonbridge: Andre Deutsch, 1965 [1930]).
Charles Carrington, *Soldier from the Wars Returning* (London: Hutchinson, 1965).
J.F.G. Fuller, *Troop Morale and Popular Culture* (Oxford: Clarendon, 1990).
Paul Fussell, *The Great War and Modern Memory* (Oxford: OUP, 1975).
Clifford Geertz, *The Interpretation of Cultures* (New York: Basic Books, 1973).
Gramophone Company, *Gramophone Records of the First World War: An HMV Catalogue 1914–18*, Introduced by Brian Rust (Newton Abbot: David & Charles, 1975).
Adrian Gregory, *The Silence of Memory: Armistice Day 1919–1946* (Oxford: Berg, 1994).
Emma Hanna, *The Great War on the Small Screen: Representing the First World War in Contemporary Britain* (Edinburgh: Edinburgh University Press, 2009).
Winifred Holtby, *South Riding* (London: Virago, 1936).
Frank Howes, *The Music of Ralph Vaughan Williams* (Oxford: OUP, 1954).
Meirion Hughes & Robert Stradling, *The English Musical Renaissance 1840–1940: Constructing a National Music (second edition)* (Manchester: MUP, 2001 [1993]).
Patrick N. Juslin & John A. Sloboda (eds), *Handbooks of Music and Emotion: Theory, Research, Applications* (Oxford: OUP, 2010).
Alex King, *Memorials of the Great War in Britain: The Symbolism and Politics of Remembrance* (Oxford: Berg, 1998).
Nick Lacey, *Image and Representation: Key Concepts in Media Studies* (London: Macmillan, 1998).
Eric Leed, *No Man's Land: Combat and Identity in World War I* (Cambridge: CUP, 1979).
Jon Mitchell, *A Comprehensive Biography of Composer Gustav Holst, with Correspondence and Diary Excerpts* (Lewiston, NY: E Mellen Press, 2001).
Pierre Nora (ed), *Lieux de Mémoire* (Paris: Editions Gallimard, 1984–92).
Graham Roberts & Philip M. Taylor (ed), *The Historian, Television and Television History* (Luton: Luton University Press, 2001).
Jeffrey Richards, *Imperialism and Music: Britain 1876–1953* (Manchester: MUP, 2002).
Martin Stephen, *The Price of Pity* (London: Leo Cooper, 1996).
Toby Thacker, *British Culture and the First World War: Experience, Representation and Memory* (London: Bloomsbury, 2014).
Dan Todman, *The Great War: Myth and Memory* (London: Hambledon, 2005).
Michael Williams, *Ivor Novello: Screen Idol* (London: BFI, 2003).
Ralph Vaughan Williams, *National Music and Other Essays* (Oxford: OUP, 1963).
Glenn Watkins, *Proof through the Night: Music and the Great War* (Berkeley: U of California Press, 2003).
Bart Ziino, ed. *Remembering the Great War* (London: Routledge, 2014).

3   *Maisons de Tolérance*
The Real and Imagined Sexual Landscapes of the Western Front

Krista Cowman

The broadening of what constitutes "war experience" in the historiography of the First World War has transformed our understanding of the spatial location of the conflict. Alongside earlier works concerned with civilian life on the Home Front, a number of studies now exist that consider what combatants did with their time away from the immediate field of battle. A variety of different spaces in which an individual soldier's war experience was shaped have thus emerged, often as a consequence of a willingness to ask different questions, shifting the attention of historical enquiry away from the single focus of the front-line trench. A century after the war broke out historians are now as likely to question why men fought as to interrogate the strategies and weaponry through which they sought to defeat the enemy. Asking new questions has led historians to look for "war experience" in previously overlooked spaces. One example of this arose from investigations into how individuals accessed the levels of social and emotional support essential to maintaining the key military concept of "morale" and mental fitness. In an early attempt to answer this question, J. Baynes' study into what kept the decimated ranks of the Second Scottish Rifles together after the battle of Neuve Chapelle revealed the complex factors of loyalty, trust and inter-dependence between ranks that provided men with critical mutual support in the front line.[1] J.G. Fuller significantly extended the spatial dimensions of Baynes' work by looking into how activities behind the line also maintained morale, showing how the recreation of aspects of civilian life by the army authorities sustained men's emotional welfare when they were out of the trenches.[2]

Looking closely at these different spaces has broadened our understanding of the types of activities which combined to constitute "war experience." As well the ability to replicate British civilian culture in the base camps and YMCA huts in Northern France, my own study of men's leisure time activities when out of the lines has suggested the importance of being able to access French civilian life for shopping expeditions or theatre trips, facilitating their engagement with a degree of "normality" when home leave was unavailable.[3] On a much wider scale, the comparative investigations into different wartime cityscapes in the "Capital Cities at War" project have emphasised the scope of distractions on offer in Paris for all allied troops serving on the Western Front.[4] Not all of the spaces providing emotional support had such a defined material reality, however. Michael Roper's work on the role of men's correspondence to upholding their psychological wellbeing argues that writing—and reading—letters had the ability to remove men from their surroundings and place them into a different, safer but invented space in ways which "sometimes felt so vivid that the awareness of the difference between the real and imaginary was suspended."[5]

The focus on men's collective and individual experiences away from the front line has been extended in a number of recent studies that consider more personal activities. Most private of all is arguably the topic of soldiers' sexual behaviour, which has only recently begun to be opened up. In an early article on this theme, K. Craig Gibson considered various types of heterosexual encounters between servicemen and French and Flemish civilian women along the Western Front.[6] Looking at numerous different relationships including flirtations, commercial sexual transactions and marriages, Gibson concluded that front-line troops were able to access sexual activity while on active service with less difficulty than may have been previously suggested. Other work has focussed more exclusively on the commercial dimensions of wartime sexual behaviour. Jean-Yves La Nour has compared the attitudes of French and American military authorities towards troops' practice of paying for sex, while Clare Makepeace has questioned British men's reasons for using licensed brothels in France.[7] Medical historians such as Mark Harrison, Edward H. Beardsley and Michelle Rhodes have approached the topic of soldiers' sexual activities through examining the different approaches of the French, British and American armies towards controlling the spread of venereal disease among troops, while Philippa Levine and others have used venereal disease as a means of interrogating the complex attitudes towards race and sexuality visible during the conflict.[8]

This chapter builds on this previous work into the more private activities taking place out of the line to consider in more detail the material space of the brothel, or *maison de tolérance*, the site framing many commercial sexual encounters on the Western Front. It shows how the wartime *maisons de tolérance* were complex spaces which were at once both real and at the same time intensely imagined, with numerous different meanings attached to them. For some of their soldier-clients the imagined space of the brothel—and what might take place there—transformed these sites into a fantasy space of pleasure away from the front line whose effect was enhanced through discussion and anticipation. At the same time, other observers imagined these spaces as degenerate sites of corruption and immorality to be fought against. This negative view was particularly evident among British civilians, but could also be deduced among soldiers, particularly those who had direct experience of *maisons* as clients when this failed to live up to their imaginings. At the same time, the French authorities in charge of regulating the actual physical space of the brothel had other preoccupations. They did not view these sites as places for escape and fantasy, or as contemporary versions of Sodom and Gomorrah, but as an unfortunate necessity to be put up with (as the name *maison de tolérance* implied) and regulated. These spaces were essential to keeping the fighting force *en bon état* but still required careful oversight and improvement if the health of men using them was to be maintained, thus French authorities encouraged significant alterations in their design during wartime.

The Pre-War *Maison de Tolérance*, its Regulation and Representation

Many of the opinions—and expectations—British troops held about French prostitution had developed before the war. The *maison de tolérance* had been part of French life throughout the nineteenth century, although access to the site had not always been as free and easy as many troops believed. As Alan Sheridan noted in his translator's introduction to Corbin's seminal study *Women for Hire*, prostitution, while it "was not legal, let alone approved" in nineteenth- and twentieth-century France, was nonetheless "in certain circumstances 'tolerated.'"[9] An essential part of this process of toleration was the attempt at spatial containment of prostitution inside the *maison de tolérance*, a legal brothel, recognised as such by the state since the early nineteenth century, and subject to strict state control. As Corbin's study has suggested, the complex regulations through which *maisons de tolérance* were regulated served both to remove the spectacle of prostitution from wider society while at the same time enabling constant state surveillance of the prostitute and her activities.[10] A number of rules surrounded the location and appearance of *maisons de tolérance*. They were to be situated in designated areas, away from schools, churches and public buildings, an arrangement first suggested by the Parisian doctor and hygiene campaigner Alexandre Parent Duchalet in 1836.[11] From the outside there would be nothing about the building on public view that suggested its function. Entry would be through a double door to prevent accidental glimpses of the interior or its inhabitants in order that men who were not already intent on visiting the *maison* would not be tempted to enter. Ground floor rooms would be kept to a minimum and shielded from view with shutters, frosted glass and "venetian blinds and curtains [that] will be continually closed."[12] The girls who worked—and often lived—inside the *maisons de tolérance* (which could only be run by women) had to be registered with the police and were subject to regular medical inspections intended to control the spread of venereal diseases.

An emphasis on segregating the commercial sexual activity of a town or city from its broader society meant that the exterior appearances of *maisons de tolérance* were designed in order to conceal their function rather than to attract clients. Yet while nothing from the outside of a *maison* was supposed to suggest its purpose, opposite principles drove the interior design. Dr Louis

Fiaux, a French admirer of Josephine Butler who favoured the stricter control or abolition of prostitution in France, published a study of *maisons de tolérance* in 1892, in which he described in detail the sumptuous interiors of some of the better-class Parisian establishments. These were luxurious and presented in ways that emphasised rather than concealed the purpose of the space. Once they were safely through the double doors and away from public view, clients would be met by an array of opulent displays. There were plush carpets and draperies and salons with "a profusion of mirrors, tapestries, chandeliers, bronzes, paintings, flowers and exotic plants" as well as ceilings adorned with painted friezes (usually depicting naked women in a variety of sexual positions) or tented with sumptuous fabrics. In the bedrooms were more draperies and mirrors, including mirrored ceilings.[13] A number of more specialised *maisons* went further and developed themed spaces with exotic décor intended to fuel a client's fantasies or to heighten their impact. Fiaux recorded rooms put together to resemble Spanish, Turkish, Egyptian or Chinese environments as well as one designed to look like the cabin of a luxury liner replete with a hammock.[14] A rich array of costumes and props were on hand to add to the overall effect of these themed spaces, blurring the reality of the space with the imagined pleasures its clients anticipated.

By the end of the nineteenth century the more expensive *maisons* were making good use of new technologies to further enhance their attempts at eroticised exoticism. Corbin cites a report from 1908, which described the role of "dazzling electric lights everywhere" in building an atmosphere of fantasy in a modern *maison*.[15] Electric lighting remained a novelty at the turn of the century, and the mirrors and chandeliers that were a feature of the interiors of many *maisons* used it to good effect. Just as important to a client's experience was the presence of adequate heating. Radiators, often adorned with sexual imagery, were an essential part of the interior design of a *maison*.[16] Fiaux explained how these innovations (which included portable electric models) provided a "gentle and temperate heat which allowed women to remain naked in the *salons* and keep the same attire as they come and go" between rooms.[17] The detailed and systematic accounts of interiors of these spaces (and the practices performed within them) that appeared in the social investigations of Louis Fiaux, Léo Taxil, Yves Guyot and others were replicated in numerous cultural representations of the inside of *fin de siècle* brothels. Popular novels including Zola's *Nana* (1880) and Edmond de Goncourt's *La Fille Elisa* (1877) offered detailed descriptions of prostitutes and their surroundings. Artists including Degas and Toulouse-Lautrec (who also undertook a number of paintings for Le Chabanais, the exclusive Parisian *maison* favoured by Edward VII where he himself was a regular customer) produced a number of paintings of prostitutes depicting the inside of *maisons de tolérance*, usually featuring an abundance of semi-nude women in finely decorated rooms.[18] Thus, while the findings of French social scientists and abolitionists may not have been widely familiar in Edwardian Britain, many of their depictions of French prostitutes and their surroundings were. Consequently, despite the presence of shutters, frosted glass and double-doors intended to shield the inside of a *maison de tolérance* from public view, knowledge of what it looked like and of what went on there was widespread by 1914 in France and abroad.

British Views of French Sexuality: The *Maison de Tolérance* as an Enticing Space

This knowledge was commonplace among the men of the British Expeditionary Force who went out to France in 1914. Lord Kitchener's advice to soldiers, famously appended to all paybooks, warned each man that while in France he would meet with "temptations both in wine and women, you must avoid both." Wine and women—and especially women—were central to the impressions of France and Frenchness of many British and allied troops who had never previously visited the continent. The sexual connotations of France and the images this invoked are well summarised in a frequently cited extract from Cecil Lewis' 1936 memoir *Sagittarius Rising* where the author explained how what came to his mind when he had the opportunity of leave in Paris in 1916 had nothing to do with

> the beautiful city of elegance and gaiety, of palaces, fountains, and boulevards where you sat under the chestnuts, munched *fraises des bois* floating in cream and sipped a *vin rosé* as clean and heady and good for the soul as anything this side of paradise. No, Paris in 1916 was to him a sort of gigantic brothel where women wore nothing but georgette underwear and extra long silk stockings.[19]

Lewis' extremely literate memoir typifies one common view of French—and in particular Parisian—sexuality that permeates many combatant's war writing both in work produced during the war and in post-conflict accounts. From the 1890s, the period of the *Belle Époque*, many British observers had developed what Stefan Slater termed "a titillating idea of 'Frenchness.'"[20] Popular cultural representations of the country, including depictions of the inside of brothels in the art and novels cited above, had helped to promote the idea of France as a site of sexual license and debauchery. This view was enhanced in wartime theatres when figures such as Jane Avril, already familiar to British audiences since her first British appearance in the 1890s, (advertised through posters by Toulouse-Lautrec) were joined on the London stage by a host of other French female performers with increasingly risqué self-presentation.[21] Some of these (including Gaby Deslys and Alice Delysia who are described in Andrew Maunder's contribution to this volume) made their names in British wartime revues where their stage costumes and performances perpetuated popular perceptions of the open sexual attitudes of French women to audiences that included large numbers of serving troops on leave or waiting to embark. In France other stage stars such as

Mistinguette, who famously had her legs insured for 500,000 francs, continued to perform in Paris throughout the war; references to her shows can be found in many British men's descriptions of their time on French leave.[22] Theatre was not the only cultural representation of free and easy French sexual behaviour available to troops. The words of popular soldiers' songs including "Mademoiselle from Armentieres" (identified by sexologist Magnus Hirschfeld as "a pretty midinette who worked in a laundry during the day and spent her evenings entertaining America soldiers at the Black Cat Café") re-enforced the popular perceptions of French women constructed on the wartime stage.[23] These perceptions were given added weight when men arrived in France through the images in numerous French publications aimed at troops such as *La Vie Parisienne*, which daringly featured sketches of naked women on its front covers. The war also saw an increase in production of the relatively new form of suggestive erotic photographs sold as postcards, a genre which was already popularly known as "French postcards" before the outbreak of war.[24] Monk Gibbon, a young subaltern, remembered the displays on the side French newspaper kiosks that were "embarrassingly intimate, and their postcards also specialised in alluring creatures in *Déshabille*."[25] All of these sites enforced the dominant impressions of French women as sexually willing, adventurous and available. Thus British troops arrived in France with deeply ingrained preconceptions, which were immediately reinforced through widely available images aimed directly at young soldiers. It was expected that French women would be exotic, extremely scantily clad (unencumbered by the long drawers, inaccessible corsets or woolen undergarments worn by women at home) and willing to engage in a variety of daring sexual behaviours, in marked contrast to English wives and sweethearts. Similar expectations were reported among American troops who arrived in 1917 equally convinced of the dissolute morals and "concentration of pleasure and debauchery" offered by France and in particular the "modern Babylon" that was Paris.[26]

Unsurprisingly many of these erotic expectations came to be centred on the space of the *maison de tolérance*. This space came to serve a number of different functions for troops. On one level it was a site where they could indulge in regular sexual intercourse, an activity that many in the army now viewed as "a physical necessity" to maintaining soldiers' health.[27] French and German military authorities certainly recognised the importance of *maisons de tolérance* in meeting this need although the attitudes of the British army were more mixed, shifting from initial acceptance to later prohibition (as a result of domestic pressure). The American authorities, by contrast, were consistently opposed to their use.[28] The French (and initially the British) authorities' pragmatic view of the *maison de tolérance* as a purely functional space for maintaining physical wellbeing overlooked its role in sustaining men's emotional welfare through providing a level of escapism which was simultaneously real and imagined. Sidney Rogerson, a young officer with the West Yorkshire Regiment, explained how as on the front line "our life was not only celibate for long periods, but it was one in which all the softer if not the finer influences were absent . . . it was not surprising, therefore, that Woman stood as a symbol of much that we were missing."[29] Visiting a *maison de tolérance* provided more than an end to enforced celibacy. It also offered men the guaranteed presence of women who could provide them with temporary respite and whose mere presence delineated this space as the opposite of the entirely male world of the front line. Thus they were sites that came to be used as much for emotional as sexual sustenance, shaping men's imaginations to provide a valuable alternative to their daily circumstance.

The emotional function of these spaces is clear in some men's writing where the presence of women appears to have been as important as the opportunity for sexual contact with them. One cavalryman's description of the *maison* nearest his French base camp paid as much attention to its gambling tables which created "a great atmosphere on [pay] nights with so much money flying about, it was very exciting" as to its ten girls who "if not actually working . . . would wander round the room and talk to the troops."[30] The majority of accounts, however, reflect the more popular views of behaviours inside the *maisons de tolérance* described above where direct engagement with women whose appearance exactly matched how it had been imagined is essential. Many men included descriptions of French women with little or no clothing in their broader accounts of French brothels. The portrait offered of the officer's brothel in Dunkirk by Lt R. Graham Dixon, a young subaltern with the Royal Garrison Artillery, shows how the interior arrangements of *maisons de tolérance* suggested a fantasy landscape both through their ornamentation and through the dress of their girls. The building featured a

> paved courtyard at the back, with a rectangular lily-pool in the centre. Here you might stroll, or sit and drink a bottle of wine with your very sketchily-clad companion—they all sported exceedingly gaudy shifts decorated with ribbons and lace, and not a stitch underneath.[31]

In this perpetual summer (presumably enhanced by the heating arrangements noted by Fiaux in Parisian *fin de siècle maisons*) Dixon found a "black-haired, black-eyed wench, whose enthusiasm was quite adequate and whose skill likewise—I stuck to her on the rare occasions when a visit seemed desirable."[32]

The eroticised attire of prostitutes served to heighten the sense of distance between the *maison* and other wartime spaces thus enhancing the sense of escapism it could provide. In *The Bells of Hell go Ting-a-Ling-a-Ling*, the memoir of Private Eric Hiscock, published in the 1970s, we find detailed accounts of a number of his sexual encounters as a teenaged soldier. One of his earliest conquests was a French girl he called "Suzy" who "didn't, she told me, fuck for money if it was with a British troop but just for the hell of it."[33] The passage describing Suzy's preparations for their night of lovemaking showed the extent to which popular perceptions of French women's sexuality gleaned from other sources helped to shape men's expectations (and in this case confirm them) of their appearance and behaviour. Hiscock recalled how, once in the privacy of her room, Suzy

> slipped off her dress (it was bright yellow) and stood in her underwear (which was black and not transparent at all which is what all the best heroines wear if the products of the Olympia Press are to be believed) and beckoned me to her bed.[34]

This anachronistic reference to the Olympia Press, a notorious Paris-based publishing house of the 1950s whose list combined post-war avant garde literature with a number of pornographic titles, suggests the potential for men's experience of erotic encounters on the Western Front to be shaped by other sources long after the events themselves had taken place. The majority of memoirs, however, were more alert to the influence of contemporary sources. Thomas Hope, another teenaged infantryman who, like Hiscock, published a much later memoir, described an advertising card he was handed in Calais for "Madame Antoine's Palace of Pleasure" which featured "a photo of one, 'Yvonne', posed in her birthday suit plus silk stockings and garters."[35] When Hope and his two companions finally arrived at Madame Antoine's *maison* they recognised the accuracy of the advertisement when they were met by three women "their complete outfit a silk shawl, barely covering their supposed charms, high heeled shoes, silk stockings and the inevitable garters."[36] Private Edward Casey found similar costumes on display at the White Star café, a recognised brothel in Le Havre. Here he was approached by a "Girly [who] wore a kind of cheese-cloth wrap-around, pinned at the shoulder. That girl (to my embarrassment) exposed every private part of her body . . . [and] sat on my knee . . . exposing one of her titties." Casey was forced to leave, lacking the necessary money to conclude the encounter, but returned some days later to be entertained by "a different [Girl] . . . wearing the same dress."[37] While each of these memoirs was written some time after the event, the dual sense of shock and excitement that they still invoke demonstrates how deep an impression such near nudity made on young British boys for whom licensed prostitution was—literally—a foreign concept.

A number of accounts suggest that the British soldiers who patronised French brothels during the war were as much struck by the opulent interiors of *maisons de tolérance* as by their prostitute's dress. Even the less affluent *maisons* catering to ordinary ranks contained some fabulous features that set them apart as a space of indulgence. Casey, who noted that even in the middle of the day, the White Star was "brightly lighted with rows of electric light bulbs," became anxious to return to "that well-lit palace of joy" as soon as his finances permitted.[38] Other descriptions included rooms, "the walls and ceilings of which were entirely covered with mirrors."[39] Such embellishments were well-established features of *maisons* before the war, as shown above, and were intended to entice custom in what was becoming an increasingly competitive market. Many of them were deliberately conceived to encourage their clients to develop complex erotic fantasies of place, as we have seen. During the war competition was no longer an issue (with the possible exception of Paris) as *maisons de tolerance* in towns close to army bases struggled to keep up with the demands of large influxes of troops. Thus the retention of interior fittings designed to convey an impression of luxury that would stimulate a client's imagination served more to enhance the sense of separation between a *maison*'s world of sensual pleasure and the all too near reality of the front line than to secure patronage in an overcrowded market.

Even those who had no intention of entering into the space of the *maison de tolérance* could find themselves drawn into its vicinity. Monk Gibbon was one of many British soldiers with memories of Le Havre's notorious Rue des Galions. He recorded how "The name was soon familiar to me, though only by repute, and its Red Lamp establishments which, it seemed, were extensively patronized. . . . The Rue de Galions must have been the fashionable quarter, but to my shocked imagination it sounded sordid enough."[40] Gibbon did not admit to joining any of his excited comrades' expeditions to the Rue de Galions himself, but he did recall joining in the conversations about these outings, recognising the importance for all of the men to be able to "get out of camp" at the weekend.

The Problematic Space: The *Maison de Tolérance* as a Source of Moral Outrage

Not all contemporary descriptions of *maisons de tolérance* were as tolerant as that of Gibbon in presenting them as enticing sites for pleasurable escapism. Some men found that what they actually encountered in the reality of this space was markedly different from the tempting landscape that rumour and cultural representation had led them to expect in their imaginings of it. In Henry Williamson's early experiential war novel, *A Patriot's Progress*, the hero, John Bullock, visited a fictionalised estaminet in Poperinghe that also functioned as a low-level brothel. Upon his arrival at the estaminet barely two hours after he left the front line, Bullock found himself perfunctorily taken upstairs by an old woman, wearing "a leather pouch like a tramdriver. It jingled with money. Beyond the open door he saw a fattish, half-dressed woman. She had thick ankles and legs in coarse black stockings. The room smelled musty. He wished he hadn't come."[41] The outfit worn by the prostitute woman here is particularly significant. While she is half-naked, the functionality of her remaining attire is not in the least bit seductive and stands in stark contrast to the delicate transparent draperies displayed in erotic postcards and seen by other men. There is nothing here to entice or embellish the senses. Diaphanous wraps are replaced by "coarse black stockings" and perfume by a "musty" smell. Consequently, Williamson's account unsurprisingly conveys a sense of regret and disappointment on the part of the soldier client.

Other literary representations suggest a more ambivalent response which also appears to have been prompted by a less imaginative approach to staging commercial sexual encounters than cultural representations had led them to expect. Having agreed to go to Madame Antoine's premises in Calais with his comrades Mac and Webster, the young Thomas Hope opted to remain watching the scene downstairs with Mac while Webster handed over some notes "to a fat greasy old woman behind the counter, then [disappeared] through the door leading upstairs" with one of the girls. Hope's account shows himself to be at once fascinated and repelled by the "utter abandonment" of the surroundings where girls would descend on a man to

> display their full bosoms, and bulging thighs or press their bodies against his until he either capitulates or transfers his affections elsewhere. There is no concealment of their trade. This is a brothel and they are harlots, willing to sell their bodies to any man who pays the price, and ready to use every trick and artifice in view of a hundred eyes to obtain a customer.[42]

Once Hope makes it clear that he has no interest in pursuing a commercial transaction with any of the girls he shifts from the role of participant to that of an outside observer of the scene. Watching the rapid comings and goings connects his disillusionment in part to the speed of the encounters and the numbers of men involved, which increase his feelings of detachment. The comparatively small numbers of licensed prostitutes working in the *maisons* close to the Western Front meant that most women were now forced to dispatch their clients as quickly as possible with no time for even a suggestion of intimacy. Spending the entire night with one man or acting out elaborately staged fantasies was out of the question, and men would have little time to notice the elements of their surroundings intended to enhance their experience. Estimates of numbers of men to each woman varied. A report by the British Association for Moral and Social Hygiene (AMSH) in December 1917 claimed that "an average of about 360 men a day" from the British convalescent camp at Cayeux-sur-Mer were visiting the town's newly-opened nearby brothel which contained a mere fifteen women.[43] Robert Graves, who by his own admission remained "puritanical" and took no part in commercial sex, claimed to have seen "A queue of a hundred and fifty men waiting" at the "Red Lamp" in Bethune "each to have his short turn with one of the three women in the house. . . . Each woman served nearly a battalion of men every week for as long as she lasted. According to the assistant provost-marshal three weeks was the usual limit" before a girl retired on her earnings.[44] Graves' figures work out at around double the numbers of clients for the girls in Bethune to those in Cayeux offered by the AMSH report, but they are roughly in line with those provided by cavalryman Ben

Clouting who claimed to have got them directly from the French doctor undertaking regular health inspections on the girls in the Cayeux brothel. The doctor recounted how during one routine inspection he asked "one of the young girls, 'You look a bit sore, how many soldiers did you have last night?' She made a quick tally and told me 'fifty six'." On hearing this, the doctor prescribed "three or four days off" and "put her on the sick list."[45]

Such lurid tales of rapidly repeated and impersonal acts of sexual intercourse fed a growing sense of moral panic in Britain that centred on the *maison de tolérance* as feared space, a site of "debauchery" rather than pleasure and the focus of moral outrage.[46] Throughout the war, authorities in all combatant nations expressed periodic general worries about the long-term consequences of what the German sexologist Marcus Hirschfeld described as "the release of sexual restraints" prompted by wartime conditions.[47] On top of the alarm prompted by a rise in both illegitimate births and venereal infections there were particular concerns in Britain attached to the introduction of conscription, which many observers felt placed a direct responsibility for young men's moral welfare onto the state. One letter from a nonconformist chaplain sent to the Secretary of State for War in 1918 explained how this might require a rethinking of previous army attitudes towards soldiers' sexual activities:

> I am receiving quite a number of enquiries with regard to the alleged house of ill-fame at Cayeux sur Mer, Somme, in connection with which certain replies to questions were recently given in the House of Commons. Would you be good enough to inform me whether any decisive step is being taken by the Army Council with regard to this matter? Now that we have conscription, and that boys are obliged to join up almost immediately after they have left school, it is intolerable that they should be exposed to the implicit incitement to immorality.[48]

The aforementioned brothel at Cayeux-sur-Mer became the focus of particular public anxiety in 1918, as this letter suggests. There were implications that the house in question—alongside one in Le Havre—was effectively being run by as well as for the British army, thus shifting the army position from acceptance to open encouragement. A formidable opposition grew up against this suggestion with prominent clergy such as the Dean of Lincoln urging their congregations not to vote for any politician who failed to support their calls for prohibition and the Archbishop of Canterbury threatening to take the matter to the Lords.[49] Feminist groups including AMSH added their voices to the protests on the grounds that the regulations imposed by French authorities on licensed prostitutes that demanded regular medical inspection and punitive action while taking no steps to check the hygiene of their clients were discriminatory and echoed the hated Contagious Diseases Acts. Questions were raised in Parliament. Eventually the British army authorities reluctantly decided to place *maisons* out of bounds to British troops (although it remains uncertain as to how widely this ban was enforced). Their decision was welcomed at home but condemned in France where the local civilian authorities were already stretched in attempting to control the growing levels of amateur prostitution that were rife across the *zone occupe*. Both the Mayor of Granville-St-Honorine and his police chief lodged protests to the War Office warning that this action would increase both amateur prostitution and venereal disease in the civilian population.[50]

The *Maison de Tolérance* as a Functional Space

The French authorities had other more practical concerns about the activity contained within *maisons de tolérance* during the war. Corbin's study suggests that while many nineteenth-century *maisons* had already closed by the twentieth century, the more specialised (and often expensive) ones continued to flourish at the outbreak of war. The first months of war in 1914 offered "a new lease of life" to surviving establishments and many new ones were opened, some providing English lessons to their employees.[51] This period also saw marked shifts in the exterior design of the *maison*. Several of the newer establishments adopted a more elaborate style that echoed their interior design and hinted at a more exotic purpose than the anonymous exteriors favoured by Parent-Duchlet. One image of a recently constructed brothel in Luçon (sent by the Parisian architect Lucien Joubin to the police authorities in Rouen as an example of his work when they were considering opening a new facility locally) was in neo-Moorish style with intricate arched windows heavily glazed and shuttered on the second floor, mosaics around the door and heavy Moroccan lanterns hanging above its entrance.[52] The lanterns were significant as they identified the purpose of a *maison* in a shift from earlier more discreet exteriors. Wartime *maisons* along the Western Front usually sported a red light outside, with a blue light designating those premises that were reserved for the use of officers.

French authorities had more pragmatic concerns regarding the interior design of *maisons de tolérance*. Studies of the French approaches to controlling venereal disease during the First World War have argued that the retention of *maisons* was viewed as having an important role in providing continuity with pre-war practices. Mark Harrison suggests that attempts to maintain licensed prostitution on the Western Front stemmed from a desire on the part of the French authorities to "reassure their citizens that the war would not result in moral or physical deterioration," thus keeping the activity clean and separate from broader society. Harrison's claim that a belief that prostitution "was inevitable and even socially necessary" had developed in France since the nineteenth century has been developed in more detail by Michelle Rhodes, whose comparative study of French and American approaches to venereal disease uncovered a strong belief among French military authorities that regular sexual intercourse was necessary to maintaining the health and vitality of fighting men.[53]

Much of the resources of the police and local authorities along the Western Front were now directed towards limiting the spread of venereal disease among the military through monitoring individual women and the cafes and estaminets in which they congregated as well as investigating and punishing those charged with spreading infection. In some areas the French authorities began to assess the potential for increasing the numbers of licensed *maisons* in their district, seeing these as being the best means of delineating boundaries for the practice of prostitution and of minimising the risk and spread of infection to allied troops through monitoring the health of the women involved. The available evidence suggests that the rise in wartime provision was extremely modest in comparison with what moral campaigners may have imagined. In the department of Seine Maritime, for example, a survey of available provision undertaken in the spring of 1918 suggested that the war may have had less impact on expanding the number of licensed premises than might have been expected. Le Havre had the largest number of *maisons de tolérance* in operation—nine—of the towns surveyed, mainly clustered in the notorious Rue de Galion, a name that was familiar to anti-prostitution campaigners in Britain as the discussions above suggest. This number was considered sufficient. Furthermore, it was considerably less than the number of *maisons* in the nineteenth-century port, that were claimed to have stood at 34 in 1870 and 12 in 1890, supporting Corbin's point that this branch of the sex industry was in decline in France by 1914.[54] Although other towns in the department had far fewer licensed *maisons* in operation, their small numbers were not always seen as inadequate. There were no plans, for example, on the part of French authorities to augment the single *maisons* operating at Fecamp, Graville and Eu, or to offer any provision at all in a number of towns including Mezidon and Pont Audemer where there were numbers of troops but no *maison* in operation. The report only offered limited evidence that the war was a driving factor in increased provision—for example in Rouen where the city's 8 existing premises were currently being augmented by "two hotels transformed into *maisons de tolérance* from 20.00 hours, reserved for English officers."[55] Other evidence was more forthcoming on the link, however. Describing the new facility in his town, capable of receiving 200 men at a time, the Mayor of Trouville explained to the military commanders at Rouen that his council had only taken the decision to build it with some "regret," to combat the numerous prostitutes congregating close to the nearby British camp in order to keep a check on the health of the women concerned, and reduce the level of general nuisance of street prostitution.[56] The regulated space of a *maison de tolérance* was seen as the best means of combating casual prostitution, placating the civilian population and maintaining a healthy fighting force.

As the actions in Trouville show, the French authorities recognised that there was some need for extra provision on this part of the Western Front, which was close to a number of training, rest and convalescent camps used by the British and Dominion forces. Sites were identified and approved, and plans discussed. The discussion took place in the light of new army regulations for the conduct and design of *maisons de tolérance* that were issued by the French government in May 1918. The guidelines went into great detail about the governance of any *maison* intended for military use with strong restrictions on the provision of alcohol, and the requirement to respect any prohibitions applicable to certain customers if a licensed house were to be placed "out of bounds" to identified ranks or units. The advice given in regard to the ideal internal layout of a *maison* was very different from either the descriptions offered by social investigators prior to the war, or from those imagined in literature and art. No scope was provided for the *maison* to provide a fantasy landscape that might offer an escape from military life. Instead many of its pre-war imaginative features were to be dulled. There were to be no exotic embellishments in *maisons* such as drapes, mirrors or chandeliers, and no suggestion that the space might shape or enhance an inner life for its (now almost entirely military) customers. Rather, the wartime brothel was to be efficient, hygienic and functional. It should have no "hidden corners, dark cabinets or secret staircases." Windows should be lined with opaque curtains or glass tiles. Corridors and hallways should be constantly lit. Walls and tables should be free from the erotic pictures and photographs that were a constant presence in memoirs of men's visits to brothels. Much emphasis was placed on the need for adequate cleanliness to assist the prophylactic function of the space. New *maisons* would contain sufficient baths, and the women should use these at least once a week; in addition, each woman would have her own bidet and wash stand and the premises should have plenty of water closets "hygienically installed and kept clean." In the reception rooms chairs and sofas would be upholstered with cloth selected to repel bugs, and elaborate wooden beds would be avoided. There would also be basins, towels (to be changed after each client) and syringes for douching that should be cleaned with *savon de Marseilles* and permanganate of potash after use. Nothing that might harbour bugs or germs was to be encouraged. There were also to be instructions on display, in each room and in communal areas, in French and English, describing the necessary precautions to be adopted by clients to escape venereal infection.[57]

This description of the state's view of an ideal interior for staging paid sexual activity close to the Western Front provides a third interpretation of the alternate space of the *maison de tolérance* in this area. The functional approach to the interior, far removed from the opulent indulgence of the pre-war *maison* removes any embellishment that might enhance the sensuality of the experience. The military *maison* is not a site for escape; rather it serves as an extension of army discipline. While the French military authorities had the greatest interest in regulating this space (which was, after all, on French soil and licensed under French law) allied army officials were equally keen to reduce its imaginative role. Contemporary accounts describe how this worked. In Richard Aldington's *Death of a Hero*, the narrator recalled a visit to the brothel in Béthune (in all likelihood the same one whose queues here recalled by Robert Graves). Here, the large numbers of men queuing outside the facility were moved efficiently through the space by their sergeant who effectively marched them in and out as if they were participating in a form of army drill. Aldington's narrator described waiting his turn for "a nice tart . . . in a 'ell of a 'urry. She kep' sayin 'urry, daypayshay'. I adn't got meself buttoned up afore I eared the Sergeant shouting 'Next two files, right turn, quick march'. But she was a nice tart, she was."[58] Although he was not sufficiently disturbed by the incident to transform it into a negative experience, recalling the woman in rather fond terms, his description is brief and brusque in comparison with the more evocative fantasies of French sensuality offered by writers such as Cecil Lewis. Stripped of its exotic accompaniments, the *maison de tolérance* on the Western Front becomes another site for military discipline, separate from the front line but essential to the overall war effort.

Conclusions

This chapter has outlined some of the different ways in which the alternative space of the *maison de tolérance* was viewed on the Western Front both during and after the war. It shows how popular impressions of the space formed and promulgated in the nineteenth and early twentieth century were fuelled by the ready availability of risqué or pornographic postcards and bawdy songs to conjure up erotic possibilities that invested the space with the ability to deliver a powerful sense of escapism and indulgence. The proximity of the front line and the contrast between the fantasy décor, scantily-clad women and the (exclusively male) world of the trench heightened the sense of pleasurable dislocation for many men. Others, however, found their senses less indulged and were disappointed by the gap between their imagined expectations, raised through literary and cultural representations of the space, and their lived experience. The squalid tone of some of these disappointments in turn fed the fearful imagination of the British public living away from the war zone whose concerns for men's moral welfare emphasised the squalor and horror of the brothel.

At the same time that different imaginative representations of the *maison de tolérance* were feeding competing discourses of these spaces as sites of either pleasure or corruption, the actual material space of the *maison* prompted different responses among contemporary observers. In the eyes of the French civil and military authorities who licensed and policed the *maisons de tolérance* of the Western Front, these spaces were about hygiene and efficiency, containing the problem of prostitution away from the eyes of broader society and managing a much-raised throughput within the facilities without endangering the health either of prostitutes or of their solider-clients. The *maison de tolérance* was a thus site of diverse meaning for troops, civilians and military and civil authorities, very different from the world of the front-line trench, but equally critical to shaping the war experience both of those who frequented it as well as those who merely imagined it.

Notes

1. J. Baynes, *Morale: A Study of Men and Courage* (London: Cassell, 1967).
2. J.G. Fuller, *Troop Morale and Popular Culture in the British and Dominion Armies 1914–18* (Oxford: Clarendon Press, 1990).
3. Krista Cowman, "Touring Behind the Lines: British Soldiers in French Towns and Cities During the Great War", *Urban History* 41, 1 (2014), 105–123.
4. Jay Winter and Jean-Louis Robert, eds., *Capital Cities at War: Paris, London, Berlin 1914–1919. Volume Two: A Cultural History* (Cambridge: Cambridge University Press, 2007).
5. Michael Roper, *The Secret Battle* (Manchester: Manchester University Press, 2009), 50.
6. K. Craig Gibson, "Sex and Soldiering in France and Flanders: The British Expeditionary Force along the Western Front, 1914–1919", *International History Review* 23, 3 (September 2001), 535–579. See also his book *Behind the Lines* (Cambridge: Cambridge University Press, 2014), 309–346.
7. Jean-Yves le Naour, "Le Sexe et La Guerre: Divergences Franco-Américaines Pendant la Grande Guerre (1917–18)", *Guerres Mondiales et Conflits Contemporains* 197 (2000), 103–116; Clare Makepeace, "Male Heterosexuality and Prostitution during the Great War", *Social and Cultural History* 9, 1 (2012), 65–83.
8. Edward H. Beardsley, "Allied against Sin: American and British Responses to Venereal Disease in World War 1", *Medical History* 20 (1976), 189–202; Mark Harrison, "The British Army and the Problem of Venereal Disease in France and Egypt during the First World War", *Medical History* 39 (1995), 133–158; Michelle K. Rhoades, "Renegotiating French Masculinity: Medicine and Venereal Disease during the Great War", *French Historical Studies* 29, 2 (2006), 293–327. See also Philippa Levine, *Prostitution, Race and Politics: Policing Venereal Disease in the British Empire* (London: Palgrave, 1992) chapter 6 "Colonial Soldiers, White Women and the First World War," 145–173; Jeffrey Greenhut, "Race, Sex and War: The Impact of Race and Sex on Morale and Health Services for the Indian Corps on the Western Front, 1914", *Military Affairs* 45 (1981), 71–74; Glendord D. Howe, "Military-Civilian Intercourse, Prostitution and Venereal Disease among Black West Indian Soldiers during World War 1", *Journal of Caribbean History* 31 (1997), 88–102.
9. Alan Sheridan, "Translator's Note", in Alain Corbin, ed., *Women for Hire: Prostitution and Sexuality in France after 1850* (London: Harvard University Press, 1990), xviii.
10. Corbin, chapter 3. See also Phil Hubbard, *Cities and Sexualities* (London: Routledge, 2012), 42–55.
11. A.J.B. Parent-Duchatelet, *De La Prostitution Dans La Ville de Paris* (Paris: J.B. Ballière, 1836) vol. 1, especially chapter 5.
12. F.F.A. Béraud, *Les Filles Publiques de Paris et la Police qui les Regit* (Paris: Desforges, 1839) vol. 2, 161, cited in Corbin, *Women for Hire*, 375 note 54.
13. Louis Fiaux, *Maisons de Tolérance, Leur Fermeture* (Paris: G. Carrè, 1892), 249–256.
14. Fiaux, *Maisons de Tolérance*, 252–253.
15. Corbin, *Women for Hire*, 123 citing Meunier, *Annexes au Rapport General Presente par M.F. Hennequin* (Melun: Imprintes Administratives, 1902).
16. An electric heater from the famous Le Chabanais brothel, decorated with four panels featuring prints of erotic scenes was put up for sale at the city's Drouet auction house in 2011 with an estimate of €3000.
17. Fiaux, *Maisons*, 255.
18. Many of these images are reproduced in Nienke Bakker, Isolde Pludermacher, Marie Robert and Richard Thomson, *Splendeurs et Misères: Images de la Prostitution 1850–1910* (Paris: Flammarion, 2015).

19. Cecil Lewis, *Sagittarius Rising* (London: Penguin, 2014 [1936]), 56.
20. Stefan Slater, "Pimps, Police and Filles de Joie: Foreign Prostitution in Interwar London", *The London Journal* 32, 1 (2007), 56. See also Raphael Samuel, "The Figures of National Myth", in R. Samuel, ed., *Patriotism: The Making and Unmaking of British National Identity* (London: Routledge, 1989), xxv.
21. On the international careers of Avril and others see Catherine Hinton, *Female Performance Practice on the Fin de Siècle Popular Stages of London and Paris* (Manchester: Manchester University Press, 2007).
22. For examples see Cowman, "Touring Behind the Lines."
23. Magnus Hirschfeld, *The Sexual History of the War* (Honolulu: University Press of the Pacific, 2006 [1941]).
24. Nigel Sadler, *Erotic Postcards of the Twentieth Century* (Stroud: Amberley Books, 2011).
25. Mark Gibbon, *Inglorious Soldier* (London: Hutchinson, 1968), 89
26. Jean-Yves le Naour, "Le Sexe et La Guerre: Divergences Franco-Americaines Pendant la Grande Guerre 1917–18", *Guerres Mondiales et Conflits Contemporains* 197 (2000), 104, my translation.
27. Makepeace, "Male Heterosexuality and Prostitution", 76.
28. For French, American and British responses see for example Le Naour, "Le Sexe et La Guerre"; Harrison, "The British Army"; Fred. D. Baldwin, "The Invisible Armour", *American Quarterly* 16, 3 (1964), 432–444. For German attitudes see Benoit Majerus, "La Prostitution à Bruxelles Pendante la Grande Guerre: Contrôle et Pratique", *Crime, Histoire et Sociétés* 7, 1 (2003), 5–42.
29. Sidney Rogerson, *Twelve Days on the Somme* (London: Frontline Books, rep. 2009), 147.
30. Richard Van Emden, ed., *Tickled to Death to Go: Memories of a Cavalryman in the First World War* (Staplehurst: Spelmount, 1996), 143.
31. IWM 92/36/1, memoir, Lieut. R. Dixon, "The Wheels of Darkness," 54.
32. Dixon, "Wheels of Darkness", 54.
33. Eric Hiscock, *The Bells of Hell go Ting a Ling a Ling* (London: Arlington Books, 1976), 97
34. Hiscock, *The Bells of Hell Go Ting-a-Ling-a-Ling*, 89.
35. T.S. Hope, *The Winding Road Unfolds* (London: Tandem Books, 1965 [1937]), 91.
36. Hope, *The Winding Road Unfolds*, 92.
37. Joanna Bourke, ed., *The Misfit Soldier: Edward Casey's War Story, 1914–18* (Cork: Cork University Press, 1999), 34, 35.
38. Bourke, *The Misfit Soldier*, 33.
39. Dennis Wheatley, *The Time Has Come . . . The Memoirs of Dennis Wheatley, Officer and Temporary Gentleman, 1914–1919* (London: Hutchinson, 1978), 153.
40. Monk Gibbon, *Inglorious Soldier* (London: Hutchinson, 1968), 1.
41. Williamson, *A Patriot's Progress* (London: Geoffrey Bles, 1930), 142–144.
42. Hope, *The Winding Road*, 94.
43. Association for Social and Moral Hygiene, "British Troops in France: Provision of Tolerated Brothels" proof copy in The National Archives (TNA) WO/32/5597.
44. Robert Graves, *Goodbye to All That* (London: Penguin, 2000 [1929]), 151, 104.
45. Van Emden, ed., *Tickled to Death to Go*, 143–144.
46. AMSH, "Provision of Tolerated Brothels."
47. Hirschfeld, *The Sexual History of the War*, chapter 1, 24.
48. Letter from Rev. J.H. Shakespeare on behalf of the United Navy and Army Board of the Four Denominations, 6 March 1918. TNA WO/32/11404.
49. Harrison, "The British Army and Venereal Disease."

50. Le Maire, Granville-Ste-Honorine to Secretary of State, 24 June 1918; Commissaire de Police to Maire, 28 June 1918.
51. Corbin, *Women for Hire*, 334, 335.
52. Postcard marked Rue Principale, Luçon (Vendée), Archives Seine Maritime, Rouen. Similar images from a *maison* at Rennes can be seen in the Gallérie Au Bonheur du Jour, Rue de Chabanais, Paris and at http://www.aubonheurdujour.net/MaisonsDecors.html (accessed 12 March 2016).
53. Harrison, "British Army and Venereal Disease", 146, 142; Michelle K. Rhodes, "Renegotiating French Masculinity: Medicine and Venereal Disease During the Great War", *French Historical Studies* 29, 2 (Spring 2006), 293–327.
54. Fiaux, *Maisons*, 12.
55. Figures taken from a series of reports into provision of *maisons de tolérance* and possible new sites, Archives Seine Maritime.
56. M. le Maire de Trouville à M le Capitaine Champrosay & l'Etat Major de la 3eme Region, 2 Juin 1918, Archives Seine Maritime.
57. Ministère de la Guerre, 4eme Bureau Ouvres Militaires no. 4179, 23 Mai 1918. Archives de Seine Maritime.
58. Richard Aldington, *Death of a Hero* (London: Hogarth Press, 1984 [1929]), 293.

Bibliography

Aldington, Richard. *Death of a Hero*. London: Hogarth Press, 1984 [1929].
Beardsley, Edward H. "Allied against Sin: American and British Responses to Venereal Disease in World War 1", *Medical History* 20, 189–202.
Bourke, Joanna, ed. *The Misfit Soldier: Edward Casey's War Story, 1914–18*. Cork: Cork University Press, 1999.
Corbin, Alain. *Women for Hire: Prostitution and Sexuality in France after 1850*. London: Harvard University Press, 1990.
Cowman, Krista. "Touring behind the Lines: British Soldiers in French Towns and Cities during the Great War", *Urban History* 41, 1, 105–23.
Van Emden, Richard, ed. *Tickled to Death to Go: Memories of a Cavalryman in the First World War*. Staplehurst: Spelmount, 1996.
Fiaux, Louis. *Maisons de Tolérance, Leur Fermeture*. Paris: G. Carrè, 1892.
Gibbon, Monk. *Inglorious Soldier*. London: Hutchinson, 1968.
Gibson, Craig. "Sex and Soldiering in France and Flanders: The British Expeditionary Force along the Western Front, 1914–1919", *International History Review* 23, 3, 535–79.
Graves, Robert. *Goodbye to All That*. London: Penguin, 2000 [1929].
Harrison, Mark. "The British Army and the Problem of Venereal Disease in France and Egypt during the First World War", *Medical History* 39, 133–58.
Hirschfeld, Magnus. *The Sexual History of the War*. Honolulu: University Press of the Pacific, 2006 [1941].
Hiscock, Eric. *The Bells of Hell Go Ting-a-Ling-a-Ling*. London: Arlington Books, 1976.
Hope, T.S. *The Winding Road Unfolds*. London: Tandem Books, 1965 [1937].
Le Naour, Jean-Yves. "Le Sexe et La Guerre: Divergences Franco-Américaines Pendant la Grande Guerre (1917–18)", *Guerres Mondiales et Conflits Contemporains* 197 (2000), 103–16.

Lewis, Cecil. *Sagittarius Rising*. London: Penguin, 2014 [1936].
Makepeace, Clare. "Male Hetrosexuality and Prostitution during the Great War", *Social and Cultural History* 9, 1, 65–83.
Rhoades, Michelle K. "Renegotiating French Masculinity: Medicine and Venereal Disease during the Great War", *French Historical Studies* 29, 2, 293–327.
Wheatley, Dennis. *The Time Has Come . . . The Memoirs of Dennis Wheatley, Officer and Temporary Gentleman, 1914–1919*. London: Hutchinson, 1978.
Williamson, Henry. *A Patriot's Progress*. London: Geoffrey Bles, 1930.

4 "The Delightful Sense of Personal Contact That Your Letter Aroused"

Letters and Intimate Lives in the First World War

Carol Acton

On Monday, 4 September 1916, Eric Appleby, an artillery officer on the Western Front, tells Phyllis Kelly, his fiancée in Athlone, Ireland: "Oh! Lady mine, I want you so very terribly badly, I want to take you in my arms and press you so hard against me that neither you nor I can breathe without the other feeling each breath. I want to give you endless kisses—long, long very gentle ones."[1] On 28 October, Appleby died of wounds in a casualty clearing station. His words to Phyllis Kelly are a vehement defiance of the impending death that haunts all the narratives discussed here. He is writing in the immediate shadow of it—his friend and Captain, Burrows, having been killed the day before. Appleby has just written to Burrows' fiancée with details of his death, all the time knowing that the intimacy he so desires with Kelly exists under the same threat. His response to witnessing Burrows die at his side, which heightens the prospect of his own death, is to use the letter to express a yearning for life and for a future that is constructed through a longing for Kelly. His desire for physical intimacy and literally for the breath that will make it possible, is constructed through a space that is at once both real, the physical place at her home in Ireland, and imagined, in that it is set in a longed for future where they will be together. Appleby is both conscious of, and denies, the terrifying possibility of death as a space that cannot be bridged by the imagined exchange with Kelly.

On the 28 October 1916, receiving the telegram "Eric . . . dangerously wounded", Kelly's immediate response is one conditioned by wartime separation—to write a letter to him in an attempt to transcend the physical separation of home and front: " I simply have sat and shivered with such an awful clutching fear in my heart. . . . Oh my love, what shall I do. . . . It will be the end of everything that matters because . . . you are all the world and life to me. . . . This writing to you is the only thing that makes the waiting easier".[2] Letters between couples thus become the means by which they negotiate the cruelty of separation and death, and construct an intimacy that defies such separation. Kelly's letter, even if it will never be sent, is an attempt to bridge the space between them through an imagined conversation. Letters thus reveal just how interdependent the connection was between home and front, in spite of the geographic separation. This interdependence goes beyond exchange of news: letters create a dialogue where the act of writing itself participates in the transcendence of the separate gendered space that prompts the letter. In his discussion of First World War letter exchanges Michael Roper finds that "[i]t was not only the news from home, but the writing of letters which drew these soldiers back into the lives they had left behind. . . . The connection sometimes felt so vivid that awareness of the difference between the real and the imaginary was sometimes suspended."[3] The correspondence explored here reveals just how much the distinction between real and imaginary spaces are blurred, as couples bring each other into their lives, men into domestic home life and women into the world of the front, as both became "structurally connected and inter-dependent."[4] It is clear from both sides of the correspondence that the emotional significance of letters lay very much in their ability to create for the couple a shared space through which they could escape the limitations of actual physical separation. They even attempt, as we see in Kelly's letter above, to transcend the final separation between life and death.

Caroline Bland and Máire Cross maintain that "[l]etters provide an access to the currency of the past."[5] For the twenty-first century reader of these letters the currency is emotional, admitting us into an intensely private experience as it takes place. Of letters and letter writing, Esther Milne argues that "much of the intimacy established between correspondents depends on their temporal and spatial distance from each other; yet it is too simple to say that such intimacy is either enabled by the physical absence of one correspondent from the other or that physical separation is an obstacle to intimacy that is overcome by letter writing. Both are evidently true."[6] In these letters intimacy arises out of the interplay between the physical space that is defined by separation and the imagined space that is created by the letter.

While we need to consider how letters develop the intimacy necessary to sustain a long courtship carried out primarily through writing, we should also keep in mind that letters can tell a story of intimacy that goes beyond language. In wartime, when women are often seen as the primary carriers of emotional labour, positioning men and women together in this private romantic space establishes men's role in the intimacy narrative. Further, examining letters as an exchange moves us beyond the privileging of "letters from the front" to position women's voices as essential to a shared narrative. Reading war letters as an exchange returns women to a space they have been denied when front-line fighting experience is privileged as the definition of war. As Hämmerle argues in her discussion of correspondence between Austro-Hungarian and German couples, examining the combatant writing in isolation

> perpetuates the hegemony of male-oriented correspondence "from the front" which was celebrated during the First World War and afterwards in popular memory. This is all the more unfortunate as the essential significance of wartime correspondence becomes clear only when one is

able to appreciate equally and simultaneously the roles of both sides in the dialogue of the sexes. When it is viewed in the proper context of the history of gender, men's and women's wartime correspondence reveals their mutual dependence and the interconnectedness of differing modes of perception and experience.[7]

In *Your Death Would Be Mine*, Martha Hanna, analyzing both sides of the correspondence between a young, recently married French couple, explores this interconnectedness at length, and shows how letters reveal this man and woman to be "at the center of two distinct but intersecting worlds."[8] In this intersecting space the letter exchanges under discussion here arguably not only represent but become that relationship.

As Phyllis Kelly's instinctive response to news of Eric Appleby's injury is to write, even though she knows the letter may never be sent, so wartime letters show how letter writing became the medium through which relationships were forged and sustained, and remain as material sites through which we can enter the intensity of the lived subjective experience of the young men and women who wrote them. Materially, letters are inherently paradoxical, signifying both presence and absence simultaneously. They become the individual who has sent them; those sent from the front affirm that, at the time of writing at least, the sender was alive and thinking of the recipient. At the same time they reinforce for the recipient the absence of the loved one and the constant threat to life, often literally carrying the mud of the trenches home, or the end of the conversation in the brutal impersonal message "Killed in Action" pencilled on the envelopes of returned letters. Letters, photographs and parcels from home bring the domestic into the trench world, and replies allow men to participate in the domestic world, as Roper and Meyer have shown.[9] Emotional exchange is communicated not only through the words, but in the material of paper, ink or pencil, the smell of perfume or tobacco, and in enclosed objects, all offering physical contact with the loved one whose recent touch and characteristic handwriting is a manifestation of that person. Milne thus argues that letters engage in a paradox where a "shared sense of immediacy and presence seems to be enabled, in part, by the physical distance between the interlocutors. What has been termed 'the intimacy of absence' (a necessarily disembodied sense of presence) has been identified as a defining feature of epistolary communication."[10]

The sample correspondence discussed here is relatively small and narrow because, although many letters from the front survive, there are few remaining exchanges. This may arise from the practicalities of carrying letters at the front, but also because letters from the front were considered more significant and thus preserved. Gender as well as practicality thus played an important role in selection even at the time of writing. Cross and Bland note of letters more generally that "[t]heir survival can be somewhat haphazard, depending on the political circumstances of their inception or the cultural and historical value attached to them."[11] These collections come from Imperial War Museum archives and published sources. They have been chosen for the completeness of the exchange, and also to explore exchanges that articulate intimacy directly. They represent most of the available published and unpublished collections written by British couples during the war. In spite of the limitations, these exchanges allow us to see how individuals negotiated a rapidly changing and unstable environment. How did they literally rewrite the script when words struggled to overcome emotional and physical distance, especially as the gendered roles imposed on men and women meant experiential as well as physical separation? How was physical desire articulated not only in the context of Edwardian prescriptions round sexual expression that were already being challenged, but where the male body was constantly threatened by death or mutilation? More broadly, this discussion explores how letters develop and sustain the intimacy necessary over lengthy separation to forge long lasting relationships.

All of the couples discussed here are very conscious of the paradoxical role of the letter in both defining and overcoming the separation that rules their interdependent lives. They affirm Milne's comments on letters more generally, that "for many correspondents 'absence' . . . opens a discursive space in which desires that might not otherwise be articulated, can be explored."[12] Will Martin writes to Emily Chitticks that letters enable the voicing of unspoken desires: "I think we can put on paper what we are somewhat shy of saying in the presence of each other" (8th Oct 1916).[13] In the same letter he reassures her as to the value of her letters: "I think your letter an ideal one, it seems to touch me everywhere." Yet the frustration at a breakdown in intimacy can be equally intense, as captured in the correspondence between Marjorie Secretan and Toby Dodgson. In September 1915, Dodgson writes that

> it's a fearful strain to write here when one feels that half the things that one would naturally say mustn't be said, and that these are just the things with which the whole of one's mind is occupied, to the exclusion of everything else. The result is one feels that letters must be hopelessly artificial and unreal . . . and if you knew how much one's nerves are on stretch here . . . you would understand.[14]

But in his response to a letter from her a few weeks later the material space of the letter and the words it contains crosses the spatial limitations imposed on them, bringing him into imagined personal contact and generating a very different reaction: "I read and reread your letter and lay there thinking about you until I dropped off to sleep—happy because I love you so and in the delightful sense of personal contact that your letter aroused."[15] Milne notes that "letter writers may refer to their physical bodies and contexts in order to convey a sense of presence, relevance and aliveness to their interlocutor."[16] Here, it is Dodgson's imagining of Secretan's physical body that transcends their separation, overcoming the dislocation he describes in the previous letter.

Letters between couples thus both rail against the separation they represent and affirm their importance in sustaining connection and intimacy in spite of it. As already noted, they can encourage a greater openness in expressing emotion than might have been the case otherwise. Sustaining a relationship of several years means that letters must create an intimacy that would otherwise have been manifest through more subtle, and often nonverbal, interaction. While most of the couples under discussion did see each other when the man was on leave, and at least four couples, Vera Brittain and Roland Leighton, Marjorie Secretan and Toby Dodgson, Dora Willatt and Cecil Slack, and Frederic Sellers and Grace Malin, knew each other as friends before the war, the romantic relationships are carried out through letters. In many cases couples exchange letters every few days, often noting a day when they do not get a letter. Thus the frequency of letters becomes shared evidence of commitment and the desire for continuous connection: they do not write because they have "news," but to reassure the other of their love and, in the case of men at the front, to indicate that they are still alive and well. The emphasis is on the immediacy of the response and the building of a conversation, no matter how difficult this was if letters were delayed or crossed. Letters are collected and reread and thus become a valued narrative of the relationship—a space to be entered into in private and returned to again and again. Where they cannot be kept, because of the practical problem of carrying them at the front, throwing them away or burning them is registered as a loss of the writer's presence since the physical letter is the container of shared intimacy. Each rereading in the context of increasing correspondence reinforces the interdependence of the two shared lives represented there. Winnie Blackburn writes to Cyril Newman on Monday, 12 July 1915, still early in their relationship:

> I woke exceptionally early on Saturday and what do you think I did? Ought I to tell you? I took all your letters—from the very first one I received out of my work-box, arranged them in order of date and read every one. It was lovely and yet- they brought tears to my eyes, and made me thoroughly "love-sick". Oh, My Darling, come home to me, let me kiss you, let me live for you. Then I put them safely away to be read again when I wake exceptionally early again.[17]

Later Newman notes sending her letters home to his mother to be kept safely. Roland Leighton sends Brittain's letters back to her to keep for him. But the difficulty of carrying letters at the front meant that women's letters were often lost or had to be destroyed. David Taylor tells May Muggridge that

> I walked out into the fields this morning with the intention of reading a whole collection of your letters and then burning them (I have a pocket full and there is not much room for any more And I must always carry them for fear of other people seeing them which I couldn't stand) but

> I read them and then found I simply couldn't burn them (they are all I have of you at present except your photo) so they are there still.[18]

However, he is later forced to burn them, so much of Muggridge's side of the early correspondence is missing. Her letters received after he became a prisoner in July 1917 have survived, presumably because he was able to store them.[19]

The candour with which conflicting thoughts about letters and the act of writing are expressed to the recipient demonstrate a closeness developed over the years of writing. Thus Blackburn writes to Newman on 28 October 1917:

> This is an uninteresting letter I feel. I just do not feel like writing. It's an awful confession to make. After three years of separation it seems impossible to write real love-letters daily, even to the best man in the world. I feel confident that you will understand, and forgive. I will try and write tomorrow.[20]

Achieving this mutual understanding occurs because the couples have achieved an intimacy that allows them to express frustration while having the confidence that "you will understand." Yet at the same time the frustration exists because, apart from the occasional leave, separation makes letters the only means of creating intimacy. Writers must rely on the limitations of the written word and their ability to express themselves through it to take the place of what psychologist Karen Praeger calls the "nonverbal" language that enhances communication between "young couples":

> physical proximity, gaze, touch, body lean . . . vocal cues such as intonation. These are called involvement behaviors because they display attentiveness, interest, and participation in interaction. Second, touch can be an intimate behaviour; touch seems to intensify, and is also prompted by, intimate experiences. (Thayer, 1988) Finally, the extensive and prolonged bodily contact involved in sexual activity is a third type of nonverbal behavior.[21]

It is not surprising then that the verbal expression of intimacy we find in these letters often includes fantasies of nonverbal behaviour, recalling incidents from moments on leave, or fantasising about such moments in the future. These rememberings or imaginings then become shared stories of intimacy that create a larger narrative which includes both verbal and nonverbal interaction. In doing so, they also develop the romantic story beyond the limitations of time and place, extending memories of the past into an imagined future.

As they construct their shared romantic story within the limitations of the written word, writers seek to overcome the difficulty and frustration of trying

"The Delightful Sense of Personal Contact" 83

to express feelings that would normally be conveyed nonverbally. Not all writers represent their physical desire as directly as Eric Appleby. Discussion of photographs appears frequently, and their ability, or lack thereof, to evoke a fantasy of the real person often becomes a way of exchanging expressions of desire. They are especially important for the combatant at the front since they allow him to carry the site of his desire, onto which he can project romantic fantasies, into the war zone and thus overcome the woman's absence. In several of the exchanges photographs become the locus of intimacy between couples, allowing imagined physical encounters that reticence and propriety might prevent in actuality. Such imagined encounters also transcend their physical separation. Soon after he arrives at the front, in April 1915, Roland Leighton ends his letter to Vera Brittain with "Goodnight and much love. I have just been kissing your photograph."[22] Brittain responds in her diary that "my eyes filled with most stinging tears . . . and when he writes such things as this—and he has never admitted so much before—I want him terribly badly."[23] She writes back, "I envy the photograph; it is more fortunate than the original. *She* never seems quite to have got past your reserve . . . I suppose it is the nearness of death which breaks down reserves & conventions."[24] Paradoxically, the distance offered by the photograph allows for an expression of closeness and desire that would not have been possible had they been together. Brittain acknowledges this, writing to him that "it is absurd that we should be so intimate in letters, and then when we are together that you should touch my hand almost as if you weren't doing it right & I even hesitate to meet your eyes with mine" (Sat and Sun Sept 11–12, 1915).[25]

Even when desire is not expressed directly, photographs indicate the man's need for the woman's presence and become the means by which she transcends the boundaries of front and home. Her careful placing in a physical space at the front indicates the combatant's reconstruction of home and is a manifestation of the "intersecting worlds" these writers inhabit. Writing from support trenches at Opp, when Charles Fair tells Marjorie Secretan that letters "bring us so much closer," her photograph in his dugout "where it is the first and last thing I see each day" emphasises that closeness (11 Oct 17).[26] Similarly, Cecil Slack's placing of Dora Willett's photographs in his billet not only brings her into his combatant space, but at the same time recreates a domestic space for himself so that the homely and erotic co-exist, retrieving a space outside the war: "This billet is the best I have had. I have a bedroom all to myself. . . . One of your photographs is on the mantelpiece and the other on the wall. I love the sepia one, and I want to kiss it every time I look at it."[27] (B.E.F. 23.2.17) As a non-commissioned officer, Cyril Newman does not have the luxury of such a billet, or even the shelf of a dugout, but returning to the relative calm of reserve trenches he tells Winnie Blackburn that he has been going through

> all the photographs I carry about with me—always a delightful pastime. In my imagination I held you in my arms and pressed my lips to yours.

> I 'ate' you with my eyes however horrid that may seem to you. And in spite of an unsatisfied 'want' I had a very pleasant interlude.
>
> (Tues 2nd April 1918)[28]

For Newman the photographs simultaneously signify absence and presence. Similarly, Muriel Harpin confesses to Neville Overton,

> Did I tell you I could never remember your face when it's away from me? I can't already you know [he had recently returned to the front from leave], and photographs don't help a bit. Isn't it funny. I can remember bits—your hair and the curly bit in front. Your eyes with their absurd curly eyelashes and your big nose that gets so in the way at times, only I like it awfully.
>
> (17.9.18)[29]

The very failure of the photograph to recreate his presence is the catalyst that allows her to show her intimate knowledge of him, and draw him into a shared remembered intimacy, "your big nose that gets so in the way at times."

Milne posits of letter writing that "since one is not physically co-present with one's interlocutor, references to the corporeal body play significant rhetorical and social functions in the production of meaning within letter-writing practice."[30] As Harpin's letter shows, evoking the presence of the "corporeal body" serves her own recall and reminds the recipient of her desire for him. For several of the writers, as in Dodgson's response to the letter from Secretan that "arouse[d]" the "delightful sense of personal contact," the letter itself evokes a physical presence. Thus Chitticks writes to Martin that "when I read your letters I feel as tho [sic] you are standing by me, talking with me yourself" (11 Nov 1916).[31] Such significance is, of course, heightened in wartime when physical longing takes place not only in the context of absence but of violence and its threat to the male body. The female corporeal presence at the front must thus be understood in the context of the conditions in which the combatant lived, the risk of death or wounding, and his desire for security in the face of constant disruption, as well as in terms of physical desire. The woman's desire for the man's presence at home takes place in the context of threat to his body. Fear on both sides may be unspoken, but it is present behind all expressions of desire. During the "push" of March 1918, Cyril Newman writes to Winnnie Blackburn:

> The strain of the last few days has, I admit, been severe and sustained. It is like joyfully entering a refreshing oasis in the desert to spend a moment or two lost in thought of YOU, my Beloved. And Oh! The longing- the foolish longing—to feel your dear arms round me—to be caressed by you. . . .
>
> One "plays the man" keeping under all sensitive, tender-hearted feelings that, if indulged in, might render one a coward. But, after the trial

has passed, or the fierceness subsided for a time, the real nature of man as nurtured in the heart—the child heart—craves of a woman's love.
(Sunday 24th March 1918 in the line)[32]

As noted earlier, the nonverbal communication of touch that separation denies these writers has to be expressed in language, and in describing it writers create a space for their correspondent to participate in an imagined scenario that goes beyond the words themselves. Although none of the letters mention sex directly, much of the language is sexualised. It is especially apparent in the imagined touching of the other's body invoked above. In Appleby's writing of his intersecting story with Kelly, his desire for physical intimacy shows how such imagining can temporarily alleviate the pain of the present in its fantasy of "the corporeal body." This is especially apparent in his response to Kelly's request that he recount to her their five days together during his leave in June 1916. Not only does he retell their time together at length, but also imagines for her his next leave, so that only the past and future exist. Central to his writing is the physical aspect of their relationship; it is as if immersing himself in this fantasy momentarily overcomes the very separation that necessitates the fantasy. On 17 October 1916, he imagines: "I would draw your head back ever so gently until you looked full in my face as I bent down. Then a wonderful love quiver would run through me and I would bend down further and kiss you full on the lips."[33] Yet even while Appleby is escaping into a nonverbal fantasy, the use of "would" draws attention to the burden of the conditional that dictates their relationship. It reveals the tension between past and future that is a constant throughout all of these exchanges: the last leave and the fragile conditional future exist only in the imagination, the words on the page an attempt to create a concrete narrative that would replace the present. He emphasises this himself on an earlier occasion, writing, "Sweetheart, don't think of the distant future at a time like this, there may never be one for me" (17 July 1916).[34] Poignantly, we know that the longed for future will never become an actuality—less than two weeks later Appleby will die of wounds. Imagined touch as an entry into the imagined space she inhabits thus exists as a defiance of death, affirming the physical self to the writer as well as to the addressee.

While Appleby's desire exists in a conditional imagined space, David Taylor and May Muggridge defy separation by creating fictional stories of physical intimacy for each other that eliminate space and time by placing them together in an imagined shared space. Writing from France on May 28 1917, Taylor tells her:

Last night was lovely.
You had your new vest on but there were no buttons on it and after I laid down as you wanted me to you insisted on cuddling my head and pressing it close to its nest. . . . But later you woke up and said

you wanted your cheek against mine and wanted to be held quite close against me and then you dropped off to sleep again.[35]

In a much later letter touch takes on a telepathic and almost mystical significance when Taylor is reported "Missing," but in fact is a prisoner of war in Germany. In her first letter to him in the POW camp Muggridge writes: "You can imagine how pleased I am to be able to write again. I felt very miserable for a day or two when your letters ceased, but one night I distinctly felt your cheek against mine, so of course took heart, and knew everything would come right in the end" (9.8.17).[36] He replies, "When your letter came I read it and re-read it until I knew it practically by heart . . . I think I know about the time when you felt my cheek for I tried for a long time to do it and once it seemed as though I did" (September 12th 1917).[37]

Their letters define their shared experience of separation. Their cessation may indicate Taylor's death; re-establishing their correspondence goes beyond renewing conversation to signify the overcoming of the absence of death. The telepathic event happens in the context of a shared space that transcends the limitations imposed on their physical bodies. Although much has been written on the importance of comradeship as a source of emotional survival in the trenches,[38] the letters discussed here suggest, as we see in the above exchange, that men turned their emotional faces towards the women at home who loved them as they sought for support and comfort and a stable sense of identity, as women did to the men at the front. They affirm the extent to which, for many men, relationships with their lovers at home were far more necessary than those with comrades at the front. Moreover, it is not just a case of men as the dependent side of the correspondence. Men reciprocated the love and support women offered to them, allowing them to participate as lovers in a companionate relationship as they entered the domestic space through their correspondence with women. Through that relationship, more than with their families, men could create a positive narrative of the romantic self, a self which allowed them to forge an identity that was more familiar and comfortable than that of soldier. Especially, the narrative created in letter exchanges meant that they could feel that their present role as soldier was temporary, whereas their imagined future role as lover and husband would be permanent. As we see in many of the letters, this imagined future could be essential to their psychological wellbeing. It differs from the imagined return home to the family in constructing a space for themselves in an autonomous post-war future, revealing the importance, as the war progressed, of close generational connections in offering support and understanding that could not be given by parents.

This generational solidarity reinforced an already existing intimacy and is demonstrated in exchanges based on practical as well as emotional needs. Thus William Wooliscroft writes to Lily Patrick who works for his family's wholesale butcher's business and to whom he would later propose marriage, asking her to find "a dose" she could smuggle to him in a corn cure

"The Delightful Sense of Personal Contact" 87

packet that would make him ill enough to be invalided out. He sends the letter dated 19 December 1915 via a friend going on leave so it will not be censored and explains this request in the context of his experience of trench warfare:

> Hell-fire Corner . . . is worse than the line itself. Now the trenches are up to the arms in places. Wet & cold it is quite enough to kill the men itself without shot or shell . . . trench foot is very common but I am sorry to say I have not had luck to get it . . . I know I shall have to go through it again & so on until eventually I either get wounded or killed & so it goes on . . . once if I had a sharp knife I intended to pierce my right eye. Any man here would give a limb gladly to get out of it as it is nothing but death & it is too late then.[39]

On another occasion he suggests that she discuss with his father the possibility of appealing for his release on the grounds that he is needed in the business at home. It is Lily, therefore, that he confides in rather than his parents and it is through her that he attempts to maintain his involvement with it. In February 1917 he was taken prisoner and spent the rest of the war in a POW camp in Germany. This probably saved Wooliscroft's life, and it also allowed him to spend time thinking about his future with the business and with Lily at home. Their letters show a relationship built on practical discussion of the business, and her concern for him includes managing the protocols of sending Red Cross parcels for her and his family. If intimacy is about drawing the worlds of home and front together with each side writing the other into their daily lives, then this is reflected in the following letter not through romantic longings, but in a very concrete and spatially situated description of the butcher's stall Lily sends to Wooliscroft while he is a POW:

> It is Saturday, market day and I am writing this at the stall. . . . Trade has been brisk, and we have got a side of Norfolk beef the best in the town, a bit of veal, pork & lamb, so we are set up, a grand display of heads, lights, liver etc at the stall. I just wish you were here, but never mind, we've a lot to be thankful for, all are well, cheer up, there's better days in store, God bless you, your loving sweetheart Lily.
>
> (June 2 1917)[40]

The present tense brings Wooliscroft into the world he longs to return to, and reinforces at the same time the wellbeing of the business and her control over it.

Letters from combatants at the front confess to their recipients just how crucial the exchange is to their emotional survival. Writing to Winnie Blackburn in October 1915, Cyril Newman tells her that her letters are "more real to my needs than physical food" (Sunday, 17 October 1915),[41] and in December: "Your letters to me are like volumes of poems; . . . during hours of blackness and solitariness on sentry-go, phrases from your letters flood into my mind, and make bearable what would otherwise be unbearable" (2–3 December 1915).[42] Almost two years later, on "Sat afternoon 8 Sept 1917" he comments more generally:

> *Four* long days without a letter from you. Lo! The mail has just arrived bringing, amongst others, two love letters from *You*. . . . The arrival of the mail is a vital factor in our happiness. I felt very unsettled last night. Others were similarly affected. "No Post" gives us a kind of malaise.[43]

For Freddie Sellers the expression of emotion seems to be therapeutic. He tells Grace Malins the day after his return from leave in February 1916:

> I am desperately lonely Gracie darling. It is foolish for me to say so. It reveals weakness but relieves me. I thought I had ceased to feel anything worse than the usual monotony but I find the "other" keeps returning in even greater force. I have waited all evening to write to you, watching others play chess & reading "Brothers" in the hope that I would grow more cheery. When this is written I shall turn in to bed. Writing to you is successful where all else has failed—I am already more cheerful.[44]

On 20 April he concludes,

> I have written at some length & I am afraid confusedly but life out here put me out of gear far more than I would wish. To me it is all incongruous & unreal & tends to make life itself seem unnatural. . . . But . . . there are days ahead which we know not but which we shall make.[45]

As Sellers' letter implies, men seem especially willing to show their emotional vulnerability when they return from leave. In such letters we find the most poignant and open declarations of love and loss. These show an intense longing for the other and an almost unbearable loneliness on both sides and, importantly, a willingness to acknowledge emotional breakdown. Cecil Slack can perform the soldier when he writes bluntly and graphically to Dora Willatt about killing Germans, but on his return from leave in March of 1918 he tells her:

> I had a little weep on the train after I said goodbye to you at Farmborough. It's horrid being parted like this. . . . Every time I leave you I hate it more, and I do love you so much. I feel very weepy tonight, darling, but I can't help it.[46]

Cyril Newman sends Winnie Blackburn a letter card from Folkstone on his return from leave on Wednesday, 25 July 1917.

9.15 am
God alone knows what the leaving of *you* means to me. My heart is numbed by the pain. We spoke not a word in our carriage on the way down. What a cruel train! What cruel towns we passed through! Cruel all! My heart cries out for you—my whole manhood rises up in protest against our separation.[47]

In a rare show of deep emotion, Roland Leighton, having confessed to Vera Brittain that he did not want to return to the front at the end of a shared leave, writes a note immediately after they part:

"London, 23rd August, 1915 7.0 p.m. I could not look back dear child—I should have cried if I had . . . I don't know what I want to do and don't care for anything except to get you back again; and that I cannot do—yet. How far it seems, sweet heart, till we may live our roseate poem through, as we have dreamed it so long. I cannot write for the pain of it."[48]

These private exchanges go some way to revealing how intimacy through letters is a crucial way of surviving the physical and psychological stress of the war for both men and women, but at the same time increases emotional vulnerability to an almost unbearably painful extent. As Martha Hanna notes, it is through letters that "the bonds of affection that made loss so painful were sustained prior to death in the face of extended absence."[49] Like so many others, Brittain and Leighton would not "live [their] roseate poem through." Leighton was killed on 23 December 1915. As women grieved for men killed at the front, letters became a site of mourning. The open expression of deep feeling that reassured each of them as to their value to the other while the man was alive, could offer a degree of consolation on his death, even in the face of such terrible loss. Moreover, as writing had transcended physical separation for some writers, so it could become a means of transcending the separation of death, since arguably the letter, in containing the presence of the writer, allows for his posthumous existence. As we saw in Phyllis Kelly's letter at the beginning of the discussion, writing could become an act of grieving. For Emily Chitticks, waiting anxiously for news of her fiancé Will, letters would become synonymous with loss and grief. Where once they had been instruments of shared intimacy, her letters become the vehicle through which she learns of his death. In the absence of an official notice, the return of her letters marked for her the brutal announcement of his death: her letter to Martin postmarked 26 March 1917 is returned with "Killed in Action 27.3.17" written on the front, and on the back, "Notified next of Kin 9.4.17."[50] The gap between death and notification is significant here, pointing to the fear of so many correspondents that the loved one would be dead before the letter reached him. The irony of the situation is reinforced in Chitticks' next letter to Martin dated 29 March 1917, which tells him: "My dearest Will, I was so delighted to get your letter this morning & to know you are quite alright." As Phyllis Kelly's response to news of Eric Appleby's dangerous wounding is to write a letter, so Chitticks' response to Martin's death is to create a memorial made up of their letters, accompanied by her private words of grief and mourning:

> **June 6th 1917**
> Sacred to the memory of my Darling Sweetheart Will. The only boy I love with my whole heart and soul, who loved me so well he gave his all, his life for me. When I die I wish all his letters to be buried with me, as my heart & love *are buried* in his grave in France.
>
>> Emily Chitticks
>> William James Martin
>> And on the back
>
>> *August 9th 1916* The Day I first met 'Will'
>> *October 27th* "Engaged to Will"
>> Nov: early. Will went to Holt and from there to Devonport
>
> Last week in Nov. Will came up on his last leave. Spent at *Southend*. *Dec: He left Devonport for Southampton: Dec 6th* sailed for *France*. *March 27th* Will fell asleep. *Killed in Action*.[51]

Although it did not happen, to have Martin's letters buried with her is her attempt to defy separation and a substitute for the shared grave they will never have. In the same way that letters become the loved one when alive, they continue to maintain the relationship after death as the space that carries his "disembodied presence."

The intimacy these letters reveal shows the extent to which they bring men and women together in an "intersecting" space that challenges wartime constructions of gender roles, as well as the post-war tendency to define the war experience in terms of experiential separation that resulted in their alienation from each other. The subjective experience is, rather, defined by a yearning for connection. As material objects, letters are at once a real space that represents connection, while at the same time each writer enters into a shared imagined space through which they construct their intimate life as a couple, a defiance of state-imposed separation. As these exchanges offer us "access" to the emotional "currency of the past" then, they demand that we pay closer attention to the connections these writers tried so hard to maintain. Reading these intimate dialogues takes us into a much richer and more complex experience than that defined through the home/front binary they resist.

Notes

1. Jean Kelly, (ed.), *Love Letters from the Front* (Dublin: Marino Press, 2000), 245.
2. Kelly, *Love Letters*, 284.

"The Delightful Sense of Personal Contact" 91

3. Michael Roper, *The Secret Battle: Emotional Survival in the Great War* (Manchester: Manchester University Press, 2009), 50.
4. Roper, *Secret Battle*, 6.
5. Caroline Bland and Máire Cross, 'Gender Politics: Breathing New Life into Old Letters,' in *Gender and Politics in the Age of Letter-Writing, 1750–2000*, eds. Caroline Bland and Máire Cross (Aldershot: Ashgate, 2004), 3.
6. Esther Milne, *Letters, Postcards, Email: Technologies of Presence* (New York: Routledge, 2010), 15.
7. Christa Hämmerle, '"You Let a Weeping Woman Call You Home?" Private Correspondences during the First World War in Germany,' in *Epistolary Selves: Letters and Letter-Writers, 1600–1945*, ed. Rebecca Earle (Aldershot, UK: Ashgate, 1999), 157.
8. Martha Hanna, *Your Death Would Be Mine: Paul and Marie Pireaud in the Great War* (Boston: Harvard University Press, 2006), 27.
9. See Roper, *The Secret Battle* and Jessica Meyer, *Men of War: Masculinity and the First World War in Britain* (Palgrave Macmillan, 2009).
10. Milne, *Letters, Postcards, Email*, 55.
11. Bland and Cross, *Gender and Politics*, 3.
12. Milne, *Letters, Postcards, Email*, 52.
13. All dates are given after the quotation in the original form. Correspondence of Emily Chitticks and William Martin, in William Martin Private papers, Department of Documents (2554), Imperial War Museum, London. Every effort has been made to trace the copyright holders and the author and Imperial War Museums would be grateful for any information which might help to trace those whose identities or addresses are not currently known.
14. Reginald and Charles Fair, (eds.), *Marjorie's War: Four Families in the Great War 1914–1918* (Brighton: Menin House, 2012), 93. Includes the letters between Marjorie Secretan (1889–1976) and Toby Dodgson (1889–1916) and Marjorie Secretan and Charles Fair (1885–1950) as well as between other members of four connected families.
15. Fair, *Marjorie's War*, 105.
16. Milne, *Letters, Postcards, E-Mail*, 15.
17. Correspondence of Cyril Newman and Winifred Newman (née Blackburn), in Cyril Newman, Private Papers, Department of Documents (03/5/1), Imperial War Museum, London. Every effort has been made to trace the copyright holders and the author and Imperial War Museums would be grateful for any information which might help to trace those whose identities or addresses are not currently known.
18. Kate Aura Hargreaves, comp. and ed., *My Dearest* (England and Wales: Property People JV Ltd., 2014), 81.
19. Keeping letters at the front was problematic because of the difficulty in carrying them. Jenny Hartley's observation on Second World War letters also applies to this war: "Letters coming from the front . . . can be and usually are preserved by their recipients, especially if they are letters going home. The letters that go out from home to those away are more vulnerable to being lost, jettisoned by those on the move . . . Letters from sweethearts and wives were more carefully tended than those from mothers." '"Letters Are Everything These Days": Mothers and Letters in the Second World War', in *Epistolary Selves: Letters and Letter-Writers, 1600–1945*, ed. Rebecca Earle (Aldershot: Ashgate, 1999), 186.
20. Newman/Blackburn correspondence, IWM.
21. Karen J. Prager, *The Psychology of Intimacy* (New York and London: The Guilford Press, 1995), 179.
22. Alan Bishop and Mark Bostridge, eds., *Letters from a Lost Generation: The First World War Letters of Vera Brittain and Four Friends: Roland Leighton,*

Edward Brittain, Victor Richardson, Geoffrey Thurlow (London: Little, Brown and Company, 1998), 80.
23. Vera Brittain, *Chronicle of Youth: War Diary 1913–1917*, ed. Alan Bishop (London: Gollancz, 1981; Fontana, 1982), 220.
24. Bishop and Bostridge, *Letters*, 83.
25. Bishop and Bostridge, *Letters*, 167.
26. Fair, *Marjorie's War*, 300.
27. Alan Wilkinson, ed., *"Thank God I'm Not a Boy": The Letters of Dora Willatt, Daughter, Sweetheart and Nurse 1915–18* (Hull: Lampada Press, 1997), 134.
28. Newman/Blackburn correspondence, IWM.
29. Correspondence of Miss H.M[uriel] Harpin and Capt Charles 'Neville' Overton, Private Papers (3051), Department of Documents, Imperial War Museum, London. Excerpts reproduced by kind permission of Susan Overton, copyright holder.
30. Milne, *Letters, Postcards, Email*, 14.
31. Martin/Chitticks correspondence, IWM.
32. Newman/Blackburn correspondence, IWM.
33. Kelly, *Love Letters*, 276.
34. Kelly, *Love Letters*, 53.
35. Hargreaves, *My Dearest*, 81.
36. Hargreaves, *My Dearest*, 174.
37. Hargreaves, *My Dearest*, 193.
38. See especially Santanu Das, *Touch and Intimacy in First World War Literature* (Cambridge: Cambridge University Press, 2005) and Roper's section, "Mothering Men" in *The Secret Battle*.
39. Correspondence of William Wooliscroft and Lily Patrick in William Wooliscroft, Private Papers, Department of Documents (09/57/2), Imperial War Museum, London. Excerpts reproduced by kind permission of Patricia Yacamini, copyright holder.
40. Wooliscroft/Patrick correspondence, IWM.
41. Newman/Blackburn correspondence, IWM.
42. Newman/Blackburn correspondence, IWM.
43. Newman/Blackburn correspondence, IWM.
44. Frederic Sellers and Grace Malin correspondence, Private Papers, Department of Documents, Imperial War Museum (09/32/1), Excerpts reproduced by kind permission of John Sellers, copyright holder.
45. Sellers/Malin correspondence, IWM.
46. Wilkinson, *"Thank God I'm Not a Boy"*, 261.
47. Newman/Blackburn correspondence, IWM.
48. Bishop and Bostridge, *Letters*, 143.
49. Martha Hanna, "A Republic of Letters: The Epistolary Tradition in France during World War One," *American Historical Review* 108 (5) (December 2003): 3.
50. Martin/Chitticks correspondence, IWM.
51. Martin/Chitticks correspondence, IWM.

Bibliography

Bishop, Alan and Mark Bostridge, eds. *Letters from a Lost Generation: The First World War Letters of Vera Brittain and Four Friends: Roland Leighton, Edward Brittain, Victor Richardson, Geoffrey Thurlow*. London: Little, Brown and Company, 1998.

Bland, Caroline and Máire Cross. 'Gender Politics: Breathing New Life into Old Letters', in *Gender and Politics in the Age of Letter-Writing, 1750–2003*, edited by Caroline Bland and Máire Cross, 3–14. Aldershot: Ashgate, 2004.

Brittain, Vera. *Testament of Youth*. London: Gollancz, 1933; London: Virago, 1978.

Brittain, Vera. *Chronicle of Youth: War Diary 1913–1917*, edited by Alan Bishop. London: Gollancz, 1981; Fontana, 1982.

Brittain, Vera. Vera Brittain Archives, William Ready Collection, Masterman Library, McMaster University, Hamilton, Ontario, Canada.

Das, Santanu. *Touch and Intimacy in First World War Literature*. Cambridge: Cambridge University Press, 2005.

Fair, Reginald and Charles Fair, eds. *Marjorie's War: Four Families in the Great War 1914–1918*. Brighton: Menin House, 2012.

Hämmerle, Christa. '"You Let a Weeping Woman Call You Home?" Private Correspondences during the First World War in Germany', in *Epistolary Selves: Letters and Letter-Writers, 1600–1945*, edited by Rebecca Earle, 152–182. Aldershot: Ashgate, 1999.

Hanna, Martha. 'A Republic of Letters: The Epistolary Tradition in France during World War One', *American Historical Review* 108 (5) (December 2003): 1338–1361.

Hanna, Martha. *Your Death Would Be Mine: Paul and Marie Pireaud in the Great War*. Boston: Harvard University Press, 2006.

Hargreaves, Aura Kate, comp. and ed. *My Dearest*. England and Wales: Property People JV Ltd., 2014.

Harpin, Muriel and Charles 'Neville' Overton Correspondence. Private Papers, Department of Documents (3051), Imperial War Museum, London.

Hartley, Jenny. '"Letters Are Everything These Days": Mothers and Letters in the Second World War', in *Epistolary Selves: Letters and Letter-Writers, 1600–1945*, edited by Rebecca Earle, 183–195. Aldershot, UK: Ashgate, 1999.

Kelly, Jean, ed. *Love Letters from the Front*. Dublin: Marino Books, 2000.

Martin, William and Emily Chitticks. The Private Papers of W.J. Martin, Department of Documents (2554), Imperial War Museum, London.

Meyer, Jessica. *Men of War: Masculinity and the First World War in Britain*. Houndsmill: Palgrave Macmillan, 2009.

Milne, Esther. *Letters, Postcards, Email: Technologies of Presence*. London: Routledge, 2010.

Newman, Cyril and Winifred Blackburn Correspondence. Private Papers, Department of Documents (03/5/1), Imperial War Museum, London.

Praeger, Karen J. *The Psychology of Intimacy*. New York and London: The Guilford Press, 1995.

Roper, Michael. '"Slipping Out of View": Subjectivity and Emotion in Gender History', *History Workshop Journal* 59 (Spring 2005): 57–72.

Roper, Michael. *The Secret Battle: Emotional Survival in the Great War*. Manchester: Manchester University Press, 2009.

Sellers, Frederic and Grace Malin Correspondence. Private Papers, Department of Documents (09/32/1), Imperial War Museum, London.

Wilkinson, Alan, ed. *"Thank God I'm Not a Boy": The Letters of Dora Willatt, Daughter, Sweetheart and Nurse 1915–18*. Hull: Lampada Press, 1997.

Part II
Voices

5 "A Certain Poetess"
Recuperating Jessie Pope (1868–1941)

Jane Potter

A poetic voice characterised by futility, satire and horror, and articulated in the poems of Wilfred Owen, Siegfried Sassoon and other "soldier-poets," has shaped a particular, dominant version of the First World War. Taken in conjunction with the graphic suffering and trauma rendered in prose, especially in nursing memoirs by such women as Mary Borden and Vera Brittain, the literary landscape of 1914–1918 is firmly rooted in a particular narrative of disillusionment and sorrow, if not protest. The priority accorded to such a resonant body of self-consciously literary work by both academics and the media alike has made it difficult to hear different voices, those of professional writers in tune with public opinion and the demands of the literary marketplace.

Lines from Wilfred Owen's Great War poem "Dulce et Decorum Est" are known by heart by scholars and countless British schoolchildren:

> If in some smothering dreams you too could pace
> Behind the wagon that we flung him in,
> And watch the white eyes writhing in his face,
> His hanging face, like a devil's sick of sin;
> If you could hear, at every jolt, the blood
> Come gargling from the froth-corrupted lungs,
> Obscene as cancer, bitter as the cud
> Of vile, incurable sores on innocent tongues,—
> My friend, you would not tell with such high zest
> To children ardent for some desperate glory,
> The old Lie: *Dulce et decorum est*
> *Pro patria mori.*[1]

As well-known as these lines is the identity of the "friend," the "you" to whom this excoriating condemnation is directed: Jessie Pope. We know from his manuscripts that Owen had Pope in mind when writing "Dulce et Decorum Est." The first draft of the poem has the dedication "To Jessie Pope, etc," then in a subsequent version, "To a Certain Poetess" (a label suggested by Siegfried Sassoon), before Owen deletes the "dedication" altogether in favour of the more general "you' and "my friend" to, in effect, universalise the poem. But his original dedication has in many ways damned Pope: her fate as a woman who seemingly ignored the suffering of soldiers was sealed when Owen achieved canonical status, his voice having become one of the main prisms through which the literary and cultural landscapes of the First World War are viewed. "Sneering at Jessie Pope has long been fashionable, the required first step towards recognizing the superiority of anti-war poets and prose-writers like Sassoon, Owen, Rosenberg, Aldington, *et al.* who had actually been in the sodden, vermin-infested trenches."[2] Pope's patriotic, enthusiastic, and jingoistic poems were frequently published in newspapers like *The Daily Mail*, in periodicals such as *Punch* and collected in volumes including as *Jessie Pope's War Poems* (1915). It is "The Call" which is most-often quoted as the example of her outlook and the standard of her verse:

> Who's fretting to begin,
> Who's going out to win?
> And who wants to save his skin—
> Do you, my laddie?[3]

"Play the Game" is equally strident with its final lines of "Get to work with a gun, / When our country's at war we must all back up / It's the only thing to be done!" Over the decades, in countless academic texts, student essays, and media discussions, Jessie Pope has been cited as *the* voice of patriotic civilian, particularly the female patriotic civilian whose war-mongering and patriotic enthusiasm is borne out of unfeeling ignorance of the "truth" of war.

Pope's reputation as an ultra-jingoistic supporter of the war is a one-sided characterisation that has obscured a more multi-faceted, popular writer, who was a successful brand in her day. This chapter aims to illuminate Pope's wartime public persona and argues that it was created by a businesswoman whose career was founded on her ability to write quickly, with wit and satire, and with a feeling for the public mood. She was neither evil nor progressive in her views, but is an example of the professional female writer in the early years of the twentieth century when the periodical press was in its heyday and readers of all classes participated in print culture in numbers greater than ever before. She earned her living by her pen and that meant appealing to popular taste and opinion, both of which were receptive to humour and clear-cut values, particularly in time of war when the rest of life was in such upheaval. Her ability to take a topical issue and turn it into verse was part of her appeal. The poems "Any Woman to a Suffragette" and "Any Suffragette to any Woman" speak to the struggle for the franchise and more specifically to the polarisation of opinion which would not have escaped anyone's notice. Such polarisation is further reinforced by the layout of the poems in the volume itself, appearing as they do on facing pages so that they can be read side by side. That Pope mimics such divided voices perhaps shows her taking a balanced view, for while "any woman to any suffragette" argues that "you see, as a class, we believe, / That brawling is vulgar, dear Madam,"[4] "any suffragette to any woman" derides the "protected shell" of non-campaigners and asserts that "when our conflict's done," "With equanimity you'll take / The vote which *we* have won."[5]

Pre-War Career

It is no small irony that Pope shares a birthday with Wilfred Owen albeit twenty-five years apart. Born on 18 March 1868, she began her writing career in her early twenties with an article about the Bushey Heath Beagles Hunt for *Punch*, and between 1902 and 1922, she contributed 170 poems to the magazine. Boasting in an interview with *The Lady's Realm* that she "never refused any work that was offered to her," she became a prolific writer of humorous verse, articles, and short stories, which were published in many other popular periodicals of the early twentieth century.[6] In addition, *The Daily Mail*, *The Daily Express*, *The Evening Standard*, *The Queen*, *The Windsor Magazine* and *The Westminster Gazette* published her work before it was collected in such books as *Paper Pellets* (1906) and *Airy Nothings* (1909). Reviewers praised Pope for her "nimble wit" and "polished facility for rhyme and scansion" (*The Evening Standard*), singling out her gender on many occasions: "an almost unique example of an Englishwoman's gift for light verse" (*Punch*); "The cynical have denied women a sense of humour, but Miss Jessie Pope has as delicate and aerial sense of humour as one can imagine" (*Daily Mail*); "Miss Pope has the unusual gift in a young lady of expressing humour in verse" (*World*); "Humourists are rare, poetic humorists even rarer, poetic humorists of the fair sex rarest of all. This makes the remarkable talent of Miss Jessie Pope all the more remarkable" (*Evening News*).[7] Given the tone of such praise, it is interesting that her gender over the years has been one of the key elements to work against her. Similarly, the reviews note a primary source of her popularity: the ability to poke fun at contemporary issues. *The Evening Standard* said that along with her "facile command of rhythm and verse," Pope had in her sense of humour a "shrewd observation of life." *The Daily Mail* noted the Shakespearean link in the title *Airy Nothings* ("As imagination bodies forth / The forms of things unknown, the poet's pen / Turns them to shapes, and gives to airy nothing / A local habitation and a name." *A Midsummer Night's Dream,* Act 5, Scene 1) when it claimed Pope "laughs at our foibles" with "the merry mischief of Puck."[8] The *Mail*'s declaration that "it is quite impossible to be angry with her" is ironic with hindsight, given how angry people have been with Pope over the intervening decades. It must be noted that such reviews come from the very newspapers that published her individual poems—a circuit of promotion that was key to her popular success.

Such success was augmented by her many illustrated collections for children, including *The Little Soldier Book* (1907), *Babes and Birds* (1910), *The*

Adventures of Silversuit (1912), *Three Jolly Anglers* (1913) and *Tom, Dick and Harry: Their Deeds and Misdeeds* (1914). Published mainly by Ward Lock and Blackie's, two of the foremost children's publishers of their day, these volumes put her firmly within a wider publishing network, and her work appeared regularly in Blackie's Annuals.

As well as being a popular writer, Pope was also a trusted publisher's reader and editor. Her most famous editorial intervention occurred in 1913 when she recommended the manuscript of *The Ragged Trousered Philanthropists* by the then-deceased Robert Noonan [*pseud.* Robert Philippe Tressell] to her publisher Grant Richards. Richards in turn asked her to cut the original 250,000-word text, parts of which he considered "damnably subversive,"[9] down to 100,000 words. Pope was later criticised for her editing in language similar to that used to excoriate her own writing: her "middle-class squeamishness" led her to make unnecessary cuts in the novel,[10] and as "a hack writer of simpering verses for children and the childishly minded," she could not perform her task "without showing her ideological slip."[11] Yet in an assessment that articulates a key motivation of her wartime verse, Peter Miles admits that her editorial interventions were not "conscious acts of political censorship," but rather "more mundane": "the outcome of a practical task for a commercial concern."[12]

Wartime Verse

Given that Pope had her finger on the pulse of the topics that dominated public concern at any given time, it is no surprise she interpreted the Great War with her characteristic gusto, firstly in newspapers and magazines as she had done before, and then in collected editions *Jessie Pope's War Poems* (1915), *More War Poems* (1915) and *Simple Rhymes for Stirring Times* (1916). Her verse also appeared in charity gift-books such as *The Fiery Cross* (1915) and her articles and short stories in popular periodicals like *Pearson's Magazine*.

It is, in fact, an article for *Pearson's* that provides a key insight to her professional personality and her attitude to her work. "Verse-Making without Tears" is primarily a "how-to" essay on becoming a versifier and a versifier who can make money from their creative efforts. In every sense it can be seen as her public manifesto. From her opening declaration that "Not being a genius," she is unfettered by the constraints of artistry, she positions herself clearly within the popular marketplace. Pope situates herself in a very different realm from literary poets. Indeed, throughout the article she refers to her craft, not as poetry, but as "verse-making." So simple is this activity, she declares,

> that I can never understand why the large number of people who often feel a secret craving to express their thoughts in rhyme should give up the attempt as utterly beyond their power.
>
> Verse-making is a pretty habit, it passes many a dull hour with advantage, and impresses one's friends as being an extraordinarily gifted

accomplishment. Perhaps it is greatest virtue, though, for more sordid minds may be added a further attraction—there's money in it![13]

This equating of money-making with "sordid" minds is an interesting deflection, but that she mentions money with an emphatic exclamation-point reveals her own key motivation for writing as she does. Moreover, if one is to make money from verse, one must be shrewd in selecting "the subject-matter for your muse": "If you hope to write for pecuniary profit, the ability to reject unmarketable ideas is almost as valuable as the ability to put the more saleable ones on paper."[14] In addition, the would-be professional versifier "must have a sense of rhythm" to know "if a poem scans," and to "acquire an 'ear'" for this, Pope recommends "reading plenty of verse."[15] In other words, one must do one's homework—divine intervention is not enough. On the subject of rhymes, she falls foul of Owen's experiments with pararhyme when she declares that "you must not think because two words have more or less the same sound they are true rhymes"—she preferred "to keep on less perilous ground, as a general rule."[16] Topics for verse are not lacking in "these stirring times" of war, so it can be "a very pleasant business, this crystallising a topical event into a set of verse." She describes her own success in warlike, military terms as "having fired forty-four shots in topical verse at editorial targets up to date, and scored forty-one hits."[17]

Having been "tolerably lucky" herself in this regard, Pope seeks to impart some of her wisdom. The rest of the article is therefore dedicated to examples of how to recognise a good rhyme and good scansion and how her "mechanical machinery gets busy when there is poetry in the air." She argued that "simplicity of expression" was a key to selling her work because "Simplicity is the key to the public heart." It is this very simplicity that damned her, but she recognised that

> The public won't waste time in pondering over the meaning of a minor poet; they will only suffer unintelligibility from genius. If you can get hold of a new idea, and express it in fresh rhythmic verses, each one of which creates an appetite for the next, then you will, I was going to say, "find a ready market," but that sounds a little too sordid, so I will say instead, you will please your reader and yourself—and after all that is the end and aim of a minor poet.[18]

Pope claims literary greatness neither for herself nor her readers who might take up their pens. In a similar way, she defends the decisions of editors and urges her readers not to "malign a man because he knows what he wants and he doesn't want your stuff": "I agree he may be missing the opportunity of his editorial career, but that's his look-out."[19] Her keen sense of the day-to-day business of popular publishing is everywhere evident in this article.

Thus Pope was in her heyday during the Great War: "it was the war that allowed Pope to come into her own, in which she did a persuasive and very popular turn as a writer of patriotic verse. Her poetry found a ready outlet; her verses were sprightly, hopeful, winning, easily understood and easily able to tap into the public mood."[20] Widely disseminated and widely read, her poems touched a public consciousness, so much so that the opening page of *Jessie Pope's War Poems* reproduces a facsimile of a letter sent from "a soldier at the front." While its authenticity may be suspect, its contents merely a marketing ploy, it nevertheless proclaims that Pope's poems are "much admired by us all out here" and "will be such a 'buck up'" for the soldier's wife: "bucking up means so much to those at home as well as for us. Really, they need it most, as after all, there is the most worrying suspense." Poems such as '"No!"' with the insistent line "Are we downhearted?" and its resounding affirmation of steadfastness from Tommy and General French, Jack the sailor, and even "the girl who is left behind / And the wife who misses her mate" may have indeed "bucked up" those on the home front. And as Douglas Kerr has asserted,

> there were large numbers of men who had seen the fighting and who, even so, produced war poetry that endorsed the official view that war was necessary, and the civilian believed that it could be glorious. And standing behind them were countless other soldiers who, at least, offered no protest.[21]

Moreover, "contrary to popular belief, Pope was not insensitive to the seriousness of the situation ... like many columnists of the time she voiced disapproval of self-indulgence and of moping around."[22] Her commercial success was based on this ability to cheer people up, to encourage her readers to face hardship with the stoicism and good humour exhibited by Tommy Atkins.

This is certainly the overriding tenor of the three volumes of war verse that were published in 1915 and 1916. Closer examination and careful reading of these books' contents reveals they contain more than simple invective. Jane Dowson, for instance has noticed how in the poem '"No!"', "among the compliant clichés and facile rhythms it is possible to hear a subtle denial of chivalric platitudes."[23] If Pope was scathing about so-called "slackers," again mimicking much of popular culture at the time, she expressed equal disgust for war profiteers and rumour mongers. She poked fun at women who used Zeppelin raids for excitement, for instance "Mariana" who "each night" "waves her hair"

> And spreads a négligé of charm
> (The very thing for air-raid wear)
> Beside her pillow, on a chair,
> And waits for the alarm.[24]

Pope urged readers not to forget the sick children at Great Ormond Street Hospital when considering outlets for their wartime charity and she asked readers to spare a thought for older women left behind in "The Loan Widow."

While she satirised fashionable and showy young men in such poems as 'The Nut's Birthday," she could be every inch as critical of women as Sassoon. Nowhere is this more evident than in "The Beau Ideal":

> The lad who throth with Rose would plight,
> Nor apprehend rejection
> Must be in shabby khaki dight
> To compass her affection.
> Who buys her an engagement ring
> And finds her kind and kissing,
> Must have one member in a sling
> Or, preferably, missing.[25]

While some critics have used this poem to point to Pope's callousness and her glorying in men being, as Sassoon noted, "wounded in a mentionable place," it can also be used to point to Pope's satire if we take into account her other verse and the varying subjects in the public consciousness she took as inspiration. "The Beau Ideal" can be seen to be not just poking fun at the outrageous attitudes of some romantic women, but also actively condemning them, with pointed humour.

Pope also cajoled women on the home front to economise and to be upbeat. For instance, "Heads Up, Girls" appeals to "Sisters" who before the war were ruled by fashions that made them "broken-kneed / And spinal cords convex," to turn their attention to the "military cut" of dress, and by extension their attitudes:

> It's up to us to do our bit
> Each time we take the road,
> For if we wear a warlike kit,
> The mien must match the *mode*.[26]

The poem appeals to them to be in a "mien" that is upbeat, upright, and vigorous: "We've finished with the 'Slinker Slouch.' / Heads up, girls, if you please!" Pope also depicted the ways in which women could be active and "show their grit." "Ready, Aye Ready!" declares "When our men went to fight / And war gripped us tight / The women were much to be pitied." But they soon realise "it's up to us all / To answer the call / To keep the Motherland going." The poem's last two stanzas itemise the various tasks women have taken up: "hands for the plough," "in workshop or garden," serving and selling, punching "tickets as well":

> No labour or toil we're afraid of.
> Though the jobs may be rough
> We'll show you the stuff
> That the women of Britain are made of.[27]

The poems "Socks," "The Knitting Song," "War Girls," and "V.A.D." are similarly laudatory, while '"Sister"' portrays the bond between nurse and patient so common in fiction, non-fiction, letters and diaries as well as autograph books:

> "Sister" has taken him under her wing—
> She's a white-capped, slender slip of a thing,
> She has frank eyes and capable hands,
> And a job that she thoroughly understands.[28]

The Sister mothers every one of her soldiers "And parts from her boys with real regret," but whilst these boys display the characteristic reticence of the Tommy, "they won't forget!"

Pope also recounts what were then familiar tales of men who regain their faith on active service among "Hell's own music" ("Dick Devil-may-care") and was attune to current events, satirising, for instance, Italy's indecisions in "Oranges and Lemons" and Turkey's treaty with Germany in "There's Many a Slip." "Sea Sorrow" responds to the sinking of Lusitania on 7 May 1915 with its opening lines, "The sea is kinder than the Hun" as its "sunlit billow tolls / A requiem for passing souls" and ends with the scathing final line: "God save us from our fellow-man!"[29] The grit of sons of the empire is lauded in such poems as "The Lads of the Maple Leaf," who "Ripe for any adventure, sturdy, loyal and game / Quick to the call of the Mother, the young Canadians came"[30] while in "Anzac," the All Blacks, once known as "sportsmen" ("At footer and cricket you're cracks") now have "weightier matters to settle":

> To-day, amid bullets and shells;
> And the world stands amazed at the mettle
> You've shown in the far Dardanelles.

The disastrous nature of that campaign is recognised, but from within the context of the "mettle" and sacrifice: "you poured out the best of your blood."[31] Like many writers at the time, Pope was part of the climate of opinion that attempted to refashion the campaign into a success story.

In "My Bit," the speaker gives voice to (presumably) Pope's own and other women's frustration:

> I may not quell the Kaiser
> Nor castigate the Hun;
> By stronger folk and wiser
> The business must be done.
> I cannot fight the German
> Nor brevet rank annex,
> I have no chance across in France
> By reason of my sex.[32]

The ease by which Pope seemingly towed the patriotic line is complicated in her final volume *Simple Rhymes for Stirring Times*. It has the same layout as previous two volumes, but it is soft rather than hard cover (presumably a product of wartime paper rationing) and published not by Grant Richards but by Pearson. The cover illustrations present an interesting shift.

On the first, *Jessie Pope's War Poems*, a man in civilian dress, a golf-bag slung over his shoulder, watches as lines of soldiers, *rifles* slung across *their* shoulders, marches past. On the second, *More War Poems*, Britannia is featured against a backdrop of billowing clouds, in her hand her unsheathed sword ready to strike. For the third volume cover, the focus is a soldier, reading outside a dug-out, presumably a magazine like Pearson's, rifle propped up next to him. These paratextual elements suggest a shift in emphasis that is discernible in the poems themselves, from recruitment to resilience, for whilst the volume does contain poems such as "Who's For the Game?" and "The Shells" with their characteristic function of encouraging action on the part of men and women, the tone of the majority of poems is more sombre and reflective. The unlike opening poems of the first two volumes, "The K.A. Boys" and "For England," "The Rumourist," which opens *Stirring Rhymes* is hardly rousing. Instead it takes on the man met "every morning in the street," agitated "with tidings of importance," who "embroiders" stories "as he goes," from "secrets of the State" to "dreadful doings in the Tower" and "German spies," all because "he knows a man who knows a man who *knows*!"[33] Similarly, instead of the slacker, it is "Dismal James," "Secure from battles' deadly roll" who is satirised for his negative outlook.[34] Also in this volume, Pope asks the reader not to forget those "Unmentioned in Dispatches," the average soldiers, who don't perform great acts of heroism but hold the line and do their duty, quietly. "The Seaport Road" is reflective, understated as is the "Soldier's Button" which recounts the simple way a woman remembers her serving solider. The penultimate poem of the volume, "Au 'voir," is sober and subtle as the speaker, realising that the swallows have gone for the winter, hopes that "At the end of your oversea lease, / May you find our dear land in a garland of spring, / And may her scarred heart be at peace!"[35]

Wartime Short Stories

Pope's voice was heard not just through poems but also through equally popular short stories, the topics of which echoed those of her prolific verse. Published first in magazines and then collected in the volume *Love On Leave* (1919), her short stories are, like her poems, "more double-edged than they first appear."[36] In these "little courtship tales," just as in her verse, Pope's "presentation of her heroines show that she expected her heroines to be as feisty as the men, and to take charge of the situation."[37] In "Allotment Bride," it is middle-aged rather than youthful romance that is at the heart of the story. The opening is an interesting recognition of the more subtle effects of war service, for the main protagonist, an army Major on leave,

> was very brown and very thin and very weary, and the servants remarked to each other that Master looked a goodish bit older. His long leave had been so hardly earned that there was a decided flavour of sick leave about it, with the prospect of light duties for the duration.[38]

He finds rest in "a hammock slung in the 'wilderness' at the bottom of the old garden, the slackest suit of 'civies,' silence, solitude, the drowsy hum of the bees, a copy of the *Angler's Gazette*—this was the sum total of his desire."[39] Conveniently for the love story, he is "a bachelor of independent means." As "tranquil spell of summer worked its charm, the *Angler's Gazette* slipped through his thin brown fingers," he falls asleep to dream in a way that presages the opening lines of Owen's "Strange Meeting" ("It seemed that out of battle I escaped / Down some profound dull tunnel"):

> For some hours his repose was peaceful, then he began to dream, and once more he was working along in a close, clammy, underground tunnel, laying an electric wire. When it was at last in position there came a sound of digging just the other side of the end of the tunnel—faint at first, then louder, till the air became full of the clamour of picks and shovels. The earth rose round him in a colossal explosion, and he awoke to find the birds flitting in the chequered sunshine of the green branches overhead. . . .[40]

Yet although he was now awake, "strange to say, the digging still continued" and he irritated by the "infernal sound of digging" that was disturbing his "well-earned peace and quiet." We quickly learn its source:

> She was sturdy-built and square shouldered, her hair on the carroty side of red, her pleasant, capable face shining with perspiration and sprinkled with freckles, her eyes very blue and determined, and her age well over forty. She was dressed in well-worn but well-cut tweeds: she had shed her coat and turned up her sleeves, and the ginger she was putting into her spadework evoked the Major's reluctant admiration.[41]

As she attempts to remove a hen who is destroying her tomato plants, she trips over her rake, much to the Major's—but not her—amusement. Picking herself up from having tumbled into her plants, she angrily suggests that instead of idly reading his *Angler's Gazette* and laughing at her "you would be much better employed in serving your country than getting gratuitous amusement out of a tired woman who is trying to do her bit."[42] He tries to make amends by replanting her tomatoes overnight, "healthy young tomato plants—finer, bigger, and bushier than ever before."[43] Seeing them in the morning, the woman gardener is amazed—and rather ashamed—as she finds the Major near the riverbank, Pope again emphasising his "careworn" features. She tells him that "what worried me most afterwards was my impertinence to you, and I hope you will forget it. Whether a man fights or stays at home is *his* business, not mine." When he reveals he has been a soldier for 26 years, her shame is complete: "Just like me!" she said, "put my foot into it again! Old enough to know better!"[44] This is not Pope the war-monger, but Pope telling women to mind their own business, not to make snap judgements or to berate men about whom they know nothing. Of course, all of this neatly tied up by a proposal, after some further misunderstandings, but what is key about this tale is the description of the Major, "he was a very tired man," whose desires are just like any other soldier's, just returned from war—peace and quiet. Everyone reading this story would have known what Pope meant. She many not have been privy to the realities and sufferings of the battlefield, but she would have seen its aftermath and how she writes here, quietly, of the Major, is telling in its simplicity.

In "Cornstalks," too, there is an apt recognition of the "before" and "after" of war experience, but it is not triumphal as is the case in much of the (early) verse. Again, in a strange echo of another of Owen's poems "The Send-Off," the opening of the story recounts how Garry, an Australian, leaves him home amidst drums and cheers and returns to England from service in France creeping back. In the next paragraph we are told he has been wounded and that he thanked his stars he was alive, an attitude mirroring that of many soldiers who were lucky enough to have only a "blighty." Garry is contrasted with his cousin Kenneth who "had seen no fighting and was still training at Salisbury Plain" so much so that he can still whistle "Australia will be there."[45] The crucial similarities and differences of these two men will have consequences for the outcome of the love story that follows. Just as Pope takes women to task for their presumptions about men not in uniform, she mocks their enthusiasm for the glory of war, but in a characteristic understated way:

> "I read all about the Dardanelles and the magnificent things the Anzacs did. That charge of the Australian Light Horse, for instance. Balaclava wasn't in the same street with it."
> "Yes, it was a bit of a scrap," he remarked indifferently.
> "A bit of a scrap!" she replied with some heat.
> "Did you know any of the men?"
> He nodded. "Did you see it?' He nodded again.
> "Didn't you think that it was simply glorious?"
> "No," he said. "I don't think I thought that."[46]

This is not only corrective to women to curb their enthusiasm, but a clear example of how what is not said is often more telling that what is said. His almost matter-of-fact, "I don't think I thought that" is at once a put-down to her ideas of glory and a nudge to the reader that what he has seen is beyond words. Pope knew her audience would understand such taciturnity and that they needed to re-adjust their previous expectations, partly formed by Pope's own early verse, about the glory of war. It is possible to suggest that Pope shifted her view as time passed, if not as explicitly as other writers. Garry in this story, or the Major in "Allotment Bride" do not have to go into the kind of detail Owen describes in "Dulce et Decorum Est"—this is unsaid but understood.

If early twenty-first century scholars "could only manage" a few of Pope's short stories at any one time, "in small doses,"[47] at least one reviewer in 1919 also felt the same: "if you wish to avoid feeling like a matrimonial agency, you will be well-advised to take it by instalments rather than in bulk." (*Punch*)[48]

Pope followed her short story collection with a further volume of verse entitled *Hits and Misses* published in 1920. Some of her war poems were reprinted here, but the edition mainly contained poems about gardens, motor-cars, the weather, and characters such as a van boy and a "would-be M.P." Much of published work in the 1920s centred on verse and stories for children including a series of picture postcards, *A Day at the Fair* (1928) and *Fairy Wings* (1928), and stories for illustrated books such as *Animal Fun & Frolic* (1930).

In 1929, Pope at the age of sixty-one married Edward Babington Lenton (1866–1942), a widowed retired bank manager, and left London to settle with him near Great Yarmouth. That she did so just at the time that the second "war books" boom was in full swing with its texts characterised by disillusionment and the futility of war, seems no small coincidence. She also purchased the remaining back-copies of her books from her publisher Grant Richards and asked that the rights be reverted to her, knowing, perhaps, that her books were now out-of-step with popular opinion and interest: "It is not that I have any plans with regard to them, but I feel a mother's craving to have my children home again, when they have ceased to be of service elsewhere."[49]

Recuperating Jessie Pope

How much, then, was Pope mimicking or sending-up rather than asserting her own pro-war views? What if she was not so much pro-war, as simply a ventriloquist of popular opinion? It is difficult to establish for certain, but a transition, however subtle, is discernible between her 1915 and 1916 volumes of verse and in her 1919 series of short stories. Unlike May Wedderburn Cannan and Berta Ruck, who wrote reflections on their war experience and writing—Cannan from the point of view of it not being a useless waste, Ruck regretting earlier jingoism/enthusiasm—Pope left no such written record. Her personal feelings beyond what we may read into the verse and stories were not recorded. The image we have of her is as a brand and not as a person. We want her to atone, but she cannot. She gave the market what it wanted. It is the law of successful publishing, especially periodicals that exist on the relationships with their audiences, that if her writing was not in tune with public opinion, she would not have been published.

Jessie Pope and Wilfred Owen were indeed opposites. Owen was a serious young man who longed for literary immortality; Pope was a professional writer who was more concerned with earning a living through her work as a humourist. Her idea of penning a poem in fifteen minutes is so contrary to Sassoon's dictum "sweat your guts out writing poetry" that it is no wonder that, next to Owen, he was one of her staunchest castigators. Writing verse didn't make Pope sweat, at least according to her public declarations. Rather, it seemed easy, just as her popularity and her financial success also seemed easy. But, as all professional writers will attest, the ease is deceptive. Pope worked hard even if the outcome seemed trivial—this was her job, not a higher poetic calling, and it was pragmatic. For her to have tried to imagine Owen's experiences would have been disingenuous and perverse. She did not experience the spacial landscape of the Western Front, but an all-together different home front landscape. She wrote, published and earned a living from themes such as love, outdoor activities, energetic women, foppish "nuts," and popular pastimes—and caricatured society as she saw and lived it within her middle-class purview. Owen aspired to move beyond this and indeed the war facilitated such a move where a class-bound society in normal circumstances would not. We only have to look at his efforts before the war to see his struggles as vicarage assistant and language teacher, operating on the margins of the literary life. As an aspiring man of letters, Owen was unsuccessful. Pope, on the other hand, although not a "woman of letters," was successful. Sassoon looked down on her from his patrician height; Owen looked down upon Pope and her kind from his position of lower-middle-class aspirational snobbery. But Pope never claimed to be anything other than what she was, whereas Owen aspired to be something else. But for being noticed and criticized by a coterie of male poets, Pope would have gone the way of many professional women writers like Berta Ruck, Ruby M. Ayres and others, fading into obscurity to be noticed only in reclamations of popular literature. Having become notorious, perhaps she would have preferred to be forgotten.

It is highly unlikely that Pope would have been unaware of the opinions made about her. A professional writer, switched into the market, she could not have been oblivious to, for instance, Gilbert Frankau's condemnation of her in his short story "Initiative," where a character declares that "subalterns who really *want* to observe fire from the forward trenches [. . .] exist only 'Histories of the Great War' or the imagination of a Jessie Pope."[50] And in later years, she could hardly fail to notice Owen's scathing attack, as his reputation grew. Is this why she retreated into children's books, then into married life in Norfolk, far from the literary world she inhabited so boldly for so many years? Did she retreat to escape the limelight, having found herself out of step with opinion in the late 1920s and early 1930s when the second wave of war literature was at its peak and the tide of disillusionment at its highest? In the absence of Pope's own words on the matter, we can only speculate.

Jessie Pope did not send men to war. To suggest her verses did so would be ridiculous. They would have played only a small part in the vast propaganda effort to convince Britons of the righteousness of the fight against "the Hun." As Argha Bannerjee has convincingly argued,

> Pope's poems serve as evidences of political exploitation of women during the early years of the war. They serve as stereotypical expressions of female poets, who internalised prevalent patriarchal notions of the time [. . .] Being conditioned to respond and be exploited, they were later accused for their efforts, suffering the sad ignominious fate of being criticised and cast into oblivion.[51]

And as Claire Buck asserts, it is this "ideological work for the British nation at war that has negatively influenced their reputations in the twentieth century."[52]

What do we want from women's voices? It seems that we expect them to be pacifist, oppositional, disillusioned, more in the manner of Borden, Brittain and others who explicitly challenged the patriotic platitudes that sent young men to war. Yet confined by their gender, women were only privy to certain experiences. And Pope's experience was one of a civilian, middle-aged woman writer with no sons of her own. Better that she were silent? Should she have used her popularity to denounce the war and its suffering? This would have been totally out of keeping. Owen's dictum of "true poets must be truthful" for Pope was truthful to her own experience: she experienced neither a gas attack, nor forth-corrupted lungs—Owen had to show her—and he did not do that until after his own death when the war was over.

W.G. Bebbington in his illuminating 1972 article suggests that Owen may have cancelled his original "dedication" to Pope because he recognized "a tongue in a cheek":

> She has no place in the history of literature, for all her undoubted skill as a writer of light, topical, satirical verse and parody [. . .] She has her place in the whole story of 1914–18 [. . .] She has her mysterious place in the whole story of Wilfred Owen too, and we at least know enough about her now to see that she is some sort of symbol, an alter ego perhaps, another and easier personification of his—or perhaps her own—ambivalent attitude to the war.[53]

That Pope's sense of wit and satire rang hollow in light of the carnage of the Western Front was a fate not unique to this "certain poetess." It is perhaps the reason why she returned in her later years to the gentler subjects of animals and fairies in her verse and stories for children. Presumably she lived quietly in retirement in Norfolk, but when she died in the midst of World War II in December 1941, she was not sufficiently important to warrant an obituary in a national newspaper.

The war generated a multiplicity of voices and in literature these voices are not always the voice of the writer him/herself, at least not for the professional, popular writer who was writing for a market. By the time of the First World War Pope was a brand—it would have been nigh on impossible for her to change tack even if privately she would have wanted to. We can never be sure if Pope held the opinions she articulated—she may have been as bellicose as the verses she penned, but it is more likely that like many in the war years, she felt loss deeply, and regretted the deaths even as she attempted to bolster the mood of the nation. Like many voices from the Great War, Jessie Pope's voice creates a more complex and interesting alternate space. Her writing problematizes our view of the war as a useless waste, at least for those experiencing it at the time, a great many of whom welcomed the kind of humorous, witty, and simple escape from the seriousness of the cataclysm, if only for the few minutes it took to read one of Jessie Pope's poem in the morning paper.

Notes

1. W. Owen, *The War Poems*, edited by Jon Stallworthy (London: Chatto & Windus, 1994), 29.
2. A. Maunder, *The Short Story and the Novella*, British Literature of World War I, vol. 1. (London: Pickering & Chatto, 2011), 171.
3. J. Pope, *Jessie Pope's War Poems* (London: Grant Richards, 1915), 38.
4. J. Pope, *Airy Nothings* (London: Grant Richards, 1909), 66.
5. J. Pope, *Airy Nothings*, 67.
6. Miall, Agnes M. 1915. 'A Humourist at Home Being an Interview with Miss Jessie Pope, The War Poet'. The Lady's Realm (May): 72–75.
7. J. Pope, *Hits and Misses* (London: Grant Richards, 1920), flyleaf.
8. J. Pope, *Hits and Misses*, flyleaf.
9. G. Richards, *Author Hunting, by an Old Literary Sportsman: Memories of Years Spent Mainly in Publishing* (London: Hamish Hamilton, 1934), 280.
10. F. Swinnerton, *The Adventures of a Manuscript, Being the Story of "The Ragged Trousered Philanthropists"* (London: The Richards Press, 1956), 28. Despite criticism, however, Swinnerton called Pope's efforts for the novel "beyond price" and that without her it might never have seen the light of day.
11. P. Miles, 'Introduction', *The Ragged Trousered Philanthropists*, edited by Robert Tressell (Oxford: Oxford University Press, 2005), xi. Miles also admits that this "most curious midwife imaginable to *The Ragged Trousered Philanthropists*" deserves credit for recommending it to Richards in the first place.
12. P. Miles, 'Introduction', xi.
13. J. Pope, 'Verse-Making without Tears', *Pearson's Magazine*, March 1915, 282.

14. J. Pope, 'Verse-Making', 283.
15. J. Pope, 'Verse-Making', 283.
16. J. Pope, 'Verse-Making', 283.
17. J. Pope, 'Verse-Making', 283.
18. J. Pope, 'Verse-Making', 284.
19. J. Pope, 'Verse-Making', 286.
20. Maunder, *The Short Story and the Novella*, 171.
21. D. Kerr, *Wilfred Owen's Voices: Language and Community* (Oxford: Oxford University Press, 1993), 322.
22. Maunder, *The Short Story and the Novella*, 172.
23. J. Dowson, 'Jessie Pope', In *The Encyclopedia of British Women's Writing, 1900–1950*, edited by F. Hammill, E. Miskimmin, and A. Sponenberg (Basingstoke: Palgrave, 2006), 189.
24. J. Pope, *Simple Rhymes for Stirring Times* (London: C. Arthur Pearson, 1916), 40.
25. J. Pope, *More War Poems* (London: Grant Richards, 1915), 43.
26. J. Pope, *More War Poems*, 16.
27. J. Pope, *More War Poems*, 38. For important academic discussions of women's war work, see J.S.K. Watson, 'Khaki Girls, VADs, and Tommy's Sisters: Gender and Class in First World War Britain', *The International History Review* 19, no. 1 (1997): 32–51 and K. Robert, 'Gender, Class, and Patriotism: Women's Paramilitary Units in First World War Britain', *The International History Review* 19, no. 1 (1997): 52–65.
28. J. Pope, *More War Poems*, 30.
29. J. Pope, *More War Poems*, 48.
30. J. Pope, *More War Poems*, 44. For a detailed analysis of this poem, see A.D. Araujo, 'Jessie Pope, Wilfred Owen, and the Politics of Pro Patria Mori in World War I Poetry', *Media, War & Conflict* 7, no. 3 (2014): 326–341.
31. J. Pope, *Simple Rhymes for Stirring Times*, 18.
32. J. Pope, *More War Poems*, 46.
33. J. Pope, *Simple Rhymes for Stirring Times*, 9.
34. J. Pope, *Simple Rhymes for Stirring Times*, 22.
35. J. Pope, *Simple Rhymes for Stirring Times*, 45.
36. Maunder, *The Short Story and the Novella*, 173.
37. G. Simmers, Great War Fiction Blog, https://greatwarfiction.wordpress.com/
38. J. Pope, 'The Allotment Bride', 183.
39. J. Pope, 'The Allotment Bride', 183.
40. J. Pope, 'The Allotment Bride', 183.
41. J. Pope, 'The Allotment Bride', 184.
42. J. Pope, 'The Allotment Bride', 185.
43. J. Pope, 'The Allotment Bride', 185.
44. J. Pope, 'The Allotment Bride', 185.
45. J. Pope, 'Cornstalks', *The Short Story and the Novella*, 175.
46. J. Pope, 'Cornstalks', 178.
47. G. Simmers, 'Jessie Pope's "Love on Leave"', Great War Fiction https://greatwarfiction.wordpress.com/2009/07/09/jessie-popes-love-on-leave/ (accessed 10 June 2016).
48. G. Simmers, 'Love on Leave Reviewed', Great War Fiction https://greatwarfiction.wordpress.com/2009/07/15/1413/ (accessed 10 June 2016).
49. Archives of Grant Richards, 1897–1948, incoming correspondence.
50. G. Frankau, 'Initiative', *Fortnightly Review*, Jan 1917, 138–146, 138.
51. A. Banerjee, *Women's Poetry and the First World War* (New Delhi: Atlantic, 2014), 124, 127.

52. C. Buck, 'Reframing Women's War Poetry', *The Cambridge Companion to Twentieth-Century British and Irish Women's Poetry*, edited by Jane Dowson (Cambridge: Cambridge University Press, 2011), 31.
53. W.G. Bebbington, 'Jessie Pope and Wilfred Owen', *Ariel: A Review of International English Literature* 3, no. 4 (1972): 82–93, 92.

Bibliography

Archives

Grant Richards Ltd.,1897–1948, incoming correspondence.

Published Sources

Araujo, A.D. 'Jessie Pope, Wilfred Owen, and the Politics of Pro Patria Mori in World War I Poetry'. *Media, War & Conflict* 2014, 7(3): 326–341.
Banerjee, A. *Women's Poetry and the First World War*. New Delhi: Atlantic, 2014.
Bebbington, W.G. 'Jessie Pope and Wilfred Owen'. *Ariel: A Review of International English Literature* 1972, 3(4): 82–93.
Buck, C. 'Reframing Women's War Poetry'. *The Cambridge Companion to Twentieth-Century British and Irish Women's Poetry*, Ed. Jane Dowson. Cambridge: Cambridge University Press, 2011. 24–41.
Dowson, J. 'Jessie Pope'. *The Encyclopedia of British Women's Writing, 1900–1950*, Eds. F. Hammill, E. Miskimmin, and A. Sponenberg. Basingstoke: Palgrave, 2006. 189.
Frankau, G. 'Initiative'. *Fortnightly Review*, January 1917: 138–146.
Kerr, D. *Wilfred Owen's Voices: Language and Community*. Oxford: Oxford University Press, 1993.
Maunder, A. *The Short Story and the Novella*. London: Pickering & Chatto, 2011.
Miall, A.M. 'A Humourist at Home Being an Interview with Miss Jessie Pope, The War Poet'. *The Lady's Realm*, May 1915: 72–75.
Miles, P. 'Introduction'. *The Ragged Trousered Philanthropists*, Ed. R. Tressell. Oxford: Oxford University Press, 2005. x–xxxvii.
Owen, W. *The War Poems*, Ed. J. Stallworthy. London: Chatto & Windus, 1994.
Pope, J. *Airy Nothings*. London: Grant Richards, 1909.
Pope, J. *Jessie Pope's War Poems*. London: Grant Richards, 1915.
Pope, J. *More War Poems*. London: Grant Richards, 1915.
Pope, J. 'Verse-Making without Tears'. *Pearson's Magazine*, March 1915: 282–286.
Pope, J. *Simple Rhymes for Stirring Times*. London: C. Arthur Pearson, 1916.
Pope, J. *Love on Leave*. London: Grant Richards, 1919.
Pope, J. *Hits and Misses*. London: Grant Richards, 1920.
Potter, Jane. 'Pope, Jessie (1868–1941)'. In *Oxford Dictionary of National Biography*, online ed., edited by David Cannadine. Oxford: OUP, October 2008. Online ed., edited by David Cannadine, May 2014. http://www.oxforddnb.com.oxfordbrookes.idm.oclc.org/view/article/98109 (accessed June 10, 2016).
Richards, G. *Author Hunting, by an Old Literary Sportsman: Memories of Years Spent Mainly in Publishing*. London: Hamish Hamilton, 1934.

Simmers, G. 'Jessie Pope's "Love on Leave"'. *Great War Fiction* https://greatwarfiction.wordpress.com/2009/07/09/jessie-popes-love-on-leave/ (accessed 10 June 2016).

Simmers, G. 'Love on Leave Reviewed'. *Great War Fiction* https://greatwarfiction.wordpress.com/2009/07/15/1413/ (accessed 10 June 2016).

Swinnerton, F. *The Adventures of a Manuscript, Being the Story of "The Ragged Trousered Philanthropists"*. London: The Richards Press, 1956.

6 Ventriloquizing Voices in World War I
Scribe, Poetess, Philosopher

Margaret R. Higonnet

This essay explores how women as civilians voice the experiences of the soldiers who fought in World War I. More specifically it asks, how do nurses, close to the front themselves, present the voices of men? Do stories of war written by and about women whose medical service placed them beside the torn bodies of men displace or distort men's voices as if in an echo chamber? How is "voice" itself constituted through word choice, tone, irony and non-verbal actions? Do class, age, and gender lines figure in our critical analyses of this problem, as a narrator tells another character's story and perhaps destabilizes the relationship of voice to self? Does war queer any conventionally "masculine" or "feminine" voice? Whose "truth" is at stake—that of actors or of observers, of survivors or of artists? To borrow from Gayatri Spivak, I suggest we need to know who constitutes the "subaltern" in war literature.

One of my premises is that a woman's voice in the war zone of 1914 is *a priori* represented as subaltern. An overview of several sets of nursing war sketches suggests that they draw on three types of narrative voice, all three to some degree in service to the man's voice. This paradigm draws on the satire in Edith Wharton's "Writing a War Story" (1919), a metanarrative that recounts how an old French governess has jotted down stories as an amanuensis, "just as the soldiers told them to me—oh, without any art at all."[1] "Mademoiselle" then assists a young "authoress" named Ivy Spang to improve the grammar while Ivy adds fashionable style and "sentiment," thereby "mauling" her "awfully good subject," as a soldier-writer reproaches her.[2] While the governess has served as scribe, Ivy has served as a poetess who mistakes the true art of fiction. If those two roles constitute Wharton's comic binary, a third, more honorable role of nurse-philosopher appears in a number of sketches by women who had performed medical service. This third type of voice, I will suggest, not only figures prominently in Ellen La Motte's story "Heroes," but helps us to understand some of the baffling features of La Motte's sketches that confront readers with their own complicity in the construction of war narratives.

Jean Norton Cru's canonizing study of war testimonies, *Témoins* (Witnesses, 1929), promoted the soldier-author as the only writer capable of recording empirically knowable experience, or the "truth" about war.[3] He explained his focus on "confessions of soldiers who have seen and proclaimed the truth" as a practice of reading "war books as documents" selected for the "reliability of their testimony."[4] He deliberately excluded civilians and all those who were not eyewitnesses.[5] In his rejection of writers who had not been soldiers in the front lines, Cru privileged one kind of voice, and it was male. Moreover, his critique of war fiction, as opposed to autobiography, objected to the complicated structures of fiction by male writers like Henri Barbusse, who decentred an authoritative singular narrator in his novel *Le Feu* (*Under Fire*, 1916), introducing the voices of many members of a squad. Literary artistry became suspect as a source of deviation from documentary truth. As extreme as Cru's premises may seem,[6] with his sharp gender distinctions, both Wharton and Barbusse respond to similar problems of voice.

Thus Barbusse, whose "truth" Cru doubted, also challenged the capacity of civilians to understand the reality of war. Even within the male realm of front-line experience, an epistemological gap opens up: Who speaks for whom? As Barbusse wrote in *Under Fire*, which won the Goncourt Prize, but was condemned by Cru as "a concoction of truth, half-truth, and total falsehood,"[7] only the (foot-) soldier's *argot*, with its dirty words, could testify truthfully about the war experience. The *poilu* Barque, his mouth full of a bar of chocolate, stammering, asks the narrator, "If you get the squaddies in your book to speak, will you make them speak like they really do, or will you tidy it up . . . I'm talking about swear words." Barbusse's narrator replies, "I'll put the swear words in, because it's the truth."[8] The simple voice of the *poilu* or "troufion" is thus linked to the truth of war: "la vérité."[9] Yet censors, as Barque reminds the narrator, would cut out some of that voice, that truth, leaving asterisks in place of soldiers' insistently scattered "gros mots." The impact of censorship has become manifest in re-editions of texts such as Frederic Manning's anonymous *Her Privates We*.[10] And class differences do separate the teller from his comrades, even though Barbusse was a communist who would move to Moscow at the end of the war.[11] As we shall see, censorship is not the only problem facing those who wish to voice the truth about war.

The would-be identification of the soldier's voice with truth-telling must be set against many war writers' lively concern for the problematic nature of representation, often expressed through metanarrative that complicates the "truth." The soldier cannot cross the gap between battle front and home front to tell his story. One factor is that language wears out. As Henry James put it, war uses up words.[12] One of the narrator's comrades in *Under Fire*, Paradis, explains that the abuse of language by civilians silences the soldier: "When you talk about the war . . . it's as though you didn't say anything. It stifles words."[13] Communication becomes problematic because the tale depends upon its audience; civilian ignorance or even indifference incenses the speaker. Another comrade in *Under Fire*, Volpatte, returns from a leave stuttering in a rage, because of the profound ignorance among civilians. Such different experiences of war fragment language. Similarly, in Erich Maria Remarque's *Im Westen Nichts Neues* (*All Quiet on the Western Front*, 1928), Paul cannot speak to his father and his older friends, who refuse to believe his account, because it differs from propaganda. At the same time, rather than being worn out, words risk carrying too much meaning: "It is too dangerous for me to put these things into words: I am afraid they might then become gigantic and I be no longer able to master them."[14] These passages suggest that voice is not a transcendental absolute or unhindered vehicle of truth (whether truth of testimony about the self or about the world). The wide diffusion of this theme in fiction by men complicated the reception of fiction by women as *prima facie* civilians who had lacked a "true experience" of the war. Furthermore, trauma itself makes us tongueless, undercutting the issue of agency altogether.

In contrast to the situation of men, gender conventions enforced in publishing meant that women could not use "les gros mots" or dirty language that corresponded to the violence of war at all. Reviewers of Mary Borden's nursing sketches in *The Forbidden Zone* (1929) repeatedly condemned her for descriptions that were "too unsparing" in their "graphic" depiction of "ghoulish" scenes, and for language (such as "mangled testicles") that constituted "breaches of good taste."[15] Yet new kinds of work assigned to women in 1914–1918 had marked a turning point in women's roles, and especially medical work close to the front lines led to their gaining a public and even political voice in many of the nations that had fought. In the face of critical doubts, therefore, women's memoirs and fictions about women's contacts with combat and combatants proliferated.

This essay considers a few women's texts about nurses that staked claims of authenticity due to their own proximity to the front and to soldiers themselves who had just come from the front. These texts raise the question of how to narrate the soldier's voice. While the nurse outside military medicine was typically understood to be feminine, when nurses served close to the front lines, the conventional spatial and documentary contrast between soldiers' accounts from the battle front and women's accounts from the home front became blurred. In a spectrum of texts about the nurses' witnessing of war and recording of men's tales, we can roughly distinguish three modes of narrator: the amanuensis, the poetess, and the philosophic night nurse carrying a lantern in her search for truth, like Diogenes, whose inner dialogue splits open her own voice and sheds light on the night-side of war work. These different narrative personae and voices, I suggest, destabilize gender identities, both of nurses and of the soldiers whose voices they record. Incrementally, these narrative paradigms challenge the norms by which women had conventionally been excluded from the making of the war story, and they do so by drawing attention to the problematic nature of voice itself.

My first paradigm, the nurse as amanuensis, represents the most conventional understanding of a woman's voice in relation to that of the soldier. In part, this genre is the natural extension of the nurse's service to a soldier whose injuries, illness, or illiteracy made it necessary for him to dictate a letter home. The role was further institutionalized by the Red Cross when it assumed the task of reportage, as recorded in the widely read memoir by Elsa Brändström, the memoir of Anne-Marie Wenzel, or the diary of Countess Nora Kinsky (published later) about their inspection trips to Siberia.[16] The submissive scribal role in hospitals at the rear became a stock narrative feature of nursing accounts, and it slipped rapidly from the task of writing for the soldier a letter addressed to his family, to writing for soldiers to an audience at home.[17]

One of the most admired examples of an amanuensis who transcribed the kind of voices that Cru sought—"witnesses of the humblest sort"[18]—was Russian nurse Sofia Fedorchenko (1888–1959), who in 1917 strung together brief conversations by wounded soldiers, many of whom could neither read nor write. Extremely popular, her volume entitled *Narod na voinie* (The people in war) appeared in many editions and was excerpted and translated into English as *Ivan Speaks* in 1919 by one of Gertrude Stein's friends, Thomas Whittemore, as well as into German, French and Spanish.[19] Whittemore explains that Fedorchenko set down "talks which she overheard," in shorthand.[20] Her vignettes capture the lively texture of peasants' language and the melancholy of these victims of the war. In a number of the sketches the men contrast their lives before war with their experiences as soldiers.[21] One of the first short texts, in a section devoted to the mobilization of the Russian army, recounts the shock of war for a gardener: "They dug me up by the roots from my garden, like an old pear tree. What sort of a soldier am I?"[22] In reply to the sempiternal question, "Why war?" another soldier answers: "One's soul has been sold, and no man is guilty of the war. War itself has come from the other world, and war itself will finish itself."[23] Even the impact of soldiers on a local population pours out spontaneously in a startlingly reflexive lament:

> How many ruined children I have seen here! One was so thin that I cannot get her out of my mind. Think of it! In a single hour soldierdom made a wreck of her life. Her mother was beaten to death, her father hanged, and her sister outraged and tortured to death. She was left—not more than eight years old.[24]

Likewise, in another account of abandoned small children, wandering, lost amid the cornfields where the dead were lying, the soldier observes that they were "as silent as dolls," then reflects, "War is hard on the children."[25] Nurses like Fedorchenko were particularly struck by the astonishing transcendence of enmity by some men: "The land is fertile with blood, and it will yield good crops. People will soon forget the war."[26] Significantly, the nurse-scribe rejects poetic accounts by young soldiers who attempted to impress a woman of her class ("niveau"), by recounting in elegant language that was too boring to write down, unlike the integrity of accounts by the simplest, oldest soldiers. One of these said to her "It is not surprising that you only like to listen to simple folk. For you we are like a foreign land, all new."[27] Even before Fedorchenko's work was translated, a text like this stark record must have stood as a model for many nurses who wished to communicate what they had experienced.

Whittemore's selected forty-seven pages offer a non-militarist nurse's version of the "soldier's tale" that Samuel Hynes calls a master-narrative, one that condenses and then juxtaposes all the specific variations of individual encounters with the conflict into a single sequence of suffering. Yet as recorded by a nurse, these injured soldiers' memories differ sharply from the military autobiographies that Hynes synthesizes. Since the English version presents no framing narrative at all by Fedorchenko (the French translator writes that "Fedortchenko completely effaced herself"),[28] one can read these free-floating paragraph-length reflections as stages in a communal suffering life. The pathos of each moment, without introduction for readers of the translation, unpremeditated, emerges from the absolute anonymity of the nursing scribe. Whittemore's succinct assessment in his preface was that "these detached utterances . . . penetrate and reveal the mystery of Russian character."[29] In the longer German translation of a wider selection, the short preface by Fedorchenko explains that she gathered the material for the book while serving at the front in 1915–1916, transcribing in shorthand the conversations that took place among the soldiers.[30] Her patients, she says, paid her little attention as they spoke to each other, since they were accustomed to nurses who wrote down prescriptions, certificates of release, a daily record of their temperature, or a letter for one of them. When reviewers encountered these simple peasants' reflections and fragments of conversation, they were shaken: "It burns us in the gut."[31] When Walter Benjamin reviewed the 1923 German translation, he found the sketches enabled the reader to recognize "the true face of war" ("das wahre Antlitz dieses Krieges festzuhalten"), albeit accessible only in shrapnel-like fragments of testimony.[32] It may be that Fedorchenko's collage offered Benjamin a model for the "small disparate notes" or fragments that he himself would use to challenge readers.[33] In his essay "The Storyteller" (1936), he commented on the increasing poverty in communicable experience that became apparent during the war, the disappearance of accounts "from mouth to mouth," of the great tales that scarcely differ "from the speech of the many nameless storytellers."[34] Fedorchenko's nameless speakers fulfilled such an ideal for many readers like Benjamin.

An intermediate model of soldiers' speech mediated by a nurse can be found in *Ames françaises* (1917), by Marie Dugard. In her Preface Dugard declares that her book is not a collection of imaginary accounts but an album of "unposed sketches" ("croquis pris sur le vif"). Recorded truthfully ("reproduites dans leur vérité") these scenes of daily life, she assures us, offer nothing like the war literature of violent combat in a flood of fire.[35] Each of her vignettes outlines the character of one of the soldiers: Jadieu, a silent man who nonetheless always noticed the presence of the night nurse; Lopez, who regrets that he did not take the decaying body of his best friend from the barbed wire, even though the captain ("capiston") had threatened to shoot him as an example, to prevent such a dangerous sortie; or the amputee Lissol, who refuses to wear his uncomfortable prosthesis, yet insists he will wear it on his return home, in order to spare his mother the shock of his lost leg. Dugard captures the idiom of the conversation around Lissol when the prosthesis is delivered: "As for a fine leg, that's a fine leg! . . . no doubt, it's f . . . g good work."[36] Dugard's self-censorship reinforces the cheerful force of the chorus that encourages this comrade to reenter life at home. Each sketch presents an anonymous recording nurse, someone who typically writes for the wounded patient to his family.[37] The collection takes shape as a kind of narrative scrapbook, like the notebooks to which patients would often contribute signed drawings, poems, or tributes. Sketches such as these by Dugard, even though they are drawn by a third person (the observing nurse), may seem to come closer to the voice of the soldier than the actual artwork that soldiers composed for commemorative scrapbooks, especially when they strove for elegance. Very few such scrapbook poems or sketches retain interest today.

One of the most striking examples of a mediated narrative is "Sister Vera's Story," a story inserted into the memoir of nurse Mary Britnieva, a half-British, half-Russian volunteer. This brief but intricately framed three-page chapter recounts the official mission of Sister Vera from Russia to German POW camps; she had been sent to bring the men news, and to take back letters for their families. "I will try to write it down as I heard it from her," says Britnieva. To retain its epistemological value, Britnieva's printed word must be faithful to the spoken word, and the educated Vera to the peasant whom she serves as scribe. The story is recorded at two removes, translated from the Russian into Britnieva's maternal language, English. Sister Vera had recounted how she listened to Russian prisoners, one of whom stretched out a hand that was terribly mutilated—all of the fingers missing. At first the man won't speak, but his comrades encourage him. The reassuring *Sestritza* draws him to sit down beside her: "Tell me how it happened—I want you to tell me yourself."[38] Petruha, whose name we know from his comrades, shyly tells that he had worked in a prison factory, until he realized that he was making shells that would kill his own brothers. When he refused to continue, he was tortured, being hung by his wrists for twelve hours. Still, he refused to work and was tortured again, then hospitalized for three months. Petruha pairs German violations of the laws of war (which prohibit such work for POWs) with German violence—evidence that Sister Vera was tasked with collecting. Finally, fearful of another punishment, on his way to work he caught sight of an axe shining "almost as a mirror." Inspired by the thought that God had put that axe there to help him, "I made the sign of the cross and saying to myself: 'For Faith, Tsar and Country,' I seized the axe in one hand, and placing the other on the stump, with one blow I chopped off my fingers."[39] The words leap from the page, asking us to understand the plight and the agony of the soldier, and perhaps war itself. Vera does not need to elaborate further the words she has heard.

Although doubly framed, this story seems to transmit the soldier's own words and act, factual and unchallenged: no words follow that sentence. Yet the implied originary "real" hidden within the Russian-doll frame story is more complex. The hand speaks before the man speaks. Once Petruha begins to talk with Vera, there is no interruption, no narrative framing. Even Petruha's own account embeds metanarrative features that imply a double articulation of his self-portrait: the axe that shines like a mirror reflects Petruha as well as the God to whom he prays, exposing the strangely contradictory combination of pacifism and violence that are knotted together in his story. Oddly then, the voice joins a mirror, slipping from one sense to the other, to tell Petruha's story. The violent gesture on which the story closes compresses feeling with a power of surprise and trauma beyond words. The silence of closure authorizes the voice that has preceded, giving Petruha himself the last word. Here, I suggest, Britnieva's narrative art and passion paradoxically convince us that these simple words and their erasure capture the patriotism and pain of Petruha.

The movement from the scribe who records the soldier's experience to the voice of the poetess, my second paradigm, is the comic topic of Edith Wharton's well-known sketch "Writing a War Story" (1919), which traces the re-writing and appropriation of the soldier's story by an ambitious young modernist woman. As Alice Kelly has argued, Wharton's war sketches written in 1918 satirise society women (ironic analogues of Wharton herself) who perform relief work. At the same time Wharton questions how a war story comes to be written at all. Hidden within this narrative lies a model like that of Fedorchenko or Sister Vera. Tongue in cheek, Wharton describes the struggles by would-be writer Ivy Spang, who while nursing in Paris, has contracted to produce an apparently female mixed genre: a "rousing ... tragedy with a happy ending," for a monthly.[40] But Ivy succumbs to writer's block, once she realizes that she does not know *how* a war story is written, *why* (and *where*) stories begin, or whether the "*subject*" matters at all. Part of Ivy's problem, of course, is that a conventional "war" story has a masculine subject. "How could your reader know what you were talking about when you didn't know yourself?" she worries.[41]

To solve her problem of knowledge, Ivy turns to the voices of others. Mademoiselle, her old French governess and now a nurse, offers Ivy a "shabby copybook" containing stories that the poor soldiers had told her "without any art at all." Mademoiselle has served as a nurse-amanuensis, who jotted down words "just as the soldiers told them to me" in the hospital ward.[42] The copyist cannot be an artist, if the result is to be true to life. In Ivy's view, the words that "poured on and on without a paragraph—a good deal like life," must now be transformed into "Literature."[43] So Ivy and Mademoiselle embellish the "rustic speech" of the soldier Emile Durand with academic flourishes and a sprinkling of "heart interest."[44] The result, a story titled "His Letter Home," doubly ventriloquizes and re-genders the soldier's account: first Mademoiselle turns it into grammatically correct academic French, then the poetess turns it into English "literature." This "re-voicing" of a soldier's oral account through the machinery of gender and of aesthetic conventions is precisely Wharton's satiric point. Truth and Art cannot coincide. Captain Harbard, one of the soldiers whom Spang visits in the ward laughs: "it's queer—it's puzzling. You've got hold of a wonderfully good subject . . . but you've rather mauled it, haven't you?"[45] Like his comrades, Harbard (himself a writer) asks for a photograph, substituting Ivy's body for her voice.

Wharton's ironic depiction of the woman writer as a parasitical "ivy," dependent on the male speaker, seems to confirm the gendered hierarchy, in which a man's autobiographical narrative provides the most authentic and powerful "war story," by contrast to a woman's esthetic fabrication. Jean Gallagher argues that women have traditionally been viewed as audiences rather than authors of war narratives. She writes that Wharton in "Writing a War Story" satirically "suggests that when they participate in the discourses of war, women must always be either the mimics of a soldier's voice or pure image, the silent objects of a soldier's desiring gaze."[46] Ivy Spang can be the subject of a story, as the novelist Harbard tells her, but cannot become an author herself. Yet Wharton gives that truth a twist by suggesting that Ivy's artistic incapacity is in part produced by the gendered genre she has been assigned by her male editor at the outset, when he told her what he needed was "a tragedy with a happy ending" for a Christmas issue.[47] Her effort has also been doomed in part by her male audience's insistence on reading and possessing her body rather than her words. And the old governess collaborates in educating Ivy into the flat conventions of academia that erase voice. Ultimately, however, Ivy is responsible for having made the soldiers' experiences "queer" without *queering* them. For she has taken the radical wartime paradigm of simple oral narrative and re-conventionalised it, banalised it, as a vehicle for the "charming" photograph. She has turned the screw in the wrong direction.

A similar theme opens Wharton's newly discovered "Field of Honour," which lay unpublished nearly one hundred years, in the impersonal third-person line, "It is over a year since the war began; and in that year some life-histories have got themselves written."[48] This ostensibly anonymous process of getting one's "history" written pointedly mocks how war experience is recorded. The life history Wharton has in mind is that of an American woman, released to enjoy herself by the departure of her French aristocratic husband for the front. This odd phrasing, which occults authorship, also momentarily deceives us by substituting the experiences of a woman for the memories men bring back from the front.[49] The fragment thus depicts the frivolity of a woman who profits from the war but does not understand it or the man who will find meaning in a senseless war.

So what would it mean to "queer" a soldier's voice? I suggest that we may find a third position in the self-division of an observer who listens, or who casts light, like Diogenes, with her lantern, as she asks herself questions. By splitting the voice of the narrator, such narratives make possible a rupture in our understanding of war and the meaning of men's stories about war. A number of women's medical accounts use dialogues with soldiers to revise the memoirist's understanding of war and of her own task as a doctor or nurse, sworn to neutrality. Thus Doctor Tatiana Alexinsky ponders "the kindly attitude of our soldiers towards the enemy," which troubles her.[50] While she had felt hatred, "Our soldiers have given me, an 'intellectual,' a lesson.... 'What enemy, Sister? They have no arms,' our men said reproachfully."[51] When she receives kindness and help from a czarist officer whom she bitterly opposes, she is forced to recognize the complicated social alignments in war. While Alexinsky's record of her own growth in understanding lends depth to her narrative, it does not significantly challenge our understanding of voice or of the grounds of narrative.

My third paradigm, then, comes from Ellen La Motte's "trenchant and sometimes bitter" sketches in *The Backwash of War* (1916), which destabilize the voice of the nurse-narrator when she retells what she hears from the soldiers and medical workers. A trained nurse herself and a friend of avant-garde writers Gertrude Stein and Mary Borden, La Motte's sketches were so ironic that they were suppressed when the United States entered the war. Reviewers from the *New York Times* and other papers found the book "revolting—even sickening at times," "unbearably horrible"—although one or two praised it because La Motte "exhibits with painful frankness the septic, gangrenous aspects of war, which are, after all, just as true as its inspiring, red-blooded side."[52] The reviewers thus perceived a dual, even antithetical truth in La Motte's narrative. That duality can be traced in her depiction of men's voices as well as in her representation of the narrative voice. "Heroes," La Motte's opening story, exemplifies her almost cubist narrative approach to multiplying the voices of male experience in war. Most important, the patient does not speak at all, although his primary act is read as a form of speech. While La Motte opens omnisciently from inside the soldier's mind with a description of his suicide attempt, that action is then immediately judged in the second half of the sentence, from outside: "When he could stand it no longer, he fired a revolver up through the roof of his mouth, but he made a mess of it."[53] Before the doctors can operate to extract the bullet, the patient must be bound and gagged to control his violent resistance. That physical symbol of the repression of his mutiny breaks two teeth. The doctor then works to save his life, in order to allow the military command to execute him for betraying the nation. The nurse-narrator seamlessly juxtaposes annoyed reports by the ambulance men, the contempt of the surgeon in command, the disgust of the *Directrice* of the mobile hospital unit (on whom the patient spits out clots of blood, in an alternate mode of speech) and the voices of two patients, in order to compose her scene from multiple perspectives.

A night nurse carrying a lantern, like Diogenes, who may have overheard those voices in the surgical unit, then reflects during her rounds on the behaviour of her other patients and the meaning of heroism. Her third-person presence within a narrative that voices her perceptions resembles the cinematic experiments in "camera off" techniques by early filmmakers such as Dziga Vertov. She disturbs commonplace assumptions about what is "natural" in wartime, such as healing a man in order to execute him. "Since he had failed in the [suicide attempt], his life must be saved, he must be nursed back to health, until he was well enough to be stood up against a wall and shot. This is War. Things like this also happen in peace time, but not so obviously."[54] Ethical purpose in wartime becomes a tangle. The narrative voice seems here both to endorse the military command and to doubt its authority. The surgeon, who finds the soldier's implied desertion "incomprehensible"—since "in these days, it was so easy to die with honor upon the battlefield", highlights another underlying paradox.[55] A suicide mission is acceptable, but not suicide itself. The nurse contrasts the "joy" of nursing those who have been "mutilated for life" to the "nuisance" of nursing a man so he can be court-martialed. "Truly," she comments, "that seemed a dead-end occupation."[56] La Motte's enigmatic voice invites her readers to explore paths such as the defamiliarisation of a military medicine that heals a self-inflicted wound so that a man can be "stood up against a wall and shot."[57]

As she observes the flaws among her other patients, treated as heroes, she poses a series of questions: Had not they ideals? "Did they contrast, after all?" She wonders how their beliefs can fail to influence their daily lives, which seem "so ignoble, so petty, so commonplace."[58] Her questions pass the task of interpretation on to the reader, as they suggest the suicide may even be the true hero. In the final sentence La Motte moves from free indirect discourse to direct quotation: one nameless patient confidentially repeats a rumor to his friend: "Dost thou know, *mon ami,* that when we captured that German battery a few days ago, we found the gunners chained to their guns?"[59] By closing her story on that canard, a question that is also a metaphor for the plight of all soldiers, imprisoned by military service and political propaganda, La Motte challenges the soldier's knowledge. Like cropping in contemporary photography, or the *Neue Sachlichkeit,* La Motte's truncated narrative-frame forces that final soldier's sentence to the foreground, and strips away the sentimental clichés that obscure our view of war.

The privileged, quasi-omniscient position of the nurse shapes an even more disturbing sketch that La Motte titles "Women and Wives." Set in a field hospital ward during a rainstorm in Flanders, the story comes to life when one of the patients shows the nurse a photograph of his wife and child, triggering an exchange of images among the whole group. Such snapshots of family play iconic roles in war fiction: *All Quiet on the Western Front* lingers on the moment when Paul Bäumer is trapped in a shellhole with the Frenchman he has killed, and finds the amateur photographs of Gérard Duval's wife and daughter. In that intimacy, with that documentation of printer Duval's life in peacetime as a family man, Paul is forced to understand that "you are a man like me . . . now I see your wife and your face and our fellowship."[60] Not only does the photograph humanise the French enemy in Remarque's novel, but it also reveals the humanity of his killer, Paul, who values life rather than death and fellowship rather than enmity. The photos suggest the peacetime "real" that has been blurred and crumpled in soldiers' pockets and kits.

In La Motte's sketch, however, the scene of family photographs exchanged by the patients lying in their beds at "queer angles" evokes a bitterly ironic series of reflections by the nurse narrator. First, she comments negatively on the "pathetic little pictures . . . of common, working-class women," in order to underscore bitterly that in this "democratic" war "some serve in better places than others," and "the trenches are mostly reserved for men of the working class."[61] The shabby little pictures trigger longing, pathos and resignation. The narrator's voice harshly judges the "stupid" "little" home lives represented by the photographs, but also re-tells the account each man provides of his wife and his devotion to her. In a second section, the narrator turns to draw a contrast between certain "women" permitted at the front, and "wives," who are not permitted into the war zone, because they are "bad for the morale of the Army." Because a wife might reveal "disquieting, disturbing things" about the home front "she herself must be censored, not permitted to come."[62] Yet there are many women at the front, some Belgian, others who come on various pretexts, in order to "cheer and refresh the troops," "better ones for the officers, naturally." The narrator then explains how each of these loving soldier husbands has a woman at the front—the orderly, the clean blond surgeon, and even the old doctor (a grandfather) who "visits" "a little girl of fourteen"—as if a sexual night out were an innocent social visit. Her comment on her colleagues and her patients: "No, no, I don't understand." The narrator's incomprehension builds on the contrast between the soldiers' words and their actions to expose to us what she calls "the other side, the backwash" of war.[63]

La Motte goes beyond this double image of the men's stories, to treat transgressive sexual relations as a system in which women too are implicated as actors as well as victims. Her own life in a lesbian partnership with art collector Emily Chadbourne may have provided her with the ironic distance allowing her to play with inconsistent discourses about sexuality at the front.[64] She interpellates the readers, asking "Have you ever watched" girls greeting a regiment of men, and invites us to expose our views of women who "make fools of themselves" by prostituting themselves to soldiers, or who are forced by the occupying army to serve the men.[65] The narrator's voice has perplexed many readers, because she cynically judges the women at the front as well as the men, and insistently asks us to observe the matter for ourselves. Just as the story "Heroes" opens with a narrator whose voice seems aligned with the prejudices of those she works with, here too the narrator *performs* patriotic anti-German judgments, in order to underscore the logical inconsistencies embedded in such moralistic judgments. "Can't you see?" is one of her closing questions—and such oscillation between reaffirmation and questioning of conventional wartime discourse functions not just as a by-product of the self-contradictory positions she is exploring, but as an exhortation to the readers to examine ourselves.

We must, La Motte's question suggests, look at how gender is implicated in the war system. It is for this reason that she blurs the false distinction between common women and prostitutes, good women and "ruined" ones, as well as testing the relationship between men's words and their actions. La Motte's brief sketch about "Women and Wives" not only undercuts the soldiers' voices but challenges conventional hypocrisy about sexuality, about the soldier as a "bon père de famille," and about the hippocratic oath "Do no harm" in the context of war. The twists and turns in La Motte's narrative voice, I would suggest, disturb the truth claims that attach to soldiers' accounts of war, and queer the normative heterosexual foundations of militarist discourse. The classic neutrality, even neutered quality of the professional nurse's voice, the quality that Jane Marcus calls "anesthetic esthetic," undoes itself in order to undo assumptions about objectivity in the representation of war.

*

If we review the three different types of narrative position that I have outlined here, one of their most striking features is the reversal of several conventions of aesthetic and moral value. The ostensibly transparent transcription of the soldier's voice, exemplified by Fedorchenko, gives priority to the simple, illiterate soldier, whose scribal account appears to present a poetic yet primal image of war experience. Not a canonical high genre, but the low form of the peasant's tale achieves the greatest impact. By contrast, the second type of narrative, with its pretensions to aesthetic elegance and its self-conscious cultivation of the image of the "high" modernist artist herself, is mocked as a feminized misrepresentation of men's experiences. The third type, which I have exemplified here through the shifting, self-contradictory and self-doubting perspective of a nurse-philosopher, challenges the reader to recognize both the contradictory situation of a nurse practicing military medicine and the unreliability of the voice of the soldier in the stresses of war as well. Omnipresent qualities of greed, selfishness, or hypocrisy—the qualities that La Motte describes as "the backwash of war"—undercut any idealistic notion of truth and authenticity in the voices of both men and women. Her irony does not provide a clear perch for the reader, since it undercuts the narrator as well as the soldiers on whom her gaze falls.

The twists in La Motte's narrative voice, I suggest, disturb the truth claims that attach to soldiers' accounts of war. But we need to ask whether we should take the voices of literature as the Real. The images that signpost these narratives are all clues to the complexity of representation. Petruha's axe is both a mirror of God and the instrument of a cut that depicts identity as self-mutilation. The photo of Ivy interposes her body as an impediment to communication. And the lamp of the night nurse in "Heroes" very simply "goes out." We cannot overlook the machinery of representation in these stories, with their mirrors, displacements and deformations or rumors. The concept of "voice" itself has been queered.

Notes

1. Edith Wharton, "Writing a War Story," in *Lines of Fire: Women Writers of World War I*, ed. Margaret R. Higonnet (New York: Penguin Plume, 1999), 395.
2. Wharton, "Writing," 400.
3. Cru himself translated into English and modified his monumental work (he condensed the documentation but expanded his theses).
4. Jean Norton Cru, *War Books: A Study in Historical Criticism*, ed. Stanley J. Pincetl, Jr. and Ernest Marchand (San Diego, CA: San Diego State University Press, 1976), vi.
5. Cru, *War Books*, 3.
6. See Leonard Smith, *The Embattled Self: French Soldiers' Testimony of the Great War* (Ithaca: Cornell, 2007), 5.
7. Jean Norton Cru, *Témoins: essai d'analyse et critique des souvenirs de combattants édités en français de 1915 à 1928* (Paris: Les Étincelles, 1929).
8. Henri Barbusse, *Under Fire*, trans. Robin Buss (New York: Penguin, 2003), 155.
9. Henri Barbusse, *Le feu, journal d'un escadron* (Paris: Flammarion, 1965). "Y a quéqu'chose que j'voudrais te d'mander. Voilà la chose: si tu fais parler les troufions dans ton livre, est-ce que tu les f'ras parler comme ils parlent, ou bien est-ce que tu arrangeras ça, en lousdoc? C'est rapport aux gros mots qu'on dit . . ." "Je mettrai les gros mots à leur place, mon petit père, parce que c'est la vérité," 221–222.
10. Albert Thierry's heavily censored *Conditions de la paix* (1916) was printed after the 1918 armistice in a complete version. The Bibliothèque de France holds a copy of Marcelle Capy's published journalism with the original text restored. It is thought that Mary Borden's *Forbidden Zone* was not published because of censorship concerns.
11. The narrator gently calls Barque "mon petit père," substituting size for class difference and inflecting the relationship as familial.
12. See Hazel Hutchison, *The War That Used Up Words: American Writers and the First World War* (New Haven: Yale University Press, 2015).
13. Barbusse, *Under Fire*, 303. *Le Feu*, "Quand on parle de toute la guerre, songeait-il tout haut, c'est comme si on n'disait rien. Ça étouffe les paroles," 414.
14. Erich Maria Remarque, *All Quiet on the Western Front* (New York: Random House/Fawcett, 1929), 165. In German: ". . . es ist eine Gefahr für mich, wenn ich diese Dinge in Worte bringe, ich habe Scheu, dass sie dann riesenhaft werden und sich nicht mehr bewältigen lassen." Erich Maria Remarque *Im Westen nichts Neues* (1929; Frankfurt/Main: Ullstein 1992), 119–120.
15. Margaret R. Higonnet, *Nurses at the Front: Writing the Wounds of the Great War* (Boston: Northeastern UP, 2001), xxvii.
16. Elsa Brändström, *Unter Kriegsgefangenen in Russland und Sibirien, 1914–1920*, trans. Margarete Klante, (Berlin: Deutsche Verlagsgesellschaft für Politik und Geschichte M.B.H., 1922); Elsa Brändström, *Among Prisoners of War in Russia & Siberia*, trans. C. Mabel Rickmers; Pref. Nathan Söderblom (London: Hutchinson, 1929). Anne-Marie Wenzel, *Deutsche Kraft in Fesseln: Fünf Jahre deutscher Schwesterndienst* in Sibirien (1916–1921) (Potsdam: Ernte-Verlag,

1931). Gräfin Kinsky Nora, *Russisches Tagebuch: 1916–1918*, Pref. Fürstin Gina von Liechtenstein, ed. Hans Graf Huyn. (Stuttgart-Degerloch: Seewald, 1976).
17. Nurses' sketches shape a different genre from the group portrait painted by George Duhamel, whose control or mastery as doctor shapes the tone and narrative curve of the sketches. For French transcriptions of conversations, see Jeanne Antelme's group autobiography *Soldats de France; simples esquisses*, 2e éd. (Paris: Delagrave, c1915); also Mme Emmanuel Colombel, *Journal d'une Infirmiere d'Arras, aout-septembre-octobre 1914* (Paris: Bloud et Gay, 1916), 72–73, 100–102.
18. Cru, *War Books*, 2.
19. Sofia Fedorchenko, *Ivan Speaks*, trans. Thomas Whittemore (Boston: Houghton Mifflin, 1919). Sofia Fedorchenko, *Narod na voinie*: frontovyĭa zapisi (Kiev: Izd. Izdatelsk, 1917). [N.B. Harvard Library transliteration of Russian name Софья Федорченко]
20. Whittemore, iii. Her preface explains that she gathered her material in 1915–1916 while in Poland and Galicia, largely recording conversations among the soldiers in shorthand. Extracts appeared in a Petrograd journal in January 1917, then in 1919 in the volume published at Kiev. The French translator praises it as the greatest Russian war book, marked by its fidelity and exactitude.
21. Karen Petrone calls the book a "fictionalized ethnography." *The Great War in Russian Memory* (Bloomington: Indiana University Press, 2011), 139.
22. Fedorchenko, *Ivan*, 3.
23. Fedorchenko, *Ivan*, 5.
24. Fedorchenko, *Ivan*, 20–21,
25. Fedorchenko, *Ivan*, 22.
26. Fedorchenko, *Ivan*, 26.
27. Fedorchenko, *Der Russe Redet: Aufzeichnungen nach dem Stenogramm*, trans. Alexander Eliasberg (Munich: Drei Masken, 1923), 9.
28. Sophie Fedortchenko, *Le peuple à la guerre. Propos de soldats russes recueillis par une infirmière*, adapted by Lydia Bach and Charles Reber (Paris: Valois, 1930), 7. My translation.
29. Sofia Fedorchenko, *Ivan Speaks*, trans. Thomas Whittemore (Boston: Houghton Mifflin, 1919), iii.
30. "Das Material für dieses Buch habe ich an der Front in den Jahren 1915–16 gesammelt. . . . In den meisten Fällen sind es Gespräche von Soldaten untereinander." Author's preface, *Der Russe redet: Aufzeichnungen nach dem Stenogramm von Ssofja Fedortschenko*, trans. Alexander Eliasberg (Munich: Drei Masken V, 1923), v.
31. See Eugenie Schwarzwald, *Neue Freie Presse* 12. November 1926, 13–14. "Es brennt unser Eingeweide."
32. Benjamin finds telling compression of the voices, whose narrative breadth has been condensed into fragments "in ihren unscheinbarsten Fragmenten noch liegt." The brief sketches enable the reader, "das wahre Antlitz dieses Krieges festzuhalten und sogar dies als das der Kreatur in Leiden . . . noch zu erkennen." http://www.textlog.de/benjamin-kritik-fedortschenko-russe-redet-aufzeichnungen-stenogramm.html (accessed March 28 2016).
33. Walter Benjamin, *Gesammelte Briefe, vol. 3, 1925–30*, ed. Christoph Gödde and Henri Lonitz (Frankfurt: Suhrkamp, 1997), 233. See Ansgar Hillach, "'Der Russe Redet', Das Dokument einer Lazarettschwester im Ersten Weltkrieg," in *Was nie geschrieben wurde, lesen: Frankfurter Benjamin-Vorträge*, ed. Lorenz Jäger and Thomas Regehly (Bielefeld: Aisthesis, 1992), 51.
34. Walter Benjamin, "The Storyteller," in *Illuminations*, ed. Hannah Arendt, trans. Harry Zohn (New York: Schocken, 1969), 84.

35. Marie Dugard, "Avant-propos," in *Âmes françaises, pages vécues*. Illus. Andrée Karpelès (Paris: Fischbacher, 1917), v–vi.
36. Note the self-censorship: "Pour une belle jambe, c'est une belle jambe! . . . y a pas à dire le contraire, c'est du travail bien f . . tu!" Dugard *Âmes*, 33.
37. Dugard, *Âmes*, 14.
38. Maria Britnieva, "Sister Vera's Story," in *One Woman's Story* (London: Barker, 1934), 46–47.
39. Britnieva, "Sister Vera's Story," 48.
40. Wharton, "Writing," 392.
41. Wharton, "Writing," 393.
42. Wharton, "Writing," 395.
43. Wharton, "Writing," 395.
44. Wharton, "Writing," 396.
45. Wharton, "Writing," 400.
46. Jean Gallagher, *The World Wars through the Female Gaze* (Carbondale: Southern Illinois UP, 1998), 13.
47. Wharton, "Writing," 392.
48. Edith Wharton, "The Field of Hour," *TLS*, 4 November 2015 http://www.the-tls.co.uk/tls/public/article1628382.ece
49. See Alice Kelly. Yale Nov 2015 "The Field of Honour."
50. Tatiana Alexinsky, *With the Russian Wounded* (London: T. Fisher Unwin, 1916), 64.
51. Alexinsky, *With the Russian*, 66.
52. Margaret R. Higonnet, "Introduction," in *Nurses at the Front: Writing the Wounds of the Great War*, ed. Margaret R. Higonnet (Boston: Northeaster University Press, 2001), xxv.
53. Ellen La Motte, "Heroes," *Nurses at the Front*, 5.
54. La Motte, "Heroes," 5.
55. La Motte, "Heroes," 6.
56. La Motte, "Heroes," 7.
57. La Motte, "Heroes," 5.
58. La Motte, "Heroes," 8, 9.
59. La Motte, "Heroes," 11.
60. Remarque, *All Quiet*, 223. "Jetzt sehe ich erst, dass du ein Mensch bist wie ich—jetzt sehe ich deine Frau und dein Gesicht und das Gemeinsame." Erich Maria Remarque *Im Westen nichts Neues* (1929; Frankfurt/Main: Ullstein, 1992), 158.
61. La Motte, "Women and Wives," *Nurses at the Front*, 41.
62. La Motte, "Women and Wives," 43.
63. La Motte, "Women and Wives," 44.
64. Robert S. Nelson, "The Art Collecting of Emily Crane Chadbourne and the Absence of Byzantine Art in Chicago," in *To Inspire and Instruct, a History of Medieval Art in Midwestern Museums*, ed. Christine Nelsen (Newcastle: Cambridge Scholars, 2008), 131–148.
65. La Motte, "Women and Wives," 45–46.

Bibliography

Alexinsky, Tatiana. *With the Russian Wounded*. London: T. Fisher Unwin, 1916.
Barbusse, Henri. *Le feu : journal d'un escadron*. Paris: Flammarion, 1965.
Barbusse, Henri. *Under Fire* trans. Robin Buss. New York: Penguin, 2003.
Benjamin, Walter. "The Storyteller." *Illuminations*. Ed. Hannah Arendt, trans. Harry Zohn. New York: Schocken, 1969. 83–109.

Benjamin, Walter. *Gesammelte Briefe, vol. 3, 1925–30*. Ed. Christoph Gödde and Henri Lonitz. Frankfurt: Suhrkamp, 1997.

Benjamin, Walter. Rreview of Fedortchenko, "Der Russe redet," *Die literarische Welt*. http://www.textlog.de/benjamin-kritik-fedortschenko-russe-redet-aufzeichnungen-stenogramm.html. Internet. March 28 2016.

Britnieva, Maria. *One Woman's Story*. London: Barker, 1934.

Cru, Jean Norton. *Témoins: essai d'analyse et critique des souvenirs de combattants édités en français de 1915 à 1928*. Paris: Les Étincelles, 1929.

Cru, Jean Norton. *War Books: A Study in Historical Criticism*. Ed. by Stanley J. Pincetl, Jr. and Ernest Marchand. San Diego, CA: San Diego State University Press, 1976.

Dugard, Marie. "Avant-propos." *Âmes françaises, pages vécues*. Illus. Andrée Karpelès. Paris: Fischbacher, 1917. v–vi.

Fedorchenko, Sofia. *Ivan Speaks*. Trans. Thomas Whittemore. Boston: Houghton Mifflin, 1919.

Fedorchenko, Sofia. *Der Russe redet: Aufzeichnungen nach dem Stenogramm von Ssofja Fedortschenko*. Trans. Alexander Eliasberg. Munich: Drei Masken, 1923.

Fedorchenko, Sofia. *Le peuple à la guerre. Propos de soldats russes recueillis par une infirmière*. Adapted by Lydia Bach and Charles Reber. Paris: Valois, 1930.

Gallagher, Jean. *The World Wars through the Female Gaze*. Carbondale: Southern Illinois UP, 1998.

Higonnet, Margaret R. *Nurses at the Front: Writing the Wounds of the Great War*. Boston: Northeastern UP, 2001.

Hillach, Ansgar. "'Der Russe Redet', Das Dokument einer Lazarettschwester im Ersten Weltkrieg." *Was nie geschrieben wurde, lesen: Frankfurter Benjamin-Vorträge*. Ed. Lorenz Jäger and Thomas Regehly. Bielefeld: Aisthesis, 1992. 43–58.

Hutchison, Hazel. *The War That Used Up Words: American Writers and the First World War*. New Haven: Yale University Press, 2015.

La Motte, Ellen. "Heroes." *Nurses at the Front: Writing the Wounds of the Great War*. Boston: Northeastern University Press, 2001. 5–11.

La Motte, Ellen. "Women and Wives." *Nurses at the Front: Writing the Wounds of the Great War*. Boston: Northeastern University Press, 2001. 39–48.

Nelson, Robert S. "The Art Collecting of Emily Crane Chadbourne and the Absence of Byzantine Art in Chicago." *To Inspire and Instruct, a History of Medieval Art in Midwestern Museums*. Ed. Christine Nelsen. Newcastle: Cambridge Scholars, 2008. 131–148.

Petrone, Karen. *The Great War in Russian Memory*. Bloomington: Indiana UP, 2011.

Remarque, Erich Maria. *All Quiet on the Western Front*. New York: Random House/Fawcett, 1929.

Remarque, Erich Maria. *Im Westen nichts Neues*. 1929; Frankfurt/Main: Ullstein, 1992.

Schwarzwald, Eugenie. *Neue Freie Presse* 12. November 1926, 13–14.

Smith, Leonard. *The Embattled Self: French Soldiers' Testimony of the Great War*. Ithaca: Cornell, 2007.

Wharton, Edith, "Writing a War Story." *Lines of Fire: Women Writers of World War I*. Ed. Margaret R. Higonnet. New York: Penguin Plume, 1999. 390–400.

Wharton, Edith. "The Field of Honour." *TLS* 4 November 2015. http://www.the-tls.co.uk/tls/public/article1628382.ece.

7 Pacifist Writer, Propagandist Publisher
Rose Macaulay and Hodder & Stoughton[1]

Lise Jaillant

Although Rose Macaulay (1881–1958) was a prolific, well-known and well-connected writer, few of her texts are remembered today. As Hermione Lee notes, "she is read now, if at all, for her haunting post-war novel, *The World My Wilderness*, for two excellent travel books, *They Went to Portugal* and *Fabled Shore* (on Spain) and her last novel, *The Towers of Trebizond*, partly set in Turkey."[2] One of her earlier novels, *Non-Combatants and Others* (1916), is nearly forgotten, and yet, it offers a rare opportunity to listen to voices that have been excluded from the dominant representations of the First World War. "In the years after the Armistice," Janet Watson notes, "women and non-combatants were pushed out of the history of the war, which became exclusively a 'soldier's story,' incomprehensible to everyone else."[3] Written during the conflict, *Non-Combatants and Others* tells an alternative story from a female perspective, a story dominated by pacifism. As Sarah LeFanu argues, it is a striking example of a disillusioned narrative on the war—published more than ten years before the boom of debunking war books by Siegfried Sassoon and others.[4]

Surprisingly, the novel appeared under the Hodder & Stoughton imprint. Macaulay, a vocal pacifist, and Hodder & Stoughton, a publisher closely associated with propaganda—this has always seemed an improbable match, but nobody has ever scrutinized this partnership. Why did Macaulay choose such a firm for her anti-war novel? Why did Hodder & Stoughton accept to bring out a novel that was so critical of the war? Although Macaulay had already published two books with this firm before 1916, Hodder & Stoughton was under no obligation to issue a novel that did not fit in its list. The history of publishing, on both sides of the Atlantic, is full of examples of publishers rejecting books from established authors, even when under contract. For instance, Macmillan turned down H.G. Wells' controversial novel *Ann Veronica* (published by Unwin in 1909) while Horace Liveright rejected Ernest Hemingway's *The Torrents of Spring*, ignoring his contract with the author.

So why did Macaulay and Hodder & Stoughton continue with such an unlikely partnership? It is difficult to answer this question conclusively, because the Hodder & Stoughton archive was bombed during the Second

World War (only a profit and loss ledger survives in the London Metropolitan Archives). The Rose Macaulay papers at the University of Cambridge do not contain any correspondence with her publisher. There are a few letters for the year 1916 in the archive, but they do not tell us anything about the publishing history of *Non-Combatants and Others*. The same could be said of the Macaulay letters at the Harry Ransom Center in Austin, Texas. Yet, it is possible to piece together parts of the story by looking at quantitative information (including sales figures and advertising figures) in the Hodder & Stoughton profit and loss ledger. Advertisements and reviews of the book show that the publisher did not market *Non-Combatants and Others* as an anti-war novel, but rather as a "romance" probably for a female readership. Macaulay's novel was advertised alongside the short stories of "Sapper"—a writer who has often been described as a propagandist.

Rose Macaulay's Association with Hodder & Stoughton

That Rose Macaulay chose a career as a writer came as no surprise to anyone in her family. Her father was a lecturer in English at the University of Cambridge and she was also related to the historian T.B. Macaulay. As LeFanu puts it, "in a household with a father who was a published scholar and where both parents valued literary culture, Rose had been the most bookish of the children, the one in whom her parents' literary aspirations were most clearly expressed."[5] Macaulay went to Somerville College, Oxford, where she read modern history. Her first poems appeared in the *Westminster Gazette*, and in 1906, John Murray IV, a very traditional publisher who was also an Eton contemporary of her father, issued her first novel, *Abbots Verney*. Macaulay stayed with the same publisher for her first five novels, from 1906 to 1911.

In N.N. Feltes' words, John Murray was a "list publisher" that focussed on its backlist as a steady source of income.[6] The main objective was not to make money, but to avoid losing money. Unsurprisingly, John Murray spent little to advertise the books of a young unknown writer such as Rose Macaulay. A search in the *Times Literary Supplement* reveals that her name did not appear in the newspaper until 1912—when her novel *The Lee Shore* was published by Hodder & Stoughton, an "entrepreneurial" imprint turned towards literary coups.

The thirty-one-year-old Rose Macaulay had just won the first prize of the £1,000 Hodder & Stoughton competition (open to all authors) for this intellectual novel about the opposition between the "Haves" and the "Have Nots." Despite having already written and published several novels, Macaulay was still presented as "the daughter of Mr G.C. Macaulay, Lecturer in English at Cambridge University."[7] It was not uncommon for a woman to be branded under male tutelage, and the reference to the Macaulay family name might have been a cheap way to get attention and publicity.[8] For an almost unknown writer, the widely advertised prize was of course excellent publicity. It also placed Hodder & Stoughton in the spotlight, at the time when an increasing number of would-be and beginning writers were competing for a chance to get published. The *Bookseller* thus declared: "the supply of moderately meritorious fiction is nowadays so exceedingly ample that its producers are in the same position as all other persons who are unfortunate enough to have for sale an article with which the market happens to be overstocked."[9] For all these literary aspirants, the Hodder & Stoughton prize offered the promise of money and fame. Macaulay was awarded £600—the equivalent of £53,000 today[10]—which helped her buy a flat in London and live on her own for the first time. Not only did she suddenly become financially independent, her novel was widely advertised (including in the *Daily Mail*—whose circulation figure was approaching 950,000)[11] and reviewed. The *TLS* thus described it as "a very charming story."[12]

After six years of obscurity, Macaulay must have felt very grateful to Hodder & Stoughton for helping her break through as a successful writer. Responding to a message of congratulations from S.C. Roberts (an old family friend and head of Cambridge University Press), she wrote "I am extremely delighted to have so much money all at once."[13] John Murray also magnanimously congratulated her, and she wrote him:

> The book isn't a good one, as a matter of fact, but fortunately the taste of the judges can't be very good either, so all was well. **Perhaps it may make my future books sell better than the past ones—Hodder and Stoughton seemed to think it probably would, so I hope it will.** Though I don't believe my books will ever sell really well. The results of this competition surprised me very much. I sent in mine because I thought it was more fun to, and I never thought it had a chance and was contemplating approaching you with it in the autumn after I got it back rejected![14] (emphasis added)

Here, Macaulay insisted on Hodder & Stoughton's confidence in the commercial potential of her books, but she perhaps underestimated the risks attached to working with such a commercially orientated publisher. Up to 1912, Macaulay had positioned herself as a serious writer published by a venerable, "list" publisher. The £1,000 competition placed her in an entirely different category—that of the bestselling author associated with an "enterprising" publisher eager to maximize profit. The transition between these two extreme positions in the literary field was so brutal that it inspired this unflattering commentary in the *Saturday Review*:

> The astonishing and perplexing thing is to find a book of this class winning a competition that is presumably run on sound commercial lines. Its class is that of the book charming rather than good, sympathetic rather than provocative; a class in which there exist many novels better than this, some of them published during this year. In saying this we have no intention of decrying Miss Macaulay's work, but we cannot

help suspecting that she must feel surprised at this novel having earned at a blow at least as much as any of her previous books.[15]

The reviewer implied that the Hodder & Stoughton prize was a mixed blessing for Macaulay: it boosted the sales of her novel, but it also associated her with a different sub-section of the literary sphere traditionally seen as unsophisticated (*"symbolically* excluded and discredited," in Pierre Bourdieu's terms).[16] On 3 August 1912, for example, readers of the *Daily Mail* encountered an advertisement for *The Lee Shore* (Figure 7.1) on the same page as a sensational new feuilleton, "Every Woman's Sin." Whether or not Macaulay was aware of the risks of being associated with the "field of large-scale production,"[17] she made the decision to leave John Murray and went on to publish her next novel, *The Making of a Bigot*, with Hodder & Stoughton in 1914.

The modernity of Macaulay's topics and style is arguably what attracted Hodder & Stoughton. For a firm known for popular page-turners, publishing a trendy modern writer added prestige to its list but also carried some risks. Perhaps to reassure readers who might be intimidated by or hostile to the new literature, one advertisement mentioned *The Making of a Bigot* below Morice Gerard's *A Heather Mixture*—"a fascinating romance of love and adventure" (Figure 7.2). In sum, the partnership between Macaulay and Hodder & Stoughton was mutually beneficial—but also risky due to their different positionings in the literary field. The publication of *Non-Combatants and Others* in 1916 made these differences particularly obvious.

Non-Combatants and Others and Pacifism

Macaulay's novel tells the story of Alix—a young disabled woman who refuses to engage with the war at all, and spends most of her time drawing and socializing with her friends in art school. Her mother Daphne Sandomir is an important figure in the peace movement, although her exact allegiance is disputed: "she was called by some a Pacificist, by more a Pacifist."[18] As Sybil Oldfield puts it, "the pacifists totally renounced participation in any war; the 'pacificists' concentrated on the means of preventing war and of bringing wars to an end.'"[19] The name "Sandomir" is itself highly symbolic: Daphne's late husband was a "Polish liberationist,"[20] and as Shafquat Towheed points out, "Sandomir is the Latin of the Polish Sandomierz, which literally means 'to judge peace.'"[21] Alix's mother travels around the world, goes to peace conferences, and tries to convince important stakeholders that the war can be stopped. Her sister Eleanor (Alix's aunt) also leads a busy life. But instead of trying to stop the conflict, Eleanor takes part in the war effort as a member of various committees. Both Daphne and Eleanor are presented as healthy and full of purpose, if in opposition—whereas Alix is described as self-centred and neurotic through her lack of engagement either way ("narrow-hearted, selfish and indolent," in her mother's opinion).[22] In a

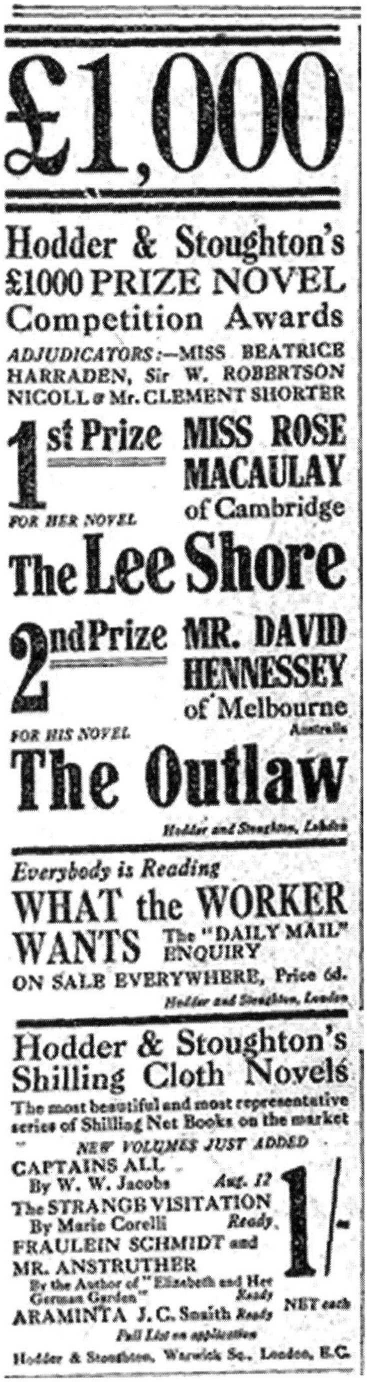

Figure 7.1 Advertisement for *The Lee Shore*, *Daily Mail*, 3 August 1912, 9.

Figure 7.2 Hodder & Stoughton advertisement, *Times Literary Supplement*, 12 March 1914, 123.

wartime context, the fact that she is disabled is highly significant. As Debra Rae Cohen points out, "writing in midwar, when disability cannot help but be read as an analogue for woundedness, Macaulay uses Alix's lameness to unsettle the distinctions between soldier and civilian, wounded and unwounded, male or female war experience, and ultimately to deconstruct the very notion of noncombatancy itself."[23]

The young woman is particularly shattered after the death of her brother Paul in France. She learns the true cause of his death by chance, when a soldier who had known her brother tells her:

> Of course there are some men out there who never ought to be there at all; not strong enough in body or mind. There was a man in my company; he was quite young; he'd got his commission straight from school; and he simply went to pieces when he'd been in and out of trenches for a few weeks.... I believe he saw his best friend cut to pieces by a bit of shell before his eyes. He kept being sick after that; couldn't stop. And ... it was awfully sad ... he took to exposing himself, taking absurd risks, in order to get laid out; every one noticed it. But he couldn't get hit; people sometimes can't when they go on like that, you know—it's a funny thing—and one night he let off his revolver into his own shoulder. I imagine he thought he wasn't seen, but he was, by several men, poor chap. No one ever knew whether he meant to do for himself, or only to hurt himself and get invalided back; anyhow things went badly and he died of it....[24]

Alix realizes that the man who has died of a self-inflicted wound is in fact her brother. This life-changing event forces her to question her passivity and to become gradually more involved in efforts to stop the war. Likewise, Alix's surviving brother, a journalist, rejects the jingoism of the press and the sentimentality of war poetry (a "flood of cheap heroics and commonplace patriotic claptrap").[25]

Macaulay's description of the peace movement is grounded in the historical context of the time. For example, we learn that Daphne Sandomir "tried, but failed, like so many others, to attend the Women's International Congress at the Hague."[26] The Congress was an actual event that took place in April 1915 with female delegates from most combatant nations.[27] One hundred eighty British women applied to attend, including many well-known political personalities such as Emmeline Pethick Lawrence—although the government took punitive measures and refused passports to most of them. Despite the obvious difficulty in organising an international conference in war-torn Europe, the congress took place as planned in the neutral territory of the Hague and produced resolutions that may have been influential. As "the first international meeting to outline what the principles of any peace settlement should be,"[28] it allegedly inspired the Fourteen Points outlined by the American president Woodrow Wilson after the conflict. When Macaulay was writing her novel, the peace movement was still highly controversial. Accused of being "pro-German," Daphne Sandomir struggles to convey her message as hecklers interrupt her meetings: "those who believed themselves to differ would shout 'Fight to a finish,' and 'Crush all Germans,' and 'Smash the Hun, *then* you may talk of peace,' and 'Here's some soldiers back here, you hear what *they've* got to say about it,' and other things to the same purpose; and once or twice they sang patriotic songs so loud that the meeting closed in disorder."[29] *Non-Combatants and Others* can therefore be seen as a space of dialogue on the peace question, at the time when the issue could hardly be discussed in the public sphere.

The title of the novel is also a reminder that "non-combatants" are in fact immersed in the conflict. Susan Grayzel notes that the term "home front" appeared at that time: "as the innovation of applying the adjectives 'home' or 'domestic' to the military term 'front' would suggest, the First World War involved civilians in a way not found in any previous modern European war."[30] It is precisely this involvement in the war that Alix tries to avoid, without success. For the hyper-sensitive young woman, the war is felt as an attack on her senses. Visual reminders are everywhere—from the uniforms of her cousins (Dorothy "in her V.A.D. dress" and Margot "in the khaki uniform of the Women's Volunteer Reserve")[31] to the Kitchener posters on the walls of a recruiting station ("Alix, looking down, met the hypnotic stare of the Great Man pictured on the walls").[32] Walking through Chancery Lane—which has been devastated by an air raid—Alix is stopped by a newspaper vendor: "*Star*, lady? *Globe, Pall Mall, Evening News*? British fail to hold conquered trenches. . . ."[33] These visual and aural stimuli have a direct impact on Alix's nerves (a term repeated twenty-two times in the novel). As the sociologist Georg Simmel had noted in his 1903 essay "The Metropolis and Mental Life," the experience of modernity is characterised by an over-stimulation of the senses. The war adds new stimuli to the existing chaos of modern life, leaving Alix in a state of "nervous breakdown." Her brother Nicholas tells her:

> The war's playing the devil with your nerves, that's what it means. You do things and feel things and say things, I dare say, that you wouldn't have once, but that you can scarcely help now. You're only one of many, you know—one of thousands. The military hospitals are full of them; men who come through plucky and grinning but with their nerves shattered to bits.[34]

Here, Alix's experience is explicitly compared to that of soldiers, blurring the distinction between non-combatants and combatants. Like Julia in H.D.'s *Bid Me to Live*—a character that Trudi Tate has described as "a civilian war neurotic"[35]—Alix is unable to maintain a sense of balance. Having failed to isolate herself from the conflict, she decides to join her mother's peace campaign, a campaign set in military terms. "We're fighting war, to the best of our lights, and with the weapons at our command," as Daphne tells her daughter.[36]

In the novel, the fight for peace is closely related to a feminist agenda.[37] Before the war, Daphne Sandomir was active in the defence of a wide range of causes—including the "economic and constitutional position of women."[38] When explaining her vision for a peaceful society, she presents women as individuals rather than "the guardians of the race or the custodians of life."[39] Unlike other militants, she refuses to essentialise women's role: "she took women as human beings, not as life-producing organisms."[40] Alix is herself deeply influenced by the women's rights movement. During her stay at a distant cousin's in London, she meets people who hold a much more conservative outlook than that of her close family and friends. Having "hitherto moved in circles where every one thought, as a matter of course, that [women] ought to have the vote,"[41] Alix observes these acquaintances making fun of Rachel Simon, a young woman with a suffragette past. Despite Alix's lack of reaction, Rachel feels they share the same vision. After being publicly ridiculed, she bursts into tears and says: "You won't *see* . . . You, none of you *see*. Except her—she indicated Alix—and she won't talk; she only smiles to herself at all of us."[42] As the novel progresses, Alix gradually reconciles her feminist vision and her actions—with a commitment to join her mother's fight for peace and for women's rights, and in so doing, rejects silence.

By the time she completed the novel, Rose Macaulay had become entirely disenchanted with the war. In April 1915, her friend Rupert Brooke, who had joined the navy, was bitten on the lip by a mosquito and quickly died of blood poisoning. As LeFanu points out,

> he was six years younger than her but very much more sophisticated. For some time, they'd been rivals in the poetry pages of the *Westminster Gazette* and he'd introduced Rose—who still lived at home with her parents—to his friends in literary London.[43]

In May, shortly after learning about Brooke's death, Macaulay enrolled as a VAD at a military convalescent home in Great Shelford near Cambridge. Her sister Jean thought it was "a mad choice" because Rose could not stand the sight of blood or even distressing stories. Then in July, her father suffered a stroke and died suddenly. For LeFanu, "the novel that she started writing soon afterwards was imbued of a sense of personal grief, alongside a simmering anger at a society that preferred not to listen to the testaments of the soldiers sacrificing their lives on its behalf."[44]

Macaulay's disastrous experience as a volunteer nurse undoubtedly inspired the character of Alix. When her cousin John Orme (on leave after being wounded at the front) wakes up in his sleep, his eyes "now wide and wet, and full of a horror beyond speech," Alix reacts by being "suddenly and violently sick."[45] The author and her character also share their gradual evolution towards pacifism. At the beginning of the war, Macaulay wrote several poems that present the war as an exciting adventure. For example, her poem "Many Sisters to Many Brothers" deals with a woman's sense of being excluded from the action:

> Oh it's you that have the luck, out there in blood and muck:
> You were born beneath a kindly star;

> All we dreamt, I and you, you can really go and do,
> And I can't, the way things are.
> In a trench you are sitting, while I am knitting
> A hopeless sock that never gets done.
> Well, here's luck, my dear;—and you've got it, no fear;
> But for me . . . a war is poor fun.[46]

As Nicoletta Gullace notes, this "feeling of being left behind and left out that was experienced by many women at home" led to "demands for female combatant service."[47] For many middle-class women, nursing came to be seen as a parallel to military service, a chance to contribute to the war effort at home and abroad.

Like Vera Brittain, Macaulay's initial enthusiasm for the war was replaced by a long-standing commitment to pacifism. But whereas Brittain's disillusionment is a product of the post-war years, Macaulay adopted an anti-war position in the middle of the conflict. In a recent radio interview, Sarah LeFanu has presented *Non-Combatants and Others* as a precursor to the disillusioned war novels of the late 1920s:

> It came out in 1916—predating by more than ten years those memoirs and novels by Edmund Blunden, Siegfried Sassoon, Robert Graves and others that alongside the works of the war poets have become the foundational texts for our perception and understanding of the war. Those books of course were written by men who served as soldiers. Each was shaped and mediated through a later post-war process of reflection. Rose Macaulay's novel is very different. Not only was it written and set in 1915 but unlike those canonical works of fiction and memoir that show the war as experienced by those fighting it, it shows us the war as experienced by those watching it: the non-combatants.[48]

Indeed, Macaulay's novel gives us a chance to listen to voices from the margins, voices that we do not traditionally associate with the Great War. *Non-Combatants and Others* is not a "soldier's story," unlike later accounts of the war. Janet Watson notes that from the late 1920s, "veterans who were not in the infantry, other active non-combatants, and especially women reimagined themselves as survivors surrounded by devastating carnage (whether physical or emotional). They were writing their own soldier's stories."[49] In addition to presenting nursing as a form of military service, Brittain's *Testament of Youth* also carries an unambiguous pacifist message—whereas *Non-Combatants and Others* echoes a wider range of voices. Commenting on the "polyphonic nature" of Macaulay's novel, Angela K. Smith associates this formal experimentation with other modernist texts such as Virginia Woolf's *To the Lighthouse*.[50] For Smith, these multiple voices diminish the authority of the omniscient narrator, resulting in an ambivalent message. I would add that Alix's disillusioned voice remains dominant in the novel and gives it a strong pacifist tone.

Macaulay became an enthusiastic supporter of the work of the League of Nations Union and from 1936, an active member of the Peace Pledge Union (PPU). But, as Martin Ferguson Smith points out, "she found it hard to be consistent and thoroughgoing in her advocacy of pacifism."[51] Her six-page PPU pamphlet *An Open Letter to a Non-Pacifist* (1937) is riddled with contradictions. "No pacifist (that I know of) objects to a certain amount of coercion," declared Macaulay. "What pacifists object to is the use of savage and murderous weapons of injury and assault to gain victory over their opponents."[52] Macaulay resigned her PPU sponsorship in March 1938, when German troops invaded Austria. However, she never entirely renounced her pacifist convictions. In 1951, she wrote to her friend, the Reverend John Hamilton Cowper Johnson:

> When do we get to the point of rejecting War? I have long felt that one great international gesture would be worth while; saying, just once, to potential aggressors, "Go ahead if you must and do your worst; we do not intend to behave like barbarians, whatever barbarians may do to us." This might mean occupation and domination by some barbarian power like Russia; very unpleasant, pernicious and horrible; but could not be more so than waging war ourselves, with all its cruel atrocities.[53]

This echoes a central theme of *Non-Combatants and Others*: the commitment to "the principles of international justice and permanent peace."[54]

Hodder & Stoughton's Marketing Strategy

Although it did not call for an immediate end to the war, *Non-Combatants and Others* can be described as a pacifist novel—but Hodder & Stoughton downplayed this pacifism and marketed the book as a romance, presumably for an audience of female readers. An announcement in the *Times Literary Supplement* thus declared:

> The war . . . colours the autumn fiction to come from Messrs. Hodder and Stoughton, whose forthcoming announcements include a new volume by "Sapper," entitled *Men, Women and Guns*, to come next month; a smaller collection of soldier stories by A. Neil Lyons, entitled *A Kiss from France*, intended as a companion volume to *Kitchener Chaps*; and *Non-Combatants*, by Rose Macaulay, **a romance of England during the war**. Mr John Buchan is also bringing out with the same publishers a companion story to *The Thirty-nine Steps* entitled *Greenmantle*, in which Mr Hannay recounts his further adventures on a mysterious mission to Berlin, Constantinople and the East."[55]

Macaulay's novel appeared on a list dominated by male writers who presented the war as a great adventure: "Sapper," A. Neil Lyons and John

Buchan. This is hardly surprising, considering Hodder & Stoughton's close links with propaganda. As Jane Potter has argued, the firm's director, Ernest Hodder Williams, and its editor and literary adviser, Sir William Robertson Nicoll, "had close personal ties to the corridors of power."[56] The Schedule of Wellington House Literature, kept at the Imperial War Museum, shows that Hodder & Stoughton published more than 130 pamphlets and books for the War Propaganda Bureau, a number unmatched by any other publishers.

Advertisements also show that Macaulay's novel was sold alongside books that offered a very different picture of the war. One advertisement in the *Manchester Guardian* is placed next to a photo of a British bombardment of the German trenches. It also includes a list of "some new and really worth while books on the war"—including *Doing their Bit*, about munitions factories at home, and Frances Wilson Huard's *My Home in the Field of Honour*: "This graphic and picturesque book is the first to pay adequate tribute to the glorious heroism of the women of France." *Non-Combatants and Others*, which is listed in the fiction category, is described as:

> A brilliant novel by a very clever author. The story deals especially with the point of view of a girl, and the different ways in which she tries taking the War, and the different attitudes of the people round her, and her relations with a man who is fighting.

There are two interesting things here: the first is the focus on the female voice (both the author and the main character are women); and the second is the emphasis on the romance between Alix and Basil. This focus on the love story shows that the publisher was probably targeting a female audience, in order to maximize the novel's commercial appeal. Novels such as *The Zeppelin Destroyer* appeared in the same fiction category. Again, the war is presented as an exciting adventure: "The War has produced no book more thrilling or more full of vivid pictures of exciting fights and hair-breadth escapes than *The Zeppelin Destroyer*."[57]

Post-War

Non-Combatants and Others was released at around the same time as Sapper's new collection of short stories, *Men, Women and Guns* (both books were sold for five shillings). "Sapper" was the pen name of Herman Cyril McNeile, a professional subaltern officer, who joined the army in 1907 and retired in 1919. His entire writing career and persona were influenced by the conflict: "Sapper" is a reference to his battalion, the Royal Engineers; he became famous for his short stories about the war ("amongst the very best that have come to us from the trenches," as the *Spectator* put it);[58] and he later sustained his popularity as the creator of Bulldog Drummond, an ex-officer who fights against England's post-war enemies. While Sapper did not shy away from describing the horrors of the conflict, he often used humour to tone down its most appalling aspects. For example, in the introduction to *Men, Women and Guns*, the narrator's old aunt asks him to describe what it feels like to be shelled:

> I drew her a picture—vivid, startling, wonderful. And when I had finished, the dear old lady looked at me.
> "Dreadful!" she murmured. "Did I ever tell you of the terrible experience I had on the front at Eastbourne, when my bath-chair attendant became inebriated and upset me?"[59]

In contrast, *Non-Combatants and Others* uses a style that contemporary reviewers often described as dry and unsentimental. Winifred Holtby thus declared that after the publication of *The Lee Shore*, "[Macaulay's] manner changed. She became, it seemed, frightened of sentiment, even of kindliness."[60] This modern style was well suited to convey her pacifist message, which anticipates the "War Books boom" of the late 1920s. As I have argued elsewhere, Sapper never came to share the disillusioned view on the war.[61]

Sapper's non-disillusioned narration fitted well with Hodder & Stoughton's list, and the publisher invested important resources to create interest in *Men, Women and Guns*. Sapper's book thus included an attractive coloured dust jacket, which contributed to its commercial appeal. *Non-Combatants and Others* had a much smaller print run, and it seems that there is no extant copy of its dust jacket. A *TLS* review mentions the contrast between the "charming" landscape represented on the paper cover and the rather depressing content of the book—another indication that Hodder & Stoughton was trying to downplay Macaulay's criticism of the war.[62]

Hodder & Stoughton spent four times more on advertising *Men, Women and Guns* than on *Non-Combatants and Others*.[63] In one advertisement, Sapper is presented as the author of *The Lieutenant and Others* and *Sergeant Michael Cassidy*—"of which over 200,000 have already been printed."[64] And like Sapper's previous books, *Men, Women and Guns* went on to become a bestseller, selling more than 146,000 copies in the ten years following its publication. In contrast, printing and advertising figures show that the publisher invested fewer and fewer resources to promote Macaulay's work. *The Lee Shore* was well advertised, it had a first printing of 9,000 copies (of which 7,873 were sold before the end of the financial year ending 31 March 1913), and it was reprinted in 1914 and 1915. For *The Making of a Bigot*, the advertising budget was a third less than for *The Lee Shore*,[65] the first printing was also lower (at around 5,000 copies), and there was no reprinting. For Macaulay's next novel, *Non-Combatants and Others*, the first printing was only 3,000 copies (three times less than the first printing of *The Lee Shore*), of which 2,586 had sold by 31 March 1917. The advertising budget plummeted to £49, which was 40% less than the advertising budget for *The Making of a Bigot*. The publisher made a modest profit of less than £49. This semi-failure probably explains why Macaulay moved to Constable for her next novel, *What Not*, and her poetry collection, *Three Days* (both published in 1919).[66]

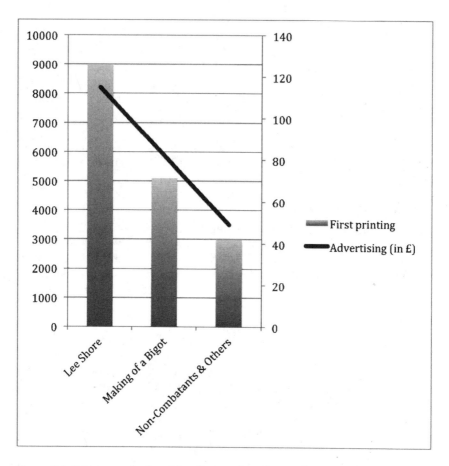

Figure 7.3 Printing and advertising figures, *Lee Shore*, *The Making of a Bigot* and *Non-Combatants and Others*.

Critical Reception

In *Virginia Woolf and the Great War*, Karen Levenback has argued that Macaulay's novel was a critical failure, which convinced Woolf to avoid any explicit criticism of the war when she was writing *To the Lighthouse*. According to Levenback:

> Woolf could not have forgotten that for all the post-war recognition afforded Macaulay (including being awarded the *Femina-Vie Heureuse* Prize in 1922), she would not have garnered such distinction had her reputation depended on the reception afforded to her civilian war novel *Non-Combatants and Others* (1916), an anti-war book so blasted by

the wartime press that when the smoke cleared, Macaulay had lost not only her publisher but her readers.[67]

Although it is certainly true that *Non-Combatants and Others* attracted some criticisms, there was no consensus. Negative reviews often described the book as too grim to be realistic. The *Times Literary Supplement* declared: "impossible as it is to exaggerate the misery and horror of these times, we feel that her note is, somehow, forced, and that her very style, with its careful elimination of sentimentality, contributes toward a general effect of exaggeration."[68] While the *Aberdeen Daily Journal* generally recommended Macaulay's book, the reviewer also pointed out that the "incident on pages 159–160" (when Alix feels sick after hearing the truth about her brother's death) "might have been omitted. The artist need not follow the photographer in including everything in his picture."[69] Interestingly, the reviewer did not question the truthfulness of this episode, but seemed to reject it on the ground of taste. The *Englishwoman*'s reviewer said Alix Sandomir's misery downplayed "all that is splendid or pitiful in life or death, belittling those who fight." The journalist also criticized Daphne Sandomir as one of those "who act from a nervous desire to be doing something different from the common task ... without any clear idea of the result of their activities." In real life, the reviewer argued, the conscientious home-front volunteers enjoy exhilaration and the comfort of "a good conscience."[70]

The *Dundee Courier* was much more enthusiastic. The review appeared alongside various news of the war, including the news of two "Dundee brothers killed in action." The reviewer wrote:

> Miss Rose Macaulay's new story, *Non-Combatants*, tells of the war as it reacts on people left at home; ... To anyone (and who has not?) having connections with the lads at the front this stirring volume will go far to heal many of the scars that now marr the mental outlook. Here, too, the afflicted one will find not a little to comfort at those moments when the brain goes out into the wilderness of despair.[71]

In this review, Macaulay's novel is presented as realistic rather than too gloomy. Similarly, *Everyman* described the novel as "one of those few novels which people will read in years to come in order to gain some idea of what the years 1914–16 really felt like to those who lived through them in England."[72] Unlike war books by Sapper or John Buchan, *Non-Combatants and Others* offered a female perspective on the domestic front. For the *Bookman*, "Alix of *Non-Combatants* ... is the woman of the war, with the 'blank misgivings of a creature' who looks on a mad world and its broken delights."[73]

These mixed reviews show that pacifism and disillusionment were discussed in mainstream venues, even during the conflict. This important fact has been largely neglected in histories of the war. For example, Janet Watson suggests that "novels and memoirs, in small but clearly noticeable numbers, began to be critical of the war soon after the Armistice." She adds: "they were still very much a minority view, however, and they failed to trigger a more general cultural response, despite their visibility in the literary community."[74] The phrase "minority view" could well apply to the alternative voices echoed in *Non-Combatants and Others*, a novel that failed to reach the mass audiences who read war books by Sapper or John Buchan.

Readers did not wait until 1928 and the "War Books boom" to become interested in non-heroic narratives on the war. "Traditional notions of 'heroism,'" as Angela K. Smith puts it, "are already presented as meaningless in this early novel."[75] Although there was a (small) audience for *Non-Combatants and Others*, Hodder & Stoughton was probably not the right kind of publisher for the book. As a mass-market publishing enterprise, it was ill prepared for a novel that foregrounded a range of voices from the margins. The publisher was very good at presenting the war as a great adventure: the dust jackets of Sapper's short stories, for instance, often show jovial characters smiling and having fun. This representation of the war could not apply to *Non-Combatants and Others*. Faced with a book so different from the rest of its list, Hodder & Stoughton tried to emphasise its most marketable aspects (such as the love story between Alix and Basil), ignoring its pacifist undertone. After the release of Macaulay's novel, the firm continued to issue propaganda that presented pacifists as politically naïve—for example Elizabeth Robins' 1919 novel *The Messenger*.[76] So why did Macaulay choose such a publisher for her anti-war novel? Why did Hodder & Stoughton accept to publish a novel that was so critical of the war? My answer is that Macaulay and Hodder & Stoughton were like an ill-assorted couple. They had a brief honeymoon in 1912, when *The Lee Shore* was published. And after that, cracks started to appear. The relative commercial failure of *Non-Combatants and Others* was the final blow that led to their divorce.

Notes

1. I am grateful to Ann-Marie Einhaus, Shafquat Towheed and the editors of this volume, who have read and commented on earlier versions of this essay.
2. Hermione Lee, "'Chattery, Chittery…Lean as a Rake,'" review of *Rose Macaulay*, by Sarah LeFanu, *Guardian*, June 14, 2003, accessed October 25, 2015, http://www.theguardian.com/books/2003/jun/14/featuresreviews.guardianreview11
3. Janet S.K. Watson, *Fighting Different Wars: Experience, Memory, and the First World War in Britain* (Cambridge: Cambridge UP, 2004), 10.
4. The edition edited by Sarah LeFanu (Capuchin Classics, 2010) has contributed to a recent critical revival, but the novel remains little known among ordinary readers.
5. Sarah LeFanu, *Rose Macaulay* (London: Virago, 2003), chap. 3.
6. N.N. Feltes, *Literary Capital and the Late Victorian Novel* (Madison: U of Wisconsin P, 1993), 28.
7. "News Notes," *Bookman*, August 1912, 185.
8. I am grateful to Shafquat Towheed for this suggestion.

9. Omnium, Jacob, "Under Cover." *Bookseller*, September 13, 1912.
10. Lawrence H. Officer and Samuel H. Williamson, "Purchasing Power of British Pounds from 1270 to Present," *MeasuringWorth*, 2015, accessed October 25, 2015, http://www.measuringworth.com/ppoweruk/.
11. John M. McEwen, "The National Press during the First World War: Ownership and Circulation," *Journal of Contemporary History* 17, no. 3 (July 1, 1982): 468.
12. Review of *The Lee Shore*, by Rose Macaulay, *Times Literary Supplement*, October 24, 1912, 464.
13. Rose Macaulay, letter to S. C. Roberts, August 4, 1912, Harry Ransom Center, Austin, Texas, qtd in LeFanu, *Rose Macaulay*, chap. 4.
14. Rose Macaulay, letter to John Murray, n.d., John Murray archive, National Library of Scotland, qtd in Jane Emery, *Rose Macaulay: A Writer's Life* (London: Murray, 1991), 136.
15. Review of *The Lee Shore*, by Rose Macaulay, *Saturday Review of Politics, Literature, Science and Art*, November 16, 1912, 617.
16. Pierre Bourdieu, *The Field of Cultural Production: Essays on Art and Literature*, translated by Randal Johnson (New York: Columbia UP, 1993), 39.
17. Bourdieu, *The Field of Cultural Production*, 39.
18. Rose Macaulay, *Non-Combatants and Others* (London: Hodder & Stoughton, 1916), 21.
19. Sybil Oldfield, *Spinsters of This Parish: The Life and Times of F. M. Mayor and Mary Sheepshanks* (London: Virago, 1984), 176.
20. Macaulay, *Non-Combatants and Others*, 21.
21. Towheed, email to author, November 7, 2015.
22. Macaulay, *Non-Combatants and Others*, 22.
23. Debra Rae Cohen, *Remapping the Home Front: Locating Citizenship in British Women's Great War Fiction* (Boston: Northeastern UP, 2002), 31.
24. Macaulay, *Non-Combatants and Others*, 156–57.
25. Macaulay, *Non-Combatants and Others*, 71.
26. Macaulay, *Non-Combatants and Others*, 232–33.
27. Anne Wiltsher, *Most Dangerous Women: Feminist Peace Campaigners of the Great War* (London: Pandora, 1985), 82. See also Jo Vellacott, *Pacifists, Patriots, and the Vote: The Erosion of Democratic Suffragism in Britain during the First World War* (New York: Palgrave Macmillan, 2007), 53–82.
28. Wiltsher, *Most Dangerous Women*, 92.
29. Macaulay, *Non-Combatants and Others*, 279.
30. Susan Grayzel, *Women's Identities at War: Gender, Motherhood, and Politics in Britain and France during the First World War* (Chapel Hill: U of North Carolina P, 1999), 11.
31. Macaulay, *Non-Combatants and Others*, 5–6.
32. Macaulay, *Non-Combatants and Others*, 58.
33. Macaulay, *Non-Combatants and Others*, 64.
34. Macaulay, *Non-Combatants and Others*, 219.
35. Trudi Tate, *Modernism, History and the First World War* (Manchester: Manchester UP, 1998), 40.
36. Macaulay, *Non-Combatants and Others*, 269.
37. This reflects an historical reality, as "a significant portion of the nation's women in 1914—including over half the leadership of the National Union of Women's Suffrage Societies [NUWSS] in Britain—were either pacifists or at the very least 'pacificists'" (Oldfield, *Spinsters of This Parish*, 176). On the divisions among the NUWSS, see Vellacott, *Pacifists, Patriots, and the Vote*, 36–58.
38. Macaulay, *Non-Combatants and Others*, 231.
39. Macaulay, *Non-Combatants and Others*, 268.
40. Macaulay, *Non-Combatants and Others*, 268.

41. Macaulay, *Non-Combatants and Others*, 87.
42. Macaulay, *Non-Combatants and Others*, 91.
43. Sarah LeFanu, "Non-Combatants and Others," *Minds at War*, BBC Radio 3, June 24, 2014.
44. LeFanu, "Non-Combatants and Others."
45. Macaulay, *Non-Combatants and Others*, 28.
46. *Poems of Today: An Anthology* (London: Published for the English Association by Sidgwick & Jackson, 1915).
47. Nicoletta F. Gullace, *The Blood of Our Sons: Men, Women, and the Renegotiation of British Citizenship during the Great War* (New York: Palgrave Macmillan, 2002), 61.
48. LeFanu, "Non-Combatants and Others."
49. Watson, *Fighting Different Wars*, 220.
50. Angela K. Smith, *The Second Battlefield: Women, Modernism and the First World War* (Manchester: Manchester UP, 2000), 148.
51. Rose Macaulay, *Dearest Jean: Rose Macaulay's Letters to a Cousin*, edited by Martin Ferguson Smith (Manchester: Manchester UP, 2011), 173 n13.
52. Rose Macaulay, *An Open Letter to a Non-Pacifist* (London: Issued by Wm. Collins Sons for the Peace Pledge Union, 1937), 4.
53. *Letters to a Friend from Rose Macaulay, 1950–1952*, edited by Constance Babington Smith (London: Collins, 1968), 74.
54. Macaulay, *Non-Combatants and Others*, 265–66.
55. "Autumn Announcements," *Times Literary Supplement*, August 10, 1916, 380 (emphasis added).
56. Jane Potter, "For Country, Conscience and Commerce: Publishers and Publishing, 1914–1918," in *Publishing in the First World War: Essays in Book History*, edited by Mary Hammond and Shafquat Towheed (Basingstoke: Palgrave Macmillan, 2007), 16.
57. *Manchester Guardian*, July 20, 1916, 3.
58. Qtd in Hodder & Stoughton advertisement, *Times Literary Supplement*, November 23, 1916, 559.
59. Sapper, *Men, Women and Guns* (London: Hodder & Stoughton, 1916), 15.
60. Winifred Holtby, "A Woman of the Day: Rose Macaulay," *Yorkshire Post*, December 10, 1926, 4.
61. Lise Jaillant, "Sapper, Hodder & Stoughton, and the Popular Literature of the Great War," *Book History* 14 (2011): 137–66.
62. Review of *Non-Combatants and Others*, by Rose Macaulay, *Times Literary Supplement*, August 31, 1916, 416.
63. The total advertising budget for *Men, Women and Guns* was 187–1–6. Hodder & Stoughton spent 49–3–1 to advertise *Non-Combatants and Others* (Hodder & Stoughton Profit and Loss Ledger, Ms. 16312, London Metropolitan Archives).
64. Hodder & Stoughton advertisement, *Manchester Guardian*, August 31, 1916, 3.
65. The total advertising budget for *The Making of a Bigot* was 81 pounds and 17 shillings (versus 114–10–9 for *The Lee Shore*).
66. In his house history, John Attenborough suggests that Macaulay left Hodder & Stoughton because she "did not like to be typed or even labelled 'popular,'" thus highlighting the different positionings of author and publisher. John Attenborough, *A Living Memory: Hodder & Stoughton Publishers, 1868–1975* (London: Hodder & Stoughton, 1975), 103.
67. Karen L. Levenback, *Virginia Woolf and the Great War* (Syracuse, NY: Syracuse UP, 1999), 84.
68. Review of *Non-Combatants and Others*, by Rose Macaulay, *Times Literary Supplement*, August 31, 1916, 416.
69. "Current Literature," *Aberdeen Daily Journal*, September 25, 1916, 2.

70. Qtd in Emery, *Rose Macaulay*, 155.
71. "New Books," *Dundee Courier*, September 25, 1916, 4.
72. Qtd in Hodder & Stoughton advertisement, *Times*, October 6, 1916, 4.
73. Katharine Tynan, "The Bookman Gallery: Rose Macaulay," *Bookman*, November 1916, 37–38.
74. Watson, *Fighting Different Wars*, 188.
75. Smith, *The Second Battlefield*, 144.
76. See Smith, *The Second Battlefield*, 157–58 n20.

Bibliography

Attenborough, John, *A Living Memory: Hodder & Stoughton Publishers, 1868–1975*. London: Hodder & Stoughton, 1975.

Bourdieu, Pierre. *The Field of Cultural Production: Essays on Art and Literature.* Translated by Randal Johnson. New York: Columbia UP, 1993.

Cohen, Debra Rae. *Remapping the Home Front: Locating Citizenship in British Women's Great War Fiction*. Boston: Northeastern UP, 2002.

Emery, Jane. *Rose Macaulay: A Writer's Life*. London: Murray, 1991.

Feltes, N.N. *Literary Capital and the Late Victorian Novel*. Madison: U of Wisconsin P, 1993.

Ferguson Smith, Martin. Ed. *Dearest Jean: Rose Macaulay's Letters to a Cousin*. Manchester: Manchester UP, 2011.

Grayzel, Susan. *Women's Identities at War: Gender, Motherhood, and Politics in Britain and France during the First World War*. Chapel Hill: U of North Carolina P, 1999.

Gullace, Nicoletta F. *The Blood of Our Sons: Men, Women, and the Renegotiation of British Citizenship during the Great War*. New York: Palgrave Macmillan, 2002.

Holtby, Winifred. "A Woman of the Day: Rose Macaulay." *Yorkshire Post*, December 10, 1926.

Jaillant, Lise. "Sapper, Hodder & Stoughton, and the Popular Literature of the Great War." *Book History* 14 (2011): 137–66. doi:10.1353/bh.2011.0011.

Lee, Hermione. "'Chattery, Chittery . . . Lean as a Rake.'" Review of *Rose Macaulay*, by Sarah LeFanu. *Guardian*, June 14, 2003. Accessed October 25, 2015. http://www.theguardian.com/books/2003/jun/14/featuresreviews.guardianreview11.

LeFanu, Sarah. "Non-Combatants and Others." *Minds at War*, BBC Radio 3, June 24, 2014.

Levenback, Karen L. *Virginia Woolf and the Great War*. Syracuse, NY: Syracuse UP, 1999.

Macaulay, Rose. *Non-Combatants and Others*. London: Hodder & Stoughton, 1916.

Macaulay, Rose. *An Open Letter to a Non-Pacifist*. London: Issued by Wm. Collins Sons for the Peace Pledge Union, 1937.

McEwen, John M. "The National Press during the First World War: Ownership and Circulation." *Journal of Contemporary History* 17, no. 3 (July 1, 1982): 459–86.

Officer, Lawrence H., and Samuel H. Williamson. "Purchasing Power of British Pounds from 1270 to Present." *MeasuringWorth*, 2015. Accessed October 25, 2015. http://www.measuringworth.com/ppoweruk/.

Oldfield, Sybil. *Spinsters of This Parish: The Life and Times of F. M. Mayor and Mary Sheepshanks*. London: Virago, 1984.

Omnium, Jacob. "Under Cover." *Bookseller*, September 13, 1912.

Poems of Today: An Anthology. London: Published for the English Association by Sidgwick & Jackson, 1915.

Potter, Jane. "For Country, Conscience and Commerce: Publishers and Publishing, 1914–1918." In *Publishing in the First World War: Essays in Book History*, edited by Mary Hammond and Shafquat Towheed, 11–26. Basingstoke: Palgrave Macmillan, 2007.

Reynolds, Nigel. "Last Chapter as Oldest Publisher Is Bought Out." *Telegraph*, May 11, 2002. Accessed October 25, 2015. http://www.telegraph.co.uk/news/uknews/1393853/Last-chapter-as-oldest-publisher-is-bought-out.html.

Sapper. *Men, Women and Guns*. London: Hodder & Stoughton, 1916.

Sapper. *Sapper's War Stories*. London: Hodder & Stoughton, 1930.

Simmel, Georg. "The Metropolis and Mental Life [1903]." In *The Sociology of Georg Simmel*, edited by Kurt H. Wolff, 409–26. Glencoe, IL: Free Press, 1950.

Smith, Angela K. *The Second Battlefield: Women, Modernism and the First World War*. Manchester: Manchester UP, 2000.

Smith, Constance Babington. Ed. *Letters to a Friend from Rose Macaulay, 1950–1952*. London: Collins, 1968.

Tate, Trudi. *Modernism, History and the First World War*. Manchester: Manchester UP, 1998.

Tynan, Katharine. "The Bookman Gallery: Rose Macaulay." *Bookman*, November 1916.

Vellacott, Jo. *Pacifists, Patriots, and the Vote: The Erosion of Democratic Suffragism in Britain during the First World War*. New York: Palgrave Macmillan, 2007.

Watson, Janet S.K., *Fighting Different Wars: Experience, Memory, and the First World War in Britain*. Cambridge: Cambridge UP, 2004.

Wiltsher, Anne. *Most Dangerous Women: Feminist Peace Campaigners of the Great War*. London: Pandora, 1985.

8 From Collusion to Condemnation
The Evolving Voice of "Woodbine Willie"

Stuart Bell

One consequence of the significant place of the Christian Churches in Edwardian society was that some of the most prominent British voices during the Great War were those of clergy and ministers. A measure of their influential position was weekly church attendance that had declined relative to the total population since 1850, but which still represented approximately a quarter of the population, with around two-fifths worshipping at least monthly.[1] Furthermore, as Callum Brown has argued, "what made Britain Christian" was not primarily church-going but "the way in which Christianity infused public culture" and shaped individuals' identities.[2] That infusion took many forms, from the close engagement of many bishops with the affairs of state, seeking to influence the political leaders with whom they had been educated at school and university, to the status still accorded to local clergy in villages and towns, reflected in the prominence given to their views in local newspapers.[3] The influence of the Churches' voice—or perhaps voices—should not be underestimated. Nevertheless, many recent discussions of the social history of the First World War have played down or even ignored the significance of religious voices during the war. Robert Beaken recently suggested that some modern writers underestimate the significance of Christianity in wartime Britain simply because it is no longer a "meaningful factor" in the lives of those writers.[4]

The broad brush-strokes of the response of the British Churches and church-goers to the outbreak of the Great War are well-documented and largely uncontested: support for Britain's engagement was very strong across all the major denominations, with the exception of the Society of Friends (Quakers) and the Churches of Christ. There were very few dissentient Anglican clergy, and while opposition was stronger in some Nonconformist denominations, most leaders publicly supported the declaration of war. Given the number of people who were regular worshippers, it is unsurprising that their response simply reflected that of the whole nation.[5] For some, such as Cosmo Lang, Archbishop of York, several weeks of reflection preceded public endorsement. For many others, such as the Bishop of Salisbury who on the first Sunday of the conflict declared it to be a Holy War, reflection was unnecessary.[6] Many former advocates of neutrality, such as the Bishop of Lincoln, fell in with the majority view, especially after the widespread publication of accounts of German atrocities in Belgium. The fundamental question for many thinking Christians was well expressed in one of the best of the torrent of books that the conflict elicited. George Bell, who would later become Bishop of Chichester, introduced a collection of essays on *The War and the Kingdom of God* with these comments: "All the writers in this book are at one in their belief that on 4 August, 1914, England was morally bound to go to war", and yet, "War seems to be and is incompatible with that Kingdom [of God]."[7] How Churches, clergy and church-goers dealt with that paradox determined their response to the Great War.

Geoffrey Anketell Studdert Kennedy was born in St Mary's Vicarage, Quarry Hill, Leeds, in 1883, the seventh son of the Rev W.S. Studdert Kennedy.[8] That the vicarage was surrounded by the workhouse, the board school, the brick quarry and a public house is indicative of the nature of the parish in which Studdert Kennedy would later assist his father as a curate.[9] Education at Leeds Grammar School and Trinity College Dublin culminated in his taking first class honours in both classics and divinity. Two years' teaching at West Kirby were followed, in October 1907, by a year at Ripon Clergy College.[10] On leaving Ripon, his first curacy was in Rugby, where, it was said, "his sermons, from the first, displayed that oratorical quality for which he was to become famous."[11] If Rugby shaped Studdert Kennedy's oratorical style, it was in his first incumbency in Worcester where the scale of the poverty motivated a zeal for social justice that became the primary focus of his post-war work.

When war broke out in August 1914, Studdert Kennedy's support for Britain's engagement in the conflict was clear and unambiguous.[12] In his parish magazine he urged every able-bodied man to volunteer for service, while those who could not volunteer should, he wrote, pray.[13] Studdert Kennedy's voice was entirely consistent with that of the denomination he served. As we shall see, his attitude and declarations supporting Britain's engagement in the conflict remained consonant with the vast majority of both clergy and the wider population throughout the conflict. Only afterwards did his publicly expressed views change. Towards the end of 1915, Studdert Kennedy obtained permission from his bishop to serve as a chaplain, and he arrived in France just before Christmas. He was sent to the large army base in Rouen by the New Year, where he soon developed a daily pattern of duty, mixing with the men at a large canteen set up by the railway sidings, making impromptu addresses, writing home to families on behalf of soldiers heading for the Front and then going with them to the trains and handing out New Testaments and packets of cigarettes, the practice which led to the "Woodbine Willie" soubriquet.[14]

His oratorical skills having been recognized by his superiors, arrangements were made in Lent 1916 for him to preach in the *Hotel de Ville*, which he did to great crowds. The meetings were widely advertised among the troops—see figure 8.1.[15] Studdert Kennedy's addresses exemplified a

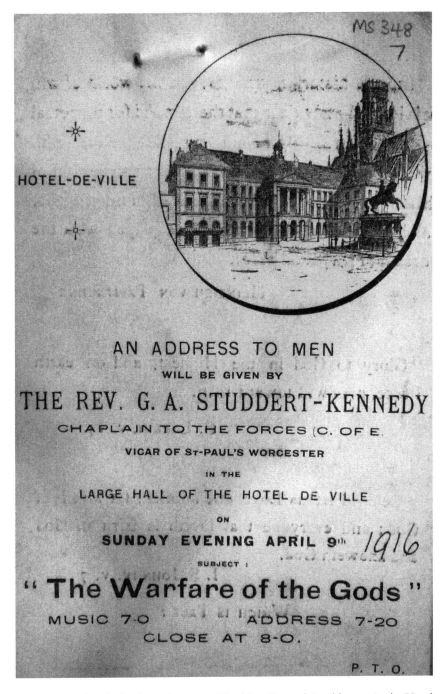

Figure 8.1 A handbill advertising one of Studdert Kennedy's addresses in the Hotel de Ville at Rouen, April 1916. Reproduced with the permission of the Library of Birmingham, MS 348/7.

Christian Patriotism which assimilated the purposes of God and his Kingdom with those of the Allies, who were engaged in battles of right against might, freedom against Germanic militarism, and the Kingdom against an enemy which had turned from God. Together, they represented some of the most vociferous advocacy of the morality of the Allies' cause and of its religious justification offered by any chaplain or clergyman during the conflict. Across the Church of England, support for the war was expressed with varying degrees of bellicosity. At one extreme, the Bishop of London, Arthur Winnington-Ingram, revelled in his role as chaplain to the London Rifle Brigade and preached many pro-recruitment sermons.[16] In contrast, the interventions of Randall Davidson, Archbishop of Canterbury, were always measured and considered, free of the rhetorical flourishes so beloved by his colleague.

Characteristically, Studdert Kennedy asserted, "Our enemies are the enemies of Man as Man, and therefore the enemies of God, and so we are prepared to fight to the last man and to the last drop of British blood."[17] He contrasted the pugnacity of the British people with the militarism of Germany, and declared,

> The individual German is the most easily governable, easily biddable, do-as-I'm-toldable, get-and-get-underable person in the world. The individual Briton is the most independent who-the-devil-are-ye-talking-toish, I won't-be made-a-door-mat-of-for-nobodyish person in the world.[18]

That conflation of divine and human causes was exemplified in the climax of his first address:

> You ask me what we are fighting for, and I say: the Freedom of the Peoples, the Honour of the Nations, and the Peace of the World. You ask me what we are fighting for—I give it you in three words: Freedom, Honour, and Peace. You ask me what we are fighting for, and I give it to you in one word: Christ.[19]

In another of his Rouen addresses, Studdert Kennedy recited part of a long dialect poem, *What's the Good?*, which would be published (with minor textual changes) in his first anthology, *Rough Rhymes of a Padre*:[20]

> Gawd knows well I ain't no thinker,
> And I never knew afore,
> But I knows now why I'm fightin',
> It's to put an end to war.
> Not to make my country richer,
> Or to keep 'er flag unfurled
> Over ev'ry other nation,

Tyrant mistress of the world.
Not to boast of Britain's glory,
Bought by bloodshed in 'er wars,
But that Peace may shine about 'er,
As the sea shines round 'er shores.[21]

The rhetoric of a "war to end all wars" would not be associated with the American president Woodrow Wilson for another year, but that was clearly the basis of Studdert Kennedy's support for the conflict. It should be noted that it was founded on a desire for peace, not for "Britain's glory." However, Studdert Kennedy, like the vast majority of his fellow clergy, was absolutely confident of the divine endorsement of the Allied cause.

In May 1916, during a period of home leave, preaching at Worcester Cathedral, Studdert Kennedy proclaimed the need "to crush this damnable curse of Germanic militarism clean out of the world." He declared that

> Tommy was . . . the finest and greatest gentleman in the world; he is the important man. And although he salutes the padre, the padre in his soul takes off his hat to Tommy. He is the most wonderful and admirable person in the world.[22]

Such hagiography of the British soldier was commonplace during the conflict. On his return to France, Studdert Kennedy spent three comparatively short periods in the front line, first in June 1916, then in 1917 when he was attached to a brigade involved in the attack on Messines Ridge and finally in 1918 as part of the Allies' final advance.[23] His experience was far from unique, and over the period of the war a significant proportion of British military personnel never saw action at the Front. After Rouen, Studdert Kennedy continued to preach, his subsequent postings being to units perceived to be performing unsatisfactorily.[24] In the last year of the conflict, he was attached as a chaplain to the School for Physical and Bayonet Training. This "school" travelled around the British Expeditionary Force, training soldiers in the use of the bayonet and seeking to raise morale.[25]

In 1917, Studdert Kennedy was awarded the Military Cross for "conspicuous gallantry and devotion to duty" during the attack on Messines Ridge, searching out the wounded while under heavy fire and helping them to the dressing station, one of more than 200 Anglican chaplains similarly honoured.[26] Friend and Assistant Chaplain General D. F. Carey recalled meeting Studdert Kennedy soon after he received the award: "He told me he had seen things. . . . Then he added: 'You know, this business has made me much less cocksure of much of which I was cocksure before.'"[27] The certainties that he had proclaimed at Rouen had, it would seem, been challenged by what he had seen in the trenches. One ordinary soldier identified Studdert Kennedy as "the only Chaplain I ever saw in the trenches" and while he was far from alone in taking such a risk, those three spells of front-line duty were hugely influential on his attitude to the conflict.[28] Hence, when that first book of poems, *Rough Rhymes of a Padre*, was published, only "What's the Good?" and "What are We Fighting For?" could have been characterised as having a strongly patriotic tone.[29] The latter started,

> Sure we're off to see the Kaiser
> Just to make him somewhat wiser,
> And to tell him what we think of sich [sic] as he.
> For he's clane [sic] outrageous barmy,
> And we'll give him British Army,
> When we've made a way to Berlin-on-the-Spree.[30]

It continued in the same vein for seven more verses, each with a similar last line. One can but wonder how that poem was received in its month of publication, March 1918, when the start of the Spring Offensive by a Germany now no longer needing to defend its Eastern Front was marked by what Malcolm Brown described as "the greatest concerted utterance of modern industrialised warfare to date."[31] Britain and her allies lost 20,000 men with 35,000 injured on the first day. However, the dominant emphasis of the poems in *Rough Rhymes of a Padre* was on making some sense of human and divine suffering. Indeed, his advocacy of a God who shares in human suffering was founded on a recognition of the true nature of the warfare of 1914–1918.

At the end of the war, Studdert Kennedy returned to his church in Worcester. However, such were the demands for him to speak elsewhere that maintaining a parish ministry became impracticable and in 1921 he accepted an undemanding living in London. This enabled him to serve the Industrial Christian Fellowship as its "crusader".[32]

While that first collection of poems had reflected a more nuanced response to the war than had the militantly patriotic sermons preached at Rouen in Lent 1916, in 1918 there was nothing to suggest that, beyond simply moderating his support for Britain's engagement in the Great War, Studdert Kennedy would subsequently become fiercely critical of it. However, in 1920, this poem was published in his second collection, *More Rough Rhymes of a Padre*:

> WASTE of Muscle, waste of Brain,
> Waste of Patience, waste of Pain,
> Waste of Manhood, waste of Health,
> Waste of Beauty, waste of Wealth,
> Waste of Blood, and waste of Tears,
> Waste of Youth's most precious years,
> Waste of ways the Saints have trod,
> Waste of Glory, waste of God,—
> War![33]

If his *Rough Talks* are taken as being indicative of his attitude to the conflict in 1916 and the above poem, *Waste*, as revealing a quite different perspective in 1920, then the two books that, like *Rough Talks*, were also published in 1918, *The Hardest Part* and *Rough Rhymes*, may well reflect staging posts in that change of voice. In *The Hardest Part*, he wove together a narrative of experiences at the Front with reaction to it and reflections on the nature of God. A key theme was that of the suffering of God: "It's funny how it is always Christ upon the Cross that comforts; never God upon a throne . . . my only real God is the suffering Father revealed in the sorrow of Christ."[34] Other chapters offered reflections "in a tent two days after a big battle" or after discovering a body in a shell-hole.[35] In *Waste*, his focus was the nature of war and its failure to produce tangible political and social benefits, rather than on its morality. Indeed, the argument of many of his poems, that the eternal salvation of those who died in battle was assured, was founded on a belief in the sacred nature of their cause. His *Rough Rhymes* included this single-stanza poem:

> There's a soul in the Eternal,
> Standing stiff before the King.
> There's a little English maiden
> Sorrowing.
> There's a proud and tearless woman,
> Seeing pictures in the fire.
> There's a broken battered body
> On the wire.[36]

The gruesome reference was to the sight of bodies tangled with the barbed wire which was commonly stretched across no man's land, the location of the bodies, unprotected by trenches, often making their recovery impossible until the next advance. Studdert Kennedy was aware of the horrors of war and did not shrink from sharing them. There was not yet condemnation, but there was a realism that had been totally absent from the addresses given at Rouen. In *His Mate*, he wrote of one of the main tasks of chaplains attached to units near the front line:

> . . . And that night I'd been in trenches,
> Seeking out the sodden dead,
> And just dropping them in shell holes,
> With a service swiftly said.[37]

It should be noted, however, that that volume of addresses full of patriotic fervour, *Rough Talks of a Padre*, continued to be published alongside Studdert Kennedy's collections of poetry, so that a reader in 1920 could have purchased both those combative talks and that poetic condemnation of the waste inherent in war. In the case of some writers, that could be attributed to an author's enlightened self-interest. However, since Studdert Kennedy was renowned throughout his ministry for giving almost everything away, including the royalties from *Rough Rhymes*, that is not a tenable explanation.[38] More likely, it reflects the fact that his attitude to the conflict was evolving. In the last years of the war and for a time afterwards he tried to hold in tension on the one hand his belief in the moral and religious justification for the war and on the other, the self-evident catastrophic horror and waste which it had involved. His biographer William Purcell suggests that in the immediate post-war years, his subject had not yet "sorted out his own ideas" on pacifism. "But he was in the process of doing so, and that is the significance of this period of Geoffrey's life."[39]

Studdert Kennedy kept no diary. Moreover, he seems to have rarely shared his own thoughts and beliefs in personal conversations. We cannot be certain, therefore, about the factors that contributed to his change of attitude to the war. Many analyses of the reasons for public support for the conflict have noted the slow transition from an emphasis on the need to respond to the brutal invasion of "brave little Belgium" to the argument that the war must be won to validate and make worthwhile the loss of so many lives.[40] Once the war was over, the reality of the scale of those losses began to sink in. For Studdert Kennedy, returning to his poverty-stricken parish in Worcester, it must have seemed that little had changed and that there was no evidence of conditions having improved in those three years. While, as Adrian Gregory has shown, many people gained financially and materially during the war, the poorest sections of society remained in poverty.[41] Such factors may well have contributed to Studdert Kennedy's change of voice. In 1919, he also published his first book that sought to address the post-war world, rather than having as its primary focus his wartime experiences. In *Lies!*, he argued that no political system offered a solution to the problems of post-war Britain.[42] He reflected on those experiences and his naivety in 1915:

> Battles were just the movements on the chess-board of the world to me. I was as innocent, as fatuously, idiotically innocent as most young men of my generation. I carried the interesting facts into my first battle. . . . They stood up before me like obscene spectres, beckoning with bloody hands, laughing like fiends at my little parochial religion, and my silly parochial God.[43]

Lies! was typical of Studdert Kennedy's early post-war work, written hurriedly and expressing anger at the injustices of a Britain in which the veterans of the conflict were not being respected and the pre-war tensions between "Capital" and "Labour," which had largely been quiescent during the conflict, were growing apace. Such was the demand that *Lies!* was reprinted on a near-annual basis throughout the 1920s. Determining his intended audience is somewhat problematic. Certainly, his books were advertised in the main church newspapers. However, it would seem that he was simply a popular writer, with a large but diverse readership. After Studdert Kennedy's death, a paperback version was published in 1932—and again regularly reprinted—with a cover carrying the text, "He being dead yet speaketh," words used in Hebrews 11:4 to refer to Abel, who according to Genesis was the son of Adam and Eve who was murdered by his brother Cain. The book's continued popularity may be to a large extent attributable to the increasingly ambivalent attitude to the war during the post-war period, fuelled by the work of the war poets. However, it should be noted that Robert Graves' *Poems (1914–1926)* was published in 1927, with *Goodbye to All That* following two years later.[44] Similarly, it was Edmund Blunden's anthology of the work of Wilfred Owen, published in 1931, which established Owen's reputation as one of the greatest of the war poets.[45] This is the period generally associated with the post-war disillusionment. In contrast, Studdert Kennedy's critique of the war, published a year after the Armistice, was offered to a British society still immersed in the memorialization of the fallen and still affirming their "noble sacrifice." Although strongly expressed *mea culpas* occur throughout *Lies!*, its primary focus was not his renunciation of his earlier patriotic support for the war, nor the offering of political solutions to the problems of British society. Indeed, he was clear that there was no purely political solution: "There is a lot of sickening cant and claptrap talked about Democracy. . . . Except ye vote for Mr. Snooks and the Coalition ye cannot see the Kingdom of God."[46] Rather, the primary thrust of *Lies!* was, just like so much of his wartime writing, his advocacy of true Christianity as offering a solution to the world's problems. He called for "a Public Opinion which is prepared to bet its life, its liberty, and its bottom dollar that Christ is the Way, the Truth, and the Life."[47]

In a chapter on industrial relations, Studdert Kennedy likened industrialised society to a hen-run in which both employers and employees were hens, the former being the larger ones, allowing the labourers to have only the smallest worms. Then came one of those paragraphs which probably made it inevitable that, despite his repeated denials to the contrary and his refusal to endorse any specific political actions, he would be labelled by some as a socialist, arguing that the "burden of shame" for the "evils" of the present day

> ... must be shouldered by the Employers of the nineteenth century, many of whom were as greedy and as brutally stupid as barn-door fowls. The Employer sowed the wind in those early days, and his children reap the whirlwind now.[48]

In 1921, Studdert Kennedy commenced his work for the Industrial Christian Fellowship (ICF). The ICF had been formed by the amalgamation of the Christian Social Union and the Navy Mission, and his role was to tour the country, urging greater harmony and cooperation between "Capital" and "Labour" and making the case for better working conditions, not least for the men who had been served their country in 1914–1918. It could be said that Studdert Kennedy, in his concern for social justice and for the wellbeing of the working men of Britain, was a Christian Socialist. However, the first of those two words was always far more important for him than the second. In *Lies!* his admission of naivety during the conflict was succeeded by explicit denunciations of war; war in general as a human activity rather than the Great War in particular. Such a distinction is critically important in understanding the development of Studdert Kennedy's thought. His desire was primarily that war be eradicated from human civilization and he expressed it in a telling metaphor: "What we did during the War was to kill mad dogs. What we have to do now is to cure rabies."[49] War was wrong because it was contrary to God's intention for humanity. He wrote, "Does God will War? . . . If God wills War, then I am morally mad, and I don't know good from evil. War is the most obviously wicked thing I know." Later, he wrote of war:

> I can see no good in it; it does not cleanse, and it does not purify, and it does not uplift the nations; it kills the noble and the strong, it leaves the weak and vicious to breed their kind; it is wasteful, cruel, and inhuman; it is vile . . .[50]

Studdert Kennedy published two more highly polemical volumes: In *Food for the Fed-Up* (1921) he offered a Christian apologetic structured around the Apostles' Creed, taking on "those arch enemies of faith—materialism, determinism, pessimism, cynicism—with which he was to be in frequent conflict in print . . . for the rest of his life" as Purcell put it.[51] In this volume, he was critical, too, of capitalism and the consequences of unrestrained free markets, lamenting that, "a world of selfishness grows more selfish."[52] For Studdert Kennedy, no political system offered a solution to the world's problems; only society modelled on the Kingdom of God could do that. In *Democracy and the Dog Collar*, also published in 1921, Studdert Kennedy examined the relationship between organised religion and organised labour.[53]

While Purcell may well have been right to identify the immediate post-war years as a period in which Studdert Kennedy was sorting out his own ideas about pacifism, it is clear than within a year of the end of the conflict, he had made up his mind about the immorality of war. Studdert Kennedy apparently felt no need to explain his change of view. It may have been that once the guns were silent, he had, for the first time, an opportunity to re-examine thoroughly those earlier "certainties" of which his time in the trenches had made him less "cocksure." Certainly he was no longer bound by loyalty to the army which he had served as a temporary chaplain, and post-war critiques of the conflict would not have been seen as being quite so un-patriotic as they would have before the Armistice. Nevertheless, the vast majority of the British public were not yet ready to hear a denunciation of a war which had had such an immense cost.

In a short time, to Studdert Kennedy's critique of the concept of war as a means of solving disputes or as an inescapable component of human progress was added forthright condemnation of the Great War. This was the obvious logical development of his earlier more general argument. However, in moving from the general to the specific example of the still very-recent conflict, it was inevitable that there would be an adverse reaction from those who believed that to challenge the war was to bring into question the sacrifices made. In a Remembrance Day address in 1921, Studdert Kennedy made his first public statement criticizing the Great War, in what he described as "a public act of contrition" for what he had said during the conflict.[54] In its critical report, the writer for the *Yorkshire Evening Post* commented, "Probably no one will regret more than Mr. Studdert Kennedy himself that he let such a despairing cry escape from the arena of his own spiritual conflict."[55] The article suggested that, in contrast, the "sane view" of the war was to be found in Studdert Kennedy's books: "Our dead did not die in vain. They did fight for freedom and honour." On the evening of Remembrance Day, Studdert Kennedy attended a service at the Methodist Central Hall, Westminster. In his address, he said of the combatants of the Great War, "They were all mad; they were all mad out there; they were given decorations for what they did when they were mad."[56] On Sunday, 13 November, speaking in Leamington Spa, he repeated the indictment, appealing for those who had lost loved ones to forgive their enemies.[57] Studdert Kennedy's general criticism of the cost of warfare had now become an unambiguous denunciation of the Great War.

To mark the eighth anniversary of the outbreak of the conflict, a "No More War" demonstration was held in Hyde Park in July 1922. A large number of organisations were represented, including the National Peace Council, the National Free Church Council, the Church of England Sunday School Institute and the Young Women's Christian Association. Studdert Kennedy was one of almost twenty speakers, including four other clerics and Maude Royden, the Anglican peace campaigner.[58] This was merely the first of several such controversial demonstrations in which Studdert Kennedy would participate. In May 1923, anticipating a public meeting in Tonbridge Wells at which Studdert Kennedy would speak, M. B. Backhouse wrote to the *Kent and Sussex Courier* asserting that an apology was still needed for that address in November 1921 and complaining that

> these inexcusable words, striking a blow at the heart of our national patriotism still stand ... and until they are retracted or apologised for it is somewhat wonderful that he has the courage to address any audience of right-minded men and women.[59]

The meeting went ahead and the same correspondent reported in the next week's issue that Studdert Kennedy had informed his hearers that he had gained his Military Cross "during a fit of lunacy," claiming that "Patriotism would crush the nations: Patriotism would destroy this country if we let it." She complained that "not a man was found to raise his voice against this iniquitous utterance" and concluded, "Emphatically, it is not the message of Christ, though it undoubtedly is of Socialism."[60] The correspondence continued a week later with a letter from Studdert Kennedy, confirming his assertion about the "madness" of the war. He wrote,

> The words, of course, are sober, accurate and very terrible truths. . . . Thousands of those who wear decorations, if you got them alone, would tell you that at the time of the deed or deeds they were utterly and completely unconscious of what they were doing. . . . The words are deliberately meant to strike a blow at the very heart of our national patriotism . . . [that] is even now destroying the world.[61]

In those responses to Studdert Kennedy's declarations, we see clear evidence of the widely held belief that to denounce the war was to denounce the sacrifice of the fallen. No longer was he trying to hold in tension his sanctified patriotism and his views on the waste of war. No longer was he critical only of war as a concept. While he still loved his country, he had rejected the nationalism that had led to near-universal support for the Great War.

In July 1923, Studdert Kennedy spoke at another "No More War" demonstration in Hyde Park. According to *The Times*, around five to ten thousand people gathered to hear speakers including Oswald Mosley, George Lansbury, Studdert Kennedy and, again, Maude Royden. According to *The Times* correspondent, "Girls with hair cut too short were associated with young men whose hair was too long."[62] Studdert Kennedy "said trades unions, churches and the League of Nations Union should be bonded together so as to make the war attitude impossible."[63]

Further evidence of his changed attitude can be found in an introduction to *The Hardest Part*, first published in 1918. In his biography of Studdert Kennedy published in 2013, Bob Holman quoted it:

> When they are old enough I am going to teach *The Hardest Part* [the poem which gave the book its title] to my sons, and hope it will make them uncompromising and bitter rebels against the cruelty and folly and waste of war . . .[64]

However, there was no such introduction in the original 1918 edition and Studdert Kennedy's second son, Christopher, was not born until January 1921.[65] Although he did not make this explicit, Holman was quoting from a "new edition" which had been published with a preface that stated that, "Seven years have come and gone since first this book was written . . .," indicating a date of 1925 and not 1918 for that fully developed personal critique of war.

From Collusion to Condemnation   163

Finally, in his last collection, *The Unutterable Beauty*, Studdert Kennedy published in 1927 "all the poems which he himself wished to live."[66] That phrase in itself is clearly significant, indicating that there were other poems that he did not wish to live. Predictably, there is no sign of "What are We Fighting For?" although "What's the Good?" still found a place, with its justification for fighting:

> Not to boast of Britain's glory,
> Bought by bloodshed in 'er wars,
> But that Peace may shine about 'er,
> As the sea shines round 'er shores.[67]

In *The Unutterable Beauty*, after a short poem about his nick-name, *Woodbine Willie*, the first of any significance was *The Suffering God*, in which Studdert Kennedy expressed his belief in a God who shares in human suffering, a belief that was at the heart of his theology.[68] The collection included *Waste*, poems addressed to his sons Patrick and Christopher and many from his later books.[69] The vast majority were religious—even devotional—in nature. Some of the dialect poems spoke of "Fritz," or a "Jerry" sniper with a square head, but that section started with *The Sorrow of God*, another extended poetic essay on a suffering God. Studdert Kennedy had indeed become "less cocksure."

Studdert Kennedy's change of voice from patriotic and uncritical collusion with Britain's involvement in the Great War to a robust and controversial challenge of war was now complete. His lamenting of the waste of war had developed into an unequivocal damning of its cruelty and a condemnation of its madness, directed at his own opinions of 1914–1918 and all who had agreed with him. He spent his last years working tirelessly for the ICF, touring the country from one speaking engagement to another, despite his failing health.[70] Finally, when he died in 1929, aged 45, his association with anti-war and trade union groups would lead to him being denied a funeral in Westminster Abbey on the grounds that the Dean deemed him to have been a socialist.[71]

How might we locate Studdert Kennedy's change of voice within the broader picture? Certainly, his denunciation first of the idea of war as a solution and then of the Great War itself pre-dated the rise of pacifism in the 1930s. Moreover, the context for his advocacy was the period in which grief, both public and private, was still raw and across the country memorials were being raised in thousands of communities. Studdert Kennedy's critique could only be heard as questioning the rhetoric of "sublime self-sacrifice" which characterised innumerable acts of commemoration.

While the influence of the war poets in the late 1920s and the growth of pacifism in the 1930s have been well documented, it is less clear how more critical responses to the war developed in its immediate aftermath. As Charles Raven, the former Great War chaplain who became a pacifist in the 1930s, recalled, "Until 1928 it needed some courage to renounce war from a public platform.... That autumn saw a definite change."[72] That year, of course, saw the tenth anniversary of the Armistice. From 1926, the National Peace Council, which had organised the demonstrations in 1922 and 1923 at which Studdert Kennedy had spoken, moved the annual anti-war rallies to the week after Armistice Day in order to gain more prominence for the pacifist cause. However, the evidence is that support for the League of Nations Union, which supported limited disarmament rather than the elimination of armed forces, was far stronger than that for the absolute pacifism. As Martin Ceadel observed, "The dozen years after the Great War were a paradoxical time for pacifism; many of its ideas were received with unprecedented sympathy; but as a distinctive position it was more than ever engulfed by the flood tide of *pacificism*."[73]

While a broad survey of pacifism in the early 1920s is beyond the scope of this chapter and, indeed, already exists in Ceadel's work, two short case studies set alongside the story of Studdert Kennedy cast further light on the changing attitudes to war of the 1920s. Firstly, C. E. Montague had worked for twenty years for the *Manchester Guardian* and was its assistant editor when war broke out. In a leading article published on 24 August 1914, he wrote, "Europe must either smash Prussian Junkerdom or be smashed by it" and before the end of the year he eagerly enlisted for military service at the age of 47, famously dying his hair so as to appear under the then maximum enlistment age of 38.[74] The son of a former Catholic priest, Montague is perhaps best known for his book, *Disenchantment*.[75] It was published in 1922, several years before the more widespread disillusionment when it had become clear that so many of the hopes and dreams of the immediate post-war years had not been fulfilled. As we shall see, there was a continuity of thought connecting his diaries and *Disenchantment*, the content of which was primarily drawn from leading articles published in the *Manchester Guardian* between October 1920 and November 1921.

Montague's wartime diary and letters reflected an engagement with the ethical and religious issues raised by the war, in stark contrast to the apparent unwillingness exhibited by the vast majority of wartime diarists and correspondents to consider such matters, even many chaplains and clergy. Consistently, Montague refused to seek to reconcile his own support for Britain's engagement in the war with his understanding of the teaching of Jesus. At the end of 1916, he wrote a short poem of which the opening stanza was:

Yes, of course it was sin
And no Christ would say "Fight
For the right"—
But we had to win.[76]

On 26 November 1917, he wrote to his wife that

Christ's opposition to all war seems to be almost indisputable, and yet I *can't* apply it to this war. I don't feel that Christ was ever wrong, and yet I do feel that to fail in resisting our enemy in this war would be wrong.[77]

The contrast with Studdert Kennedy, who at Rouen had clearly demonstrated that at the time he saw no inconsistency between the teaching of Jesus and his sanctified patriotism, is stark. Later that year, Montague recorded in his diary,

> To take part in this war cannot, I think, be squared with Christianity. . . . But I am more sure of my duty of trying to win this war than I am that Christ was right in every part of all that he said. . . . Therefore I will try . . . to win the war, not pretending meantime that I am obeying Christ.[78]

Here was no change of attitude but rather an accommodation of two quite contradictory ethical views of the conflict. Four years later, in a critique of army chaplains in *Disenchantment*, Montague expressed a similar view in what is clearly an autobiographical comment:

> "I've been a Christian all my life, but this war is a bit too serious." So saying, a certain New Army recruit had folded up his religion in 1914 and put it away, as it were, in a drawer with his other civil attire to wait until public affairs should again permit of their use.[79]

Frequently, Montague wrote with admiration of the Quakers, critical of the "institutional side of religion." While his publication of *Disenchantment* was contemporaneous with Studdert Kennedy's denunciation of the war, the pathways by which they had arrived at that common perspective could hardly have been more different.

In contrast, H.R.L. ("Dick") Sheppard, a friend of Studdert Kennedy, supported the conflict while vicar of St Martin-in-the-Fields in central London during the Great War, but then founded the pacifist Peace Pledge Union in 1934. Before taking up that wartime appointment, he had spent just over two months as a chaplain at a military hospital in France. In letters to Cosmo Lang, Archbishop of York, Sheppard wrote of holding limbs as they were amputated and fighting a drunken Tommy: "I've missed a thousand opportunities and lived through a life's experiences in five weeks."[80] Those experiences shaped his pioneering and hugely popular ministry in London. Health problems caused Sheppard to resign his living in 1926 and in the following year he published a radical critique of institutional religion, *The Impatience of a Parson*.[81] In that volume, he made his first declaration of pacifism, writing, "War cannot be reconciled with Christianity; there is no such thing as a Christian war."[82]

Sheppard played a major role in the British pacifist movement until his death in 1937, aged 57. In the many books which he wrote in his last decade he made much of his relatively brief experience in France, typically in 1935 telling of kneeling by a soldier: "He was the first soldier I saw die."[83] This was one of those experiences that, in Martin Ceadel's judgment, "haunted him for the rest of his life."[84] In a letter to Laurence Houseman in 1927,

Sheppard stated "I cannot but identify myself with pacifism, for I am a pacifist . . .," although in the last year of his life he claimed that he had become one in 1919.[85] Linda Parker has recently drawn attention to Maud Royden's clear statement that during the conflict, Sheppard had no doubts at all about the war's legitimacy: "War seemed to him to be then absolutely necessary and therefore right, even though he, as a Christian priest, must not take a sword in his hand."[86] In 1925 he had famously managed to have an Armistice Day Ball at the Royal Albert Hall cancelled in favour of an "In Memory" meeting, raising money for former combatants in a less ostentatious way. However, that was not necessarily indicative of a change of heart about the war itself. Clive Barrett, in a narrative of Anglican pacifism during and immediately after the Great War clearly written from a pacifist perspective, has suggested that the first signs of Sheppard's pacifism did not come until that period in 1926 when he was convalescing between appointments.[87] Martin Ceadel's somewhat critical assessment was that Sheppard's "main inspiration seems to have been the need to find an issue which could revitalize the Church of England."[88] The inescapable conclusion is that, notwithstanding his own claim and P. T. Kirk's observation that Sheppard had organised the 1921 meeting at which Studdert Kennedy had denounced the conflict, Dick Sheppard was not at the forefront of that movement to renounce war which would gather pace in the latter part of the 1920s. Although Sheppard's place in the historiography of pacifism between the wars is well established, Studdert Kennedy's *volte-face* preceded Sheppard's by perhaps five years.

Clearly in the account of Studdert Kennedy's change of voice, set alongside the narratives of Montague and Sheppard, we find three quite different responses to the paradox that George Bell had enunciated in 1915. For Montague there was an almost immediate recognition that war and the teaching of Christ were incompatible and there was no point trying to argue otherwise. For Studdert Kennedy, the transition from vociferous collusion with Britain's war aims to post-war condemnation had its origins in his front-line experiences but could only be completed once peace had come. For Sheppard, there would elapse almost eight years after the Armistice before he would publicly declare for the cause of pacifism that came to play such a significant part in his life and which led to his prominent place in the story of the inter-war pacifist movement. Together, these narratives exemplify some of the ways in which increasing numbers of clergy and church-goers came to repudiate armed conflict in the post-war period.[89] However, Sheppard, Montague and Studdert Kennedy had all died before an impending war would in the late 1930s cause the British Churches to re-visit George Bell's paradox.

Notes

1. Clive Field, "'The Faith Society'? Quantifying Religious Belonging in Edwardian Britain, 1901–1914", *Journal of Religious History*, vol. 37, no. 1 (2013), 39–63.
2. Callum Brown, *The Death of Christian Britain* (London: Routledge, 2001), 8.

3. Albert Marrin documented the similar public school education of bishops, the peerage and landed families (and, indeed, their familial connections) in *The Last Crusade: The Church of England in the First World War* (Durham, NC: Duke UP, 1974), 12–16.
4. Robert Beaken, *The Church of England and the Home Front 1914–1918: Civilians, Soldiers and Religion in Wartime Colchester* (Woodbridge: Boydell & Brewer, 2015), 2.
5. See Albert Marrin, *The Last Crusade*; Alan Wilkinson, *The Church of England and the First World War* (London: SPCK, 1978); Edward Madigan, *Faith Under Fire: Anglican Chaplains and the Great War* (Basingstoke: Palgrave, 2011); Stuart Bell, "The Church and the First World War" in *God and War: The Church of England and Armed Conflict in the Twentieth Century*, eds. Stephen Parker and Tom Watson (Farnham: Ashgate, 2012); Catriona Pennell, *A Kingdom United: Popular Responses to the Outbreak of the First World War in Britain and Ireland* (Oxford: OUP, 2012); Michael Snape and Edward Madigan, eds., *The Clergy in Khaki: New Perspectives on British Army Chaplaincy in the First World War* (Farnham: Ashgate, 2013), 33–55.
6. John G. Lockhart, *Cosmo Gordon Lang* (London: Hodder & Stoughton, 1949), 246; "A Just and Righteous War", *Western Gazette*, August 14, 1914, 5.
7. Henry L. Goudge et al., *The War and the Kingdom of God*, ed. George K.A. Bell (London: Longmans, Green, 1915), 4 and 6.
8. John K. Mozley, "Home Life and Early Years of His Ministry" in *G.A. Studdert Kennedy by His Friends*, ed. John K. Mozley (London: Hodder & Stoughton, 1929), 13.
9. Ibid., 40.
10. Michael W. Brierley, "Ripon Hall, Henry Major and the Shaping of English Liberal Theology" in *Ambassadors of Christ*, ed. Mark Chapman (Farnham: Ashgate, 2004), 89–155.
11. Mozley, "Home Life", 56.
12. See John K. Mozley, ed., *G.A. Studdert Kennedy by His Friends* (London: Hodder & Stoughton, 1929); William Purcell, *Woodbine Willie: An Anglican Incident* (London: Hodder & Stoughton, 1962); Bob Holman, *Woodbine Willie: An Unsung Hero of World War One* (Oxford: Lion, 2013).
13. William Moore Ede, "Studdert Kennedy: His Life in Worcester" in *G.A. Studdert Kennedy by His Friends*, ed. John K. Mozley (London: Hodder & Stoughton, 1929), 99.
14. D.F. Carey, "War Padre" in *G.A. Studdert Kennedy by His Friends*, ed. John K. Mozley (London: Hodder & Stoughton, 1929), 115–124.
15. See Stuart Bell, "'Patriotism and Sacrifice': The Preaching of Geoffrey Studdert Kennedy ('Woodbine Willie')" in *Delivering the Word: Preaching and Exegesis in the Western Christian Tradition*, ed. William Lyons and Isabella Sandwell (Sheffield: Equinox, 2012), 190–208.
16. See Stuart Bell, "Malign or Maligned?—Arthur Winnington-Ingram, Bishop of London, in the First World War", *Journal for the History of Modern Theology / Zeitschrift für Neuere Theologiegeschichte*, vol. 20, no. 1 (2013), 117–133.
17. Geoffrey A. Studdert Kennedy, *Rough Talks by a Padre* (London: Hodder & Stoughton, 1918), 72.
18. Ibid., 39–40.
19. Ibid., 66–67.
20. Geoffrey A. Studdert Kennedy, *Rough Rhymes of a Padre* (London: Hodder & Stoughton, 1918).
21. Studdert Kennedy, *Rough Talks*, 64–65.
22. "Rev. G.A. Studdert Kennedy at the Cathedral—Appreciation of Tommy Atkins", *Berrow's Worcester Journal*, June 3, 1916, 3.

23. Carey, "War Padre", 125.
24. Michael Snape, *God and the British Soldier: Religion and the British Army in the First and Second World Wars* (London: Routledge, 2007), 107.
25. Michael Snape, *The Royal Army Chaplains' Department, 1796–1953: Clergy under Fire* (Woodbridge: Boydell & Brewer, 2005), 108.
26. Ibid., 143; Madigan, *Faith Under Fire*, 148.
27. Carey, "War Padre", 154.
28. Thomas J. Higgins, *Tommy at Gommecourt* (Leek: Churnet Valley Books, 2005), 45.
29. Studdert Kennedy, *Rough Rhymes*.
30. Ibid., 92–94.
31. Malcolm Brown, *The Imperial War Museum Book of 1918: Year of Victory* (London: Pan, 1999), 48.
32. Holman, *Woodbine Willie*, 111.
33. Geoffrey A. Studdert Kennedy, *More Rough Rhymes of a Padre* (London: Hodder & Stoughton, 1920), 80.
34. Geoffrey A. Studdert Kennedy, *The Hardest Part* (London: Hodder & Stoughton, 1918), 8–9.
35. Ibid., 75 and 143.
36. Ibid., 39.
37. Studdert Kennedy, *Rough Rhymes*, 68–69.
38. Moore Ede, "His Life in Worcester", 92.
39. Purcell, *Woodbine Willie*, 159.
40. See, for example, Stuart Bell, "'Soldiers of Christ Arise': Religious Nationalism in the East Midlands during World War 1", *Midland History*, vol. 39, no. 2 (2014), 226–234.
41. Adrian Gregory, *The Last Great War: British Society and the First World War* (Cambridge: CUP, 2008), 187–212.
42. Geoffrey A. Studdert Kennedy, *Lies!* (London: Hodder & Stoughton, 1919).
43. Ibid., 4–5.
44. Robert Graves, *Poems (1914–1926)* (London: Heinemann, 1927); Robert Graves, *Goodbye to All That; An Autobiography* (London: Cape, 1929).
45. Edmund Blunden, *The Poems of Wilfred Owen* (London: Chatto & Windus, 1931).
46. Studdert Kennedy, *Lies*, 7.
47. Ibid., 9.
48. Ibid., 28.
49. Ibid., 103.
50. Ibid., 160.
51. Geoffrey A. Studdert Kennedy, *Food for the Fed-up* (London: Hodder & Stoughton, 1921); Purcell, *Woodbine Willie*, 166.
52. Studdert Kennedy, *Food for the Fed-up*, 29.
53. Geoffrey A. Studdert Kennedy, *Democracy and the Dog-Collar* (London: Hodder & Stoughton, 1921).
54. "A Momentary Aberration", *Yorkshire Post*, November 12, 1921, 4.
55. "A Momentary Aberration", *Yorkshire Evening Post*, November 12, 1921, 4.
56. Words confirmed in letter by Studdert Kennedy, "To the Editor", *Kent and Sussex Courier*, June 8, 1923, 7. The *Hartlepool Mail* offered a slightly different transcript, "'No Freedom and No End to War'—'Woodbine Willie's' Open Confession", November 12, 1921, 6.
57. "'Woodbine Willie' and Leamington—Remarkable Statements at Y.M.C.A. Musical", *Leamington Spa Courier*, November 18, 1921, 8.
58. "Church Reform", *The Times*, July 17, 1917, 3; "No More War—Demonstration in Hyde Park", *The Times*, July 31, 1922, 5.

From Collusion to Condemnation 169

59. "An Apology Still Awaited", *Kent and Sussex Courier*, May 25, 1923, 11.
60. "The Apology That Was Not Given", *Kent and Sussex Courier*, June 1, 1923, 11.
61. "To the Editor", *Kent and Sussex Courier*, June 8, 1923, 7. A letter was also published from P. T. Kirk, General Director of the Industrial Christian Fellowship, correcting several errors in the original letter, stating that the 1921 Central Hall meeting had been organised by the Rev H.R.L. ("Dick") Sheppard from St Martin-in-the-Fields, and distancing both that meeting and the ICF from a disturbance to the two-minute silence which had occurred earlier that day.
62. "'No More War Movement'—Demonstration in Hyde Park", *The Times*, July 30, 1923, 12.
63. "'No More War' Demonstration", *Aberdeen Journal*, July 30, 1923, 4.
64. Holman, *Woodbine Willie*, 74.
65. Purcell, *Woodbine Willie*, 157.
66. Geoffrey A. Studdert Kennedy, *The Unutterable Beauty* (London: Hodder & Stoughton, 1927) later republished as *The Rhymes of G.A. Studdert Kennedy* (London: Hodder & Stoughton, 1940), 5.
67. Studdert Kennedy, *The Rhymes*, 142–146.
68. Stuart Bell, "The Theology of 'Woodbine Willie' in Context" in *The Clergy in Khaki: New Perspectives on British Army Chaplaincy in the First World War*, eds. Michael Snape and Edward Madigan (Farnham: Ashgate, 2013), 95–110.
69. Geoffrey A. Studdert Kennedy, *Peace Rhymes of a Padre* (London: Hodder & Stoughton, 1920) and *Lighten our Darkness: Some Less Rough Rhymes of a Padre* (London: Hodder & Stoughton, 1925).
70. Gerald Studdert Kennedy, *Dog-Collar Democracy 1919–1929* (London: Macmillan, 1982).
71. Purcell, *Woodbine Willie*, 178.
72. Charles Raven, *Is War Obsolete?* (London: George Allen & Unwin, 1935), 22–23.
73. Martin Ceadel, *Pacifism in Britain 1914–1945: The Defining of a Faith* (Oxford: Clarendon, 1980), 62. "Pacificism" denotes an ethical objection to war, except when it is absolutely necessary to bring peace.
74. Oliver Elton, *C.E. Montague a Memoir* (London: Chatto & Windus, 1929), 101.
75. Charles E. Montague, *Disenchantment* (London: Chatto & Windus, 1922).
76. Elton, *Montague: A Memoir*, 165.
77. Ibid., 169.
78. Ibid., 167.
79. Montague, *Disenchantment*, 71. Grieves identified this material as originally having been published in the *Manchester Guardian* on 20 August 1921; Keith Grieves, "C.E. Montague and the making of Disenchantment", *War in History*, vol. 4, no. 1. (1997), 35–59 at 38.
80. Madigan, *Faith under Fire*, 206.
81. Hugh R.L. Sheppard, *The Impatience of a Parson* (London: Hodder & Stoughton, 1927).
82. Sheppard, *Impatience*, 52.
83. Hugh R.L. Sheppard, *We Say "No": The Plain Man's Guide to Pacifism* (London: Murray, 1935), 1.
84. Ceadel, *Pacifism in Britain*, 59.
85. Laurence Houseman, ed., *What Can We Believe?* (London: Peace Pledge Union, 1939), 82; Sheppard's claim about 1919 reported at www.ppu.org.uk/learn/infodocs/people/pst_dick.html, retrieved February 24, 2014.
86. Maude Royden, "Dick Sheppard, Peace Maker" in *Dick Sheppard: An Apostle of Brotherhood*, ed. William Paxton (London: Chapman and Hall, 1938), 45, cited in Linda Parker, *Shellshocked Prophets: Former Anglican Army Chaplains in Inter-War Britain* (Solihull: Helion, 2015), 212.

87. Clive Barrett, *Subversive Peacemakers: War Resistance 1914–1918; An Anglican Perspective* (Cambridge: Lutterworth, 2014), 217.
88. Ceadel, *Pacifism in Britain*, 59.
89. See Alan Wilkinson, *Dissent or Conform? War, Peace and the English Churches, 1900–1945* (London: SCM, 1986), 137–189.

Bibliography

Barrett, Clive. *Subversive Peacemakers: War Resistance 1914–1918; An Anglican Perspective*. Cambridge: Lutterworth, 2014.

Beaken, Robert. *The Church of England and the Home Front 1914–1918: Civilians, Soldiers and Religion in Wartime Colchester*. Woodbridge: Boydell & Brewer, 2015.

Bell, Stuart. "The Church and the First World War". In *God and War: The Church of England and Armed Conflict in the Twentieth Century*, edited by Stephen Parker and Tom Watson, 33–60. Farnham: Ashgate, 2012.

Bell, Stuart. "'Patriotism and Sacrifice': The Preaching of Geoffrey Studdert Kennedy ('Woodbine Willie')". In *Delivering the Word: Preaching and Exegesis in the Western Christian Tradition*, edited by William Lyons and Isabella Sandwell, 190–208. Sheffield: Equinox, 2012.

Bell, Stuart. "Malign or Maligned?—Arthur Winnington-Ingram, Bishop of London, in the First World War." *Journal for the History of Modern Theology / Zeitschrift für Neuere Theologiegeschichte*, vol. 20, no. 1 (2013): 117–133.

Bell, Stuart. "The Theology of 'Woodbine Willie' in Context". In *The Clergy in Khaki: New Perspectives on British Army Chaplaincy in the First World War*, edited by Michael Snape and Edward Madigan, 95–110. Farnham: Ashgate, 2013.

Bell, Stuart. "'Soldiers of Christ Arise': Religious Nationalism in the East Midlands during World War 1." *Midland History*, vol. 39, no. 2 (2014): 219–235.

Blunden, Edmund. *The Poems of Wilfred Owen*. London: Chatto and Windus, 1931.

Brierley, Michael W. "Ripon Hall, Henry Major and the Shaping of English Liberal Theology". In *Ambassadors of Christ*, edited by Mark Chapman, 89–155. Farnham: Ashgate, 2004.

Brown, Callum. *The Death of Christian Britain*. London: Routledge, 2001.

Brown, Malcolm. *The Imperial War Museum Book of 1918: Year of Victory*. London: Pan, 1999.

Carey, D.F. "War Padre". In *G.A. Studdert Kennedy by his Friends*, edited by John K. Mozley, 115–124. London: Hodder & Stoughton, 1929.

Ceadel, Martin. *Pacifism in Britain 1914–1945: The Defining of a Faith*. Oxford: Clarendon, 1980.

Elton, Oliver. *C.E. Montague A Memoir*. London: Chatto & Windus, 1929.

Field, Clive. "'The Faith Society'? Quantifying Religious Belonging in Edwardian Britain, 1901–1914." *Journal of Religious History*, vol. 37, no. 1 (2013): 39–63.

Goudge, Henry L. et al. *The War and the Kingdom of God*, edited by George K.A. Bell. London: Longmans, Green, 1915.

Graves, Robert. *Poems (1914–1926)*. London: Heinemann, 1927.

Graves, Robert. *Goodbye to All That: An Autobiography*. London: Cape, 1929.

Gregory, Adrian. *The Last Great War: British Society and the First World War*. Cambridge: CUP, 2008.

Grieves, Keith. "C.E. Montague and the Making of Disenchantment." *War in History*, vol. 4, no. 1 (1997): 35–59.

Higgins, Thomas J. *Tommy at Gommecourt*. Leek: Churnet Valley Books, 2005.
Holman, Bob. *Woodbine Willie: An Unsung Hero of World War One*. Oxford: Lion, 2013.
Houseman, Laurence, ed. *What Can We believe?* London: Peace Pledge Union, 1939.
Lockhart, John G. *Cosmo Gordon Lang*. London: Hodder & Stoughton, 1949.
Madigan, Edward. *Faith under Fire: Anglican Chaplains and the Great War*. Basingstoke: Palgrave, 2011.
Marrin, Albert. *The Last Crusade: The Church of England in the First World War*. Durham, NC: Duke UP, 1974.
Montague, Charles E. *Disenchantment*. London: Chatto & Windus, 1922.
Moore Ede, William. "Studdert Kennedy: His Life in Worcester". In *G.A. Studdert Kennedy by His Friends*, edited by John K. Mozley, 87–111. London: Hodder & Stoughton, 1929.
Mozley, John K., ed. *G.A. Studdert Kennedy by His Friends*. London: Hodder & Stoughton, 1929.
Overy, Richard. *The Morbid Age: Britain and the Crisis of Civilisation, 1919–1939*. London: Penguin, 2010.
Parker, Linda. *Shellshocked Prophets: Former Anglican Army Chaplains in Inter-War Britain*. Solihull: Helion, 2015.
Paxton, William, ed. *Dick Sheppard: An Apostle of Brotherhood*. London: Chapman and Hall, 1938.
Pennell, Catriona. *A Kingdom United: Popular Responses to the Outbreak of the First World War in Britain and Ireland*. Oxford: OUP, 2012.
Purcell, William. *Woodbine Willie: An Anglican Incident*. London: Hodder & Stoughton, 1962.
Raven, Charles. *Is War Obsolete?* London: George Allen & Unwin, 1935.
Royden, Maude. "Dick Sheppard, The Peacemaker". In *Dick Sheppard: An Apostle of Brotherhood*, edited by William Paxton, 73–81. London: Chapman and Hall, 1938.
Sheppard, Hugh R.L. *The Impatience of a Parson*. London: Hodder & Stoughton, 1927.
Sheppard, Hugh R.L. *We Say "No": The Plain Man's Guide to Pacifism*. London: Murray, 1935.
Snape, Michael. *The Royal Army Chaplains' Department, 1796–1953: Clergy under Fire*. Woodbridge: Boydell & Brewer, 2005.
Snape, Michael. *God and the British Soldier: Religion and the British Army in the First and Second World Wars*. London: Routledge, 2007.
Snape, Michael and Edward Madigan, eds. *The Clergy in Khaki: New Perspectives on British Army Chaplaincy in the First World War*. Farnham: Ashgate, 2013.
Studdert Kennedy, Geoffrey A. *The Hardest Part*. London: Hodder & Stoughton, 1918.
Studdert Kennedy, Geoffrey A. *Rough Rhymes of a Padre*. London: Hodder & Stoughton, 1918.
Studdert Kennedy, Geoffrey A. *Rough Talks by a Padre*. London: Hodder & Stoughton, 1918.
Studdert Kennedy, Geoffrey A. *Lies!* London: Hodder & Stoughton, 1919.
Studdert Kennedy, Geoffrey A. *More Rough Rhymes of a Padre*. London: Hodder & Stoughton, 1920.
Studdert Kennedy, Geoffrey A. *Peace Rhymes of a Padre*. London: Hodder & Stoughton, 1920.

Studdert Kennedy, Geoffrey A. *Democracy and the Dog-Collar*. London: Hodder & Stoughton, 1921.

Studdert Kennedy, Geoffrey A. *Food for the Fed-up*. London: Hodder & Stoughton, 1921.

Studdert Kennedy, Geoffrey A. *Lighten our Darkness: Some Less Rough Rhymes of a Padre*. London: Hodder & Stoughton, 1925.

Studdert Kennedy, Geoffrey A. *The Unutterable Beauty*. London: Hodder & Stoughton, 1927.

Studdert Kennedy, Geoffrey A. *The Rhymes of G.A. Studdert Kennedy*. London: Hodder & Stoughton, 1940.

Studdert Kennedy, Gerald. *Dog-Collar Democracy 1919–1929*. London: Macmillan, 1982.

Wilkinson, Alan. *The Church of England and the First World War*. London: SPCK, 1978.

Wilkinson, Alan. *Dissent or Conform? War, Peace and the English Churches, 1900–1945*. London: SCM, 1986.

Part III
Landscapes

9 First World War Nursing Narratives in the Middle East

Nadia Atia

Lured by the call of duty or the promise of adventure, and apparently undeterred by the region's reputation for dangerous Arabs, dirt, dust, heat and disease, Allied women from Britain and the Dominions provided medical care in the Middle East under some of the most challenging circumstances of the First World War. The Middle East presented women with an unreliable landscape: both deeply alien and disconcertingly familiar. The ancient civilizations of Egypt and Mesopotamia; Biblical sites such as Babylon, the Garden of Eden, or the Holy Land, and the Oriental mystique of a region so associated with the *Arabian Nights* stories in the Western imagination, combined to offer a plethora of mythologies on which to draw. In Britain, and throughout the British Empire, recruitment posters depicted women and girls seemingly in need of protection and carried slogans such as "WOMEN OF BRITAIN SAY GO!" or images of mothers holding infants with the words "45,000 AUSTRALIAN FATHERS ARE FIGHTING! WILL YOU HELP?" While these constructions of gender were being used to shame or persuade men into military service, Allied commanders were preventing women's physical presence on, or close to, the front line, to the detriment of the medical care provided for serving men. Despite this reluctance to have much needed, medically trained women near the battlefields, many women eventually made their way to the Middle East, with nurses reaching Mesopotamia (modern-day Iraq) in 1916. Drawing on published and unpublished life writing and interviews held in British archives, this chapter examines the war service of Allied nurses in the Middle East.

The tendency to overlook women's service in the so-called sideshows of the First World War has its roots in some of the first histories that emerged after the war. Elizabeth Haldane in *The British Nurse in Peace and War* (1923) reminds her readers on page 247 of her 282-page study that "[i]t must be recollected that the nursing work to done in France during the Great War was but one part, though the most important part, of the whole."[1] In the last few years, we have begun to fill these gaps in our knowledge, but our understanding of the experiences of Allied nurses outside Europe remains limited.[2] Women nursed in Malta and Lemnos in the Mediterranean, to which the wounded from Gallipoli's beaches were evacuated. Many nurses were stationed in Egypt, which was a central hub, providing medical equipment, hospitals and nursing care for nearby theatres. Eventually, women cared for the wounded in Mesopotamia, Palestine, Syria, in the Sinai desert and on hospital ships that traversed the waters between these and European or Indian shores, taking wounded men from the Middle East for treatment or convalescence elsewhere. The majority of British nurses in the Middle East fell into two categories: trained nurses who had signed up to Queen Alexandra's Imperial Nursing Service (QAIMNS) or its reserve QAIMNS(R), and Voluntary Aid Detachment Workers (commonly referred to as VADs). This second category of women had volunteered with the Red Cross and Order of St John of Jerusalem either before or at the outbreak of war. Such women had little or no experience of nursing before the war. While many women from the Dominions were also recruited into each of these "British" services, either by choice or because they were seconded to them, each of the Dominions also had their own nursing service. Most Canadian nurses served as part of the Canadian Army Medical Corps (CAMC); Australians in the Australian Army Nursing Service (AANS); and New Zealanders in the youngest of the three: the New Zealand Army Nursing Service (NZANS).

Angela K. Smith describes "a kind of double censor" at work in the life writing of serving women during the First World War: the combination of military censorship applied to all military personnel, and of a particular, gendered, pressure "to escape from the tight social control of their upbringing." In order to overcome this, women, Smith argues, "often drew on their literary heritage in order to discover a means for authentic self-expression. Where their education failed them, they searched further, often devising new literary techniques in order to articulate their experience adequately."[3] Smith's analysis of the restrictions, both internal and external, that came to bear on serving women, and—in particular—the importance of a literary heritage to women's expression of their experiences is central to my reading of these archives. These women were not only responding to a "double censor," but also drawing on a host of literary texts to represent a complex and often contradictory mixture of duty and pleasure in their life writing. To her astute summary of the tensions such texts embody, I would add the effects of hindsight in relation to the sources I use here. In interviews conducted, or memoirs written, many years after the war, the passing of time may have inflected memories with more modern attitudes, especially in relation to gender, race or Empire.

The Middle East was rich in significance for women educated within a still predominantly British, Judaeo-Christian context, even—or perhaps especially—in the so called "Kith and Kin" Dominions before the First World War, where an idealized version of kindred "Britishness" was actively cultivated. Egypt, with its world-famous sites and its relatively large contingent of nurses and troops, was a particularly rich source of touristic experiences and their re-telling and documentation. As a result, the travelogue and guidebook serve as important intertexts in these women's wartime life writing.

Perhaps especially in the memoir with its retrospective gaze, the tone of the travelogue is often consciously or unconsciously reproduced. Sadie Apperley, later Mrs S.T. Wilsdon, was a VAD who began her service in Britain and later nursed in Egypt and India. Apperley's diary of 1918 describes her experiences in the Middle East vividly. On arrival in Cairo she writes,

> We gave in our papers to Matron and wandered away to view the Pyramids—we went around them on camels, and mine developed a yen for home and took me, willy-nilly, into its village—scattering scrawny hens, children and goats in every direction. My native guide on recovering me told my fortune. I am to be married to a large man in about 4 months—quick work that.[4]

In fact, Apperley married Ray Wilsdon in September the following year and much of the rest of her diary describes her trips around the Middle East with Ray. Apperley continues that, later that day, she and her colleagues "watched the sun set over the desert—far away the Pyramids of Memphis were outlined by a flaming sky—along the banks of the Nile, men, camels and oxen were trudging home."[5] Her combination of humorous tales and more romantic descriptions of the landscape and life of the Middle East is evocative of travelogues of women in the nineteenth century such as that of the American Sarah Rogers Haight and the British writer and journalist Harriet Martineau.

Having said this, it must be acknowledged that Apperley and her colleagues were much more impressed by the sights of Egypt than these more famous travellers. Haight at least found the Pyramids an impressive sight, concluding that "it would require objects of more than ordinary interest . . . to divert one's attention from them."[6] But Harriet Martineau confessed herself "disappointed in the Pyramids now . . . as we approached, they became less and less wonderful,"[7] and Florence Nightingale, perhaps the most apt comparison, found them "vulgar" and concluded that their offensive "come-look-at-me appearance" was only tempered by the fact that as ancient mausoleums they were softened "by the shadow of death which reigned over the place, as moonlight makes everything look beautiful."[8] In contrast to the measured, or even disappointed, responses of these famous women travellers, most nurses visited the Pyramids on numerous occasions, often marking each trip with new photographs. It is ironic, too, that the associations this iconic nurse traveller makes between the Pyramids and death are not to be found in any of the nursing narratives I have seen so far, despite their wartime setting and the women's daily encounters with the human cost of war. Despite their wartime setting, the life writing of these women elides all mention of war, death or suffering. Christine Hallett suggests that the centrality of touristic experiences to women's accounts might be explained by the simple fact that "[n]ursing work was a commonplace; travel was an adventure—something that, without the opportunity to offer 'war service', they might never have experienced."[9] While she is no doubt right about the attraction of sending news of desert adventures as opposed to dysenteric wards, the emphasis on discourses of travel is so pervasive, and the lack of comment or even association with the war is so stark, that I would argue it warrants further analysis. In a context such as this, where the associations with death are so readily available, the omission is suggestive of the fact that—as I shall go on to discuss—what these women are not saying may be more indicative of their real preoccupations.

Mary Millicent Rumney recalled that in her time off she saw the Sphinx and Pyramids, and discovered sea bathing: "bathing: bathing was a great thing," she told her interviewer. In an interview for the Imperial War Museum recorded some 60 years after the war, an elderly Mary Rumney reflected on the opportunities for travel and adventure the war had offered her: "We went through the Grecian archipelago, which of course was a thing that I could never have done otherwise [. . .] and I was seeing the beauties of the world, and fortunately I knew it."[10] It is difficult for the modern reader to encounter war memoirs that are full of fun and adventure; they seem incongruous in the extreme. Not only did Mary Rumney retrospectively consider herself incredibly fortunate to have had these experiences, but she knew it at the time. This was not simply a monetary issue, but the route was one she was unlikely to encounter again: these were, in other words, simply adventures not offered by the travel agents Cook and Sons, even to those with the means to visit the Mediterranean of their own accord.

Sarah Anne (Annie) Hills' diaries and letters held at the Imperial War Museum describe her service with QAIMNS (July 1915–June 1918) on a number of hospital ships and at the 21st General Hospital in Alexandria. Like many others, her letters and diaries are full of trips to see the sights. She writes, for example: "[s]aw Pompei's [sic] pillar and two sphinxes near the catacombs were most interesting also the river Nile. We also saw a lot of sheep & two cows."[11] The list of sights here stretches from ancient archaeological sites, through geographical icons, to live stock. The inclusion of the latter is suggestive of the ways in which even everyday life in the Middle East held a fascination for many women, as I shall go on to discuss. Hills writes home that she found Egypt "most fascinating" and longed for more sightseeing than time allowed her: "[w]e have not done much sight seeing in the native bazaars yet, such quaint things there are to be seen."[12] Even after several months she asserted that although "[s]ome say the novelty will soon wear off . . . if I stay here months I am sure it won't."[13] Later, when volunteers are requested for Mesopotamia or East Africa, Hills writes that she "could not miss the opportunity & put down my name for East Africa."[14] With very little said about her life on the wards or ships, one cannot help but note her excitement and her appreciation of the opportunity to travel, all of which seems very far from the war zone in which she was of course located.

At first glance Patt (Martha) Tuckett, a Canadian nurse with the QAIMNS who served at the New Zealand Hospital and No. 21 General Hospital in

Egypt (1915–1916), seems to have done nothing but have days out, dine at hotels, have afternoon tea, get manicures, pedicures and otherwise enjoy her visit to Egypt. Tuckett's diary, so laconic as to suggest a text intended only as an aide-memoire, is full of extremely brief, but detailed, descriptions of her everyday life in Egypt. Visits to the "oriental stores," "catacombs and Pompey's [sic] pillar"[15] are regularly interspersed with the taking of photographs and their development, for instance: "off for ½ day. Went in bathing with Janet and Ethel . . . had tea at Groppi's. Went to Kodak."[16] So rarely does Tuckett mention her work or the war that, taken out of context, her diary would be difficult to identify as war service. These—and numerous other examples—read as uncanny travelogues in a war zone. The reality of Tuckett's regular pampering, teas, outings to a variety of leisure and touristic activities and trips to Kodak and Cook and Sons, serve to disrupt the reader's expectations of war service, and suggest a leisured, even luxurious, experience that sits at odds with the received and idealized image of the nurse as a ministering and self-sacrificing figure.

Sadie Apperley describes two trips to Palestine in tones reminiscent of the travelogue. She and Ray visited the major sights: Jerusalem ("a most grubby place"); Bethlehem, where they "went to the Church of the Nativity and saw the place where Christ was laid in a manger—a little crypt under the church with a British sentry ever on guard"; "The Church of the Holy Sepulchre [sic]—full of majesty; the Garden of Gethsemenie [sic] . . . the Zion Gate to the Pool of Bethzida. [. . .] More places of interest until we finished up on Solomons [sic] stables." Her diary is filled with romantic descriptions of "blue hills and orange groves with the golden globes shining in the moonlight." Apperley also notes the ubiquity of "Lily of the field,' making "a gay splash of colour amongst the green—vivid crimson, they look like drops of blood in the sunshine." Despite making the association with bloodshed herself, Apperley makes no reference to the men who lost their lives in the Allied advance on Jerusalem, or elsewhere in the Middle East, although she would have had intimate knowledge of their suffering.[17]

Ida Cliffe, Ida Jefferson when she served in QAIMNS, self-published a memoir of her service in Egypt, India and Mesopotamia. Although often evoked in women's writing, guidebooks are rarely referenced. Ida Cliffe's memoir, perhaps because it was edited later for publication, recreates the tone of the travel guide more closely than most. Cliffe added detail less frequently available to those writing contemporary accounts of their time in the Middle East. Of her visit to the Sphinx, for example, Cliffe writes:

> The Sphinx represents the Egyptian God 'Horus', the midday sun of the Horizon. Some authorities consider it is older than the Pyramids. [. . .] Its body of one hundred and fifty feet long, paws fifty and head thirty feet. It measures seventy feet high to the top of its head. Its countenance is semi-negro. Nearby is the Temple of the Sphinx, the earliest known temple.[18]

Elsewhere, she includes quotations from famous travellers to the region: the words of Byron, Napoleon and others pepper her own memories of the war in the Middle East. If we compare her account to that of Karl Baekdeker in *Egypt and the Sudan: Handbook for Travelers* (1914), we find a similarly factual tone and equivalent, if different, details about the Sphinx:

> The Sphinx, which next to the Pyramids themselves is the most famous monument in this vast burial-ground, is hewn out of the natural rock . . . The entire height of the monument, from the pavement to the crown of the head, is said to be 66 ft. while its length from the fore-paws to the root of the tail is 187 ft. The ear, according to Mariette, is 4 ½ ft., the nose 5 ft. 7 in., and the mount 7ft. 7 in. in length; and the extreme breadth of the face is 13 ft. 8 inches.[19]

In a guidebook such as Baedeker's, the inclusion of these facts presumes a reader who might benefit from the information on their own visit to the sight being described. In a war memoir such as Cliffe's, we might interpret their inclusion as an assertion of authority; these details assert Cliffe's knowledge of the region and landscapes, just as they do in any other guidebook. As such, they feel particularly misplaced. It is the missing details of her work as a nurse that would evidence the authenticity of her account—a memoir of her war service, after all—but in Cliffe's memoir, as in so many other women's accounts, these details continue to remain elusive. This lacuna is especially noticeable in memoirs such as these where the author has had the opportunity to retrospectively add details missing from sources written contemporaneously. While Cliffe invests her memoir with extraneous details of the physical landscape and monuments of Egypt, it is the emotional, the everyday, landscapes of her war work that remain hidden from view.

In his book, *Belated Travellers*, Ali Behdad traces the shift from travelogue to guidebook, which he situates in the mid-nineteenth century. What Behdad calls "[t]he 'informational' nature of the guide"[20] marks a change in the power structure between orientalist traveller and reader. As Behdad acknowledges, the rise of the guidebook by no means ushered in the disappearance of the travelogue. However, more accessible and affordable travel to the Middle East necessitated a less romanticized, more practical tone that, Behdad argues, presumed the possibility that the readers might one day themselves undertake the journey being described. For Behdad, a marked change in tone and purpose can be identified in the shift from travelogue to tourist guide in the nineteenth and early twentieth centuries, but the discourses that Edward Said identified as Orientalism—namely a homogenisation and sexualisation of the lands and people regarded as oriental, which operate within discursive power structures that presume knowledge and, consequently, control of the region and its people—continue to shape both modes of representation for the European traveller. The guide, for Behdad, 'is in a relation of coexistence with the precursory discourse [the travelogue] in reproducing similar elements and concepts.[21] These discourses, and the power dynamics inherent within them, are very much at work in the ways that Allied women represented their time in the Middle East. In their descriptions of leisure time, these "belated travellers" reproduced the power dynamics of these genres in their letters, diaries and memoirs. Descriptions of their relationship with the places they visited and, perhaps especially, the people whom they encountered—whether it was on their travels, as patients, or colleagues—were marked by predictable discourses of race and empire, often grouped by critics under the term "Orientalism."

If the war brought women to unfamiliar geographical landscapes, perhaps all the more novel were the cultural and religious landscapes to which it also exposed them. Their work ensured that they met, treated or worked alongside men and women of many different races and creeds, whom they might otherwise have never encountered. Particularly in the Middle East, partly because its campaigns were seen as "sideshows" and staffed by colonial and imperial troops and native (Indian, Chinese and local) labour, and partly because travel to the Middle East necessitated long sea journeys through South East Asia, women were exposed to new and different ways of life. These accounts, therefore, offer us a timely reminder of some of the people we know least about: the non-white soldiers, nurses and labourers upon whom Allied forces depended, but whose presence is so elusive in our narratives of the war. Mary Schofield, who served as a VAD on hospital ships in the Mediterranean, caring for the men who fought around the Middle East between 1914 and 1917, was interviewed for the Imperial War Museum in 1975. Schofield served aboard the HMT *Aragon* and the 21st General Hospital in Alexandria. She was one of the nurses aboard the *Aragon* when it was torpedoed in December 1917. She remembered working with Egyptian men: "we called them 'gypo' orderlies—they were very good too." She also remembered "very few Egyptian soldiers."[22] Winifred Lea served from September 1915–July 1916, with the QAIMNS(R) on Lemnos, but also on hospital ships around the Mediterranean. Lea remembered Indian patients being cared for: "happy in their palatial looking place." She wrote home to her family that "the Sikhs are such fine looking men—& I was horribly disgusted at seeing a Tommy dead drunk the other day being looked at in contempt & surprise by Sikhs & French soldiers passing."[23] Here and elsewhere in her letters, Lea shows an extraordinary amount of understanding of the racial and religious tensions that the war brought into play in Britain and around the Empire. Her awareness that not all Indians were of one creed, for example, is far more sophisticated than that of a good many of her male colleagues during the war. Even those commanding large numbers of Indian men often conflated race and creed.[24] Later, she writes worriedly that Britain's "Indian question too is difficult—Mohammedans don't like fighting Mohammedans!"[25] Again, few men, even those in command of large Indian forces, showed as much understanding of the problems caused by the declaration of war, and especially of the declaration of *jihad*, by the Ottoman

Sultan in November 1914. These were mixed with the very real fears of those with large numbers of Indian Muslim soldiers under their command. Given their religious beliefs, to whom would Indian Muslims really owe allegiance, especially when asked to fight in Muslim lands, against a Muslim enemy?

In her description of her trip to Palestine in 1918, Effie (Euphemia) Ross Gardner, who served in Cairo during the war, noted the sight of "officers (British, Egyptian, Indian, Jewish, Australian, New Zealand, and one grand Italian so well dressed that he lent quite a tone to the motely group) going on leave."[26] On arrival at Bombay, Miss Campbell toured the city, taking in the "native quarters—very dirty"; "snake charmers" and "Lady Hardinge's war hospital for wounded Indians" where she watched as a "batch of wounded came in as we were there from hospital ship. A ward of Turkish prisoners was guarded by two policemen. [Nursed by] [m]ostly English educated Indian nurses."[27] In her autobiography, Margherita De Walden recalled the "enormous Maoris" among the myriad men that she and her staff cared for in a private convalescent home for officers that she set up in Cairo to be near her husband. Although she herself was not a nurse, she played a hands-on role in the care of the men there.[28] These brief observations remind us of the existence of some of the people whose service is most hidden in First World War studies. Nurses' interactions with non-white men and women—some of whom they must have worked with or even cared for on a daily basis—are most often banal; the people they describe are either predictably racialized, or problematically blended into an exotic back drop, but we nevertheless have a duty to acknowledge them, and to read them a reminder of the existence of a multi-cultural landscape, so often obscured from our view of the war.

However, given the prominence of travel in these accounts of war service, more frequently ordinary life and people in the Middle East were themselves a source of fascination and exoticism for these women. Examples of seeing the quotidian as exotic are almost ubiquitous in their accounts, as we have already seen. In his analysis of the *Blue Guide*, Roland Barthes argued that discourses of travel over-emphasise the monumental at the expense of the human. As a result in such writing, "men exist only as 'types' . . . they are a mere introduction, they constitute a charming and fanciful décor, meant to surround the essential part of the country: its collection of monuments."[29] For Barthes, this reductive practice "suppresses at one stroke the reality of the land and that of its people," ushering in a "process of vanishing," which acts as "an agent of blindness," obscuring real, ordinary life at the expense of the spectacle.[30] Although Barthes was thinking specifically about the ways in which the politics, history and people of Spain under Franco's rule are elided by the *Guide*, his analysis of the flattening effects of discourses of travel are equally applicable in this context. Ali Behdad distinguishes his own reading of the common ground between travelogue and guide from Barthes', but I read the discourse of Orientalism as an equally flattening ideology—in both a place is reduced and its people dehumanised in a touristic discourse where they themselves are one of the most exotic sights to behold, an oriental "type" in Barthes' terms.

References to the many different people women encountered either on their travels around the Middle East, or during their service as objects of curiosity are manifold. In an example of the ways in which the First World War enabled moments of cultural exchange, Miss Campbell recalled her first glimpse of "Cingalese [sic] running beside us selling flowers *singing* it's a long way to Tipperary" (emphasis in original).[31] Miss E. Campbell was an Australian nurse who served in QAIMNS between 1915 and 1919. It must have sounded particularly apt, if somewhat strange, to Campbell far from her own home as it was sung quite so far from Tipperary by Sri Lankans, who presumably had picked the song up from Allied men serving very far from their own homes.

Other women's recollections of native peoples were more predictable. Hills recalled a trip to the bazaars where she saw "people [who] are so very Eastern. Just what you read about but have never seen before. Most of the women wear a veil which hides three parts of their face."[32] It is clear from her comments that the people are as much an exotic sight as the bazaar itself. What is rarer, but also recorded by Hills, is the return gaze of the "types" she describes. She recalls that the people she was ogling were themselves ogling her: "The people would say to each other as we passed 'English'!" She and her party were, it seems, a source of equal fascination to those they encountered in the bazaars; far from blending into the landscape within which they formed one of many "sights," the return gaze asserts an alien, but still human, subjectivity. Winnie Lea was clearly delighted by her first sight of Arabs: "Landed at Alexandria at last Hurrah! All so quaint—the Arabs with their long dressing gown sort of garments & the women with their faces covered by those long black things."[33] The everyday dress and customs of the Arabs were a constant source of fascination for Allied women, especially the women's custom of wearing a veil as indicated by both Hills' and Lea's comments here. Lea lacks the vocabulary to describe what she sees, but she is not frightened or disapproving, rather somewhat patronizing in viewing the scene as "quaint." Sadie Apperley reproduced a more troubling tone in her recollection of seeing "the Jews [sic] Wailing place where a few of them with side locks were intent on howling and rocking as they read their old Testaments."[34] Apperley's tone hints at anti-Semitism with her use of a rather derogatory "howling."

Sometimes women actively sought out Middle Eastern people, or ways of life as exotic sights and experiences, just as they sought out any other elusive sight or place of interest. Lea recalls driving "about 7 miles out with Walter [...] we wanted to [go] into the Desert a see something of the tribes but we only touched the fringe of the real Desert & saw some Bedouis [sic] in tents about 4 ft high covered with rags."[35] Ida Cliffe devoted long sections to the people she encountered or sought out on her travels around the region. "[A]ttractive" Greek women, the "Lovely eyes [that] peep at one as the 'Moslem' women pass by—over the yasmak—and they leave behind a delicious fragrance."[36] At one point Cliffe and her colleagues actually pay to observe a "Moslem wedding," which she describes at great length. These stereotypical and Orientalized scenes pepper her narrative, culminating in "a wonderful and unforgettable experience and one I should not have liked to have missed, inside of an Arabian Harem."[37] We might situate Cliffe's enthrallment with the harem, which she discovers by chance on a trip to Kuwait, in a long line of European "Harem narratives." Cliffe's is typical of the genre in its fixation on entering and describing a forbidden, oriental, feminine space. Accompanied by the Sheik's "small grandson," who acted as an interpreter, she and her female friends visited the Sheik's wives:

> I believe there were about sixteen wives, some of them quite young and some very lovely indeed. The latest and youngest one was very lavishly adorned with anklets and bangles, and her robes seemed gay. Their quarters were quite spacious and off a very large courtyard, and seemed very wonderful and fully of precious embroideries and carpets.
>
> We visitors could not speak Arabic, so we did not understand what was being said, but the grandson translated and he told us that one of them was very curious to know why we were travelling in a car alone with gentlemen who were not our husbands. It was very strange to them. News evidently travels fast in a harem. They asked us to take off our hats and stroked our hair and faces. It was all very embarrassing and rather amusing.[38]

Cliffe's recreation of the harem narrative complete with numerous beautiful wives, oriental carpets and accoutrements, also offers us an account of the return gaze and equal fascination of the women she and her friends have gone to see. The women themselves, first posited as an oriental spectacle, find Ida Cliffe and her occidental friends a bizarre and fascinating curiosity. The Kuwaiti women's disapproval of the British women's travelling arrangements, and requests to touch their bodies and hair reveal an equal, and equally objectifying, attitude towards Cliffe and her friends that—inadvertently I would suggest—subverts the classic harem adventure that she wishes to recount. In place of the placid, or even oppressed, harem of wives, Cliffe's account suggests a lively and confident group of women, happily subverting the oriental gaze with an "occidantalising" gaze of their own.

Although the emphasis of women's war writing, and consequently ours, has been on the pleasures and novelty of travel—on the touristic landscape most readily and easily evoked in letters home—the vast majority of serving women's time was taken up with the difficult business of caring for wounded men, often under almost intolerably strained circumstances: a hidden and equally if not more uncharted landscape of war work and grief. However, if carefully examined this latter landscape asserts its presence, most often in women's diaries, or later interviews, but occasionally also in letters home.

Six months into her service, Hills writes on New Year's Day 1916 of a rare "whole day off today. The first I have had."[39] Sadie Apperley wrote to her mother of the eerie nights she spent alone on night duty afraid of "ghosties and ghoulies and things that go bump in the night—Good Lord deliver us—I am sitting in a horrid little bell tent at 1.30am on a cold and windy night."[40] "This address looks very grand," Lea wrote to her father, "but oh! It is a filthy Hotel!"[41] On arrival she needed to ask for money to tide her over while the War Office processed her pay so that she might "at least buy eggs here."[42] Ida Cliffe recalled limited water and "few fresh food stuffs . . . our food was 'tinned'. Even the butter and the milk!"[43] Although they rarely mentioned it, it is clear that their living conditions were basic at best.

Apart from the hardships of climate and sub-standard accommodation, women serving in the Middle East were also subject to the many diseases to which their patients succumbed. Ida Cliffe remembered the impact of Malaria and Sandfly fever: "we had three thousand beds in tents—the shortage of staff—badly off as we were at the best of times—made matters rather worse, but we all did our best."[44] Eventually, Ida Cliffe had to leave the Middle East because the impact of the climate on her own health became too detrimental. Our critical focus on the fun these women had, recorded so evocatively in photographs and letters, has led us perhaps a little too far from the realities of wartime nursing in the Middle East. Contained, but not so prominent, in these women's life writing are also descriptions of sometimes sad, or even harrowing, often simply mundane war experience. Patt Tuckett's very brief, laconic diary entries are a difficult mixture of stark war experience and tourism. She writes for example: "[t]wo patients died in 21a [. . .] bathing in Mediterranean after dinner. Beautiful moonlight night."[45] Or, "I had a manicure and a hairdress. Received convoy of frozen feet from peninsula today."[46] It is difficult to interpret these stark facts, thrown in among the everyday, and the sometimes rather indulgent, activities listed alongside them. The list—which was most likely a reflection of nothing more than Tuckett's own attempts to process and record her overwhelming experiences—seems to reduce everything contained within it to the same magnitude, equating the deaths or injuries of her patients with her trips to Kodak. In his examination of nursing narratives set on the Western Front, Santanu Das observes that women had "to create a protective layer of callousness between themselves and the suffering of the men they treat."[47] We might read Patt Tuckett's lists of fun interspersed with the very real horrors of war in light of this.

While it is clear that many women used their spare time to visit the sights, the reality of war service could very quickly catch up with them. No matter how many trips to the Pyramids or the catacombs they went on, these women—particularly those serving with QAIMNS—had signed up for war service and were not free to come and go, as tourists would have been. For many months Lea's letters suggest a leisured life, filled mainly with trips to see the sights. She wrote to her sister of a trip where "far away in the distance were the pyramids of Gizeh looking so mysterious." Her letters stretched on for days echoing the tones of the travelogue, but while describing the scene above, Lea received news of her mother's unexpected death. Immediately, she was plunged into grief and longing to go home. She writes again to her sister—in a continuation of the same letter containing the touristic scene quoted above:

> How *can* I go on with this letter? Yesterday evening matron brought the [wire] from Walter, telling the sad sad news!!! It is so sudden & unexpected—& oh dear! I do feel such a horrible long way from home—I keep wishing & wishing that I had never come—& now I shall not hear anything for a fortnight—such an age to wait!!! [48] (emphasis in original)

From this point on, the realities of being miles from home, of communications that took weeks, or months, to catch up with life events became all too prominent, all too important. For weeks after her mother's death, for example, Winnie Lea continued to receive letters from her deceased mother. She writes of the strangeness of "receiving little short letters from mother written in such a bright way feeling quite herself."[49] Lea was desperate to go home, but without the independent means to do so and tied to her war service with QAIMNS, she was forced to continue to serve in Egypt. While these memoirs, letters and diaries bear the hallmarks of the travelogue, to dismiss them as trivial would be to miss the reality of the war that was central to these women's experiences, even if it remains peripheral in their—and our—narratives of them.

Photographs of women enjoying themselves and letters, perhaps tellingly, empty of all reference to the war that waged around them have kept us from noting that they also nursed men on all surfaces of hospital ships, under tarpaulin in makeshift hospitals in the desert for long shifts, constantly on the move as the war moved and with varying, but consistently poor, standards of accommodation. This reluctance to describe their service might be partly explained by a sort of stoicism. Ida Cliffe insists from the beginning of her memoir that she was "on War Service, not on a voyage of pleasure."[50] Later, when describing her time in Mesopotamia caring for 3,000 men with few staff, Cliffe uses a turn of phrase, often repeated by nurses, insisting that no matter how difficult the circumstances "we tried to be cheery and bright and make the best of things."[51] This is a sentiment echoed by many, including Mrs A.G. Elliot (née Gordon-King), an Australian nurse who served with the Army Nursing Service and was interviewed by the historian Peter Liddle about her experience of nursing on hospital ships around the Gallipoli peninsula during the evacuation of Allied troops. "[Y]ou don't consider yourself," Elliot insists throughout, "you put yourself out of it if you are a good nurse. You think of the patient."[52] Liddle insistently questions Elliot on the emotional toll taken by her work. Reluctantly, she reveals that "it was all horrible. Twice I broke down and wept but most of the time I managed to keep going and smiling. Smiling was very important because you had to cheer the boys."[53] This insistence that one must put one's patients first, that one must remain strong, indeed "cheery" (the word is tellingly repeated by both women) and never allow one's feelings to intrude fits well with narratives of war service, which elide all pain and hardship and focus only on the cheery travel their work made possible. Pushed repeatedly on the question by Liddle, Mrs Elliot reveals the two incidents that led her to lose the self-control and stamina that she understood as hallmarks of her professionalism.

She recalled "a tall New Zealander" with '[M]ultiple wounds. Compound fractures of the legs as well as other wounds and [he] was not conscious. We didn't even have a bed that was long enough for him.'[54] Like the failed suicide described in Mary Borden's story "Rosa," it is this man's size and strength (Elliot repeats the word tall in her interview as Borden repeatedly uses words such as "huge" and "immense") that most upsets her; Elliot emphasises the fact that he was too big to be contained by the war machine that had broken his limbs.[55] Like Borden's "Rosa" the man is too big for hospital beds; many years later Elliot remembers his compound fractures, the multiplicity of his wounds, and gestures towards more, hidden, wounds to his awesome body: as Borden's nurse narrator reflects "[b]ecause he was so big, his helplessness was the more helpless."[56]

Elliot's second example also evokes Borden, both "Rosa" in her continued lament of the broken strength of the male body, but also Borden's sexualized appreciation of the same in "Enfant de Malheur." Elliot recalls "a beautiful young fellow" who was dying on arrival. "[W]hen I went over" she tells Liddle, "he was just going. He was such a fine looking fellow, beautiful physique and everything and he just went before I could do anything for him."[57] Once again it is the loss of a vital, beautiful (she repeats this, the only adjective she uses to describe the young man) male body that breaks her resolve. As Pim in Borden's story marvels at the black man's body, reflecting that "[n]ot even his wounds could disfigure him," so the youth and beauty of these young men's bodies seem to have been preserved in Elliot's awed memory of them.[58] Elliot's final comment on her emotional responses to the deaths of the men is that a nurse's "duty wasn't to think of ourselves. Our duty to attend to the patients and do what we could to cheer them and help them." Her discomfort at revealing her feelings is clear.[59]

Perhaps it is this insistence on service, on cheer in the face of all hardships that has led women to downplay their often difficult and dangerous work in their narratives of war service. Mary Schofield described the sinking of the *Aragon* in remarkably understated tones: "we'd had boat drill every day, so we knew just what to do."[60] An elderly Schofield seems reluctant to suggest that she had been frightened, even several decades after the event. Ida Cliffe recalls being transported home on a troop ship—a dangerous place to be—by a reluctant captain. Although her ship was attacked ("We saw the torpedo coming, but our boat was only slightly damaged"), the incident gets barely a sentence in her memoir of the war.[61] Similarly, Sadie Apperley notes the fact that Egyptian riots in the aftermath of the war had "killed two sisters and a good many of our men in Cairo," but only in the context of her disappointment that she was not allowed "leave for Luxor for a train load going there was attacked."[62]

These curiously conflicted texts offer us glimpses of multiple hidden landscapes of the First World War. As a corpus of life writing, they assert the importance women's work in the Middle East, too long overlooked in our understanding of the war in that region. Contained in Sadie Wilsdon's papers at Leeds is a letter from Yvonne Cross, editor of the *Nursing Mirror*. Although Cross enjoyed the diary very much and "toyed quite seriously with the idea of publishing it" she decides against it because of the "dearth of description of actual *nursing*" (emphasis in original). Perhaps because they contain so little description of nursing, perhaps because they contain so many incongruous descriptions of travel and fun, perhaps because they are narratives neither of battlefield experience—so central to First World War studies—nor located on the Western Front, these women's war service has been neglected in our understanding of the war. There is no question that the Middle East, its people, and the non-white men and women that their work brought them into contact with form another hidden landscape, far from fully mapped in our understanding of the war. These men and women are often a problematic source of idle fascination in these women's narratives. Most often, what small glimpses they offer us of them are related through the prism of predictable discourses of race and gender, typical of the travel narratives that so often formed their templates. But among the predictable, beneath the veneer of the travelogue, lies evidence of important labour too often hidden from view and a very real, three-dimensional humanity, too complex to be contained in the template a travelogue offers. Whether it was their own, often dangerous, always difficult work or the work of native labourers, nurses, or soldiers, these women's accounts allow us to see—sometimes very fleetingly—aspects of cultural, physical and human landscapes of the war in the Middle East that have remained obscured for too long.

Notes

1. Elizabeth Haldane, *The British Nurse in Peace and War* (London: Murray, 1923), 247.
2. See for example: Christine E. Hallett, *Containing Trauma: Nursing Work in the First World War* (Manchester: MUP, 2009); Hallett, *Veiled Warriors: Allied Nurses of the First World War* (Oxford: Oxford University Press, 2014) and Yvonne MacEwen, *In the Company of Nurses: The History of the British Army Nursing Service in the Great War* (Edinburgh: Edinburgh University Press, 2014). See also Leah Leneman, 'Medical Women at War, 1912–1918', *Medical History* 38 (1994), 160–177; Billie Melman, *Women's Orients: English Women and the Middle East, 1718–1918* (Basingstoke: Macmillan, 1995); Anne Powell, *Women in the War Zone: Hospital Service in the First World War* (Stroud: History, 2009).

First World War Nuring Narratives in the Middle East   189

3. Angela K. Smith, *The Second Battlefield: Women, Modernism and the First World War* (Manchester: Manchester University Press, 2004), 18.
4. S.T. Wilsdon née Apperley, Liddle Collection, Leeds: LIDDLE/WW1/WO/134 (hereafter Wilsdon), 3–4.
5. Wilsdon, 4.
6. Sarah Rogers Haight, *Letters from the Old World, by a Lady of New York, Vol. 1* (New York: Harper, 1840), 123.
7. Harriet Martineau, *Eastern Life, Past and Present* (Philadelphia: Lea and Blanchard, 1848), 217.
8. Cited in: Michael D. Calabria, *Florence Nightingale in Egypt and Greece: Her Diary and 'Visions'* (New York: State University of New York Press, 1997), 415.
9. Hallett, *Containing Trauma*, 127.
10. Mary Milicent Rumney, IWM Sound.739.
11. Miss A. Hills, IWM, Documents.9601, Letter 25/7/1915. (Hereafter Hills).
12. Hills, 26/9/1915.
13. Hills, 26/9/1915.
14. Hills, 17/2/1916.
15. M.L.P. Tuckett, IWM, Documents.11751, 26/9/1915. (Hereafter Tuckett).
16. Tuckett, 24/9/1915.
17. Wilsdon, 11–12.
18. "S R N at War: A Nurse's Memoir" by Ida E. Cliffe, Cliffe (née JEFFERSON), Ida E, LIDDLE/WW1/WO/017, 19. Hereafter, Cliffe.
19. Karl Baekdeker, *Egypt and the Sudan: Handbook for Travelers* (London: Peter Unwin, 1914), 135.
20. Ali Behdad, *Belated Travelers: Orientalism in the Age of Colonial Dissolution* (Cork: Cork University Press, 1994), 36.
21. Behdad, *Belated Travelers*, 38.
22. Mary Schofield, IWM, Sound. 690—my transcript.
23. WEB Lea, IWM, Documents. 510, 6/2/1916.
24. I have explored these ideas elsewhere, particularly in relation to the siege of Kut and the Mesopotamia campaign see for example chapters 3 and 4, Nadia Atia, *World War I in Mesopotamia* (London: IB Tauris, 2016).
25. Lea, 29/2/1916.
26. Miss E. Ross Gardner, IWM, Documents.12984, 5–6.
27. Miss E. Campbell, IWM, Documents.947, 5/6/1915. (Hereafter Campbell)
28. Lady Margherita Howard De Walden, *Pages from My Life* (London: Sidgwick and Jackson, 1965), 127.
29. Roland Barthes, *Mythologies*, trans. Annette Lavers (New York: Noonday Press, 1972 [1957]), 74–75.
30. Barthes, 75–76.
31. Campbell, 2/6/1916.
32. Hills, 25/7/1915.
33. Lea. n.d.
34. Wilsdon, 11–12.
35. Lea, 4/2/1916.
36. Cliffe, 3.
37. Cliffe, 16.
38. Cliffe, 15.
39. Hills, 1/1/1916.
40. Wilsdon, 13.
41. Lea, 4/2/1916.
42. Lea, 10/ 10/1915.
43. Cliffe, 14.
44. Cliffe, 14.

190 *Nadia Atia*

45. Tuckett, 27/8/15.
46. Tuckett, 7/12/15.
47. Santanu Das, *Touch and Intimacy in First World War Literature* (Cambridge: CUP, 2005), 176.
48. Lea, 10–11/3/16.
49. Lea, 22/3/16.
50. Cliffe, 1.
51. Cliffe, 14.
52. King, LIDDLE/WW1/ANZAC/AUST/051, 5 (hereafter King).
53. King, 5.
54. King, 6.
55. Mary Borden, *The Forbidden Zone* (London: Hesperus, 2008), 63.
56. Borden, 64.
57. King, 6.
58. Borden, 47.
59. King, 6.
60. Schofield.
61. Cliffe, 21.
62. Wilsdon, 13–14.

Bibliography

Baekdeker, Karl. *Egypt and the Sudan: Handbook for Travelers*. London: Peter Unwin, 1914.

Barthes, Roland. *Mythologies*, trans. Annette Lavers. New York: Noonday Press, 1972 [1957].

Behdad, Ali. *Belated Travelers: Orientalism in the Age of Colonial Dissolution*. Cork: Cork University Press, 1994.

Borden, Mary. *The Forbidden Zone*. London: Hesperus, 2008.

Calabria, Michael D. *Florence Nightingale in Egypt and Greece: Her Diary and 'Visions'*. New York: State University of New York Press, 1997.

Das, Santanu. *Touch and Intimacy in First World War Literature*. Cambridge: CUP, 2005.

De Walden, Lady Margherita Howard. *Pages from My Life*. London: Sidgwick and Jackson, 1965.

Haight, Sarah Rogers. *Letters from the Old World, by a Lady of New York, Vol. 1*. New York: Harper, 1840.

Haldane, Elizabeth. *The British Nurse in Peace and War*. London: Murray, 1923.

Hallett, Christine E. *Containing Trauma: Nursing Work in the First World War*. Manchester: MUP, 2009.

Hallett, Christine E. *Veiled Warriors: Allied Nurses of the First World War*. Oxford: Oxford University Press, 2014.

Leneman, Leah. 'Medical Women at War, 1912–1918.' *Medical History* 38 (1994): 160–177.

MacEwen, Yvonne. *In the Company of Nurses: The History of the British Army Nursing Service in the Great War*. Edinburgh: Edinburgh University Press, 2014.

Martineau, Harriet. *Eastern Life, Past and Present*. Philadelphia: Lea and Blanchard, 1848.

Melman, Billie. *Women's Orients: English Women and the Middle East, 1718–1918*. Basingstoke: Macmillan, 1995.

Powell, Anne. *Women in the War Zone: Hospital Service in the First World War.* Stroud: History, 2009.

Smith, Angela K. *The Second Battlefield: Women, Modernism and the First World War.* Manchester: Manchester University Press, 2004.

Liddle Archive, Brotherton Library, Leeds

Cliffe (née Jefferson), Ida E., LIDDLE/WW1/WO/017
King (Mrs Elliot), LIDDLE/WW1/ANZAC/AUST/051
Wilsdon (née Apperley), Liddle Collection, Leeds: LIDDLE/WW1/WO/134

Imperial War Museum Archives, London

Campbell, Miss E., IWM, Documents.947
Gardner, Miss E. Ross, IWM, Documents.12984
Hills Miss A., IWM, Documents.9601
Lea, W.E.B., IWM, Documents.510
Rumney, Mary Milicent, IWM Sound.739
Schofield, Mary, IWM, Sound. 690
Tuckett, M.L.P., IWM, Documents.11751

10 Cars in the Desert
Claud H. Williams, S.C. Rolls and the Anglo-Sanusi War

Lisa Regan

On 5 November 1915 the HMS *Tara* was torpedoed and sunk by a German U-Boat while on patrol just North-East of the Egyptian garrison town of Sollum. Ninety-two of the crew survived and swam to shore where they were taken prisoner by the German-Turk forces and placed in the custody of a devout Muslim confraternity called the Sanussiyya who marched them starving, thirsty, sometimes wounded and often barefoot across the most hostile landscape the Welsh crew had ever seen: an "immense red-brown sea of desert [. . .] featureless [. . .] its monotony unbroken by a single rock or tree."[1] In this space, tortuous to mind and body, the crew were, in the Captain's words, "like [. . .] the spirits of the damned mov[ing] through Hades."[2] After the sinking of HMS *Tara* other attacks on British ships came to light, and before the month was out Bedouin tribes led by the Sanussiyya massed in force to retake Sollum.[3] It marked the opening of hostilities between the Sanussiyya and British forces that would bring other soldiers from across the British Empire to an alien, hellish landscape.

The Anglo-Sanusi War as it became known was short-lived. British military intelligence interpreted such maneuvers as part of a German-Turk campaign to exert concerted pressure on British-occupied Egypt from the Western desert and draw forces from the Dardanelles and the Suez Canal. Sollum and another coastal town, Barani, were evacuated. British troops regrouped further up the coast at Mersa Matruh and then rode out in December to meet Sanussiyya forces led by Turkish commanders Nuri Pasha and Ja'far Pasha. The Battle of Wadi Majid on Christmas Day scattered Sanussiyya forces, including their trained militia, the *muhafizia*, and further military engagements routed them further, sending them into the desert interior. By mid-March 1916 the British had re-acquired Sollum and Barani.[4] T.E. Lawrence remarked as early as January 1916 that "on the West the little flare up seems nearly over."[5] Certainly this conflict was overshadowed by his success with the Arab Revolt. In June 1916 Sharif Husayn initiated the Arab nationalist uprising against the Turks to secure Mecca. From autumn that year Lawrence worked with the Sharif's son, Faysul, to unite the disparate nomadic tribes of the Arabian Peninsula, raiding Turkish forces along the Hijaz Railway from Mecca through to Akaba and finally taking Damascus in October 1918.[6] But the Anglo-Sanusi war or "reverse Arab Revolt,"[7] was more than just a prelude to Lawrence's campaign or a "sideshow" of the war at large. As the war correspondent W.T. Massey was to insist, this "campaign had an importance to the Empire far beyond that of relieving the Egyptian seaboard of the presence of an enemy invader. It was an object in Imperial unity."[8] Massey refers to the fact that this particular spot of desert brought together troops from four continents: Sikhs supported by English yeomanry led South Africans and New Zealanders into battle. Massey's observation suggests this war ought to be read, as recent studies illustrate, as part of the wider sweep of imperial history.[9] And this is what I do here by focussing on another remarkable aspect of this desert conflict, which was that it marked the first extensive use of armoured cars and the Model T Ford by the British military. The "cars struck terror in Senussi hearts" and secured victory in an otherwise impossible landscape.[10]

The Western Egyptian and Libyan Desert was a landscape that demanded a different kind of warfare from the Western Front. From the outset it became evident that traditional battle tactics could cause unnecessary casualties in this desert terrain. Early in December yeomanry on reconnaissance encountered the enemy and charged, only to discover a wadi or dry-riverbed in their path with "an abrupt and precipitous drop of about fifty feet" over which many soldiers fell to their deaths.[11] Indeed, as one account details, the "broken nature of the ground" meant that the Sanussiyya could often hold off the British infantry and escape into caves, while the heat rising from the ground generated "mirages in every direction and an object on the horizon was so distorted that it was impossible to make out whether it was a bush, a man, a camel, or a tree."[12] Even the very notion of victory had to be recalibrated, for Sanussiyya forces were not defeated in the usual sense but merely dispersed to remote oases in the desert interior, and the leader of the Sanussiyya at this time, Sayed Ahmed, was never captured. Although the war was considered largely over by March 1916, British patrols continued to track the Sanussiyya and only eventually drove them out of the Western Egyptian Desert at the oasis of Siwa in February 1917.

Siwa was cause for celebration not only for the victory itself but also for how that victory was achieved. The "Siwa show was probably unique in this or any other war," Claud H. Williams insisted; "[i]t was purely a motorcar affair, for the great distance of barren, waterless country precluded the use of any other force."[13] Williams was the New Zealand captain of one of the 15 Light Car Patrols established in Spring 1916.[14] These Light Car Patrols used Model T Fords, and although they were jocularly referred to as "Flying Bedsteads," their value in the desert terrain was beyond compare:[15] as Andrew Goudie notes, the "high quality vanadium" used by Ford for these cars gave them "a remarkable reputation for durability."[16] Light Car Patrols could cover the vast distances required in desert conflict impossible for ordinary yeomanry dependent on water and fodder for horses, and were even capable, as the desert explorer R.A. Bagnold would later remark, "of supplanting the camel in certain areas, notably in the Western Desert"; at a time when troops were desperately needed elsewhere these cars "armed with machine guns, guarded the whole eight hundred-mile frontier against a possible recrudescence of the Senussi menace."[17]

At Siwa the Light Car Patrols fought alongside the Armoured Car Division, led and developed by the second Duke of Westminster, Sir Hugh Richard Arthur Grosvenor. These were an armour-plated 40–50 hp Rolls Royce chassis with a "revolving gun turret" that was, Goodie points out, "an essentially naval feature," fitting given that they were initially to be used by the Royal Navy Air Service.[18] Although these cars were "little or no use in trench warfare" they found their apogee in the desert, chasing down a highly mobile enemy.[19] Not only were they essential to the triumph at Siwa—Williams describes them trading fire and holding their positions all through the night until the Sanussiyya disbanded at dawn—but also to the rescue of the *Tara* prisoners on 17 March 1916, during which they were reported to have made a desert run of 250 miles in 22 hours "without casualties and without incident."[20] A letter written by the second officer of the *Tara* recalls the "glorious sight" of "armoured motorcars dashing up to us" and declares the Duke of Westminster "a champion of champions."[21]

But there is a disturbing end to the second officer's account: "as soon as the party greeted us, two of the cars dashed off, and in a few moments we heard machine guns speaking or pom-pomming. The flying Arabs were all killed."[22] S.C. Rolls, an armoured car driver at the rescue, returns to this moment in his war memoir, *Steel Chariots in the Desert* (1937), and sees this killing in retrospect as an unjustified act of vengeance. Shocked by the sight of the prisoners as "a throng of living skeletons," he recollects, "there was no room left in us for compassion. [. . .] Men, women, and even children were mown down ruthlessly with our guns, in that mad hustle for revenge" and only two babies survived.[23] Rolls would later become the driver for T.E. Lawrence, and his admiration for Lawrence—for the man "who knew the desert and its inhabitants so well"—is clear.[24] So too is Lawrence's influence on Rolls' reassessment of the Arab peoples in *Steel Chariots* which Rolls only wrote with Lawrence's encouragement in the wake of Lawrence's own *Seven Pillars of Wisdom* (1935).

In what follows I compare Rolls' and Williams' memoirs to explore the ways in which they engaged with this landscape in their different vehicles and how this generated sometimes divergent perspectives on the conflict, the enemy and imperial identity. For Williams the car often seems able to defy and master the landscape, and much of his experience using the car to map unknown desert space is articulated in terms which continue the narrative of European imperial expansion in Africa. But for Rolls his mastery over the landscape seems in fact to be compromised rather than facilitated by the armored car he drives. His is an imperial sensibility that appears much more akin to Lawrence's, sharing in the "schizoid discourse," to borrow Ali Behdad's term, of late imperialism, whereby imperial superiority is asserted at the same time as identifying with the racial and cultural "Other":[25] a perspective that destabilizes even as it affirms imperial identity. By analyzing these two accounts as examples of war memoir as well as travel and exploration narratives, I consider how the desert landscape of the Anglo-Sanusi War becomes a site for the continuation and subversion of imperial conquest and cross-cultural encounter.

Conquering "Blank Space"

"But for the war and the consequent establishment of the car Patrols the greater part of the Western Desert must have remained a blank for generations, for the country is well nigh valueless and could never justify the expense of proper surveying."[26] Such was Williams' retrospective conclusion to his 1920 account of service in the Light Car Patrol. The emphasis on empty space highlights the scale of the impediment that the cars were able to overcome. In his memoirs of serving with the Imperial Camel Corps in Western Egypt, Geoffrey Inchbald makes similar observations. He recalls how operations against the Sanussiyya were severely hampered by lack of knowledge of the terrain: "Such maps as existed were virtually useless and there were thousands of square miles of desert which appeared on the maps either as a completely blank space or with just one word 'unexplored'."[27] Although Inchbald documents instances of mapping undertaken by the camel corps, these it seems were not without the risks that the cars seemed able to surmount.[28] For Williams, it was less a case of avoiding and rather a case of seeking the enemy. Notions of the enemy being close at hand were, Williams explains, mostly fearful fantasy. Or as the commanding Major of the Mersa Matruh camp, C. S. Jarvis would later put it: "As a nation, we dearly love the bogy of a fanatical army of millions of desert Arabs yelling 'Allah!' and putting infidels to the sword."[29] But the truth was that Sanussiyya secret agents grossly exaggerated numbers of the enemy in their reports to the British, no doubt to keep themselves in paid service, and the result was that the Light Car Patrols reported "with monotonous regularity no enemy in sight."[30] It "was only when our increasing radius of activity failed to disclose trace of man or beast," Williams confesses, "that we [. . .] grasped the fact that if we wanted a fight we must go and look for it."[31]

Even though Williams describes a literal "blank" space, there is no escaping the imperial connotations of his description. Why this particular section of the Western Egyptian and Libyan Desert remained a "blank" when most of the African continent had by the early twentieth century been mapped and brought under European administration lay partly in the difficult terrain, impenetrable dunes and waterless stretches, and partly in the history of local resistance to colonial incursions. France had claimed administrative control over the majority of the Sahara by the end of the nineteenth century, but the territory that would later form the Eastern side of Libya, Cyrenaica, was the last to be colonized by Italy in 1912, and even then Italy's presence remained largely confined to the coastal towns, leaving the desert interior much as it had been under the Ottoman Empire, a law unto itself controlled by the Sanussiyya.[32] So when Williams calls this space a "blank" he performs the kind of imperialist erasure of indigenous peoples that Dane Kennedy suggests characterised European cartographic practices from the early nineteenth century—an approach, Kennedy explains, that would "permit explorers and their sponsors to conceive of continents, like oceans, as vast and seemingly empty spaces that could be truly known only after they had been made unknown."[33]

Williams suggests the call to fill in the "blank" and map the desert space—"to chart [their] information and to build up gradually a fairly reliable map of the country"—was part of the war effort to locate and track an elusive enemy, as well as identify water sources for troops.[34] To accumulate knowledge of an "unknown" landscape the drivers became specialized in the use of compasses and speedometers, even designing a sundial that would reduce the need to continually stop and get out of the car to check compass bearings. But the call to exploration was more than duty for Williams; it was also a means of filling time and, moreover, atoning for his sense of distance from active conflict, as well as his own doubts about his efficacy as a soldier.[35] He admits to manipulating his commanding officer into ordering the Light Car Patrol to find and fix a local landmark on the map, Mount Iskander, reputedly a cliff scaled by Alexander the Great when he became lost on his journey from Alexandria to consult the oracle at Jupiter Ammon in Siwa. This particular expedition stands out because Williams' crew took with them Major C.S. Jarvis who was to describe it decades later in his account of military service in *Three Deserts* (1936), recalling the extremely difficult low country terrain ("what the Arabs call *shabak* (net) desert, i.e. a network of sharp limestone ridges flush with the surface with the hollows in between filled with the finest limestone powder").[36] By a process of "[z]igzagging along ledge after ledge of gypsum," they reach Mount Iskander by midday on the second day of the expedition.[37] But even this achievement fails to satiate their appetite for discovery, and so when they strike upon an unknown "masrab" (trade route) "unsulllied by the foot of white man and undefiled by the wheel-mark of the desecrating Ford car," Williams declares, "the demon of exploration entered into us."[38]

This particular episode indicates the extent to which Williams felt able to master the "blank" space of the desert. He and his patrol navigate the worst country yet to find Mount Iskander and, using theodolite and stars, "nailed it securely to the map."[39] They follow the unknown "masrab" only to find themselves in a very narrow valley in severe heat, which they scale with difficulty to a plateau pitted with soft sand, in which Williams is yet able to discern a rocky causeway to guide them through before water supplies fail. And even when a shortage of petrol causes the cars to stop suddenly and crash into each other, they rebuild the battered cars on the spot with heavy stones. "It is difficult to put a Ford car out of action," Williams later reports, "and makeshift road repairs of the most drastic nature can be carried out."[40] Indeed, it was precisely such forays, later with the highly regarded Dr John Ball of the Egyptian Survey, which earned Williams praise from his superiors. General M. Yorke was to write to Williams assuring him that "General Allenby appreciates what you did, not only by keeping the peace, but also the excellent cartographical work which was accomplished."[41]

But for all this, there are yet indications in this narrative that Williams is not a confident, imperialist surveyor, despite his success with mapping. The scaling of Mount Iskander presents the perfect opportunity for what Mary Louise Pratt calls the "monarch-of-all-I survey-scene", in which the European explorer takes possession of a hitherto unknown landscape, often from a promontory, and makes a "non-event" narratively speaking into the event of discovery through aestheticisation of the scene and layering of meaning with numerous adjectival modifiers.[42] But in Williams' account such processes are entirely absent. The ascent is recounted in flat, pragmatic prose: "we climbed the hill and put in some good work with the theodolite on its wide, flat summit."[43] Partly this is explained by the fact that in not promoting himself as an explorer, Williams has little need to adopt narrative devices in order to earn recognition by a reading public or institutional authority such as the Royal Geographical Society. But comparison with Jarvis' response to reaching the top of this 700 ft massif also suggests that there is something about this landscape, however successfully it is mapped or explored that simply resists the element of "*mastery* predicated between the seer and the seen" that Pratt detects in Victorian explorers' accounts of the Nile.[44] Jarvis approaches "a monarch-of-all-I survey scene": "From the top one looked out across a harsh forbidding stretch of truly frightening desert shimmering in the heat haze of noon and one could understand Alexander the Great feeling appalled at the prospect."[45] Although appalling, the landscape is still aestheticized through attention to distance and light, while modifiers pile up before the nouns. But even so, the sense of "mastery" is undercut by the reference back to Alexander the Great. For although the trip to see the oracle at Siwa was a success for Alexander who was thereafter proclaimed the son of Zeus, the desert landscape of Western Egypt is still alarmingly resistant to becoming another Alexandria. Perhaps Jarvis imagines this because of long-standing scholarly debate about whether Alexander had ventured to this highly respected oracle to seek knowledge of his divine birth or whether it was to seek justification for his kingship of Egypt, which was not given.[46] Not even one of the most notable of military commanders and conquerors in history, it seems, could easily emerge from this space victorious. Although the Model T Ford inspired further desert exploration after the war, and although Bagnold would declare the Light Car Patrols' "exploits, with the crude vehicles they had [...] astonishing," this "blank" yet exceeds Williams' ability to, and perhaps inclination to, fully master it by car or compass in ways which bring his war account closer to that of S.C. Rolls.

Seeing the "Clever Choice of Ground"

While Williams' doubts about "mastery" are only detectable in textual absence, Rolls self-consciously foregrounds his lack of visual conquest in *Steel Chariots in the Desert*. Acutely aware that his armoured car, particularly in battle, offers very limited vision, Rolls describes "the dash-plate consist[ing] of an armour-plate lid with narrow horizontal slits in it."[47] When negotiating terrain in battle he must move "forward, dodging the larger stones, which were difficult to see through the narrow slits."[48] This lack of vision at the moment of conflict seems to motivate Rolls to see more clearly in other ways. And this is reflected in the style of his memoir, which atones for previous blindness through a frequently proleptic narrative.

When Rolls describes the armoured car at the beginning of *Steel Chariots in the Desert*, he anticipates its vulnerability rather than immunity to the rigours of the landscape. "The heat in the Libyan desert in summer was found to be so great," Rolls explains, "that men inside the cars were in danger of being cooked like rabbits in a saucepan."[49] This danger of being "cooked" is brought home to the reader mid-battle outside the contested garrison town of Sollum. The combination of heat from three men in a crowded space, the engine and the sun along with the noise of gunfire and red-hot empty cartridges stinging bare skin make conditions inside the car "infernal."[50] These same cramped conditions later lead to Rolls being temporarily disabled after knocking over the primus stove and scalding himself. Similarly, the revolving gun turret that ought to have guaranteed dominance on the battlefield is highly precarious: in the battle outside Siwa it gets stuck while they are on an incline leaving them temporarily unable to return fire, while bullets pierce the gun jacket, compromising its cooling system and leaving it liable to explode. Not only must Rolls always have water reserves at hand because the car's engine boils away vast quantities of their supply, but there must always be a bottle of water kept for the gun's cooling jacket which cannot be drunk on penalty of court martial. Rolls must keep to this rule even when he finds South African troops dying of thirst and stranded on the plateau.

This sustained sensitivity to the alien and potentially overpowering aspects of this desert landscape that cannot simply be mastered by the car's technology surfaces variously in Rolls' account, but particularly when recollecting moments of travelling at speed. At these moments, this is less of the futurist exultation in velocity we might expect, and more often a heightened sense of maladaptation to the terrain. At three points in the campaign he sees the Turkish leader of the Sanussiyya army, Nuri Bey "like a streak of light on his piebald mare," both seemingly "unreal apparitions flitting in the grim desert."[51] The romanticized imagery is consolidated by Rolls' obvious appreciation for his quarry's ability to evade him on horseback—"Nuri had chosen his ground well"—and Rolls answers by "charg[ing] the dunes with a terrific roar," but a burst tyre brings the chase to an end.[52] Nuri's skill in "flitting" is less annoying than admirable—a feature of Rolls' narrative that gestures to identification with the desert "Other" over the technologically advanced European soldier, which intensifies once Rolls is redeployed to serve in the Arab Revolt with T.E. Lawrence after February 1917. Serving under Lawrence, Rolls was to meet Nuri again, although by this time, Nuri had defected to the Allied side. On meeting Nuri again, his first thought is that "but for his clever choice of ground I should certainly have caught him," but, as it transpires, with Lawrence in the car Rolls too can make the same "clever choice."[53]

Rolls has the opportunity of giving Nuri a ride in the very car which chased him at Bir Wair as they travel through Wadi Rumm on their way to raid the Turkish railway. At this moment, Rolls recalls racing with one of the other armoured cars at 65 miles an hour, but when he starts to fall behind and resigns himself to losing, Lawrence suddenly directs him off track. They avoid a hidden watercourse, known to Lawrence because he has ridden the terrain on his camel, Ghazala. The watercourse waylays their opponent, and Rolls, Lawrence and Nuri are victorious. The incident affects Rolls' understanding of his relationship to this landscape, and leads him to conclude that "when you ride or walk you see more than what lies just under your nose. Car travelling is too fast and busy for close observation of surroundings."[54] This realization steers Rolls towards an account which idealizes those like Nuri and Lawrence for their ability to integrate with the landscape by horse, camel and on foot, for learning to see like the Bedouin themselves. As Old Ali, the guide who assists them on their missions finds, he can see a Sanussiyya caravan in the distance long before the English drivers can: "the English are blind," he tells them, "They have eyes in their heads, but they see nothing."[55] That Rolls leaves this to resonate in the text is a testament to his determination to retrospectively see this landscape through the eyes of the desert dweller. The result is a narrative studded with humane and ethical insights.

These emerge strongly with that bitter recognition of the violent revenge brought against the Arabs holding the *Tara* prisoners. Contrary to Inchbald who states the prisoners "had received very bad treatment,"[56] Rolls believes "it was all a mistake" and seems influenced here by what he learns from the *Tara's* captain.[57] Captain Rupert Gwatkin-Williams rode back with Rolls from the prison camp, and, like Lawrence, saw the desert peoples differently after living among them during his internment. In his account, *Prisoners of the Red Desert* (1919), Gwatkin-Williams expresses profound regret at being unable to save the prison guards: "dead, like the brave and fearless outlaws they were [. . .] There they lay, for ever sleeping on the open plain, the plain on which we first slept, swept by the bitter winds during our first tent-less week at Bir-Hakkim."[58] Although the chiasmic sentence structure here might easily imply an Old Testament notion of justice, it works rather to suggest the desert as a levelling space in which racial and cultural differences are elided and where individuals suffer equally. Gwatkin-Williams stresses too that although the prisoners had to resort to eating desert snails to survive, food was also scarce for their captors in that remote location. And Rolls adopts a similar attitude to reports of Sanussiyya starvation after discovering the emaciated British prisoners, highlighting the hypocrisy of the British blockade of the coast and Egyptian frontier: "A well-known way of taming lions and other wild creatures," he notes, "starve them thoroughly first and then offer them a dole food."[59]

The desert landscape's ability to erase distinctions between Allied troops and Arabs was in other respects seemingly welcome. After being assigned to Lawrence's command, Rolls quickly notices the change in the soldiers' appearance "with the Arab kefiya on our heads and heavy army boots on our sockless feet" as "the outward sign of our fitness to do the work we had in hand."[60] The "work" to which Rolls refers is the destruction of Turkish railway lines along the Western Arabian Peninsula, one of the irregular military strategies deployed so successfully by Lawrence. As Rolls rather wryly observes, when his armoured car unit reached Akaba in August 1917, "the Arab campaign was beginning to be organised in the European style. The organisation never got much beyond a beginning, which partly accounts for the success of the campaign."[61] Traditional European battle tactics had already shown themselves unsuited to the terrain of the Western Egyptian and Libyan Desert. And Lawrence's guerilla tactics were designed not to fight against the desert but to use the landscape known so well to the nomadic tribes to Allied advantage. *Seven Pillars* is still regarded as one of the key texts on the military advantage of the "flash attack" over conventional battle encounter.[62] And such guerilla warfare was, as Lawrence recognized, better fitted to a landscape such as the desert which resembled the sea: "Camel raiding parties, self-contained like ships, might cruise confidently along the enemy's cultivation-frontier, sure of an unhindered retreat into their desert-element."[63] Speed, fluidity and distance were pivotal to Lawrence's success in pitting desert tribesmen against Turkish troops. As he put it, "[o]urs were battles of minutes, fought at eighteen miles an hour."[64]

But Lawrence's identification with the Arab peoples and their desert far exceeded Rolls' connection with the landscape. Indeed, although Rolls is able to see "the clever choice of ground" by which the desert dweller can evade or attack a more technologically advanced army, he does so only with the help of Lawrence. Rolls might understand the benefit of seeing the desert through the eyes of its inhabitants for military gain or critique of military discipline or misguided strategies, but he does not form any personal connection even to the extent that we see with Gwatkin-Williams or Claud H. Williams. Gwatkin-Williams describes one of his kindlier guards, a Sanussiyya officer in uniform—"Mahomet Zoué by name, and a fine-looking specimen standing six feet in height"—who gives Gwatkin-Williams reason "to modify [his] views as to the savagery and untamable-ness of the Senussi."[65] Although Claud Williams finds the Bedouin "dirty," unwashed, verminous and, moreover, "cruel,"[66] he yet builds a rapport with a Sanussiyya officer, "an attractive, clean looking chap" who "much to [his] sorrow" is tried and shot as a spy.[67] Rolls' engagement with the landscape and its peoples seems entirely mediated by Lawrence, and this is brought to the fore later as Rolls waits with the Arab tribes outside of Akaba. He admits that he and the other British soldiers increasingly hate the Arabs and their "beastlike" customs as the war goes on, but when Lawrence arrives at the outpost a change comes over the whole camp as he kisses Prince Faysul.[68] Arabs and British equally hail him as hero. "There is now a visible link between us and the Arabs," Rolls writes; "We do not like them more than before, but we feel for them a sort of respect."[69] Rolls' slip into present tense at this moment creates an enduring tableau that underscores Lawrence's lasting legacy for cross-cultural understanding between the British and the desert dweller. Indeed, at this moment in the narrative, Rolls presents Lawrence as "the visible link [. . .] between us and England," and signals how Lawrence symbolizes a bridge between two very different landscapes, at a personal level here for Rolls and his fellow servicemen, and, later, at a cultural and international level in the post-war period.[70]

Although Lawrence reveals to Rolls "a very little, of those far-reaching political hopes of his for the Arabs," by which we might understand Lawrence's commitment to Arab nationalism, *Steel Chariots* continues to preserve those hopes after Lawrence's death in 1935 by reading the Anglo-Sanusi War as part of a long and continuing history of European imperialism in North Africa and the Middle East.[71] As Rolls admits with an eye to Mussolini's aggressive imperial designs in the 1930s, the campaign in the western desert "eventually made Cyrenaica safe for the willful tricks of infant fascism."[72] Although Rolls might not identify with the Arab peoples as Lawrence does, he yet articulates a shift in imperial consciousness honed by his experiences of navigating and surviving a desert landscape that could not simply be mastered by European technology. Williams too, despite his mapping success, also exhibits similar concerns about the imperialist project. Returning to furnish his 1920 account with a conclusion in the 1960s in light of Egyptian independence, Williams felt bound to add some of his experiences of the Egyptians he had known and express his understanding for why nationalism had taken hold: "is it not probable that the high-class cultured leaders got tired of hearing their people alluded to as 'Wogs' or 'Dogs' and themselves relegated to a level of permanent inferiority in their own country," he asks.[73] Perhaps his own experiences as one of the Dominion troops informed this insight or else the 1,200-mile motor trip he took across the desert, escorting dignitaries to negotiate with Sidi Idris, who would become the new leader of the Sanussiyya and later King of an independent Libya in 1951. Without doubt, though, for both Rolls and Williams, it was the experience of the desert landscape itself—"sand, gravel, rock, gravel, sand for ever and ever"—which exercised a "fascination" that both allured and challenged the imperial imagination in this theatre of war.[74]

Notes

1. R.S. Gwatkin-Williams, *Prisoners of the Red Desert: The Adventures of the Crew of the Tara during the First World War* (London: Leonaur, 2008), 61.
2. Gwatkin-Williams, *Prisoners of the Red Desert*, 72.
3. This strategically important port had been acquired for "Anglo-Egypt" while the Sanussiyya and Turks were fighting during the Italian invasion of Tripoli in 1911. See Russell McGuirk, *The Sanusi's Little War* (London: Arabian Publishing, 2007), 27.
4. For a contemporary concise overview of the Anglo-Sanusi War see Anon., "In the Western Desert of Egypt," *Blackwood's Edinburgh Magazine*, February 1917, *passim*. See also McGuirk, *The Sanusi's Little War*, 132–246.
5. T.E. Lawrence to his family, 4 January 1916, *T.E. Lawrence Studies*. Available at *http://www.telstudies.org/writings/letters/1915–16/160104_family.shtml*. (Accessed 01/06/2016).
6. See Eugene Rogan, *The Fall of the Ottomans: The Great War in the Middle East 1914–1920* (London: Allen Lane, 2015), 275–309; 365–7; 378–80.
7. This is a phrase used by Lisa Anderson, although she qualifies it by distinguishing the Sanussiyya revolt as "not in fact 'Arab' at all but Islamic." "The Development of Nationalist Sentiment in Libya, 1908–1922," in *The Origins of Arab Nationalism*, ed. Rashid Khalidi, Lisa Anderson, Muhammad Muslih, and Reeva S. Simon (New York: Columbia University Press, 1991), 234.
8. W.T. Massey, *The Desert Campaigns* (New York and London: G.P. Putnam's Sons, 1918), 148.
9. Challenging interpretations of the Sanussiyya attack as solely the product of a German-Turk military strategy, John Slight argues for the broader consideration of this jihad as a response to historical European encroachment into Muslim territory. His article "seeks to demonstrate how incorporating aspects of imperial and Islamic history, especially through a focus on British perceptions of the Sanussiyya which have remained understudied, can contribute new insights into future studies of the war in the Middle East that move beyond the concerns of older military histories." See John Slight, "British Understandings of the Sanussiyya Sufi Order's *Jihad* against Egypt, 1915–1917," *The Round Table*, 103:2 (2014): 234.
10. Massey, *The Desert Campaigns*, 147.
11. "In the Western Desert of Egypt," 207.
12. "In the Western Desert of Egypt," 209, 212.
13. Claud H. Williams, "Light Car Patrols in the Libyan Desert (1920)," in *Light Car Patrols 1916–19: War and Exploration in Egypt and Libya with the Model T Ford: A Memoir by Captain Claud H. Williams*, ed. Russell McGuirk (London: Silphium Books, 2013), 176. For more detail on the "battle at Qirba" just outside Siwa, see McGuirk, *The Sanusi's Little War*, 264–8.
14. For details on the establishment of the Light Car Patrols from Spring 1916 to allow British and colonial soldiers to be withdrawn from the Western Desert, see Russell McGuirk, "The Formation of the Light Car Patrols," in *Light Car Patrols 1916–19*, 28–32.
15. C.S. Jarvis, *Three Deserts* (London: John Murray, 1936), 6.
16. Although Henry Ford and initially objected to the use of his Ford car in the war, he eventually relented and Britain went on to deploy some 19,000 of them not only in the Anglo-Sanusi War but also elsewhere in the Middle East and France. See Andrew Goudie, *Wheels across the Desert: Exploration of the Libyan Desert by Motorcar 1916–1942* (London: Silphium Press, 2008), 49–57.
17. R.A. Bagnold, *Libyan Sands: Travel in a Dead World* (London: Eland, 2010; first published 1935), 14.

18. Goudie, *Wheel across the Desert*, 60.
19. S.C. Rolls, *Steel Chariots in the Desert: The First World War Experiences of a Rolls Royce Armoured Car Driver with the Duke of Westminister in Libya and in Arabia with T.E. Lawrence* (London: Leonaur, 2005; first published 1937), 14.
20. Anon. "Starving in Captivity in the Desert: Welsh Seamen's Life among the Bedouin," *Manchester Guardian*, 22 April 1916, 6.
21. This appeared in "Tara Survivors: Second Officer's Account," *Irish Times*, 9 April 1916, 4 and shortened in "Saved from the Senussi," *Observer*, 9 April 1916, 10.
22. "Tara Survivors: Second Officer's Account," 4.
23. Rolls, *Steel Chariots*, 47–8.
24. Rolls, *Steel Chariots*, 133.
25. Ali Behdad, *Belated Travellers: Orientalism in the Age of Colonial Dissolution* (Cork: Cork University Press, 1994), 14.
26. Williams, *Light Car Patrols in the Libyan Desert*, 243.
27. Geoffrey Inchbald, *With the Imperial Camel Corps in the Great War: The Story of a Serving Officer with the British 2nd Battalion against the Senussi and during the Palestine Campaign* (London: Leonaur, 2005; first published 1970), 70.
28. Inchbald relates the tragedy of two members of the Imperial Camel Corps: Captain Mason MacFarlane and Lieutenant Ryan. MacFarlane undertook "personal reconnaissance on foot" to discover a way through the dunes to the oasis of Baharia where the Sanussiyya were camped and returned pursued by the enemy, exhausted with thirst, but able "to reproduce a rough map of the Baharia which turned out to be substantially accurate." Weeks later, MacFarlane attempted a second reconnaissance mission on foot taking Ryan with him, but the two were killed. Their bodies, thrown over a cliff, were discovered when British troops took the oasis months later. *With the Imperial Camel Corps in the Great War*, 75–8 (76).
29. Jarvis, *Three Deserts*, 5.
30. Jarvis, *Three Deserts*, 6.
31. Williams, *Light Car Patrols in the Libyan Desert*, 170.
32. For further details, see Eamonn Gearon, *The Sahara: A Cultural History* (Oxford: Signal Books, 2011), 113–15; Knut S. Vikør, *The Maghreb Since 1800: A Short History* (London: Hurst & Co., 2012), 79–81. For detailed accounts of the Sanussiyya resistance to Italian incursions, see Edward E. Evans-Pritchard, *The Sanusi of Cyrenaica* (Oxford: Oxford University Press, 1954; first published in 1949), Chapter 5, and Lisa Anderson, "The Development of Nationalist Sentiment in Libya, 1908–1922," *passim*.
33. Dane Kenedy, *The Last Blank Spaces: Exploring Africa and Australia* (Cambridge, MA: Harvard University Press, 2013), 12, 20.
34. Williams, *Light Car Patrols in the Libyan Desert*, 171.
35. On Williams' sense that "he was not cut out to be a solider," see McGuirk, "Claud Herbert Williams: A Biographical Sketch," in *Light Car Patrols 1916–19*, 270. In September 1918, Williams wrote to his superiors on behalf of the Light Car Patrols requesting redeployment to "an active front" to abate the "monotony" of the desert and guard against the shame of "having passed through this great war without firing a shot." Williams to Major General Western, 17 September 1918, in *Light Car Patrols 1916–19*, 138–9.
36. Jarvis, *Three Deserts*, 7.
37. Williams, *Light Car Patrols in the Libyan Desert*, 196.
38. Williams, *Light Car Patrols in the Libyan Desert*, 198.
39. Williams, *Light Car Patrols in the Libyan Desert*, 198.
40. Claud H. Williams, "Report on the Military Geography of the North-Western Desert of Egypt," in *Light Car Patrols 1916–19*, 262.

41. Brigadier General Yorke to Captain Williams, Ramleh, Egypt [undated], in *Light Car Patrols 1916–19*, 140–1.
42. Mary Louise Pratt, *Imperial Eyes: Travel Writing and Transculturation*, 2nd ed. (New York: Routledge, 2008), 197–204.
43. Williams, *Light Car Patrols in the Libyan Desert*, 198.
44. Pratt, *Imperial Eyes*, 200.
45. Jarvis, *Three Deserts*, 8.
46. For the most recent intervention into these scholarly debates about Alexander's motives for the journey to the oracle at Siwa, see Andrew Collins, "Alexander's Visit to Siwa: A New Analysis," *Phoenix*, 68:1/2 (2014): 62–77.
47. Rolls, *Steel Chariots*, 19.
48. Rolls, *Steel Chariots*, 34.
49. Rolls, *Steel Chariots*, 18.
50. Rolls, *Steel Chariots*, 34.
51. Rolls, *Steel Chariots*, 34–5.
52. Rolls, *Steel Chariots*, 35.
53. Rolls, *Steel Chariots*, 141.
54. Rolls, *Steel Chariots*, 146.
55. Rolls, *Steel Chariots*, 43.
56. Inchbald, *With the Imperial Camel Corps*, 49.
57. Rolls, *Steel Chariots*, 48.
58. Gwatkin-Williams, *Prisoners of the Red Desert*, 280–1.
59. Rolls, *Steel Chariots*, 87.
60. Rolls, *Steel Chariots*, 136.
61. Rolls, *Steel Chariots*, 128.
62. Gilles Deleuze and Félix Guattari, *Nomadology: The War Machine*, trans. Brian Masumi (New York: Semiotext(e), 1986), 110, 145.
63. T.E. Lawrence, *Seven Pillars of Wisdom: A Triumph* (London: Penguin, 1962; first published 1935), 345.
64. Lawrence, *Seven Pillars of Wisdom*, 346.
65. Gwatkin-Williams, *Prisoners of the Red Desert*, 76.
66. Williams, *Light Car Patrols in the Libyan Desert*, 226–8.
67. Williams, *Light Car Patrols in the Libyan Desert*, 174–5.
68. Rolls, *Steel Chariots*, 210.
69. Rolls, *Steel Chariots*, 211.
70. Rolls, *Steel Chariots*, 211.
71. Rolls, *Steel Chariots*, 137.
72. Rolls, *Steel Chariots*, 17.
73. Williams, *Light Car Patrols in the Libyan Desert*, 248.
74. Williams, *Light Car Patrols in the Libyan Desert*, 169, 170.

Bibliography

Anderson, Lisa. "The Development of Nationalist Sentiment in Libya, 1908–1922." In *The Origins of Arab Nationalism*, eds. Rashid Khalidi, Lisa Anderson, Muslih Muhammad, and Reeva S. Simon, 225–242. New York: Columbia University Press, 1991.

Anon. "Tara Survivors: Second Officer's Account." *Irish Times*, 9 April 1916, 4.

———. "Starving in Captivity in the Desert: Welsh Seamen's Life among the Bedouin." *Manchester Guardian*, 22 April 1916, 6.

———. "In the Western Desert of Egypt." *Blackwood's Magazine*, February 1917, 206–222.

———. "Starving Senussi." *Sunday Times*, 18 February 1917, 7.
Bagnold, R.A. *Libyan Sands: Travel in a Dead World*. London: Eland, 2010. First published 1935.
Behdad, Ali. *Belated Travellers: Orientalism in the Age of Colonial Dissolution*. Cork: Cork University Press, 1994.
Collins, Andrew. "Alexander's Visit to Siwa: A New Analysis." *Phoenix*, 68:1/2 (2014): 62–77.
Deleuze, Gilles, and Félix Guattari. *Nomadology: The War Machine*. Translated by Brian Masumi. New York: Semiotext(e), 1986.
Evans-Pritchard, Edward E. *The Sanusi of Cyrenaica*. Oxford: Oxford University Press, 1949.
Gearon, Eamonn. *The Sahara: A Cultural History*. Oxford: Signal Books, 2011.
Goudie, Andrew. *Wheels across the Desert: Exploration of the Libyan Desert by Motorcar 1916–1942*. London: Silphium Press, 2008.
Gwatkin-Williams, R.S. *Prisoners of the Red Desert: The Adventures of the Crew of the Tara During the First World War*. London: Leonaur, 2008.
Inchbald, Geoffrey. *With the Imperial Camel Corps in the Great War: The Story of a Serving Officer with the British 2nd Battalion against the Senussi and during the Palestine Campaign*. London: Leonaur, 2005. First published 1970.
Jarvis, C.S. *Three Deserts*. London: John Murray, 1936.
Kenedy, Dane. *The Last Blank Spaces: Exploring Africa and Australia*. Cambridge, MA: Harvard University Press, 2013.
Lawrence, T.E. to his family, 4 January 1916. *T.E. Lawrence Studies*. Available at *http://www.telstudies.org/writings/letters/1915–16/160104_family.shtml*. (Accessed 01/06/2016).
———. *Seven Pillars of Wisdom: A Triumph*. London: Penguin, 1962. First published 1935.
Massey, W.T. *The Desert Campaigns*. New York and London: G.P. Putnam's Sons, 1918.
McGuirk, Russell. *The Sanusi's Little War*. London: Arabian Publishing, 2007.
Pratt, Mary Louise. *Imperial Eyes: Travel Writing and Transculturation*, 2nd edn. New York: Routledge, 2008.
Rogan, Eugene. *The Fall of the Ottomans: The Great War in the Middle East 1914–1920*. London: Allen Lane, 2015.
Rolls, S.C. *Steel Chariots in the Desert: The First World War Experiences of a Rolls Royce Armoured Car Driver with the Duke of Westminister in Libya and in Arabia with T.E. Lawrence*. London: Leonaur, 2005. First published 1937.
Slight, John. "British Understandings of the Sanussiyya Sufi Order's *Jihad* against Egypt, 1915–1917." *The Round Table*, 103:2 (2014): 233–242.
Vikør, Knut S. *The Maghreb Since 1800: A Short History*. London: Hurst & Co., 2012.
Williams, Claud H. "Light Car Patrols in the Libyan Desert (1919)." In *Light Car Patrols 1916–19: War and Exploration in Egypt and Libya with the Model T Ford: A Memoir by Captain Claud H. Williams*, ed. Russell McGuirk. London: Silphium Books, 2013. 159–251.

11 Murmurs of War
Grace Fallow Norton and "The Red Road"

Hazel Hutchison

Landscapes of war are not always external. In her poem "Cutting, Folding and Shaping" (1916), the American writer Grace Fallow Norton considers how, for many behind the lines, the observed or reported traces of war can open up dizzying and distressing internal perspectives. This experience, Norton suggests, is most commonly shared by women, whose sense of dislocation from the rhetoric and action of the conflict also alerts them to the personal ironies that follow in the wake of violence:

> *Cutting Folding and Shaping*
>
> We have made hundreds of oakum-pads and dressings and compresses,
> Cutting, folding and shaping, amid murmuring women's voices.
> The woman beside me has lost two brothers, so they tell.
> She tells no one. . . . She works well. . . .
> The young girl beyond knows her lover will soon be sent;
> He goes with the foreign regiment,
> But her father is serving Austria at Trente.
> They come here and make oakum-pads and dressings and compresses,
> Cutting, folding and shaping, amid murmuring women's voices.
> I wish I were a great commander of the army,
> Strong and rough and stormy.
> The spirit of Lafayette would come to me
> And I would go over the sea,
> Sure of followers, crying, "Who will follow me!"
> I am a pale Joan of Arc, seeing visions, hearing no clear voices,
> So I sit here and make oakum-pads and dressings and compresses.[1]

It is a complex and thought-provoking poem. Initially, it transmits the sense of the helplessness of women volunteers on the home front, whose place in the war is defined in terms of traditionally feminine roles: production, emotion and nurture. The oakum-pads and dressings and compresses will be shipped out to arenas of war where the women themselves cannot travel, but will project the care and healing associated with them. The speaker of the poem wishes that she might break that societal expectation, that she too might have the thrill of participation, even of violence. This wish expresses itself in a desire for a stronger voice; she longs to cry out to followers and to hear "clear voices" rallying in response. She also wishes for a new site of action "over the sea," for a new landscape in which she can have more agency. Thus, the apparently local and personal concerns of the women in the work-room provide a point of imaginative access to a landscape of heroic and historical proportions in which distinctions of time and place collapse. The present-day conflict is overlaid with the wars of medieval Europe and the American Revolution, despite these events being continents and centuries apart. In contrast with the claustrophobic "murmuring women's voices" of the work-room, the speaker's internal vision of the landscape of war creates a wide-open zone, in which action and clear speech might become possible. However, there is a swift recognition that this landscape sits beyond reality. The panoramic perspective is quickly replaced by the continuing, domestic-scale task of cutting, folding and shaping dressings for use in the distant war zone. Nevertheless, the dogged patience of those who accomplish this quiet task provides a powerful and important contrast to the destruction of war. In this poem, Norton offers us a glimpse of ordinary people whose lives, like the dressings, are being cut and remoulded by the events of war, but who in spite of their sorrows—perhaps because of them—continue to perform this small, routine and yet meaningful act of attention and kindness.

The poems of Grace Fallow Norton (1876–1962) are not widely read and rarely appear in anthologies of First World War verse. However, they provide a compelling glimpse into how the war, even in its early stages, was directing creative writers towards new techniques. They also demonstrate how poets, such as Norton, used their creative processes to explore the thorny and distressing dilemmas thrown up by the conflict, even if the war zone itself was geographically remote and remained in many ways inconceivable. America did not enter the war formally until 1917, although unknown numbers of individual American civilians did volunteer before this, perhaps as many as half a million, either as soldiers in European armies—on both sides of the struggle—or as medical personnel. And it would be wrong to assume that Americans at home took little interest from the sidelines. The problem of how to respond to the war in Europe, and how to help end it, was the most persistent and difficult issue in both political and cultural debates between August 1914 and April 1917. Many voices called for many different things: peace, war, justice for Belgium, justice for Germany, protection for transatlantic shipping, food aid to Europe, weapons for the Allies, death to German spies, better pay for war workers, money for war charities. These months were tense and volatile, and would leave a profound imprint on America's sense of national identity as it redefined its responsibilities to the international community, and shaped a new discourse that was designed to absorb the nation's many ethnic groupings into a collective feeling of being "one hundred percent American."[2] Later on, military intervention on the Allied side, and a place at the bargaining table for the Treaty of Versailles in 1919, would leave an American imprint on the landscape of Europe and would consolidate America's place as a global super-power for the next hundred years. However, as Norton was writing in the early months of the war, all this lay ahead, and the fascination of her poems lies in recovering the uncertainty and contradiction of the war's opening months. As modern readers, it is very easy to look back at the literature of the First World War with predetermined ideas of what we should find there. Our well-schooled expectations of trauma, physicality and "futility"—which are satisfied, in truth, by only a handful of writers—and our lack of patience with any expressions of political engagement or acceptance of military action, are as misplaced in their own way as the kind of wartime preconceptions and prejudices which are, these days, often blamed for the war itself. But, if we wish to understand the war better, we must listen more carefully. We must listen in particular to those who were among the first to dare to pose difficult questions about the conflict—tentative as their questions may seem in comparison with the crushing outrage of later voices.

This chapter looks at how Norton's war poems use an array of "murmuring voices" to create internalised spaces and imagined warscapes, within which she can explore the ideological confusion of the early months of the war. Her poem "Cutting, Folding and Shaping" can also be seen to provide a useful metaphor for the activities of the poet in wartime. As Norton well knew, asserting any kind of clear voice amid the upset and distortion of shifting political aims and public values was far from simple. She told her editor, Ferris Greenslet, that writing war verses made her feel "like a butterfly barking at a cyclone."[3] However, Norton's voice would emerge as one of the most distinctive and innovative American literary responses to the war in its early stages. "Cutting, Folding and Shaping" sits at the heart of Norton's poetic cycle "The Red Road," which was written as a response to her eyewitness experiences in France and England in the opening months of the war, and which appeared as the closing sequence of her third book of poems. *Roads* was published in 1916, as America debated whether it would actively engage in the conflict. In these poems, Norton explores the attitudes and assumptions that led the great powers of the world along the "red road" to war. These poems move the reader through a number of different perspectives and offer a range of voices, often in ways that dramatically cut across Norton's own views. She can also be said to be exploring new poetic landscapes in this collection. Traditional patterns of metrical verse are challenged and distended in the search for appropriate forms to convey the stress and weight of her subject matter. She is cutting, folding and shaping her experience into language, in a way that also offers a quiet defiance of the formlessness of war. The result is a series of texts which explore the operation of voice and place on both a poetic and a political level during time of war, and which offer new strategies in verse that would be more forcefully developed by other literary voices in later years.

Almost nothing has been written about Norton over the years. However, her life was eventful and her poems are powerful and innovative. Born in Northfield, Minnesota, she grew up in an extended family of fervent Congregationalists who used the money they made in banking to establish themselves as a kind of local aristocracy. After her mother's death when she was 10 years old, Grace was raised by a succession of aunts and uncles. As a teenager, Grace was sent to Abbot Academy in Andover where, in defiance of previous family codes about musical entertainment, she signed up for piano lessons in Boston—a decision which would set her on a path towards a musical career as a professional accompanist. Daringly, she also joined an Episcopalian church, a move so offensive to her Congregationalist uncles that one of them never spoke to her again.[4] After Andover, her sister's husband paid for her to study music in Germany and Norway. She then returned to the United States to settle in New York, where she married Herman de Fremery, a curator at the Museum of Natural History. Relishing her freedom and the relaxed cultural atmosphere of the Bohemian circles in which she moved, she took piano playing engagements and began to publish her poetry.

From 1910 onwards, Norton placed work in many of the major American literary periodicals of the day, including the *Atlantic Monthly*, *Century Magazine*, *Scribner's Magazine*, *Harper's Monthly Magazine*, *McClure's Magazine*, *Poetry Journal* and *Poetry*. In 1912, she published her first collection *Little Gray Songs From St Joseph's*, soon followed by *The Sister of the Wind* (1914). Both were well received. However, in 1913 her marriage to de Fremery broke down, and Norton (who continued to use her own name for professional purposes throughout her life) married the rising young painter George Herbert Macrum. In May 1914, the couple left for France and took a house at Plomarché in Brittany, so that Macrum could paint and Norton could write. This arrangement would not last for long.[5]

By November, the Macrums were back in New York. Like many other Americans who were eager to get home from the margins of the war, they had struggled to secure transatlantic tickets. The Macrums had stopped over in London and then Cornwall, trying to get away from the insistent clamour of war and the sights and sounds of mobilization. But even with these limited impressions, Norton had gathered enough material to produce some powerful poems. She did not initially think of these poems as connected to the studies in mood and colour that were supposed to form the bulk of the material for *Roads*. However, as soon as she sent them to Greenslet for a second opinion in May 1915, he reported that they had given him a "poetic thrill" and advised her to work them up as a group and include them in the collection.[6] The result was "The Red Road," a sequence of nine titles: "Is This the End of the Journey?," "The Mobilization in Brittany," "The French Soldier and His Bayonet," "The Journey," "In This Year," "The Volunteer," "Cutting, Folding and Shaping," "On Seeing Young Soldiers in London" and "O Peace, Where is Thy Faithful Sentry?" Within this series, "On Seeing Young Soldiers in London" presents seven short connected poems. So, the whole set comprises 15 poems, with "Cutting, Folding and Shaping" placed as the middle poem. This seems appropriate, as that poem's use of contrasting voices to create vivid internalised worlds is repeated throughout the whole sequence, as is the tension between imagined spaces and real nations. Norton gives as an epigraph to the series a quote from Thomas Hardy's play *The Dynasts* (1904–1908) about the Napoleonic Wars: "—a patriot cry, / A battle, bravery, ruin and no more?"[7] Anyone who recognised the line would have been able to interpret this epigraph as a reference to the downfall of Prussia—regularly used throughout the First World War as a synonym for Germany. In full, the quotation reads:

> The kingdom late of Prussia, can it be
> That thus is disappears—a patriot cry,
> A battle, bravery, ruin; and no more?[8]

However, by clipping the line to remove the overt reference to Prussia, Norton makes her nationalism less explicit. The patriot's cry, she suggests, may end in ruin, no matter which side one is fighting for. And in the poems that follow she gives plenty of examples of the kind of patriotic shouting that is likely to end in nothing more than tragedy and futility. Indeed, Norton's allusion to Hardy's epic drama gives the reader a powerful clue as to how to approach her texts. Similarly balanced between form and informality, ironic in tone, often voiced by dramatic personae, and profoundly concerned with the interplay between individual lives and cosmic forces, Norton's war poems echo both the method and mood of Hardy's work. Perhaps not surprisingly for a woman who had recently fallen in love with a painter, she also makes use of the theme of colour that runs through the whole volume of *Roads* as a powerful motif—especially the red of war.

The opening poem "Is This the End of the Journey?" was written as a link poem to connect "The Red Road" to the earlier sections of *Roads*. However, it also introduces us to the idea that Norton is going to explore the war through disparate voices and unfamiliar landscapes. Although the "journey" of the opening line is partly the poetic journey that has wound its way through the preceding poems, it is also presented as the journey from the gaiety and bravado of mobilization to the reality of the Front:

> Is this the end of the journey?
> Bright bridge and gala street
> Led but to the black shadow
> That shakes beneath our feet?

However, the war is not itself a destination, but the beginning of another, darker journey designed by some mystical "builder" who is "Paving with lives a road / That will journey onward, onward, / Over great bridges of blood!"[9] The speaking voice of this poem, with its apocalyptic tone, sets up a powerful contrast with the following two-part poem "The Mobilization in Brittany" which is much more firmly grounded in realistic observation and, perhaps not coincidently, is also more innovative in method. Here, Norton shifts dramatically to adopt a familiar, everyday, personalised voice—probably in order to relate some of what she herself witnessed in early August 1914 as France prepared for war. The speaker of this poem is first alerted to the fact of the mobilization through silence. "It was silent in the street," reads the opening line, "I did not know until a woman told me / Sobbing over the muslin she sold me."[10] As with the "murmuring women's voices" in "Cutting, Folding and Shaping," it is the inarticulacy of the woman at the market that speaks so powerfully of the coming of war. This quiet exchange is followed by the noisy crash of drums, shouting, the gathering of the townspeople, cathedral bells, and then in the second part of the poem the singing and yelling of the men bound for the Front, as their train roars out of the station. But, after that, quietness returns and there is nothing but "the weeping of the wild old women of Finistère."[11] Once more, words seem to be of little currency, and the "patriot cry" of the men heading to war rings hollow. Both parts of this long poem are experimental in their format, making use of irregular metre and line length, and unpredictable rhymes. The disorder that Norton senses in the landscape and community around her finds a reflection in the reworking and recalibrating of traditional poetic rhythms. It has become a truism to point to the nihilistic futility of the First World War as a catalyst for the rise of free-verse techniques in poetry. It is not so easy to chart exactly how or where that change took place.[12] However, it is certain that Norton's poems are among the first to explore the potential of non-metrical forms as a vehicle for the expression of the disorder and psychological strain of the conflict.

Norton also had other imaginative strategies for showing the collapse of social values in the context of war. In "The French Soldier and His Bayonet" she returns to a regular four-foot couplet form, which initially suggests a song-like security, a recourse to the ballad rhythms of the past. This sense of familiarity is short lived, however, as the content of the poem reveals it to be spoken by a soldier whose view of the world has been so twisted and brutalised by his experience of the trenches that he has fallen in love with his bayonet, the slim and vicious Rosalie:

> Farewell, my wife, farewell, Marie,
> I am going with Rosalie.
> You stand, you weep, you look at me—
> But you know the rights of Rosalie,
> And she calls, the mistress of men like me![13]

This poem offers a damning critique of the French "cult of the bayonet," which created a strangely eroticized relationship between soldier, bayonet and victim.[14] In Norton's poem, however, that triangle is diverted to include the soldier's wife, who also becomes a victim of war in a way that demonstrates emotional rather than physical violence. Neglected, disowned and abandoned by a husband who is supposed to be fighting to protect his family, his community and his way of life, Marie finds herself violated and disorientated by this reversal of values. And given that the poem is all addressed directly to the wife, the reader too finds him or herself allied with her position, and becomes the audience for the soldier's extraordinary outpouring of battle-lust.

Norton creates a powerful and disturbing voice in this poem; a dramatic monologue, intended to be read against the grain of its expression. In other poems, such as "The Volunteer," it is much less clear whether the reader is invited to oppose or to empathise with the speaker's position and views. Structured around the interwoven colours of the American flag, this poem presents the voice of the patriotic soldier, eager for action. "Sow white stars in a sky of blue," it begins, setting up the organic imagery that recurs in each stanza, transforming the stars of the Stars and Stripes into white flowers that, despite the speaker's confidence and determination, seem to prefigure some sort of funeral garland. The poem concludes, "Spill red wine on a cloth of white. . . . / I fight for freedom and France to-night!"[15] Here, the colour red obviously signifies the blood of the soldiers in the field of battle. However, the conflation of the red, white and blue of the French and American flags, which is the conceit on which this little poem turns (and which is underscored by the pun on the word "sow/sew" at the opening) also alerts us to an important political alignment which Norton senses between the two nations. The concept of *fraternité* denoted by the red in the French flag becomes a signifier for a sense of ideological compatibility with American values. Like many of her generation and social class, Norton had travelled in France before the war, and considered the nation to be the pinnacle of Western civilization. The status of France as the home of culture, art and taste was cited by scores of educated Americans, both at home and abroad, as a justification for military intervention in the European conflict.[16] Many, Norton included, felt that America's attempt to maintain a neutral position throughout the early stages of the war was a betrayal of those cultural values, a refusal to defend beauty and style against force and materialism.[17] Norton also felt profoundly that the failure to take part in the great struggle playing out in Europe was a betrayal of America's founding political values. Justice, Liberty, Freedom: these words echo self-consciously through her war poems. For Norton, the affinity between France and America was based on their shared republican values, and the attraction of those values lay in their potential to validate and improve the lives of ordinary people, and to erase distinctions between classes. To her, the cause of France seemed just, because it was the cause of a republican democracy fighting against the totalitarian monarchies of Germany and Austria. Her second cycle of war poems, *What is Your Legion?* (1916), deals more explicitly with this political theme.[18] However, there are also hints of her position in "The Red Road," and these hints suggest another interpretation of the recurring presence of the colour red throughout the series of poems. While Norton may not have overtly self-identified as a Socialist or Communist, she certainly had strong sympathies on the left of the political spectrum, and counted the anarchist Emma Goldman among her friends in New York.[19] So, while "The Volunteer" might appear on first glance to be a blithely jingoistic exercise in flag-waving rhetoric, there is a much more thoughtful consideration of international politics which underpins the poem. And, as the depersonalised title of the poem reminds us, the voice of "The Volunteer" is simply one voice among the many entitled to speak about the war—neither more nor less valid than the French soldier who loves his bayonet, or the women making dressings in the work-room. Norton's democratic principle is thus built into the structure of her poems, which, like those of Walt Whitman before her, provide a platform for a range of contrasting perspectives, without necessarily making it clear which the reader is supposed to accept or resist. Nevertheless, set among these other poems which undercut the "patriot cry" of the fervent soldier, Norton was surely aware that this poem, which voices the dreamy, flowery idealism of the Volunteer, would have been impossible to read without some level of irony. Even the most patriotic reader of 1916 must have felt unease, at least, at the tragic naivety of the young fighter whose ideas of war and national allegiance are defined by wine, fabric and flowers.

Indeed, before reaching "The Volunteer," Norton's readers have already negotiated the disparity between the flowers and wine of pre-war Europe with the destruction of the present in "The Journey." Here, Norton once more shows her sense of internationalism, and her aspiration towards a renegotiation of political boundaries, a desire to transcend class barriers and national politics:

> I went upon a journey
> To countries far away,
> From province unto province,
> To pass my holiday.[20]

This journey takes the speaker of the poem, in the manner of the cultural European tour so popular with the American upper classes in the decades before the war, through the Balkans, Eastern Europe, Germany, Belgium, France and England. But the soldier with whom the speaker once spoke in the "flower-filled garden" in Serbia, now "lies dead at Belgrade," the Russian friend "lies dead at Lemberg," the sons of Germany and Austria "lie dead at Liège" or "dead through the farms of France." The Frenchman with whom the speaker shared bread and wine "lies dead at Cambrai," and the same fate awaits the young English soldiers from Dover:

> Now they lie dead at Dixmude,
> The brave, the strong, the young!
> I turn unto my homeland,
> All my journey sung![21]

Like "The French Soldier and His Bayonet," this is somehow a much more modern and powerful poem than it has any business to be. Metrical poetry of the 1900s and 1910s is usually labelled as "Genteel" in an American context. However, as Norton ably demonstrates, there was often nothing gentle about "Genteel Verse." Designed in three foot quatrains, this poem repeats a tactic used repeatedly in an earlier time by Emily Dickinson, that of taking the seven/six syllable pattern with an ABCB rhyme-scheme, so familiar in nursery rhymes and hymns, and using this as a platform for challenging and contemporary content. This format sets up an uncomfortable tension between the predictable and the volatile within the poem, which also destabilizes the reader's sense of how to interpret the voice of the speaker. Is this the voice of the rich complacent tourist, whose journey is nothing more that the cause of a song—and an old-fashioned one at that? Does the final stanza suggest that the speaker turns away from Europe with a shrug, that the paratactic listing of the warring nations is the result of nothing more than idle curiosity? Does the matter-of-fact tone suggest that the grim fate of Europe is something about which nothing can be done? And if this is the case, is the reader invited to condemn or collude with such a viewpoint? Alternatively, the poem can be read with more warmth, as a statement of faith in the basic, shared humanity of the common people in all these nations, now needlessly warring. The everyday existence of these "simple kindly folk" has been replaced with the wounds, the heat, the thirst of the battlefield, and the death of friendship. Within this reading, the silent implication of the poem is that their rulers, whose political ambitions destroy the underlying solidarity of the workers across the continent, have foisted this wanton destruction on peaceful peoples. Such a perspective casts the poem's final stanza as a warning. If these dark outcomes have destroyed the tranquil lives of the people of Europe, the fact that the speaker now turns to his or her "homeland" invites the inference that something similar lies in store for America. The journey may be all sung, but the knowledge of the reality of war comes home with force, and in ways that have deep political implications for the turbulent political landscape of wartime America—where organised labour and anti-capitalist rhetoric were feared almost as much as the threat of external invasion. Like "The Volunteer" therefore, "The Journey" offers more than one potential voice within its lines, and the difficulty of ascertaining which of those voices lies closer to Norton's own suggests that she, like her nation, was torn between apparently incompatible perspectives on the European war in its early stages. The justice of the Allied war effort against Germany in defence of Belgium, balanced against the recognition of the brutality and the commercialisation of war, provided a powerful ideological conundrum for many in America. This conundrum was also intensified by the mixed ethnic make-up of the nation—which by 1914 included not only the British, Dutch and French settlers, who had had a presence on the continent for centuries, but also large new communities of Serbs, Russians, Scandinavians, Chinese, Italians and Germans. At the start of the war, German speakers or those of recent German descent accounted for almost a quarter of the American population.[22] "The Journey" may on first reading appear a simple statement of the pity of war, but in its unresolved complexity this poem touches on many of the ideological paradoxes at play in America in the mid-1910s.

This poem also dramatizes that tension between passionate engagement and neutral detachment which would become such a distinctive feature of American writing about the war right through to the 1930s. A character such as Frederic Henry, the protagonist of Ernest Hemingway's *A Farewell to Arms*, is continually torn, as was Hemingway himself, between a desire to be at the crux of dramatic events and a sense of detachment from them.[23] The American artist Joseph Pennell, despite his pacifist views, dedicated the four years of the war to making a visual record of the effects of the conflict, especially the industrial impact of the munitions industry. As he succinctly put it, borrowing a biblical turn of phrase: "we are in the midst of war, though some of us are not of it."[24] Malcolm Cowley, who served as a *camion* driver in France, would later describe his sense that the war engendered a "spectatorial" attitude in the young American volunteers who witnessed the European war.[25] Those who served in the front line or who worked long distressing shifts as medical personnel might well have taken issue with any suggestion that they were merely observing events. However, the idea of the American observer in Europe was a familiar one with a distinguished history, not least in the novels of Henry James and Edith Wharton, or even further back in the essays of Ralph Waldo Emerson. "The Journey" plays on the recurring idea that the American traveller is, on the one hand, at a cultural disadvantage in Europe, having much to learn about history, art and society, but, on the other hand, stands at a moral advantage, being untrammelled by the class boundaries, ornate religious practices and hidebound conventions of older, more traditional nations. Whether one reads Norton's poem with a complacent or a sympathetic tone, one cannot quite escape the speaker's sense of confidence in their own judgement and the inevitable conclusion that beautiful old Europe has made a shocking mess of itself.

Norton further explores this tension between engagement and observation in her long seven-part poem "On Seeing Young Soldiers in London." Triggered by her fleeting journey through England in 1914, these poems initially offer a fairly conventional response to the sight of youth enlisting, sorrow for those "go to die ere they have lived, their youth within their eyes."[26] Norton here invokes an idea that with hindsight seems naïve, even distasteful, that the death to which the young men march is a kind of new life: "O let them wake, laugh and unfold! For them green Paradise."[27] However, as these poems progress, it becomes apparent that Norton is not offering a static response to the war, but is once more playing with different perspectives and voices. The voices of these seven poems move through a new kind of journey from the orthodox to the experimental. This journey also moves the reader through a complex range of emotional responses, from the wistful religiosity of the opening poem to another poem that considers the way to respond to rumours of atrocity in the war zone: "I heard that old men were murdered, young children harried and hurt, / While the world's wonderful wonders were burned and turned to dirt."[28] The speaker of the poem feels the urge to vengeance, but then tempers this reaction and calls for Justice in its place. This Justice is also the focus of the third poem in the cycle. Those who fight are called to build her a throne, but it is at this point in the cycle that one begins to sense that Norton's view of war is not nearly as naïve as the early lines suggest. The throne of Justice is to be built "bone on bone, / Body on body, with blood." By the final stanza, Justice herself has become an absolute tyrant, capable in her own uncompromising way of violence and atrocity:

With steel and showering stone,
With the mortar's murderous breath,
With horror and anguish and death—
All these she must have for her throne![29]

Strikingly, it is at this point in the cycle, when Norton has reached a point in her argument that takes her away from conventionally patriotic responses to the war, that she also begins to move away from the set-piece metrical forms of the three opening poems and to work in much looser structures. There is still rhyme, but it is not always regular, the line lengths vary and the metre is less rhythmic. Characteristic techniques of free verse—repetition, assonance, intrusive punctuation—become more frequent as Norton moves into an exploration of responses to the war that may have been much less readily understood or even endorsed by her early readers. Part IV offers a dream sequence in which the speaker is haunted by the image of a sword suspended, like the sword of Damocles, by a single thread. Following on from part III, the inference is also that this is the sword of Justice, but rather than let it do its work, the speaker's mission is to prevent the sword from wounding, to "lift it and bring it to earth ere it fall." A "blue trilling bird," whose quiet song goes unexplained, replaces the image of the sword. "Is this the dream that follows you?" asks the speaker. "By this dream am I haunted too."[30]

Moving into part V, it is not clear whether we have escaped the world of dream, or whether the panicked voice of this poem faces real rather than imagined danger. "Banners and bugles! My ship is going down!" it cries.[31] However, the speaker's desperate injunctions to "Fling flags into the air!" and "Spread banners blue and red!," the repeated calls for "Trumpets and drums!" in the face of death and the fact that every phrase in the poem is accompanied by an exclamation mark raise the suspicion that Norton is not being entirely serious here. Once more, the "patriot cry" is the subject, if not of outright mockery, at least of a probing realism that questions the clichés of war rhetoric, even as it engages with them. Here, as in her mobilization poems, Norton projects an imagined voice, a persona whose hopeless, flag-flinging defiance is put forward for the reader's judgement—but what Norton intends that judgement to be is far from clear. Once more, she gives us a poem that gives no clear road map for its own reading.

Underneath these conflicting voices, however, Norton senses something more elemental and powerful. In part VI, she personifies the world as a broken-hearted woman who "Silent, bent and burdened" has "slept in a seething world." This "Lover, life-giver, woman" now is waking and facing the "red tide" of war, and this wakefulness seems to the speaker of the poem to be linked to her own fate—although she would much prefer to be "glad, gay, golden, / Lost in a murmuring verse."[32] The choice of "murmuring" is intriguing here, as the reader is already aware from the earlier poem "Cutting, Folding and Shaping" that the murmuring voices of that poem offer no clear escape from war. As in that poem, the tension in the final two parts of "On Seeing Young Soldiers in London" is between the desire to speak quietly and the impulse to make some bold, decisive statement of action. This tension, between shy decorum on the one hand and daring incision on the other is also evident throughout Norton's poetic *oeuvre*, which sometimes sits a little awkwardly between convention and innovation. It is also apparent in her letters, which reveal a very brilliant, impishly witty and sometimes outspoken woman, who nevertheless wished to give no offence, and who realised that convention would often triumph, do what one may. However, in part VII, the final part of the set, Norton's voice emerges clearly, in a Yeatsian vision of a world in which both geographical and conceptual order has been overturned by war:

> Shore breaks upon shore,
> Tide baffles tide,
> Hill rides upon hill
> Where the high hills were lying,
> And on one plain the whole of the world is dying![33]

Turned back upon itself, the physical landscape implodes, and it is only the dangerous figure of Life, who "with red lips drives her wild strong steeds," that is able to take control, crying "Go!"—a cry for action rather than observation, for clear speech rather than a murmur. "O freedom, freedom, freedom, / I did not know I loved you so!" responds the speaker of the poem.

This is one of Norton's least structured poems. As I have noted elsewhere, its fourteen irregular lines (varying from one to twelve syllables) offer a kind of bombed-out sonnet structure, as though the poem, like the landscape it describes, has somehow folded back violently upon itself.[34] It is also a surprise to note, as one reads this poem, that the heading at the top of the page remains "On Seeing Young Soldiers in London," because the cycle has moved dramatically away from those young soldiers and from the setting of London, into a much more internalised meditation about the meaning of the war. These final two poems in particular, seem to be expressed in a voice much closer to Norton's own, considering as they do the value (or otherwise) of speech in a time of conflict. This process brings Norton to a consideration of idealised and externalised forces such as Life, Death, the tyrannical Justice, and the weeping woman of the World. Like the forces that drive Hardy's play *The Dynasts*, the elemental powers that govern Norton's conception of the war take little cognisance of the individual lives and voices whose fates they battle over—which is of course the tragedy of the young men marching to war. The fervent prayer for their safety and redemption offered in the opening poem is countered, indeed almost cancelled, by the catastrophic upheaval of the final poem in which individual lives and deaths are obliterated within the cosmic scale of events. Indeed, the human participants of the war simply disappear from view. In the final coda piece to "The Red Road," Norton asks "O Peace, where is thy faithful sentry?" Perhaps to reassure her 1916 readers of her poetic seriousness, she returns for this last poem, the last of *Roads* as a collection, to a more familiar lyric register. Nevertheless, the questions posed by this poem are unsettling: while many seem willing to die "for kings or for democracy," what has happened to those who would defend Peace? On the last printed page of *Roads*, Norton places a quotation: "Jeanne d'Arc, mettez beaucoup de colère dans nos coeurs." [Joan of Arc, put a great rage in our hearts.][35] It is the final line of the poem "Jeanne" by the French symbolist Remy de Gourmont (1858–1915) from his work *Les Saints du paradis* (1898).[36] Like the opening epigraph from Hardy, this line calls the reader to look out from Norton's work to a wider literary landscape. However, facing, as it does, the hymn to Peace, it also raises the question of how best to direct public anger about the war. Invoking once more the figure of Joan of Arc, a woman of action, but also in the end a voice silenced by history, Norton leaves her readers with the tension that runs through this entire sequence of poems, the urge to speak out about the war, but the difficulty of knowing what to say.

It seems important that Norton chooses to end on this note. Despite the many different calls for violence that are voiced in "The Red Road," and despite her own conviction that America should act to support the democratic and progressive cause of France, Norton took no joy in the war. Proud of her own nation as she might be, she was not so patriotic as to lose sight of the hypocrisy, the economic opportunism, or the brutality set in motion by the war. As the war progressed, Norton would become increasingly disillusioned with the bureaucracy, jingoism and expansionism that came to dominate American attitudes to the war as it drew to a close. After America's entry into the war in 1917, she co-authored an American best seller, when her translation of *The Odyssey of a Torpedoed Transport*, shot to instant popularity. This series of anonymously published letters supposedly written by a French merchant seaman "Y." was really the fictional work of Maurice Larrouy (1882–1939). It is a poignant, personal book about the very ordinary life of a sailor on a cargo boat, whose war is not especially heroic or often at times even very interesting. Among the fleeting dramas of war, such as the rescuing of the victims of U-Boat attacks or running coal to French navy ships in action, and the endless routine of life on deck, he wonders how to get to port for a drink, and when he will get home to his wife and child. What is compelling about Larrouy's book is the powerful sense of this individual life swept this way and that by the forces of the war—like a damaged boat at sea. When the book was discovered to be a work of fiction, not a set of genuine letters, there was something of a public outcry. Norton herself claimed that she had translated the letters believing them to be real.[37] Like the voices of Norton's speakers, the voice of Larrouy's "Y." drew in and confused its readers, unsettling their judgement as a way of refocussing their attention on an unnoticed human aspect of the war. And like the landscapes of her own work, Larrouy's seascapes provided an alternative vantage point from which to consider the ironies and brutalities of the war beyond political and national allegiances.

The physical landscape of the First World War was a powerful element, which left its imprint on all who witnessed it—sometimes with startlingly creative outcomes. In contrast, Norton's poems make the case that imagined landscapes of war are also able to offer a space in which the many dark and contradictory anxieties and moral puzzles of conflict can be explored. As modern readers of war literature, our experience of the landscapes of the First World War can only ever be imaginative—one could argue illusory. Even eyewitness and participant accounts of the war zone are nothing like the real thing itself, as so many survivors of the war were keen to stress. Moreover, warscapes are just as likely to have been mediated to us through voices which may have been remote from the front-line action of the war, or which may themselves be imaginary. However, something important can still come to us out of this process. One of the privileges of literature is that it need not always speak facts in order to speak the truth. As Norton's poems so vividly remind us, the tragedy of war is the tragedy of the individual life caught up in a hostile, brutalised environment where the individual life has ceased to be properly valued. The consequences of this are so crushing as they play out, that they threaten not just the physical self but even more fundamental values, so that it is indeed as though the landscape in which we function shakes beneath our feet or folds back to devour us. Norton's poems remind to look again for what we are able to stabilise in any zone of conflict. It is by cutting, folding and shaping that something can be salvaged out of chaos.

Notes

1. Grace Fallow Norton, *Roads* (Boston: Houghton Mifflin, 1916), 78. [Ellipses sic.] *Roads* was also published in London by Constable in 1916. It has never been reprinted. However, it can be accessed online via Internet Archive at www.archive.org. Call number 151528445.

2. See Theodore Roosevelt, Foreword to *One Hundred Percent American*, edited by Arnon L. Squiers (New York: Doran, 1918), iv–vii.
3. Norton to Greenslet, 15 May 1915, Houghton Mifflin Company Papers, bMS AM 1925 (1934).
4. Donohue, Berta Schmidt, 'Aunt Grace Talking,' Family Memoir (c.1940). I am indebted to Ellen Weiss for access to private papers relating to Norton's life and family.
5. For a fuller account of Norton's biography see Hazel Hutchison, *The War That Used Up Words: American Writers and the First World War* (New Haven: Yale, 2015), 53–66 and 131–141.
6. Norton replied with amusement: "Thank you so much for getting up a 'poetic thrill' . . . Isn't it funny you are willing to buy my little, painted pig in a poke!" Norton to Greenslet, 4 June 1915, Houghton Mifflin Company Papers, bMS AM 1925 (1934).
7. Norton, *Roads*, 64.
8. Thomas Hardy, *The Works of Thomas Hardy*, 2 vols (London: Macmillan, 1913), II, 205.
9. Norton, *Roads*, 65.
10. Norton, *Roads*, 66.
11. Norton, *Roads*, 68.
12. For a wider discussion of the rise of experimental forms of expression during the First World War see Vincent Sherry, *The Great War and the Language of Modernism* (Oxford: Oxford University Press, 2003) and Trudi Tate, *Modernism, History and the First World War* (Manchester: Manchester University Press, 1998).
13. Norton, *Roads*, 70.
14. For an extended reading of this poem see Hutchison, *The War That Used Up Words*, 59–63. For a discussion of more French songs about bayonets during the First World War, see Regina M. Sweeney, *Singing Our Way to Victory* (Middletown, CT: Wesleyan University Press, 2001), 121–128.
15. Norton, *Roads*, 77.
16. See for example Edith Wharton's collection of eyewitness essays about her visits to the war zone in *Fighting France: From Dunkerque to Belfort* (New York: Scribner's, 1915).
17. For an analysis of American cultural and social responses to the war see John Dos Passos, *Mr Wilson's War* (New York: Doubleday, 1962).
18. Grace Fallow Norton, *What Is Your Legion?* (Boston: Houghton Mifflin, 1916). This pamphlet of poems was published on a non-profit basis in May 1916, to be sold at an event organised by the American Rights Committee in New York, to mark the anniversary of the sinking of the *Lusitania*. See Hutchison, *The War That Used Up Words*, 131–141.
19. In April 1914, as her second volume of verse *The Sister of the Wind* was in press, Norton insisted to her editor that Goldman's journal *Mother Earth* be included in the list of acknowledgements for previous publication of Norton's poems: "I don't care for the looks of it at all. But if it must be done kindly include *Mother Earth* in the goodly company. Not that I am an anarchist—Gott bewahre—but that I like Emma." Norton to Greenslet, 12 April 1914, Houghton Mifflin Company Papers, bMS AM 1925 (1934).
20. Norton, *Roads*, 72.
21. Norton, *Roads*, 74.
22. Meirion Harries and Susan Harries, *The Last Days of Innocence: America at War, 1917–18* (New York: Random House, 1997), 32.
23. Ernest Hemingway, *A Farewell to Arms* (New York: Scribner's, 1929).

24. Joseph Pennell, *Pictures of War Work in England* (London: Heinemann, 1917), ix.
25. Malcolm Cowley, *Exile's Return* (1951; repr. London: Penguin, 1986), 38.
26. Norton, *Roads*, 79.
27. Norton, *Roads*, 80.
28. Norton, *Roads*, 80.
29. Norton, *Roads*, 81.
30. Norton, *Roads*, 83
31. Norton, *Roads*, 83.
32. Norton, *Roads*, 84.
33. Norton, *Roads*, 85.
34. Hutchison, *The War That Used Up Words*, 65.
35. Norton, *Roads*, 87.
36. Remy de Gourmont, *Les Saintes du paradis* (Paris: Mercure de France, 1898).
37. "Others too have asked if it was fiction! Mr Greenslet, that never entered my head!" Norton to Greenslet, 11 October 1918, Houghton Mifflin Company Papers, bMS AM 1925 (1934).

Bibliography

Cowley, Malcolm. *Exile's Return*. London: Penguin, 1986 [1951].
Dos Passos, John. *Mr Wilson's War*. New York: Doubleday, 1962.
Gourmont, Remy de. *Les Saintes du paradis*. Paris: Mercure de France, 1898.
Hardy, Thomas. *The Works of Thomas Hardy*, 2 vols. London: Macmillan, 1913.
Harries, Meirion and Harries, Susie. *The Last Days of Innocence: America at War, 1917–18*. New York: Random House, 1997.
Hemingway, Ernest. *A Farewell to Arms*. New York: Scribner's, 1929.
Hutchison, Hazel. *The War That Used up Words: American Writers and the First World War*. New Haven: Yale, 2015.
Norton, Grace Fallow. *Roads*. Boston: Houghton Mifflin, 1916.
Norton, Grace Fallow. *What Is Your Legion?* Boston: Houghton Mifflin, 1916.
Pennell, Joseph. *Pictures of War Work in England*. London: Heinemann, 1917.
Sherry, Vincent. *The Great War and the Language of Modernism*. Oxford: Oxford University Press, 2003.
Sweeney, Regina M. *Singing Our Way to Victory*. Middletown, CT: Wesleyan University Press, 2001.
Tate, Trudi. *Modernism, History and the First World War*. Manchester: Manchester University Press, 1998.
Wharton, Edith. *Fighting France: From Dunkerque to Belfort*. New York: Scribner's 1915.

12 Landscapes of Memory in Centenary Fiction

Angela K. Smith

There has always been a strong connection between fiction and memory, perhaps particularly so for First World War fiction, triggered even in the 1920s and 1930s by a combination of commemoration and commerciality. Modris Eksteins, in his discussion of one of the very first and most commercially successful First World War novels, *All Quiet on the Western Front*, suggests:

> Remarque's spectacular success brought on a flood of war books and other material dealing with the war and ushered in what came to be known as the "war boom" of 1929–1930. War novels and war memoirs suddenly dominated the lists of publishers . . . they were so in demand, as public speakers and radio performers, that they could not cope with the glut of invitations. The sudden public interest in the war meant that moldy manuscripts, previously rejected by wary publishers who thought the war would not sell, were now rushed into print. New books, too, were quickly commissioned and quickly written.[1]

This first literature boom framed many of the tropes, including representations of landscape, that still shape the war for us, as people responded to literary representations of their own experience on an unprecedented scale. Memory and the need to understand were of the utmost importance, particularly as the post-war world was much less stable than anyone had foreseen. Eksteins goes on:

> The war boom of the late twenties and early thirties was a product of this mixture of aspiration, anxiety, and doubt. All the successful war books were written from the point of view of the individual, not the unit or the nation. . . . The war was a matter of individual experience rather than collective interpretation. It had become a matter of art, not history.[2]

While individual memory has now faded, individual experience remains a focal point for the art of commemoration one hundred years on. Now, as then, the individual is used to represent collective memory in different ways. There was a resurgence of interest in fiction engaging with the First World War in the last decades of the twentieth century and it is unsurprising then that the centenary of the war has already seen a wave of new work, one that continues to tread the thin line between the two motivational forces of commemoration and commerciality. Gail Braybon argues, "There is a new enthusiasm for tracing the way in which the war had been remembered—forgotten—over time, which in turn is connected with research into the nature of memory and has been influenced by the rise of 'public history.'"[3] This chapter focuses on the commemorative, exploring the ways in which centenary fiction, defined here as fiction concerning the First World War published in the three decades anticipating the centenary, redraws, adapts and develops familiar landscapes to examine the legacy of memory one hundred years on.

Collective memory and its associate cultural memory need some definition. Cultural memory is informed by collective memory, a term first coined by Maurice Halbwachs in his 1925 work, *On Collective Memory*. Collective memory, Chris Weedon and Glenn Jordan suggest, "signifies narratives of past experience constituted by and on behalf of specific groups within which they find meaningful forms of identification that may empower."[4] This builds on the ideas that individual memories combine to create group memory. Multiple group memories intermingle in the creation of collective memory, textual narratives inevitably impacting on this corroboration. Cultural memory is determined by the ways in which collective memory is translated through a society or culture. Marianne Hirsch explains: "Always mediated, cultural memory is the product of fragmentary personal and collective experiences articulated through technologies and media that shape even as they transmit memory."[5] Both collective and cultural memory can be located in what Pierre Nora terms *lieux de memoire*, sites of memory, which, in our culture, are usually manufactured: "we must deliberately create archives, maintain anniversaries, organize celebrations, pronounce eulogies, and notarize bills because such activities no longer occur naturally."[6] These definitions help to explain the importance of individual experience as component part of collective memory and perhaps justifying the continuing focus on individual memory to represent the collective. Contemporary representations of individual memory continue to be used in centenary fiction, creating the "everyman," who can embody the war experience. But decades of critical attention, and indeed feminist critical attention, on the war has had an impact. While much centenary fiction explores familiar landscapes and images, alternate perspectives emerge. The twenty-first century "everyman" comes in a range of different forms, including "everywoman."

Julian Barnes' 1995 story "Evermore"[7] confronts questions of how to remember head on. His elderly protagonist, Miss Moss, has devoted her life to the memory of her brother Sam, killed in 1917. The rituals and landscapes of commemoration shape her life and her thinking, prompting her to analyse these larger definitions:

> She wondered if there was such a thing as collective memory, something more than the sum of individual memories. If so, was it merely coterminous, yet in some way richer; or did it last longer? She wondered if those too young to have original knowledge could be given memory, could have it grafted on.[8]

In this story the individual and the collective blend against a backdrop of the homogenised Western Front: the cemeteries of the Imperial War Graves Commission. Apart from a brief, unsuccessful marriage to her dead brother's disabled comrade (itself an act of commemoration), Miss Moss has occupied her life working as a proof-reader for a dictionary, spending her annual holiday on pilgrimage to France. Always taking the same route around the cemeteries, one that concludes at her brother's grave, Miss Moss constructs her memory through the landscape and the dead who inhabit it. Her tour incorporates visits to the reclaimed landscapes of the Western Front as she re-imagines the realities of the actual trench experience. For her, memory is embedded in the new landscapes of post-war France; landscapes that are encoded with alternative meanings:

> You followed signposts in British racing green, then walked across fields guarded by wooden martyred Christs to these sanctuaries of orderliness, like dominoes on edge; beneath them, their owners were present and correct, listed, tended. Creamy altars proclaimed that THEIR NAME LIVETH FOR EVERMORE. And so it did, on graves, in the books, in hearts, in memories.[9]

The religious symbolism endorses both the Britishness of the cemetery and also the collective and ordered nature of the commemoration. The act of remembering becomes a kind of sanctuary in itself, a space in the landscape enshrined by the myths of collective grief.

Despite the generic nature of this site of memory, Miss Moss uses the individual to articulate the collective very effectively. On the one hand as she drives around the former battlefields in her old grey Morris (gun-metal grey to reflect its only destination, with blood red leather seats), Miss Moss represents a singular individual experience. "At first, back then, the commonality of grief had helped: wives, mothers, comrades, an array of brass hats, and a bugler amid gassy morning mist which the feeble November sun had failed to burn away."[10] Her early visits for Armistice Day pitch her with the crowd of bereaved, the "gassy morning mist" connecting them directly with the lost. As the years pass, however, her grief alters rather than diminishes, setting her apart from the crowd until it becomes "a calliper, necessary and supporting; she could not imagine walking without it."[11] As disabled as the male war veterans, her individual experience of grief marks her out from the crowd. Only she wishes to sleep on her brother's grave, resulting in the Imperial War Graves commission banning her from attending the annual ceremony. Only she replaces the turf on his grave with "English" turf and plants bulbs, both of which are systematically removed before her next return. Only she shapes her life around commemoration while other mourners move on. In this way she comes to embody different tropes of memory and to question what will happen to memory when she too has gone.

On the other hand, Miss Moss builds the layers of her memory by imagining the individual stories of the cemeteries. Each year, she spends time reading the names of the fallen, creating lives and identities for them as well as focussing on her brother. Sammy Moss is one of very few Jewish servicemen buried in his particular cemetery. Others have names that intrigue her and spark her commemorative imagination. On other memorials she considers the experiences of civilians. Numbers and listings of the dead are important to her, but only as a collective of individual stories. In this way Barnes uses his character to explore both the significance of memory and its formulation. He also begins to question what will happen to memory as the war falls further and further into history.

> Soon—in fifty years or so—everyone who had served in the war would be dead; and at some point after that, everyone who had known anyone who had served would also be dead. What if the memory grafting did not work, or the memories themselves were deemed shameful?[12]

The landscapes of the Somme haunted by Miss Moss in "Evermore" had already been revisited with great commercial success in Sebastian Faulks' 1993 novel, *Birdsong*, which seemed to herald the start of a new era for First World War fiction. The war was far enough removed to be beyond the living memory of most people, a real part of history, yet the emphasis on individual experience, established by the first wave of writers, continued to dominate. Faulks' Stephen Wraysford is a kind of post-modern anti-hero destroyed by the war even though he survives; he is different enough to stand out as an individual, yet his experience enables him to also function as an "everyman." But he is less uniform; an "everyman" for the post-modern age. Memory, legacy and hindsight dominate Faulks' interpretation of familiar tropes through Stephen.

The landscapes of the First World War that Faulks recreates are based upon the photographs and paintings that form the archive of memory upon which he could draw to create his fictional representation. Also available to him was 80 years of cultural memory, a developing legacy that colours the way we see the war today. In the years following the Armistice, the ways in which cultural memory categorised the war subtly changed. As the war became a part of history, as the real impact of the loss of so many men began to be felt, a kind of culture of disillusionment began to develop, compounded by the boom in war literature of the late 1920s and early 1930s. This mythology has been very powerful and is in part built around the horror of the trench experience, something that has come to embody the way the war is remembered even today. Samuel Hynes has argued, "By the time the decade of the thirties began, the myth of the war had been constructed in its essential and persisting form, and that construction may be regarded as an act of closure, both for the war and for the decade that followed it."[13] This understanding of memory has been supported by much First World War scholarship of the twentieth century. Paul Fussell's seminal study, *The Great War and Modern Memory* (1975), argues that the war, as it was enshrined in primary literary sources, has shaped political, cultural and artistic development in the twentieth century. Fussell's thesis has come to embody this mythology almost as much as the writings of Remarque, Sassoon and Owen. More recently, however, some historians have begun to question the myth, claiming it as a post-war phenomenon.[14] But this questioning of the myths of the war, of the culture of disillusionment at the heart of early representations, does not seem to have filtered into contemporary fiction as yet. On the contrary, 80 years of disenchantment, symbolised by the powerful images of the Western Front, still dominate but are now layered with and interpreted through decades of memory.

One of the best examples of how these things blend in a modern work is Faulks' representation of the battle of the Somme in *Birdsong*. In the early part of the novel he illustrates the Somme valley as a pastoral idyll in 1910. Later he explores the same landscape after the guns fall silent at the end of 1 July 1916, the first day of the battle of the Somme.

> The earth began to move. To their right a man who had lain still since the first attack, eased himself upright, then fell again when his damaged leg would not take his weight. Other single men moved, and began to come up like worms from their shellholes, limping, crawling, dragging themselves out. Within minutes the hillside was seething with the movement of the wounded as they attempted to get themselves back to their line.[15]

This is the same landscape explored by the soldier writers decades earlier, but Faulks has a different focus; it moves away from the stark, sterile desolation of their front line to present a landscape that is sensual, living, almost organic. Most importantly it is human. The technology of war has been silenced, as has the natural world, the "birdsong" that one might expect to hear. What matters now is the human aspect. The wounded and hidden soldiers are of the earth as they begin to move in the relative safety of the twilight. "Limping, crawling, dragging," the emphasis is on the human cost, of this most costly of days. At the same time the image of worms seems to suggest the earth as a dead body. It is as if humanity has killed the landscape. Faulks continues:

> Stephen noticed nothing but the silence that followed the guns. Now, as he listened, he could hear what Weir had meant: it was a low, con-

tinuous moaning. He could not make out any individual pain, but the sound ran down to the river on their left and up over the hill for half a mile or more. As his ear became used to the absence of guns, Stephen could hear it more clearly: it sounded to him as though the earth itself was groaning.[16]

The way Stephen responds to the landscape of the Somme reflects not only his own experience of the battle, but something much larger. This is a statement about the legacy of the war; it is an illustration of the way in which cultural memory has shaped our understanding of the landscape of war. As with the earlier passage, the emphasis is on the human element. The men are absorbed into the landscape; they become part of it, both living and dead. Whereas it is initially the movement of the men that animates the land, here it is their sound. The soundscape of the Somme does not elucidate any "individual pain"; it represents the anonymous voices of the many, moaning down the intervening decades, insistent to be heard. It is "as though the earth itself was groaning." The agony of men is absorbed by the earth and becomes a symbolic representation of how we understand the battle of the Somme today, the earth as a wounded body groaning for mankind. Faulks infuses his text with his understanding of cultural memory; his battlescape is different because it encompasses what the Somme will come to mean; the legacy as well as the experience.

Contemporary with *Birdsong*, Pat Barker published her *Regeneration* Trilogy, equally successful and influential in encouraging a new wave of First World War fiction. Barker again blends the individual, the collective and the legacy to develop our understanding of memory, this time by adopting a formula of fictional biography. The trilogy is constructed around the war work of psychiatrist and anthropologist W.H.R. Rivers with shell-shocked patients at Craiglockhart hospital in Scotland. These famously included Siegfried Sassoon and Wilfred Owen, allowing Barker to suggest an historical "truth" to her narrative in retelling their stories. At the same time she develops purely fictional characters (such as Billy Prior) that enable her to explore alternate aspects of the war. She again adopts this formula for her "centenary" fiction, her most recent novels, *Life Class* (2007) and *Toby's Room* (2012), which must surely have been published with an eye to both commemoration and the commerciality that can accompany it.[17]

These later novels are loosely structured around the war work of another contemporary figure, Henry Tonks. Tonks was a British surgeon who went on to be an influential teacher of art at the Slade. During the war he returned to medicine and also documented innovative developments in the treatment of facial disfigurement with plastic surgery. Tonks is a relatively minor character in *Life Class*, functional primarily to link the central fictional players, but becomes more prominent in *Toby's Room*, which does engage with facial disfigurement, for many years a great taboo of the war.

228 *Angela K. Smith*

In order to succeed "centenary" fiction needs to consider alternate spaces of war. While it is important to incorporate the familiar landscapes of war, those that will trigger memory, it is not enough to simply rewrite or reinterpret stories that have already been told. Twenty-first century writers need to find new landscapes, or at least less familiar ones; like Faulks they need to weave legacy and memory into their narratives. Barker does this in a number of ways.

When the war breaks out in *Life Class,* the fictional art students, all of whom are based on real artists to a greater or lesser extent, take a number of different positions in relation to the conflict. Troubled working-class artist Paul Tarrant may be Paul Nash or Mark Gertler or a combination thereof with his own characteristics. Kit Neville seems to be loosely based on Christopher Nevinson, and Elinor Brooke is not unlike Dora Carrington in some of her responses to the war. Elinor's refusal to engage with the war allows Barker to explore the pacifism of the Bloomsbury group, while both Paul and Kit find themselves as ambulance drivers rather than soldiers. So Barker is able to present the familiar horrors of the Western Front from an unfamiliar angle. Barker's source materials are clearly identifiable in the writings of First World War women. Mary Borden, Ellen La Motte, Katherine Mansfield, Enid Bagnold and Vera Brittain all lend their voices to the narrative giving an authenticity to the landscape. The hospital in which Paul works is clearly located in Borden's "forbidden zone" and Barker's switch to a present tense narrative (like Borden) for these sections of the novel emphasises the immediacy of the front line hospital experience. But even where Barker uses her source material most closely, she needs to alter it for a contemporary audience.

For example, here is Paul describing one of his patients to Elinor:

> "They should have met one of our patients. You'd have liked him. He was an apache."
>
> "An Indian?"
>
> "Not that kind. He was a criminal. The French have special regiments for criminals to . . . I don't know, pay their debt to society, I suppose. They're supposed to be very good on the battlefield—born killers—but not so good at sticking it out between times. But the point about him was he was covered in tattoos. Not his face and hands but literally everywhere else, every inch. And they were good. They were art. He'd used his skin as the canvas, that's all. Now that man was probably born in the gutter, knocked from pillar to post. . . . But he didn't think art was irrelevant. Or Trivial. He suffered for it . . .
>
> Oh, and by the way, he didn't need ornament. He was extraordinarily beautiful."[18]

Here is the way Borden described the same (no doubt real) individual to her own audience in 1928:

> His name was tattooed on his arm, and the head of a woman, life-size on his back. . . . He was one of a lot of some twenty *apaches* that had

Landscapes of Memory in Centenary Fiction 229

been brought in that morning. As I remember they were all handsome young men—these assassins, thieves, pimps and traffickers in drugs—with sleek elastic limbs, smooth polished skins and beautiful bones. . . . But the *Enfant de Malheur* was the most beautiful of them all . . . Excellent troops of assault, these young Parisian criminals who had been sentenced to penal servitude for life and conscripted into the army of North Africa. . . . They were born killers. . . .[19]

While Borden's "enfant de malheur" is clearly a work of art, it is primarily as a consequence of his innate, rather savage beauty. Borden forces us to engage with his criminality and the uncomfortable issues of the female sexual gaze as her nurse narrator describes, even glamorises the wounded degenerate, only to replace the physical with the spiritual as the story develops into a narrative about salvation. Barker's "apache"—and she feels the need to explain exactly what that means as her contemporary readers would have a different understanding of the term—rather than being a work of art in himself, represents a canvas. Her driving theme, alternative spaces of art in war, re-designates the wounded man, emphasising his artistic tendencies rather than his criminality, allowing the reader to see the potential alternative spaces. With twenty-first century sensibilities he is presented as a victim of circumstance; his suffering for art is blended with his suffering for war. Art almost becomes a means of escape rather than a backdrop for depravity as Borden suggests. There is no connection with spirituality here. The reference is part of the artistic thread running throughout the novel, attempting to make us "see" the war differently.

Barker continues to weave this thread in *Toby's Room*, with a focus on the ways in which Elinor uses her art to negotiate memory. Following the death of her brother she turns to landscape painting as a means of therapy.[20] She makes multiple pictures of the landscapes of their shared childhood, each one containing a shadow; the spectre-like impression of her dead brother. Only when she goes to work with Tonks, sketching and painting the work of the plastic surgeons at Queen's Hospital, Sidcup, does she find a way of expressing her grief (Kit Neville is one of the patients). Elinor explores new kinds of individual landscape. The scientific becomes the personal generating memory. The dead and wounded fit into these new landscapes reflecting the need to commemorate a range of alternative aspects of the war.

Thomas Keneally's 2012 novel, *The Daughters of Mars*, was published just in time for the centenary of the war and examines the war from a completely different perspective. It tracks the experience of ANZAC[21] nurses operating in the Middle East and on the Western Front throughout the war, focalised through the viewpoints of two sisters, Naomi and Sally Durance. The sisters, both qualified nurses, sign up for Foreign Service as soon as they are able, Sally haunted by the notion that they have killed their terminally ill mother with a morphine overdose. Their work takes them firstly to Alexandria, then onwards on their hospital ship, *Archimedes*, to gather wounded troops from Gallipoli. After the sinking of the *Archimedes*, a central event in the novel, they are posted first to Lemnos and then the Western Front. While the novel is concerned with the relationship between the nurses and the soldiers they encounter, a curious detachment in the tone of the narrative voice enables it to present a broader picture of this more "marginal" experience of the war, offering an alternate space for memory. There is at once the individual suffering of the sisters as they journey through the war sometimes together, sometimes apart. Equally they encapsulate a universal set of nursing experiences, collective memory for the contemporary reader. At the same time, the landscapes that the nurses pass through are mapped back onto their home landscapes of Australia, each emphasising the alienation, the alternative, colonial perspective; multiple memorial strands.

Christine Hallett has argued that nurses in the First World War continue to be "veiled" by a number of distorting myths. "The First World War Nurse is an icon, but, like most iconic figures, her identity is obscured and distorted by the myths and narratives of successive generations."[22] Hallett explores three dominant myths surrounding our memory of these nurses: the courageous VAD (Voluntary Aid Detachment), the romantic nurse and the nurse as heroine, arguing that these impressions are misleading and prevent us from understanding the realities of their experience. These myths, she argues, like those surrounding the trench soldier, have been formed predominantly by the literature of the 1920s and 1930s. Books such as Vera Brittain's *Testament of Youth* (1933) and Ernest Hemingway's *A Farewell to Arms* (1929) have classified the First World War nurse into these roles, obscuring their actual experience as well as perpetuating the wider mythology of disillusionment. Keneally's novel, whilst conforming to the need for romance plot strands (commerciality steps in again), does work hard to dispel some of these more rigid myths. The "heroism" of the sisters is tempered by our understanding of their fear, and the detailed information about their daily nursing lives goes a long way towards rejecting any notions of glamour attached to the roles.

Hallett argues that no adequate medical provision was factored into the military planning of the Gallipoli campaign,[23] and when casualties far exceeded expectations, nurses found themselves under extraordinary pressure. The inadequate hospitals on Lemnos quickly became the recipients of large numbers of Gallipoli wounded, as it was geographically much closer than Egypt. Hallett cites one British nurse recalling Mudros Bay on Lemnos as a "wilderness of drought," a deadly environment, lacking in essential supplies and further poisoned by a chauvinistic medical director who did not support the women, refusing them military status.[24] Keneally's fictional sisters are posted on the island following their survival of the sinking of the *Archimedes* (probably based on the sinking of the SS *Marquette* in the Aegean Sea on 23 October 1915) and their experience reflects all this hostility. However, they also act as tourists, taking in the beauties of the island, just as they have already explored the pyramids in Egypt. As colonial nurses, the landscapes of Europe serve to accentuate their alterity, offering a different perspective on the war for the contemporary reader.

The Northern Europe of the Western Front provides an even stronger contrast to home. Sally finds France a very different place to her Melbourne home. "They passed copses of elm trees and poplars which seemed to Sally to have been culled down from ancient forests into ornamental size. The dying ring-barked verticals of tall gums which marred Australian distances were utterly missing from the scene."[25] Europe is more diminutive, but older and more controlled, despite the chaos of the war raging so close at hand. The element of tourism, of not fitting in, remains, compounded later by the equally alien cold weather and the air raids that result in their complete immersion into the war. Keneally's plot weaves around many of the tropes popular in war fiction, encompassing as many experiences as possible, collective memories for the soldiers as well as the nurses. At the conclusion of the novel, the war is over and only one of the sisters survives. There are two alternate endings, enabling the reader to choose, placing the responsibility for negotiating memory on our shoulders. Memory of the war here is finally endorsed by considering the different possible pathways for the survivors, implying that their multiple experiences of war will continue to haunt them all through the post-war world.

2014, the first centenary year, saw the publication of a number of new First World War novels. Two interesting examples explore notions of memory, legacy and hindsight in complex ways. Helen Dunmore's *The Lie* (2014) and Anna Hope's *Wake* (2014) are both set in 1920 and concerned with issues of memory with a particular focus on the impact of the absence of the body on commemoration; a return to the unknown soldier so important in first wave war fiction.

The Lie tells the story of a returned soldier, Daniel Branwell, living in a cottage on the outskirts of the Cornish community in which he grew up. The first-person narrative enables Daniel to reflect back on his childhood as a displaced member of that community with his working-class outsider parents. His widowed mother took care of the children in the local landed family, resulting in his forging the closest bond of his life with Frederick Dennis, a boy of a different class and background. Later in the trenches, Frederick is his commanding officer, but is soon killed, blown to pieces by a shell so no trace of him remains. His dead friend haunts Daniel, with memories of their homoerotic bond further displacing him from society. Dunmore maps the narrative onto the Cornish landscape creating an interface between the post-war world and the trenches by using quotations from wartime soldier's manuals as epigraphs for each chapter. These epigraphs relate thematically or metaphorically to the events covered in the chapter illustrating the extent to which the war pervades the landscape of Daniel's life despite the passing of time.[26] He is unable to see the world in any other terms,

> I shade my eyes and look up the hill where the furze flares yellow. It is quiet but every inch of the land is known to someone, and any move-

ment on it is seen. Ridge. Copse. Salient. There's a shattered cottage covered with ivy, but you can't see it from here.[27]

The novel concerns itself with the absence of bodies and the importance of commemoration. The lie of the title, although open to multiple interpretations, centres on the idea of the importance of where the body rests. Upon his return, Daniel stays with an old woman he has known since childhood. She inhabits the cottage, slowly dying of natural causes; he lives in a shelter in the garden that resembles a dugout. When she dies, he takes her dying wish literally, burying her on her own land with no marker and telling no one. This failure to give Mary Pascoe a proper resting place is his undoing, but for Daniel, who has seen so many bodies buried where they have fallen, becoming part of the landscape, it seems only natural. The failure of the British government to repatriate all of the dead of the war sets a precedent; formal funeral rites no longer seem necessary.[28] The decision not to bring home any bodies was taken in 1917 by the Imperial War Graves Commission (later Commonwealth War Grave Commission). Caroline Winter notes,

> [. . .] it defined a set of principles for burials; each of the dead was to be buried in an individual grave with no distinction made with respect to military rank and civilian status. Every grave was to have a permanent headstone of uniform size and shape (white Portland stone, 2 feet 8 inches in height), which was meant to convey the comradeship and common service of the men.[29]

The problem of course, was that so many bodies were either unidentifiable, or completely absent.

Julian Barnes' Miss Moss engages with this absence. Grateful that she has a graveside to visit, she is repelled by the Edwin Lutyens' memorial at Thiepval because of what it symbolises to those even less fortunate than herself.

> She could not bear the thought of these lost men, exploded into unrecognizable pieces, engulfed in the mud-fields, one moment fully there with pack and gaiters, baccy and rations, with their memories and their hopes, their past and their future crammed into them, and the next moment only a shed of khaki or a sliver of shin-bone to prove they had ever existed.[30]

This notion of complete absence is incomprehensible. Barnes uses the smallest details, "baccy" and "gaiters," juxtaposed against the uncontainable, memory, past and future, to emphasise the individuality of this collective experience. These dead have become the landscape, but need a different kind of commemoration to those with gravesites.

Anna Hope's *Wake* identifies narratives of memory in the urban landscapes of London, but shares this focus on the physical absence of the dead.

Landscapes of Memory in Centenary Fiction 233

This novel is structured around five days in November 1920, framed by internment of the Unknown Warrior in Westminster Abbey. Adrian Gregory notes:

> Armistice Day 1920 was centred on a funeral. On that day an 'Unknown Warrior of the Great War' was buried at Westminster Abbey. Within a week somewhere between 500,000 and a million people had paid homage at the tomb. It was one of the most striking public demonstrations of emotion in British history.[31]

This emotion-drenched public ritual provides the backdrop, the landscape for Hope's novel. The journey of the "warrior" from an unmarked grave in France to his final procession through London is interwoven around the stories of three women, each representing a different generation, responding to the burial in alternate ways. The women also symbolically represent the three dictionary definitions of "wake." Ada, the bereaved mother, who has no body to bury and no real information about the death of her son, embodies the need for the wake as a ritual for the dead. Ada is unable to mourn her dead son because she has no place of mourning:

> There with her pieces of paper, with her maps of graveyards. These are the things of riches; Ivy is rich. It may well cost pounds to visit France, but if she knew that there was a patch of land that held the body of her son, she wouldn't complain about *money*. She would save everything she had until she could go and visit it. Sit by that piece of grass. Put her hands to it.
>
> It is the lack of a body.
> If she had had that, at least. . . .[32]

The reader later discovers that Ada's son has been shot for desertion, hence the lack of information about his grave, but she does not share this knowledge and finds solace in watching the procession of the unknown warrior:

> On top of the flag Ada can see the dented helmet of a soldier. It is the same helmet that Michael wore. For a stunned second she thinks it is his, that it is the helmet that was tied around his neck the last time she saw him, as he lumbered off down the road in the pale spring sun, bouncing against his back so that she was worried it would bruise; and for a second she is convinced that the body in the coffin is his. Then there's the sound of a woman's sob, sharp and uncontrolled. It echoes off the buildings on either side of the road. Then there's another sob, and another, and in the crowd opposite hundreds of handkerchiefs appear, stark white against the black. Beside her, Ivy is convulsed with silent tears.
> And then she understands. They all wore that helmet. All these women's husbands, brothers, sons.[33]

The internment of the Unknown Warrior symbolised collective memory and mourning, along with the cenotaph and the many other new memorials, inscribing the Western Front onto the landscape of post-war Britain, providing a focal point for the bereaved. Small touches like the helmet enable everyone to believe that their own lost loved one might be in the casket. But for Evelyn, approaching thirty and still mourning her dead lover, the ritual is repellent. She asks her brother, Edward Montfort, "This is supposed to make it all right, is it? This burial? This pulling a body from the earth in France and *dragging* him over here? And all of us standing, watching, weeping? Clapping at the *show*?"[34] Like Dunmore's Frederick Dennis, a shell has decimated Evelyn's lover, Fraser:

> To walk forward.
> To disappear.
> To have no body any more.
> They were sorry, they wrote, that there was no body. That there would be no burial place. But in time, they hoped, there would be somewhere to go.[35]

The "somewhere to go" could be any of the pristine new war memorials; but it is not enough for Evelyn. She needs to "wake" from the sleep of grief, but the Unknown Warrior cannot help her. Instead she learns empathy, discovering her brother's role in condemning Ada's son to death. Through this discovery she understands that although her brother has survived the war, it has still destroyed him, leaving him an impotent, alcoholic, neurasthenic, tortured by the actions his "duty" forced him to commit.

In *The Lie*, Daniel's only hope of salvation seems to lie in Frederick's sister Felicia. The third angle of their triangle, yet forever excluded by her gender, in 1920 Felicia is a war widow with a small child to care for. She seeks out Daniel and together they look for refuge in the Cornish landscapes of their childhoods, each trying to capture the part of the other that holds the dead Frederick. But he is unable to tell her the truth about Frederick's death, and he cannot separate the landscapes of home from those of his memory:

> We clip on. I've almost forgotten where we're going, and why. I went to Bass Head with Frederick. The day was so beautiful, but it's just as lovely now. Nothing cares a bit that he is dead. He doesn't take up an inch of soil. They ought to have put graveyards of all the dead over here. They ought to have covered the farms and dug up the furze and foxgloves and had nothing but crosses as far as you could see. Miles and miles of them, going from town to town. Hasty wooden crosses like the ones we made, all leaning different ways from shell-blast. Bodies blown out of their graves.[36]

Daniel's own neurasthenia ensures that he will not be able to recover. Felicia is not Frederick; she is not his love and she can never understand the things he has seen. For him all landscapes are full of the dead:

> But the landscape dances too. Men are rising lazily out of their beds. They stretch their limbs, and the soil falls off them. The uniforms are unmarked. Their faces are round, and tanned with living in the open air. They stare about them. I am afraid that one of them will catch my eye and so I lean my face into Felicia and the flank of the mare, and I shut my eyes but they are still there. Puzzled, looking about them. They don't know this place. I want them to go back. I want the earth to cover them. I want them to be blown to bits again if only it stops them coming on.[37]

Just as there seems little hope of recovery for Edward Montfort in *Wake*, it is impossible to see a resolution for Daniel. The damage runs too deep. The texts are littered with the broken shells of returned soldiers, making a living however they can, as travelling salesmen (Rowan Hinds in *Wake*), subsisting on the land (Daniel) or fighting for ever-reducing pensions (Evelyn works in a war pensions office). As Rosa Maria Bracco has argued, "Communion with the dead underlies most poignantly the concept of a race apart, a generation which is doomed to live within the emotional confines of an experience which can be understood only by those who have lived through it."[38] The forgotten survivors of the war are contrasted sharply with the "glorious dead" in both novels. Daniel's service to his country is meaningless when an angry mob forces him over a cliff at the end of the novel for his crime of burying an old woman in the resting place she has chosen.

If the Cornish landscape blends with the Western Front for Daniel in *The Lie*, the Western Front is transported to the streets of London with the Unknown Warrior in *Wake*. The crowds that pack the city streets paint the landscape black with their mourning. Among the crowds Hettie, the third woman, stands with her shell-shocked brother, another forgotten casualty of war. Hettie is nineteen and a dancer for hire at the Hammersmith Palais. She is the "consequence or aftermath," what happens in the "wake" of war. Hettie cries out for experience, embracing the "flapper" mentality, searching for excitement and adventure. Reflecting on the society of 1920, Modris Eksteins argues:

> What was true of the soldiers was true of with somewhat less immediacy of civilians. The crowded nightclubs, the frenzied dancing, the striking upsurge of gambling, alcoholism, and suicide, the obsession with flight, with moving pictures, and with film stars evinced on a popular level these same tendencies to drift towards irrationalism.[39]

Hettie embodies some of this hedonistic attitude, which is why she is attracted to the mysterious Ed (actually Edward Montfort). In fact he only wants to sleep with her to recover from his impotence; she reminds him of a French prostitute he knew in the war. The encounter fails, but does leave her reflecting on the multiple consequences of war for men and for women, "bearing witness" to what has gone before.

After the procession the crowds place their flowers around the cenotaph, carpeting Whitehall with blooms, transforming the urban landscape into one of pastoral remembrance. Eksteins argues,

> The "real war" had ceased to exist in 1918. Thereafter it was swallowed by imagination in the guise of memory. For many the war became absurd in retrospect, not because of the war experience in itself but because of the failure of the postwar experience to justify the war.[40]

The flowers help to hide the reality for those left behind. They create a fiction of the war that softens memory and enables recovery.

Centenary fiction, it seems, puts commemoration first. The myths of the war, enshrined in cultural memory for decades, remain at some levels, but at others seem to give way to something more basic. Miss Moss, protagonist of "Evermore" ends with questions. She makes no assumption that this culture of remembrance will endure. On the contrary she assumes that memory will not in the end survive death. "Then the great forgetting could begin, the fading into the landscape."[41] This is a landscape already flooded with the forgotten. Anticipating her own death she looks forward to the next century, asking, "Might there be one last fiery glow of remembering?"[42] In 1995, Barnes anticipates the centenary. "Might there not be, at some point in the first decades of the twenty-first century, one final moment, lit by evening sun, before the whole thing was handed over to the archivists?"[43] One hundred years on, fiction remembers the war, although often from unexpected or less conventional perspectives. The pathos of remembrance infiltrates the Western Front landscapes of Sebastian Faulks, Pat Barker and Thomas Keneally. But for Dunmore and Hope, the survivors, both winners and losers, take centre stage and the aftermath becomes the focus. In a world where the last survivors have now passed on, centenary fiction addresses how it felt to be an individual part of collective memory, when memory itself was still young, before, as Miss Moss anticipates, "in the space of a blink, the gap in the trees would close and the mown grass disappear, a violent indigo cloud would cover the sun, and history, gross history, daily history, would forget."[44]

Notes

1. Modris Eksteins, *Rites of Spring: The Great War and the Birth of the Modern Age* (London: Papermac, 1989), 277.

2. Eksteins, *Rites of Spring*, 290.
3. Gail Braybon, *Evidence, History and the Great War: Historians and the Impact of 1914–18* (New York and Oxford: Berghahn Books, 2003), 1.
4. Chris Weedon and Glenn Jordan, "Collective Memory: Theory and Politics," *Social Semiotics* 22.2 (2012): 143.
5. Marianne Hirsch and Valerie Smith, "Feminism and cultural Memory: An Introduction," *Signs* 28.1 (Autumn 2002): 6.
6. Nora, Pierre, 'Between Memory and History: Les Lieux de Memoire', *Representations*, Number 26, (Spring, 1989), 7–24. P. 12.
7. First published in the *New Yorker*, 13 November 1995.
8. Julian Barnes, "Evermore", in Barbara Korte (ed.), *The Penguin Book of First World War Stories* (London: Penguin, 2007), 352.
9. Barnes, "Evermore", 347.
10. Barnes, "Evermore", 348.
11. Barnes, "Evermore", 349.
12. Barnes, "Evermore", 360.
13. Samuel Hynes, *A War Imagined: The First World War and English Culture* (London: The Bodley Head Ltd, 1990), 459.
14. Sheffield, Gary, (2001) *Forgotten Victory: The First World War: Myths and Realities*, London, Headline Book Publishing Watson, Janet, (2004) *Fighting Different Wars: Experience, memory, and the First World War in Britain*, Cambridge, Cambridge University Press. Gregory, Adrian, (2008) *The Last Great War: British Society and the First World War*, Oxford: Oxford University Press.
15. Sebastian Faulks, *Birdsong* (London: Vintage, 1994), 191.
16. Faulks, *Birdsong*, 192.
17. A third novel, *Noonday*, was published in 2015, moving the same characters into the Second World War.
18. Pat Barker, *Life Class* (London: Penguin, 2007), 176–7.
19. Mary Borden, "Enfant de Malheur", in Hazel Hutchison (ed.), *The Forbidden Zone* (London: Hesperus Press Ltd, 2008 [1929]), 47–8.
20. Barker retells the story of Vera Brittain's brother Edward through Toby Brooke.
21. The nursing organisation was not actually part of ANZAC (Australian and New Zealand Army Corps), which has become an acceptable general descriptor. They were actually part of the Australian Army Nursing Service (AANS).
22. Christine Hallett, *Veiled Warriors: Allied Nurses of the First World War* (Oxford: Oxford University Press, 2014), 2.
23. Hallett, *Veiled Warriors*, 128.
24. Hallett, *Veiled Warriors*, 136–7.
25. Keneally, *Daughters*, 285.
26. For example, the chapter 1 epigraph deals with camouflage techniques and the chapter deals with Daniel's ability to blend into the Cornish landscape. The epigraph for chapter 12 deals with preparation for a raid and the need for concealment. The chapter deals with the night before their fateful raid and their kiss in a darkened garden.
27. Helen Dunmore, *The Lie* (London: Windmill Books, 2014), 53.
28. See Jay Winter, *Sites of Memory, Sites of Mourning: The Great War in European Cultural History* (Cambridge: CUP, 1995), 23.
29. Caroline Winter (2011), 'First World War Cemeteries: Insights from Visitors Books', *Tourism Geographies: An International Journal of Tourism Space, Place and Environment*, 13.3, 462–479, doi:10.1080/14616688.2011.575075.
30. Barnes, "Evermore", 349.
31. Adrian Gregory, *The Silence of Memory: Armistice Day 1919–1946* (Oxford: Berg, 1994), 24.

32. Anna Hope, *Wake* (London: Transworld Publishers, 2014), 187.
33. Hope, *Wake*, 307–8.
34. Hope, *Wake*, 283.
35. Hope, *Wake*, 140.
36. Dunmore, *The Lie*, 259.
37. Dunmore, *The Lie*, 259.
38. Rosa Maria Bracco, *Merchants of Hope: British Middlebrow Writers and the First World War* (Providence and Oxford: Berg, 1993), 95.
39. Eksteins, *Rites of Spring*, 293.
40. Eksteins, *Rites of Spring*, 297.
41. Barnes, "Evermore", 361.
42. Barnes, "Evermore", 361.
43. Barnes, "Evermore", 361.
44. Barnes, "Evermore", 361.

Bibliography

Barker, Pat. *Life Class*. London: Penguin, 2007.
Barker, Pat. *Toby's Room*. London: Penguin, 2012.
Barnes, Julian. "Evermore" in Barbara Korte, ed., *The Penguin Book of First World War Stories*. London: Penguin, 2007. 345–361.
Borden, Mary. *The Forbidden Zone*. London: Hesperus Press Ltd, 2008 [1929].
Bracco, Rosa Maria. *Merchants of Hope: British Middlebrow Writers and the First World War*. Providence and Oxford: Berg, 1993.
Braybon, Gail. *Evidence, History and the Great War: Historians and the Impact of 1914–18*. New York and Oxford: Berghahn Books, 2003.
Dunmore, Helen. *The Lie*. London: Windmill Books, 2014.
Eksteins, Modris. *Rites of Spring: The Great War and the Birth of the Modern Age*. London: Papermac, 1989.
Faulks, Sebastian. *Birdsong*. London: Vintage, 1994.
Gregory, Adrian. *The Silence of Memory: Armistice Day 1919–1946*. Oxford: Berg, 1994.
Gregory, Adrian. *The Last Great War: British Society and the First World War*. Cambridge: Cambridge University Press, 2008.
Hallett, Christine. *Veiled Warriors: Allied Nurses of the First World War*. Oxford: Oxford University Press, 2014.
Hirsch, Marianne and Valerie Smith, "Feminism and Cultural Memory: An Introduction," *Signs* 28.1 (Autumn 2002): 1–19.
Hope, Anna. *Wake*. London: Transworld Publishers, 2014.
Hynes, Samuel. *A War Imagined: The First World War and English Culture*. London: The Bodley Head Ltd, 1990.
Keneally, Thomas. *The Daughters of Mars*. London: Sceptre, 2012.
Nora, Pierre, "Between Memory and History: Les Lieux de Memoire," *Representations* 26 (Spring, 1989): 7–24.
Remarque, Erich Maria. *All Quiet on the Western Front*. London: Picador, 1991.
Sheffield, Gary. *Forgotten Victory: The First World War: Myths and Realities*. London: Headline Book Publishing, 2001.
Watson, Janet S.K. *Fighting Different Wars: Experience, Memory and the First World War in Britain*. Cambridge: Cambridge University Press, 2004.

Weedon, Chris and Glenn Jordan, "Collective Memory: Theory and Politics," *Social Semiotics* 22.2 (2012): 143–153.

Winter, Caroline. "First World War Cemeteries: Insights from Visitors Books," *Tourism Geographies: An International Journal of Tourism Space, Place and Environment* 13:3 (2011): 462–479.

Winter, Jay. *Sites of Memory, Sites of Mourning: The Great War in European Cultural History*. Cambridge: CUP, 1995.

Contributors

Carol Acton is Associate Professor of English at St Jerome's University in the University of Waterloo. Her research focuses on war, gender, and life-writing. She has written on war and grief in *Grief in Wartime: Private Pain, Public Discourse* (Palgrave, 2007). Her most recent book is on the experience of medical personnel in war zones (with Dr Jane Potter), *Working in a World of Hurt: Trauma and Resilience in the Narratives of Medical Personnel in Warzones* (Manchester University Press, 2015. She has also edited the diary of a Second World War nurse: *A Very Private Diary: A Nurse in Wartime by Mary Morris* (Weidenfeld & Nicolson, 2014).

Nadia Atia is Lecturer in World Literature at Queen Mary, University of London. Her first monograph *World War I in Mesopotamia: The British and Ottomans in Iraq* (IB Tauris: 2016) explores how ideologies of race and empire shaped the ways in which British travellers, archaeologists, servicemen and women from different classes and professional backgrounds interacted with and represented the region now known as Iraq in the early twentieth century. In particular, she examines their interactions with the Indian, African, Afro-Caribbean, Egyptian or Chinese workers and military personnel who played such a crucial role in the war, but whose presence is not a familiar one in many accounts of the First World War.

Stuart Bell is a minister in the Methodist Church and Honorary Research Fellow, St John's College, Durham University. After studying computer science at Manchester University in the era of punched cards and paper tape, he taught that subject for seven years at Plymouth College of Further Education and Plymouth Polytechnic before training for ordained ministry at Wesley House and Fitzwilliam College, Cambridge. For his MTh dissertation at the University of Oxford he examined the influence of the Great War on the Anglican Modernists, while his PhD thesis at the University of Birmingham discussed the influence of the conflict on popular faith.

Krista Cowman is Professor of History in the School of History and Heritage, University of Lincoln. She has published widely on the history of women and politics including women's suffrage and women's role in reconstruction after the First World War. She was Co-Investigator on the "Alternate Spaces" project and has been researching interactions between British servicemen and French civilians during the First World War.

Emma Hanna is a Senior Research Fellow in the School of History at the University of Kent. She has published widely on music and film from 1914–1918, and on the cultural memory of the First World War in contemporary Britain.

Margaret R. Higonnet, Professor of English and Comparative Literature at the University of Connecticut, has worked on a range of topics including the literature of World War I, feminist theory, comparative literature and women's photographically documented memoirs. Her current work on women in World War I has three focuses: nurses' memoirs, elegiac poetry and texts that inculcate a war culture for children. Her comparative study of nurses on both Western and Eastern Fronts examines issues of self-representation in relation to critiques of the military and medical commands that led to the banning of at least one book. Her study of women's elegies connects their despairing motifs to the iconography of Käthe Kollwitz. Forthcoming essays are devoted to code-switching in the representation of Indian soldiers on the Western Front, the mobilization of girls as volunteer soldiers in the nineteenth century, the Scottish Women's Hospitals and the relationships between nurses' voices and those of soldiers. Her theoretical reflections on comparative literary history will appear in the decennial assessment of the American Comparative Literature Association.

Hazel Hutchison lectures in British and American literature at the University of Aberdeen, where she is also the Director of the Centre for the Novel. She has published books and articles on fiction and poetry of the late nineteenth and early twentieth centuries, especially on Henry James and on American war literature. She is the author of *The War That Used Up Words: American Writers and the First World War* (Yale, 2015).

Lise Jaillant is Lecturer (Assistant Professor) in the School of the Arts, English and Drama at Loughborough University, UK. Most of her work has been on twentieth-century literary institutions (publishing houses, creative writing programmes). Her first monograph *Modernism, Middlebrow and the Literary Canon* (Routledge, 2014) focuses on the Modern Library, a cheap series of reprints that published works such as Virginia Woolf's *Mrs Dalloway*, James Joyce's *Dubliners* and *A Portrait of the Artist as a Young Man*, as well as "popular" literature. Her second book, *Cheap Modernism: Expanding Markets, Publishers' Series and the Avant-Garde*, will be published by Edinburgh University Press. She is currently working on a global history of creative writing programmes in the United States, Britain and Australia. More information can be found here: www.lisejaillant.com.

Andrew Maunder is Head of English at the University of Hertfordshire. He is the editor of *British Theatre and the Great War 1914–1919* (2015), and author of biographies *Bram Stoker* (2006) and *Wilkie Collins* (with Graham Law, 2010). His student guide on R. C. Sheriff's *Journey's End* was published by Methuen in 2016. He is a member of the AHRC-funded Centre for Everyday Lives in War based at the University of Hertfordshire, where he also leads the World War I Theatre Project which revives forgotten wartime plays for modern audiences.

Jane Potter is Reader in Arts in the Oxford International Centre for Publishing Studies, Oxford Brookes University. Her publications include *Boys in Khaki, Girls in Print: Women's Literary Responses to the Great War, 1914–1918* (Oxford University Press, 2005), *Wilfred Owen: An Illustrated Life* (Bodleian Library Publishing, 2014) and, with Carol Acton, *Working in a World of Hurt: Trauma and Resilience in the Narratives of Medical Personnel in Warzones* (Manchester University Press, 2015). She is currently editing a new edition of *The Selected Letters of Wilfred Owen* for Oxford University Press and for Cambridge University Press, *A Cambridge History of World War One Poetry.*

Lisa Regan is a Lecturer in English Literature at the University of Liverpool with interests in travel and exploration narratives, particularly those of British travellers to the Middle East and North Africa. Alongside T.E. Lawrence's legacy in popular culture, she is currently focussing on the rise of the desert romance and its connections with British exploration of the Sahara in the early twentieth century. She has published on the interwar, feminist writer, social reformer and traveller, Winifred Holtby: *Winifred Holtby, 'A Woman in Her Time': Critical Essays* (Cambridge Scholars, 2010) and *Winifred Holtby's Social Vision 'Members One of Another'* (Pickering and Chatto, 2012). And she has also published on E. M. Hull, Rosita Forbes and Rose Macaulay, as well as a chapter on 'Women Writing Empire' in *The History of Women's Writing, 1920–1945*, vol. 8, edited by Maroula Joannou (Palgrave, 2013).

Angela K. Smith is an Associate Professor (Reader) at Plymouth University. She specialises in war writing, with a particular interest in the First World War and gender issues. She has published extensively on the First World War, women's writing and gender as well as the women's suffrage movement in wartime. Her latest collection, *War and Displacement in the Twentieth Century: Global Conflicts* was published by Routledge in April 2014 and her latest monograph, *Women of the Eastern Front: British Women in Serbia and Russia 1914–9*, was published by Manchester University Press in 2016. She was the Principal Investigator on the "Alternate Spaces" project.

Index

Aldington, Richard 71–2, 97
Allen, Sir Henry 44
American troops 63
Appleby, Eric 77, 85
Arnold, Sir Malcolm 47
Asquith, Cynthia 36
Association for Moral and Social Hygiene (AMSH) 67, 68
Australian Army Nursing Service (AANS) 176, 186, 229

Bagnold, Enid 228
Barbusse, Henri 116
Barker, Pat 227–9, 236; *Life Class* 227–9; *Toby's Room* 227, 229
Barnes, Julien 223–5, 232, 236
Barthes, Roland 182–3
Battle of the Somme (BBC) 48
Baynes, J. 58
Beadsley, Edward 59
Bebbington, W. G. 110
Beck, Jeff 50
Behdad, Ali 180–2, 194
Benjamin, Walter 119
Bennett, Arnold 33
Bland, Caroline 78, 799
Blackburn, Winnie 81, 82, 83, 84, 87, 88
Blathwayt, Raymond 36
Blunden, Edmund 6–10, 140, 159
Bogle, Eric 51
Borden, Mary 97, 117, 187, 228–9
Bracco, Rosa Maria 235
Braybon, Gail 223
Britnieva, Mary 120–1
Brittain, Vera 10–11, 83, 89, 97, 140, 228, 230
Brooke, Rupert 139
Brophy, John 44

brothel *see maison de tolerance*
Butt, Alfred 22, 31
Butterworth, George 49, 50
Bystander 22, 26

Canadian Army Medical Corps (CAMC) 176
Carrington, Charles 1–2
Chamberlain, Neville 34
Charlot, André 22, 26, 27
Cochran, Charles 19, 21, 22, 26, 27, 33, 34, 36
Coles, Cecil 59
Community Singing 43–6
Corbin, Alain 60, 61, 69, 70
Courville, Albert de 22, 33, 34
Cowley, Malcolm 215
Cross, Máire 78, 79
Cru, Jean Norton 115, 116, 118

Daily Express 43, 44, 45
Daily Mail 133–5
Das, Santanu 185
Davies, Henry Walford 44
Defence of the Realm Act (DORA) 26
Delysia, Alice 32, 33, 62
Deslys, Gaby 21, 27–9, 31, 62
Dodgson, Toby 80, 81, 84
Dorrien, Genreal Sir Horace Smith 33
Duchalet, Alexandre 60
Dugard, Marie 119–20
Dunmore, Helen 231–2, 234–6; *The Lie* 231–2, 234–6

Eksteins, Modris 222, 235–6
Elgar, Edward 52
Emney, Fred 24
Evans, Will 24

Faulks, Sebastian 225–7, 236; *Birdsong* 225–7, 236
Fedorchenko, Sofia 118, 119, 121, 126
Fiaux, Louis 61
Findon, B. W. 20
First World War, The (Channel 4) 49
Formby, George, Sr. 24, 34
Frankau, Gilbert 109
Fuller, J. G. 58
Fussell, Paul 7, 226

Gallipoli 175, 186, 229–30
Gibson, K. Craig 59
Graves, Robert 2, 6, 140, 159
Grayzel, Susan 138
Great War, The (BBC) 47, 48
Gregory, Adrian 2, 158, 233, 237n
Grossmith, George 21
Gullace, Nicoletta 140

Halbwachs, Maurice 223
Hallett, Christine 177, 230
Hämmerle, Christa 78–9
Hanna, Martha 79
Hardy, Thomas 210, 218
Harrison, Mark 59, 69
Hemingway, Ernest 131, 215, 230
Hirsch, Marianne 223
Hirschfeld, Magnus 63, 68
Hiscock, Eric 64
Hodder and Stoughton 12, 131–6, 141–3, 146
Holst, Gustav 48, 49
Holtby, Winifred 143
Hope, Anna 231–6; *Wake* 231–6
Houseman, A. E. 49
Hynes, Samuel 7, 226

Industrial Christian Fellowship (ICP) 159, 163

Karno, Fred 30
Kellog, Shirley 24, 34
Kelly, Phyllis 70–1, 72, 85, 89
Keneally, Thomas 229–31, 236; *Daughters of Mars* 229–31
Kennington, Eric 5
Kerr, Douglas 102
Kerr, Fred 23

La Fanu, Sarah 131–2, 139–40
La Motte, Ellen 115, 123–6, 228; *The Backwash of War* 123–6; relationship with Emily Chadbourne 125
La Nour, Jean Yves 59
Lauder, Harry 51
Lawrence, T. E. 192–4, 199–201
League of Nations 141, 164
Lee, Hermione 131
Leighton, Roland 83, 89
letter-writing 78–9
Levine, Philippa 59
Lewis, Cecil 62, 72
Lillie, Beatrice 27
Littlewood, Joan 47
Lloyd, Marie 35, 36
London Council for the Promotion of Public Morality 30
Long Long Trail, The (BBC) 47
Lord Chamberlain's Office 24, 30, 31, 32

Macaulay, Rose 12, 131–46; *The Lee Shore* 132–5; *The Making of a Bigot* 134, 136, 143–4; *Non-Combatants and Others* 131–2, 134–46
McEwen, John B 45
McNeile, Herman Cyril (Sapper) 132, 141–3, 145–6
maison de tolerance 59–72; at Bethune 67, 71; British objections to 67–8; at Calais 65, 67; at Cayeux-sur-Mer 67; at Dunkirk 64; interior design of 61–2, 64, 66, 69, 70; at Le Havre 65, 66, 70; pre-war regulation of 60; at Trouville 70
Makepeace, Clare 59
Manchester Guardian 142, 164
Manning, Frederick 116
Mansfield, Katherine 228
Marcus, Jane 126
Marshall, Norman 22
Martineau, Harriet 177
Mesopotamia 175, 178–9, 186
Meyer, Jessica 79
Milne, Esther 78, 80
Mistinguett 63
Monkman, Phyllis 26, 29
Montague, C. E. 164–6
More, James Ross 21
music hall 41

Nash, Paul 5, 9, 49, 228
Nevinson, Christopher 5, 228
Newman, Cyril 81, 82, 83, 84, 87, 88
New Zealand Army Nursing Service (NZANS) 176, 229
Nightingale, Florence 177
Nora, Pierre 41, 223

Index

Norton, Grace Fallow 8–9, 206–19
nurses' writing 118–20

Oh! What a Lovely War! 47
Oldfield, Sybil 134
orientalism 180–2, 184
Owen, Wilfred 2, 21, 49, 50, 99, 101, 106, 107, 109, 159, 226–7; *Dulce et Decorm Est* 97; and Jessie Pope 97–8, 109, 110

pacifism 13, 134, 139–41, 145, 158–9, 163–6, 228
Pankhurst, E. Sylvia 11
Partridge, Eric 44
patriotism 13, 44, 160–2
Peace Pledge Union 141, 165
Pelissier, Harry 21
Pope, Jessie 12, 97–111; pre-war writing 98–100; short stories 105–8; wartime verse 100–5
Potter, Jane 142
Praeger, Karen 82
propaganda 142

Queen Alexandra's Imperial Military Nursing Service (Reserve) (QAIMNS)(R) 176, 178–9, 181, 183, 185–6

radio 47
Rathbone, Irene 11–12
Remarque, Erich Maria 6, 117, 222, 226; *All Quiet on the Western Front* 117, 124–5
remembrance ceremonies 43, 51
Rhodes, Michelle 59, 69
Rivers, W. H. R. 227
Roper, Michael 59, 79
Royden, Maud 161, 166

Said, Edward 180
Sassoon, Siegfried 2, 6, 19, 37, 97, 98, 103, 109, 131, 140, 226–7
Secretan, Majorie 80, 81, 83, 84
Shaw, George Bernard 19
Sheffield, Gary 6, 237n
Sheppard, H. R. L. (Dick) 165–6
Smith, Angela, K. 140, 146, 176

Society of Friends (Quakers) 151
sound recordings 42–3
Spivak, Gayatri 115
Stone, Joss 50
Strachen, Huw 7–8
Studdert-Kennedy, Geoffrey Ankertell (Woodbine Willie) 6, 152–66

Tatler 22, 24
theatre in wartime 19–37; theatre producers 22
Thiepval memorial 52
Thurston, Edward 21
Tilley, Vesta 11–12
Times Literary Supplement 132–3, 141, 143, 145
Tippett, Michael 50
Tonks, Henry 227, 229
Tree, Herbert Beerbohn 21, 22, 36

Vaughan Williams, Ralph 48, 49
venereal disease 59, 60, 68, 69, 70, 71
Voluntary Aid Detachment (VAD) 10, 138–9, 176–7, 181, 230

war experience 58–9
War Propaganda Bureau 142
Watson, Janet, S. K. 2, 6, 7, 131, 140, 145–6, 237n
Wells, H. G. 131
Wharton, Edith 115, 121; *Writing a War Story* 118, 121
White, Pearl 24
Whittemore, Thomas 118, 119
Williams, Gordon 22
Williamson, Henry 66
Wilson, Woodrow 155
Winter, Caroline 232
Winter, Jay 4, 6, 41, 58–9
Women's International Congress (The Hague 1915) 137
Women's Volunteer Reserve 138
Wood, Sir Henry 44
Woolf, Virginia 140, 144

Young Men's Christian Association (YMCA) 49, 58